# CULTURE CRISIS

# CULTURE CRISIS

## TRUTH SHALL PREVAIL

Robert T. Fertig

*Edited by Miriam A. Fertig, M.A.*

Library of Congress Control Number:        2020922447

PAPERBACK:            978-1-953791-33-7
EBOOK:                978-1-953791-34-4



Ordering Information:

For orders and inquiries, please contact:
1-888-404-1388
www.goldtouchpress.com
book.orders@goldtouchpress.com

Printed in the United States of America

# Contents

# Preface

Many decades of information collection and research provides you with new insights, and perhaps a fresh perspective, on a wide spectrum of "ideas" from seventy-five scientists, scholars, philosophers, and theologians. We guide readers through the maze of newly discovered facts, theories, and ideas that have led civilization to where we are today.

With the stakes of our personal choices so high, it would be prudent to make every effort to search and choose correctly. That takes knowledge from many sources. In this work and dialogue, this writer presents many key issues that have divided Scientists, Society, and Cultures, such as the formation of the Universe, the Origin of Life and Mankind, Free Will, Reason, Faith, Truth, and many other topics.

This work is a major update of my prior books: *The Beauty and Wonder of Transcendent Truths* (2010), and *Consequences* (2014). This author has also added new materials, illustrations, and photos to enhance the presentation of facts and its readability. Much of this work is "transformative;" i.e., paraphrased and the author's interpreted works from numerous scholars. (See Appendix).

This author has reached eighty-plus years of life, and have found some of my early notes from 1960s, which are incorporated in this work. This writer states that he has "moral certainty" on what is written and now desires to share with readers some of the most important lessons of life that he has learned over these eight decades.

If anyone has questions about this work and its presentation, which is *not* based "opinions" or "conspiracy theories," but are documented "facts," please respond via my web site: **www.fivestarpubs.com**

Photos and images were purchased, or created by the author. Photos from NASA are in the public domain.

# Introduction

We begin with *Being & Life Truths*, since this subject provides a "humanistic" foundation for all the other topics on truth. Science explains the "what?" and "how?" Philosophy and Spirituality, and Ideology explains the "why?" of our existence, which undeniably requires *both* reason, and faith or trust.

Subjects are thematically grouped into ten chapters. This book is a *guide* that builds a bridge between what many believe, and what skeptics' question, using theories and discoveries in various newly explored areas. We are at a special time in human history because of recent scientific breakthroughs that are changing some mistaken theories by earlier "experts." Some relevant texts also include materials compiled by this author, during the past half-century.

We not scientists, philosophers, or theologians. We are simply "thinkers," who wish to share with you "Words of Wisdom," from recognized past and present scholars that are essential and also fascinating. The major building blocks of this book edifice is what Scientists, Scholars and Scripture contributed. This writer selected, paraphrased, interpreted, and summarized what they produced, while fashioning a few thoughts of my own, and then put it all together into a style that today's generation may find more suitable.

Analogies, metaphors, anecdotes, charts and images are used to liven up the presentation for my readers. Throughout this book we have tried to faithfully present a *balanced dialogue*—both pro and con—on many difficult topics, particularly on today's Ideology. There is no real search for truth for anyone standing outside generally agreed definitions, assumptions, without considering accepted facts, traditions, and communities of truth seekers.

Today's more educated and skeptical young adults are vulnerable to many peer-pressures, and mass media blitz, that attack objective truths, and traditions. Hopefully, this book may provide *Words of Wisdom* to help defeat some of these *false ideologies* that have become "truths" in many of today's text books. To be sure, all of the burning issues of our times will not be answered fully by this work, but at least *a dialogue* will have begun for sincere truth seekers, that will empower them against some of these mistaken ideologies.

Thomas Aquinas contended in *Summa Contra Gentiles* and *Summa Theologia*, in his dialogue with Arab and Jewish thinkers of his time: *"There should not be any discrepancy between faith and human reasoning. Our heart cannot worship that which the mind cannot consent to. Both the light of reason and light of faith come from God; hence there can be no contradiction between them. Faith therefore has no fear of reason, but seeks it out and has trust in it… Faith is in a sense an 'exercise of thought' and human reason is neither annulled nor debased in assenting to the contents of faith, which are in any case attained by way of free and informed choice."*

St. Augustine put it more succinctly: *"I believe, in order to understand; and I understand, the better to believe."*

This author hopes that this wide-ranging work will help men and women—especially, today's skeptical young adults—find answers to questions about science, society, spirituality, and ideology that have serious *consequences* for our times.

This work is a kind of dialogue between me and various scholars, as well as reflections on issues that have bothered me for a half-century. This is a book for *all* people: Christians, Muslims, Atheists, which considers many perplexing questions that trouble today's youth and adults. As Augustine wrote: *In faith, unity; in doubtful matters, liberty; in all things, love.*

Some of the *proposed* answers in this book are argumentative. Nonetheless, controversy and deliberation leads to comprehension. Our need to inquire, to explore, to probe appears to be in our genes at birth, along with our urge to eat, and compulsion to have sex and procreate. If our system of knowledge has taught us anything during past centuries, it is this: retreating from the truth and human curiosity is unrealistic.

> ***"To believe is nothing other than to think with assent… Believers are also thinkers: In believing, they think and in thinking they believe… If faith does not think, it is nothing."*--Augustine.**

No single person can be an expert in all the topics covered in this book. Some topics, questions and *proposed* answers are summarized in one short paragraph, while others required multiple pages to merely scratch the surface on these complex issues. My method in this work is to give you the *"Essence of the Truth,"* while providing multiple viewpoints, wherever possible.

**NOTE: This book is structured into "topical modules," that allows readers to pursue information that suits their particular interest. We suggest readers jump to topics of specific interest to them, and later review in more detail other topics that may be of less interest.**

## Reviewed By Christian Sia for Readers' Favorite 5-Star Rating

Culture Crisis: Truth Shall Prevail by Robert T. Fertig is a compelling, thought-provoking book that invites readers to think about culture and to ponder existential issues that are prevalent in contemporary history. The reader is offered a wide selection of reflections, each crafted on a specific theme, but the overall book deals with the question of why we are here, why we experience the cultural and religious differences that have been behind the numerous tensions in modern times.

This is a powerful work that is well researched and that enters into dialogue with the best thinkers the world has ever known, experts in religious and cultural phenomena, and writers who have articulated on ideas of life, cultural, the purpose of human life, the place of culture in the evolution of life and human consciousness, and a lot more.

Robert's writing is exceptional and not like anything one sees too often. The reader is left in no doubt that, this book is well researched and that the author knows what he is talking about. It is interesting to notice the author's mastery of the different schools of thought, including the core teachings of doctrines like Christianity, Islam, atheism, and others.

# I. Being & Life Truths

*Life is like a tapestry that contains many different threads. Each thread is a thought, a dream, an experience. Some are short threads of dull pigment; others are long threads of vivid color. Reality and dreams are in the hands of that expert carpet weaver. He connects different strands of our lives to others. He weaves them together to pattern our distinctive, universal being. We are dependent on His will and skilled hands. In the end we must affirm: Thy will be done. --Author*

Parmenides (540 BC) believed *"Being is the only reality."* Heraclites (500 BC) insisted that *"Change is the only reality."* Buddha (623 BC) also believed that change is the only reality in the universe. They were all wrong! *Both* being and change are now proven to be the universal reality. All material things are changeable (matter into energy, hydrogen and oxygen into water). Some idealists claim: being comes from non-being, or something comes from nothing. Such ideas are not only irrational, they are potentially dangerous.

Humans Beings move from what is known to what is less known, *not the reverse.* Proof that something is true comes from conformity with reality, not from imagination and ideas alone. The very first thing that we know as thinking humans is: *"there is an 'is.'"* Being means to exist; it's fundamental, elementary. Our inability to define or measure something does not mean it doesn't existence. Darkness, in itself, does not exist; it is the absence of light. People blind from birth have no concept of light, yet they see things in their "minds-eye." *Nothing comes from nothingness!*

## WHAT DRIVES HISTORY?
*Politics? Economics? Might it be Culture—what men and women honor, cherish, and worship—isn't that the most dynamic element in human affairs?*

"Battle or "Crisis" are overused words these days, but in the present circumstance it is appropriate. America and Europe is depopulating itself. Generation after generation of below-replacement-level birthrates have created a demographic vacuum, filled by transplanted populations (mostly Moslems and Hispanics), whose presence is a challenge to Western Culture, and could become a threat to democracy. Democracy requires educated, informed voters, willing to assimilate and accepts our laws, *which Islam does not.*

How can we speak of, and defend "Universal Human Rights," in a cultural climate in which the very idea of "truth" is under sustained assault? These questions are of crucial importance on both sides of the Atlantic. "Culture Battles" are, in fact, an ongoing debate—and continuing political struggle—between those who believe that human beings can, however inadequately, grasp the truth of how we ought to live together, and those for whom any notion of "transcendent truth" involves an unacceptable imposition of someone's "values" on someone else.

## WHAT IS TRUTH?
Roman Governor Pilate, turned to Jesus Christ and asked: *"What is truth?"* It was a cynical response to what Christ had revealed: *"I have come into the world to testify to the truth."*

Today the entire world seems to be replaying Pilate's cynicism. Some say that truth is "relative." Others say truth is the "collective judgment" of people, and the product of our current "cultural consensus." Truth is that which is consistent with the mind; it is the way everything really is. ***Truth is both objective and subjective!*** Truth unites people. Relativism, based on "individual whims," or "group-think," separates us, causes loss of dignity, and leads to "might makes it right."

| TRUTHS | OBJECTIVE | SUBJECTIVE | REMARKS |
|---|---|---|---|
| ALL SCIENCES | X | | GENDER IS FACTUAL |
| LOGIC/MATH | X | | |
| BEAUTY/ ART/MUSIC | | X | PERSONAL TASTE |
| HISTORY | X | X | DEPENDS ON WHO WROTE IT |
| MEDICAL/ HEALTH | X | X | PART SCIENCE, MOSTLY ART |
| FERTILIZED EGG IS 100% HUMAN | X | | GENOME VALIDATION |
| FAITH/TRUST | Small x | X | BASED ON SOME EVIDENCE |
| ETHICS/ LAWS | X | X | NATURAL vs CIVIL LAWs |

> **Fig. 1 Objective & Subjective Truths***

According to Rene Descartes, in his the *Discourse on Method*, reason involves understanding, arguments, judgments, and reasoned conclusion. First, our mind must understand and agree on the terms used; and they must be intelligible and unambiguous. Second, we must accept the premise as true, if it corresponds to our current knowledge of reality. Third, the arguments must be correct.

If the conclusion(s) follow undeniably from the premises. If all the terms used are understood. If all the premises are valid. If all the arguments are logically correct, then the conclusion must be true.

By *reason*, humans are capable of understanding the natural order of all things, physically, mentally, and spiritually.

By *free will*, humans are capable of directing themselves toward seeking what is true and good.

By *intelligence*, humans are endowed with knowledge, which is an outstanding manifestation of Divine Wisdom.

By *faith*, one recognizes the revealed message of our Creator, which urges us to do what is good and avoid what is evil.

## BIOLOGICAL BIG BANG:

> ***Genesis agrees: when life first appears on the third day, the word creation does not appear. We are merely told "The earth brought forth life." Earth had within it the necessary properties for life.***

About 3.5-3.8 billion years ago, an exquisite, efficient system for encoding and of transmitting the information needed to guide all organisms development from seed to adult appeared. That same system, the double helix of genetic DNA, guides all forms of life, from algae to oak trees, from microscopic bacteria to massive elephants, and humans as well (it's an intelligent blue print). Evolution is not a free agent. The laws of biology, chemistry and physics, and the laws of nature determine which structures can evolve, and which cannot evolve. There are only 34-50 basic body plans (Phyla) for *all* animals, including humans.

During the Cambrian explosion, about 530-540 million years ago, entirely new species rapidly came into being on planet Earth. It was an "explosion of new species." Darwin stated: "If numerous species, belonging to the same ... families, have really started into life at once, that fact would be fatal to the theory of [macro] evolution through natural selection." *That's exactly what has happened!*

Evolutionist Niles Eldredge, Curator of the American Museum of Natural History, said: "Despite the evidence for very early phases of human-like evolution in Africa, the precise material samples for the appearance of Homo sapiens in that continent are obscure and difficult to draw into a coherent picture." He frankly admits of the failure of the fossil record to provide evidence for macro-evolution (however, micro-evolution *within* species does exist), stating: "No one has found in-between creatures ... and there is growing conviction among many scientists that these transitional forms never existed."

Dr. Eldredge, argues that: the fossil record shows distinct jumps or gaps in the evolution of the human species. "Darwin's Origin of species, *'Nature non facit saltum'*—that nature does not make jumps, that it

[only] evolves—*has been proven false!* The fossil record we were told to find for the past 200 years does not exist." Macro-evolution also never explained how the whole process began.

## MYSTERY OF THE GENOME:

Prior to Noah, humans lived much longer, according to Genesis. Some examples include: Adam 930, Seth 912, Enoch 905, Kenan 910, Mahalalel 895, Jared 962, Methuselah 969, Noah 950, Shem 600, Eber 474, Peleg 239, Reu 239, Nahor 138, Terah 205, Abram (Abraham) 176 (10 generations after Adam), Jacob 147, and Joseph lived 107 years.

How was this possible? What caused the decline of human lifespans?

Dr. J.C. Sanford, probably has the correct answer. He says: "Human life expectancy presently has an average of about 79 years, and a maximum of nearly 120. However, when first cousins marry, their children have a reduction of life expectancy of nearly 10 years."

Why is this so? "It is because *inbreeding* exposes the genetic mistakes within the Genome (recessive mutations), that have not yet had time to 'come to the surface.'"

## Aging Metabolic Process:

Each of the species is pre-programmed (within their DNA) for death at a given age range: fleas live five years; dogs live fifteen years; the human life span today is about 79 years. Mutations can upset the aging process. For example, Progeria disease speeds up aging process about ten-fold.

Dr. Stanford has verified *that incest causes a decrease in lifespan for each generation.* The effect of incest (which was not immoral during this ancient period) varied, and likely had a greater impact in earlier eons. The lowest average age limit was about 40-50 years, during the Roman Empire. By the 1800's, the world reached its first billion, and by 2010 we had a population of over seven billion, which might exceed nine billion by 2050. The reasons for the current increase in life-span is not only due to a rapid decline of incest, which became morally unacceptable in civilized societies; it's also because of significant improvements in healthcare, hygiene, food processing, communication, and many other technological developments.

## EPIGENETIC CONTROL:

One of the sources for a discussion on Intelligent Design, is *Mind over Genes: the New Biology*, by Bruce H. Lipton, Ph.D. Until recently, it was thought that genes were self-actualizing…that genes could 'turn themselves on and off.' Such behavior is required in order for genes to control biology. Though the power of genes is still emphasized in current biology courses and textbooks, a radically new understanding has emerged at the leading edge of cell science. It is now recognized that the environment, more specifically, our perception (interpretation) of the environment, directly controls the activity of our genes. Environment controls gene activity through a process known as "epigenetic control," according to Bruce H. Lipton, Ph.D.

### Mind and Spirit:

> *Your body is not who you are. The mind and spirit transcend the body.* --**Christopher Reeve**

This new perspective of human biology does not view the body as just a mechanical device, but rather incorporates the role of a *mind and spirit* (emphasis mine). This breakthrough in biology is fundamental in all healing for it recognizes that when we change our perception or beliefs, we send totally different messages to our cells and reprogram their expression. The new-biology reveals why people can have spontaneous remissions or recover from injuries deemed to be permanent disabilities. In addition, such external signals can send messages to the "cell antennas," that can turn on and off various cell processes. Thus, spiritual healing, is the result of biological processes that essentially correct the DNA of cells in sick people, working *within* Intelligent Designed laws.

## Multi-Cellular Communities:

The functional units of life are the individual cells that comprise our bodies. Though every cell is innately intelligent and can survive on its own when removed from the body, in the body each cell foregoes its individuality and becomes a member of a multi-cellular community. *The body really represents the cooperative effort of a community* (emphasis mine) of perhaps fifty trillion single cells. By definition, a community is an organization of individuals committed to supporting a shared vision. Consequently, while every cell is a free-living entity, the body's community accommodates the wishes and intents of its 'central voice,' a character we perceive as the mind and spirit.

## Dysfunction and Disease:

When the mind perceives that the environment is safe and supportive, the cells are preoccupied with growth and maintenance of the body. In stressful situations, cells forego their normal growth functions and adopt a more defensive 'protection' posture. The body's energy resources normally used to sustain growth are diverted to systems that provide protection during periods of stress. Thus, growth processes are restricted or suspended in a stressed system. While our systems can accommodate periods of acute (very brief) stress, prolonged or chronic stress is debilitating since its energy demands interfere with the required maintenance of the body, and as a consequence, leads to dysfunction and disease.

## Mind and Body:

Lipton continues: The principle source of stress is the system's 'central voice,' the mind. The mind is like the driver of a vehicle. With good driving skills, a vehicle can be maintained and provide good performance throughout its life. Bad driving skills generate most of the wrecks that litter the roadside or are stacked in junkyards. If we employ good "driving skills" in managing our behaviors and dealing with our emotions, then we should anticipate a long, happy and productive life. In contrast, inappropriate behaviors and dysfunctional emotional management, like a bad driver, stresses the cellular 'vehicle,' interfering with its performance and provoking a breakdown.

(If we extend this biological human system of acute stress to a higher level, it will often lead to dysfunctional families, and if not corrected, it ultimately leads to dysfunctional communities, and dysfunctional states, such as exists today in some modern societies).

## Conscious and Subconscious:

Are you a good driver or a bad driver? Before you answer that question, realize that there are two separate minds that create the body's controlling 'central voice.' The (self) *conscious mind* is the thinking 'you.' It is the creative mind that expresses free will. Its supporting partner is the *subconscious mind*, a super computer loaded with a database of (pre) programmed behaviors. Some programs are derived from genetics. These are our instincts and they represent *nature*. However, the vast majority of the subconscious (new) programs are acquired through developmental learning experiences, they represent *nurture*.

## Programmable Autopilot:

The subconscious mind is *not* a seat of reasoning, or creative consciousness, it is strictly a stimulus-response device. When an environmental signal is perceived, the subconscious mind reflexively activates a previously stored behavioral response…no thinking is required. The subconscious mind is a programmable autopilot that can navigate the vehicle without the observation or awareness of the pilot—the conscious mind. When the subconscious autopilot is controlling behavior, consciousness is free to dream into the future or review the past.

## Behavioral Programs:

We are generally consciously unaware of our fundamental perceptions or beliefs about life. The reason is that the prenatal and neonatal brain is predominately operating in delta and theta EEG frequencies through the first six years of our lives. This low level of brain activity is referred to as the hypnogogic state. While in this hypnotic trance, a child does not have to be actively coached by its parents for they obtain their behavioral programs simply by observing their parents, siblings, peers and teachers. Did your early developmental experiences provide you with good models of behavior to use in the (unfolding) of your life?

## Central Voices:

During the first six years of life a child unconsciously acquires the behavioral repertoire needed to become a functional member of society. In addition, a child's subconscious mind also downloads beliefs relating to self. When a parent tells a young child it is stupid, undeserving or any other negative traits, this too is downloaded as a 'fact' into the youngster's subconscious mind. These acquired beliefs constitute the 'central voice' that controls the fate of the body's cellular community. While the conscious mind may hold one's self in high regard, the more powerful unconscious mind may simultaneously engage in self-destructive behavior.

By being fully conscious, we become the masters of our fates rather than the 'victims' of our subconscious programs. This path is similar to Buddhist mindfulness. With conscious awareness, one can actively transform the character of their lives into ones filled with love, health and prosperity.

> *Everything, including you and me, is a field of energy, interconnected, interacting, and influencing each other physically and spiritually. Everything is a mysterious vibrating pattern of energy.* **--Author**

## Differentiation & Integration:

All natural and healthy creatures and human growth processes proceed by differentiation and integration. The best example of this is the growth of complex organisms (intelligently coded human cell which contains our unique DNA). From a fertilized single-cell egg, the zygote divides into two cells, then four, eight, sixteen, etc., until trillions of cells have developed. While this incredible differentiation is occurring, different cells are at the same time being integrated into cooperative tissues, organs, and systems that forms the human body.

This differentiation and integration process enables a single cell to evolve into multi-cellular systems of *exquisite* unity and functional integrity. This is how nature creates higher units and deeper integration. In this growth process, if anything goes wrong, with either differentiation or integration, the result is pathology (desolation). If differentiation fails to occur, the result is fusion, fixation, and arrest of growth. If differentiation begins, but gets out of control, the result is dissociation or fragmentation; the parts don't differentiate, they separate or disunite, and the result is fragmentation, repression, and alienation.

Therefore, one must not confuse differentiation with dissociation (separation, alienation), or mistaken growth for a disease, like cancer. In that case, one will be confusing dignity with disaster, and evolution with catastrophe. If differentiation (variation, diversity) was the dignity of *Modernity*, dissociation was *the real disaster*, when the sciences (the objective "It's") in recent times have dominate all aspects of human life—including cultural, artistic, moral, and spiritual life.

## LIFE IS UNNATURAL:

> ***Being alive is very unnatural. All life exists in defiance of, not in conformity with, the fundamental laws of the universe. The creation of life was an extremely unnatural act. The probability of life created by pure chance is unbelievable. The odds are far too great.***

There is the electromagnetic force, which encourages atoms to combine into molecules. This *strong nuclear force*, that holds atomic nuclei together, were it slightly stronger, a diproton, not hydrogen would be the major component of the universe, and no hydrogen means no stars, and no water which is absolutely *essential* for all forms of life.

Other objective truths are the strength of the *weak nuclear force* and the strength of *gravity*, which dominates the universe at distances greater than the size of molecules. Then there are clusters that mass into galaxies, stars, and planets, the mass and energy of the big bang, the temperature of the big bang, the rate of expansion of the universe, and much more. All of these forces have to mesh *perfectly* to produce the beautiful, wonderful universe, our solar system and the world in which we live. This could *not* be by chance, not if our understanding of the laws of nature is even approximately correct.

Consider carbon, element number six in the periodic table. Before carbon comes hydrogen, helium, lithium, beryllium and boron. After carbon, there is nitrogen, oxygen, and the rest of the 92 natural elements. All life, as we know it, is based on carbon. It is the only element that can form long and complex chains essential for the process(s) of life. Elsewhere in the universe life might be based on liquids other than water, but carbon is the necessary element for life. It is also the essential stepping stone for the production of all the other eighty-six natural elements heavier than carbon.

## Interdependency of Life:

Life is like a magnificent play (like Aristotle's orchestra, which has no score, no conductor, and no audience besides the players), and we are the actors or musicians. Each of us has a vital role to play, and we *cannot play it alone*. We exist in dependence of each other, to complete each other, in the service of each other. A complex web of *interdependency* exists in all nature—one with the other and all collectively. How well we participate and perform our roles determines the final score—*the Mystical Music of the Creator's Symphony.*

> ***Life is a beautiful wonderful adventure, a journey,***
> ***a process, a testing ground between the forces of good***
> ***and evil. The amazing thing about our journey in life***
> ***is that the events, for which we are most grateful for***
> ***now, were most painful then. Because its progress, not***

> ***perfection, its process—each and every life epitomizes
> a unique journey. --Author***

> ***The more immanent the activity, the higher the
> life: movement of execution, movement of form,
> and movement towards an ultimate and glorious
> end. –Ralph W. Emerson***

A tree is no less perfect because it is a seedling. A flower, such as a rose, is beautiful and perfect, even before it reaches full bloom. An infant child is beautiful, wonderful, and no less perfect than the adult it will soon become. Because it cannot yet do things, does not know things—does not make it less perfect. That created child is perfection itself—so too are you—as adolescents and adults. All life forms are self-maintaining, self-renewal, self-transcending and interdependent. Life follows a preconceived intelligent pattern.

Life is self-maintaining. Intelligence exists within each of us and externally in that nature knows when to do things, according to time and season: a tree knows when to grow leaves, when to flower, when to produce fruit and seeds.

> ***Don't judge each day by the harvest you reap but by the
> seeds that you plant.*** **Robert Louis Stevenson**

Life is self-renewal in that it replaces itself constantly. Our skin and other organs replace themselves slowly, continuously (a complete replacement takes about seven years). Life is self-transcending in that it's constantly evolving, creating new forms of itself, and these micro-mutations adapt to circumstances in nature. All life forms are interdependent with each other, and cannot exist alone.

## MACRO-EVOLUTION:

Small changes within microbes and creatures has been proven; that's *Microevolution* theory. However, many public school textbooks also declare that we (and all living things) are "simply objects of blind natural processes and *macroevolution*." But where is the evidence?

Two key biologists have emerged as leading skeptics of Darwinism: Jonathan Wells, in *Icons of Evolution,* shows that the scientific evidence conflicts with this textbook theory. Michael Behe, author of *Darwin's Black Box,* and *The Edge of Evolution*, demonstrates how intricate machines inside all living cells *could not* have evolved; thus they were designed. More recently, Stephen C. Meyer's book *Signature in the Cell* shows that digital code embedded in DNA points to "a designing intelligence," and helps to unravel a mystery that Charles Darwin did not address at all: *How did life begin?*

Furthermore, random mutations using many generations of malaria (among other microbes), demonstrates that mutations and natural selection *doesn't work*; if anything it's negative. There is no evidence for a molecules-to-man theory at all. Additional research by noted worldwide generic expert, Dr. John C. Sanford, in *Genetic Entropy & the Mystery of the Genome*, also demonstrates that the "ape to man via genetic meltdown [is]: *"A theory in crisis."*

## Phenomena of Life:

The universe and all its processes make up a whole, whose essential four components are matter (also dark matter), energy, space, and time. In order to cope with this vast subject, scientists divide it into different levels of analogous phenomena and work with each "level" individually. Looking back on the history of human knowledge, we see that these phenomena have been grouped according to the nature of the principles and scientific "laws" created to understand them. Thus the phenomena of life have been distinguished from those of the nonliving universe. This was done for a number of reasons, but the most basic is that life, although chemically based on the inorganic world, cannot be explained in terms of the laws of physics and chemistry. No scientist has yet produced a living thing, not even a single living cell, or bacteria from chemicals in a test tube.

Many anthropologists argue that culture, although dependent upon and growing out of life, *cannot* be completely explained in terms of biological or even psychological principles. Accordingly, there are three primary levels of phenomena: (1) Inorganic or physical universe, (2) Biological or living world, and (3) the Cultural world of societies. Each of these principles of organization requires special techniques of study, analysis, and explanation.

## HOMO SAPIENS:

Scientific evidence suggests prehistoric creatures with human-like bodies and brains, namely *Neanderthals*, existed hundreds of thousands of years before this age, and overlapped with *Homo sapiens*. The fossil evidence of Cro-Magnon (Homo sapiens), some forty thousand years ago, resembles a human, although a direct link to any past creature was missing until recently.

Recent DNA evidence also indicates that Homo sapiens and Neanderthals bred together. Interestingly, much of this inbreeding between Neanderthals and Homo sapiens occurred in Europe, according to recent gene research results. These creatures had limited intelligence. All Neanderthals suddenly became extinct after the more intelligent Homo sapiens dominated the world.

Creatures whose anatomical appearance is indistinguishable from modern man existed about 40,000 years ago, during the last *major* ice-age. The skeletal materials of these early human-like types come from Africa, Asia, and Europe. There is *circumstantial evidence* that they entered the Americas about 30,000 years ago. The earliest human-like fossil discovered in the New World, a skeleton from Midland, Texas, dates back 20,000 years.

In *Mapping Human History*, Steve Olson traces the history of humankind through mitochondrial DNA analysis. (Source: *Y-Origins*, Volume One, www.y-zine.com). By analyzing human fossils and DNA samples throughout history, new and stunning insights regarding human ancestry have been forthcoming: "With the appearance of modern humans, the large-scale evolution of our species essentially ceased." Pale-anthropologist at Cambridge University, Marta Lahr, explains, "The bulk of the chronological and genetic data indicate a single origin of all modern humans." We all descended from a single ancestor, from a single set of parents.

## Homo Naledi found in a South African cave.

A team of "underground astronauts" removed more than 1,500 bones belonging to at least 15 individuals. Homo Naledi had human-like face, feet and hands, but a short, ape-like torso and a very small brain. The new species appears to have intentionally buried its dead, a behaviour thought to be previously limited to humans.

John Hawks of the University of Wisconsin-Madison, a senior author on the paper describing the new species, said: "Naledi might be a transitional creature. It has human-like aspects but is also very primitive, so it is a mixture. It has human-like feet and lower legs, and very human teeth and cranial architecture, but the brain is much smaller than ours. The shoulders, though, are more similar to those of apes. We don't yet know when they existed or what they were doing or what their social system was like." Its brain is the size of an orange "perched atop a very slender body", said Hawks, and it appears to have weighed on average 45kg and stood 1.5m tall. It also has hands that might have been capable of using tools and curved fingers perfect for climbing, while the feet are "virtually indistinguishable from those of modern humans," said Dr. William Harcourt-Smith of City University of New York. The bones were first discovered in 2013 by Witwatersrand University (WU) scientists and volunteer cavers in the Cradle of Humankind, a UNESCO World Heritage Site. "I am pleased to introduce you to a new species of human ancestor," Lee Berger, a research professor at the WU in Johannesburg, told reporters at the site.

## CREATION HYPOTHESIS:

According to Genesis 2:22: The Lord "made" woman from the rib he had taken out of the man, and brought her to man. Man said, *"This is now bone of my bones and flesh of my flesh; she shall be called 'woman,' for she was taken out of man."* This author's hypothesis is that the Creator selected from his earlier "made" creatures, which had evolved over thousands of years, and became the prototype for man and woman. God then breathed upon them, when they reached the age of twenty, giving Adam and Eve eternal spiritual souls. This hypothesis makes Darwin's micro-evolution theory *compatible* with the Genesis.

It is further proposed, that during Cain, Abel, and Seth's timeframe, that Cain, who was evil, had sex with Neanderthals (creatures lacking spiritual souls), thus spreading his wickedness. If this hypothesis is correct, then that would explain why the Creator destroyed them by a regional flood, during Noah's time.

The really important question is this: Why were humans with souls created? If *Genesis* was science and the *Origin of Species* was religion, these two viewpoints might meet and conflict. Darwin does *not* indicate who created humans or why? He merely indicates how they could have evolved (again, it's a theory that has never been proven). Genesis in Scripture explains, *"who and why?"*

Support for my hypothesis comes from the chapter on *The Origin of Humankind*, from Dr. Schroeder's book: *The Science of God*: "The *making* of mankind relates to the *body* of Adam. The Hebrew word *Adam* has its root in the Hebrew *adamah*, meaning soil. The *creation* of Adam relates to the human soul, the *nashama*. Since legend tells us that Adam was *created* at twenty years of age, is it possible that Adam-like being [Homo sapiens] lived during those first nineteen years without *neshama*, and then became human at age twenty with the *neshama's* creation by God. Scripture also teaches that only at age twenty does one become responsible for one's actions (Num. 1:3; 14:29; Deut. 1:29)."

## Early Human History:

40,000: Nomadic tribes roam Africa, Asia, Middle East and Europe.

10,000: Ice Age ends, southern tribes move to Europe and Americas.

7,000: Hunter-gatherers become food producers and farmers.

6,000: Adam and Eve appear in history, according to the Genesis.

5,000: Bronze Age in Mesopotamia and the Middle East.

4,500: Ox-drawn plow replaces hoe.

4,100: Noah Great flood (regional) destroys much of humanity.

3,400 First written language by Sumerians.

3,300: Invention of the wheel.

3,000: Hieroglyphic writing appears in Egypt.

2,100: Abraham and Sarah travel to the land of Canaan (Gen. 12:5)

## Population Trends:

Human population has grown very slowly. Scientists currently estimate that human beings (Homo sapiens) evolved roughly 130,000 to 160,000 years ago. Threats from diseases to climate fluctuations kept the life expectancy short in pre-industrial society. It took until 1804 for the population to reach one billion. From that point forward, population growth accelerated:

| World population | Year | Time to add each billion |
| --- | --- | --- |
| 1 billion | 1804 | |
| 2 billion | 1927 | 123 years |
| 3 billion | 1960 | 33 years |
| 4 billion | 1974 | 14 years |
| 5 billion | 1987 | 13 years |
| 6 billion | 1999 | 12 years |

By 2010 we reached about 7.5 billion people. Millions have died from infectious diseases, such as the pandemic, black plague, typhoid and cholera, which spread rapidly in the crowded, filthy conditions that were common in early factory towns and major cities, or they were weakened by poor nutrition. But from about 1850 through 1950, a cascade of health and safety advances radically improved living conditions in industrialized nations. These major milestones include:

## Advances Extended Life:

- 1796 Vaccination by Edward Jenner;
- 1846 Anesthesia by Thomas Green Morton;
- 1863 Pasteurization from Louis Pasteur's germ theory;
- 1866 Plant breeding by botanist Fr. Gregory Mendel;
- 1885 Vaccines by Louis Pasteur;
- 1818 Nitrogen fertilizers by Fritz Haber, by which Norman Borlaug began the "Green Revolution";
- 1850s Sanitation systems, and refrigeration;
- 1895 X-rays by Wilhelm Conrad; and
- 1928 Penicillin by Alexander Fleming.
- 1956 DNA codes show life is preprogrammed.
- 2021 Corona-19 (Chinese virus) vaccine.

Other improvements in medical practices included researching causes and means of transmission of infectious diseases, and developing vaccines and antibiotics, and recent advanced drugs to control previously uncontrollable diseases. By the mid-20th century, most industrialized nations had passed through the demographic transition. As health technologies were transferred to developing nations, many of these countries entered the mortality transition and their population swelled. The world's population rate of growth peaked in the late 1960s, at just over two percent per year (compared to about 2.5 percent in developing countries).

## Life Expectancy:

> *No person dies before his or her hour. The time you leave behind was no more yours, than that which was before your birth, and [concerns] you no more.* --**Emperor Marcus Aurelius, *Meditations*:**

Human life expectancy at birth has increased from about 55 in 1900, to about 79 years by 2010. Heart disease has been the leading cause of death (other than natural disasters and man-made wars) for most of the past century. Although the heart disease "epidemic" peaked in the 1960s at about 350 deaths per 100,000 people, it has since been cut in half. Cancer kills as many people as heart disease.

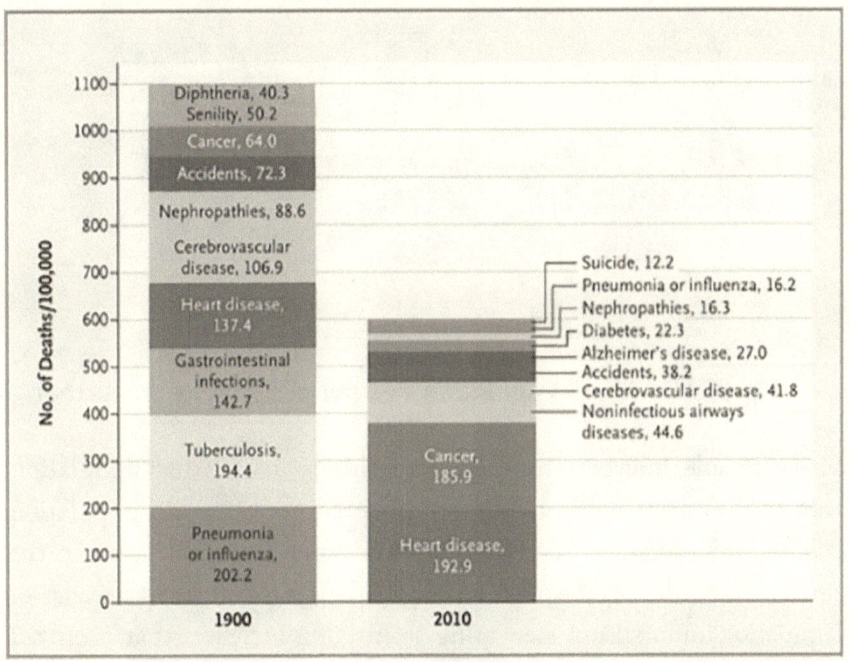


> **Fig. 2 New England Journal of Medicine. Illustrated by Author***

Human intelligence during the past century has eliminated serious diseases such as tuberculosis, flu, smallpox, malaria (except Africa), and polio. As a result, demographers currently project that Earth's population will reach just over nine billion before 2050, with virtually all growth occurring in developing countries (Africa, India, China).

Future fertility trends will strongly affect the course of population growth. This estimate assumes that fertility will decline from 2.6 children per woman in 2005, to slightly over 2 children per woman in 2050, worldwide.

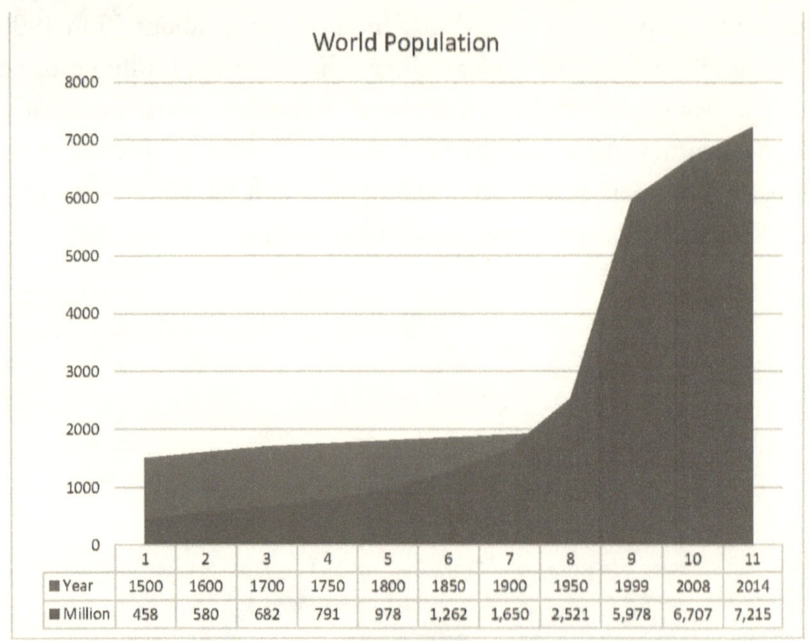



| | 1 | 2 | 3 | 4 | 5 | 6 | 7 | 8 | 9 | 10 | 11 |
|---|---|---|---|---|---|---|---|---|---|---|---|
| ■ Year | 1500 | 1600 | 1700 | 1750 | 1800 | 1850 | 1900 | 1950 | 1999 | 2008 | 2014 |
| ■ Million | 458 | 580 | 682 | 791 | 978 | 1,262 | 1,650 | 2,521 | 5,978 | 6,707 | 7,215 |

➢ **Fig. 3* UN World Population Prospects**. **Chart by the Author.**

Many people interpret forecasts like this to mean that population growth is "out of control. In fact, as noted above, world population *growth rates* peaked in the late 1960s and have declined sharply in the past four decades. The world's total population is still rising because of population momentum stemming from large increases that occurred in developing countries in the 1950s and early 1960s. But fertility rates are rapidly falling as many developing countries pass through the demographic transition, due to factors that include lower infant mortality rates, expanding human rights, better education, and labor market opportunities for women, and increased access to family planning services.

World population growth in the 21st century will be different from previous decades in several important ways. First, humans are living longer and having fewer children, so there will be an older population. In Florida, nearly 25% of the population are senior citizens (age 60 and above), for example. Second, all population growth will mostly occur in urban areas. Third, fertility rates will continue to decline.

All of these trends will affect nations' economic development. Senior citizens can be active and productive members of society, but they have many unique needs in areas ranging from medical care to housing and transportation. Growing elderly populations will strain social services, especially in countries that have not developed social safety nets to guarantee adequate incomes and support for older citizens. As societies age, demand for younger workers will increase, drawing more people into the labor force and attracting immigrants in search of work. Declining fertility rates allow more women to work outside of the home, which increases the labor supply and may further accelerate the demographic transition.

Some observers argue that declining fertility rates in both industrialized and developing countries will lead to a "birth dearth," with shrinking populations draining national savings and reducing tax revenues. However, societies can transition successfully from high mortality and fertility, to low mortality and fertility, with sound planning. Promoting good health standards (especially for children), expanding education, opening up to international trade, and supporting older citizens through retirement, are all policies that can offset the negative impacts on society of an aging population.

## GENETIC ENTROPY:

Dr. John C. Sanford writes: "What is the mystery of the genome? Its very existence is its mystery. Intelligent information and complexity which surpass human understanding are programmed into a space smaller than an invisible speck of dust. Mutation or selection cannot even begin to explain this. It should be very clear that our genome could *not* have arisen spontaneously.

> **"The only reasonable alternative to a spontaneous genome is a genome which arose by [intelligent] design. Isn't that an awesome mystery—one worthy of our contemplation?" Dr. Sanford, *Genetic Entropy*.**

Dr. Sanford continues: "We have reviewed compelling evidence that when ignoring deleterious mutations, *mutation/selection cannot create a single gene*—not within the human evolutionary time scale. When deleterious mutations are factored back in, we see that mutation/selection cannot create a single gene—*ever*. In my opinion this constitutes what is essentially a formal proof that *the Primary Axiom [evolution] is false.*

"In conclusion, the genome must have been designed, and could not have evolved. If the primary Axiom is wrong, then our basic understanding of life history is also wrong. If our genome is degenerating, then our species is not evolving, but is essentially 'aging.'"

> ***All humans evolve to every-more creativity. The process of evolution of the universe is experimental. There is not a predetermined, automaton universe. There is room for trial and error. There is opportunity for newness. There is freedom of choice.* --Author**

What we are and what we may become is determined by four factors:

(1)  Nature: genetics, our DNA.
(2)  Nurturing: parental care, early guidance.
(3)  Education: especially at an early age.
(4)  Environmental: early role models, peer groups, positive or negative experiences.

One can control some of these factors, except perhaps heredity, although whom we choose as our mate is generally a very good, or an extremely bad decision. Consider this vital point: mass killers, dictators, terrorists and bizarre characters in our history were probably lovable, adorable young children. What made them become bad guys and girls? One or more of the above four key factors were responsible for who or what they ultimately became.

Readers should *not* think that the author believes that such bad acts are justified because of any of the above factors. Nothing can be further from the truth! Human beings, who are not mentally handicapped, know right from wrong, and have free will, *choose* to do evil acts. They are responsible, and must pay the *consequences*.

## INTELLIGENT DESIGN:

> *Intelligent Design is defined as: science that studies signs of intelligence. Note that a sign is not the thing signified. Intelligent design directly challenges Darwinism (specifically macro-evolution theory) and other naturalistic approaches to the origin and evolution of life.* --**William A. Dembski**

The following excerpts are from a paper titled: *The origin of biological information and the higher taxonomic categories* by Stephen C. Meyer. (Serious students of biology and ID should review Meyer's entire paper in the *Proceedings of the Biological Society* of Washington, 117 (2): 213-239 (2004), and especially his new amazing work called: *Signature of the Cell*.

**Hierarchical Systems**: Building a new animal from a single-celled organism requires a vast amount of new genetic information. It also requires a way of arranging gene products—proteins—into higher levels of organization. New proteins are required to service new cell types. But new proteins must be organized into new systems within the cell; new cell types must be organized into new tissues, organs, and body parts. These, in turn, must be organized to form body plans. New animals, therefore, embody hierarchically organized systems of lower-level parts within a functional whole. Such hierarchical organization itself represents a type of information, since body plans comprise both highly improbable and functionally specified arrangements of lower-level parts. The specified complexity of new body plans requires explanation in any account of the Cambrian explosion. More than 500 million years ago, 95% of all species suffered *massive extinction*, probably from an asteroid or comet smashing into earth, and yet an "explosion of totally new forms of life" (numerous metazoan body plans or living phyla) developed almost immediately *after* this worldwide extinction happened.

**Developmental Biology**: The problems with the neo-Darwinian mechanism run deeper still. In order to explain the origin of the Cambrian animals one must account not only for new proteins and cell types, but also for the origin of (about fifty) new body plans. Within the past decade, developmental biology has dramatically advanced our understanding of how body plans are built during ontogeny. In the process, it has also uncovered a profound difficulty for Neo-Darwinism.

Two analogies may help further clarify the point. At a building site, builders will make use of many materials: lumber, wires, nails, drywall, piping, and windows. Yet building materials do not determine the floor plan of the house, or the arrangement of houses in a neighborhood. Similarly, electronic circuits are composed of many components, such as resistors, capacitors, and transistors. But such lower-level components do not determine their own arrangement in an integrated circuit.

**Random Mutations:** Biological systems also depend on hierarchical arrangements of parts. Genes and proteins are made from simple building blocks—nucleotide bases and amino acids—arranged in specific ways. Cell types are made of, among other things, systems of specialized proteins. Organs are made of specialized arrangements of cell types and tissues. And body plans comprise specific arrangements of specialized organs. Yet, clearly, the properties of individual proteins (or, indeed, the lower-level parts in the hierarchy generally) do not fully determine the organization of the higher-level structures and organizational patterns. It follows that the genetic information that codes for proteins does not determine these higher-level structures either. Thus, the mechanism of natural selection acting on random mutations in DNA *cannot in principle* generate novel body plans, including those that first arose in the Cambrian explosion.

Could the notion of *purposive design* help provide a more adequate explanation for the origin of (organism) form generally? Are there reasons to consider design as an explanation for the origin of the biological information necessary to produce the higher taxa and their corresponding morphological novelty? The remainder of this review will suggest that there are such reasons.

First, the possibility of design as an explanation follows logically from a consideration of the deficiencies of Neo-Darwinism and other current theories as explanations for some of the more striking "appearances of design" in biological systems. Neo-Darwinists such as Ayala (1994), Dawkins (1986), Mayr (1982: xi-xii) and Lewontin (1978) have long acknowledged that organisms appear to have been designed.

**Competing Hypotheses:** A second reason for considering design as an explanation for these phenomena follows from the importance of explanatory power to scientific theory evaluation and from a consideration of the potential explanatory power of the design hypothesis. Studies in the methodology and philosophy of science have shown that many scientific theories, particularly in the historical sciences, are formulated and justified as inferences to the best explanation (Lipton 1991:32-88, Brush 1989:1124-1129, Sober 2000:44). Historical scientists, in particular, assess or test competing hypotheses by evaluating which hypothesis would, if true, provide the best explanation for some set of relevant data (Meyer 1991, 2002; Cleland 2001:987-989, 2002:474-496). Those with greater explanatory power are typically judged to be better, more probably true, theories. Darwin (1896:437) used this method of reasoning in defending his theory of universal common descent.

**Intelligent Agents:** In the first place, intelligent human agents—in virtue of their rationality and consciousness—have demonstrated the power to produce information in the form of linear sequence-specific arrangements of characters. Indeed, experience affirms that information of this type routinely arises from the activity of intelligent agents. A computer user who traces the information on a screen back to its source invariably comes to a *mind*—that of a software engineer or programmer. The information in a book or inscriptions ultimately derives from a writer or scribe—from a mental, rather than a strictly material, cause.

Our experience-based knowledge of information-flow confirms that systems with large amounts of specified complexity (especially codes and languages) invariably originate from an intelligent source, from a mind or personal agent. As Quastler (1964) put it, "creation of new information is habitually associated with conscious activity." Experience teaches this obvious truth.

**Form and Function:** Further, the highly specified hierarchical arrangements of parts in animal body plans also suggest *design*, again because of our experience of the kinds of features and systems that designers can and do produce. At every level of the biological hierarchy, organisms require specified and highly improbable arrangements of lower-level constituents in order to maintain their form and function. Genes require specified arrangements of nucleotide bases; proteins require specified arrangements of amino acids; new cell types require specified arrangements of systems of proteins; body plans require specialized arrangements of cell types and organs. Organisms not only contain information-rich components (such as proteins and genes), but they comprise information-rich arrangements of those components and the systems that comprise them. Yet we know, based on our present experience of cause and effect relationships, that design engineers—possessing purposive intelligence and rationality—have the ability to produce information-rich hierarchies in which both individual modules and the arrangements of those modules exhibit complexity and specificity—information so defined.

**Electronic Circuit Analogy:** Individual transistors, resistors, and capacitors exhibit considerable complexity and specificity of design; at a higher level of organization their specific arrangement within an integrated circuit represents additional information and reflects further design. Conscious and rational agents have, as part of their powers of purposive intelligence, the capacity to design information-rich parts and to organize those parts into functional information-rich systems and hierarchies. Further, we know of no other causal entity or process that has this capacity. Clearly, we have good reason to doubt that mutation and selection, self-organizational processes or laws of nature, can produce the information-rich components, systems, and body plans necessary to explain the origination of morphological novelty such as that which arises in the Cambrian period.

**Random Variations:** There is a third reason to consider purpose or design as an explanation for the origin of biological form and information: purposive agents have just those necessary powers that natural selection lacks as a condition of its causal adequacy. At several points in the previous analysis, we saw that natural selection lacked the ability to generate novel information precisely because it can only act *after* new function has arisen. Natural selection can favor new proteins, and genes, but only after they perform some function. The job of generating new functional genes, proteins and systems of proteins therefore falls entirely on random mutations. Yet without functional criteria to guide a search through the space of possible sequences, random variation is probabilistically doomed. What is needed is not just a source of variation (i.e., the freedom to search a space of possibilities) or a mode of selection that can operate after the fact of a successful search, but instead a means of selection that (a) operates during a search—before success—and that (b) is guided by information about, or knowledge of, a functional target.

**Genetic Algorithms:** Demonstration of this requirement has come from an unlikely quarter: genetic algorithms. Genetic algorithms are programs that allegedly simulate the creative power of mutation and selection. Dawkins and Kippers, for example, have developed computer programs that putatively simulate the production of genetic information by mutation and natural selection (Dawkins 1986:47-49, Kippers 1987:355-369). Nevertheless, as shown elsewhere (Meyer 1998:127-128, 2003:247-248), these programs only succeed by the illicit expedient of providing the computer with a "target sequence" and then treating relatively greater proximity to *future* function (i.e., the target sequence), not actual present function, as a selection criterion. As Belinsky (2000) has argued, genetic algorithms need something akin to a "forward looking memory" in order to succeed. Yet such foresighted selection has no analogue in nature. In biology, where differential survival depends upon maintaining function, selection cannot occur before new functional sequences arise.

**Natural Selection and Foresight:** What natural selection lacks, intelligent selection—purposive or goal-directed design—provides. Rational agents can arrange both matter and symbols with distant goals in mind. In using language, the human mind routinely "finds" or generates highly improbable linguistic sequences to convey an intended or *pre*conceived idea. In the process of thought, functional objectives precede and constrain the selection of words, sounds and symbols to generate functional (and indeed meaningful) sequences from among a vast ensemble of meaningless alternative combinations of sound or symbol (Denton 1986:309-311).

Indeed, in all functionally integrated complex systems where the cause is known by experience or observation, design engineers or other intelligent agents applied boundary constraints to limit possibilities in order to produce improbable forms, sequences or structures. Rational agents have repeatedly demonstrated the capacity to constrain the possible to actualize improbable but initially unrealized future functions. Repeated experience affirms that intelligent agents (minds) uniquely possess such causal powers.

Analysis of the problem of the origin of biological information, therefore, exposes a deficiency in the causal powers of natural selection that corresponds precisely to powers that agents are uniquely known to possess. Intelligent agents have foresight. Such agents can select functional goals *before* they exist. They can devise or select material means to accomplish those ends from among an array of possibilities and then actualize those goals in accord with a preconceived design plan or set of functional requirements.

Rational agents can constrain combinatorial space with distant outcomes in mind. The causal powers that natural selection lacks—almost by definition—are associated with the attributes of consciousness and rationality—with purposive intelligence. Thus, by invoking design to explain the origin of new biological information, contemporary design theorists are not positing an arbitrary explanatory element unmotivated by a consideration of the evidence. Instead, they are positing an entity possessing precisely the attributes and causal powers that the phenomenon in question requires as a condition of its production and explanation.

**Conclusion:** An experience-based analysis of the causal powers of various explanatory hypotheses suggests purposive or intelligent design as a causally adequate—and perhaps the most causally adequate—explanation for the origin of the complex specified information required to build the Cambrian animals and the novel forms they represent. For this reason, recent scientific interest in the design hypothesis is unlikely to abate as biologists continue to wrestle with the problem of the origination of biological form and the higher taxa.

Reader Note: Dr. Stephen C. Meyer paper was *peer-reviewed* and accepted for publication by Dr. Richard Von Sternberg, who holds two PhDs in the evolutionary biology field. Dr. Sternberg subsequently experienced *serious retaliation* by his co-workers and upper management at the Smithsonian because he permitted an "open discussion of a dissenting scientific viewpoint," despite the fact that he is neither a proponent of ID nor a Creationist. (See *Washington Post*, August 19, 2005, "Editor explains reasons for ID article."

## UNIVERSAL HIERARCHY

Interview with George Gilder (abridged). Source: Ruthie Blum, *The Jerusalem Post*, June 20, 2007

George Gilder has been famous in the United States for more than three decades. Infamous would be a more accurate adjective — considering the political-cultural climate in which he emerged and to which he has devoted his life's research and writings-- Gilder's best-selling book was *Wealth and Poverty* (1981).

Dozens of books, hundreds of articles, an influential newsletter and a think-tank later (the Seattle-based Discovery Institute, which he co-founded with Bruce Chapman, who accompanied him on a trip to Israel), the 68-year-old expert in microchips is raising more eyebrows than ever. Being a techno-scientist who opposes Darwin's theory of evolution will do that. Gilder's lengthy and diverse resume includes, having been a fellow at the Kennedy Institute of Politics at Harvard (from where he graduated), serving as a speechwriter for Nelson Rockefeller and Richard Nixon and receiving the White House Award for Entrepreneurial Excellence from president Ronald Reagan, he says that everything he has examined points to the same "top-down" model. "The universe is hierarchical," says Gilder, with the intensity of someone racing to keep up with a mind constantly in overdrive. "And hierarchy points to a summit. The summit remains enclosed in fog, but this doesn't exclude the possibility that behind the fog is a divinity that we, through our faith, might worship."

In an hour-long interview with *The Jerusalem Post*, Gilder clarifies how his scientific reasoning, political positions and religious faith are not only consistent with one another, but converge in a way that makes sense out of life — and, makes life make sense.

### You're a scientist who questions evolution. Can you explain that?

The Darwinians essentially uphold that the human brain is all the intelligence in the universe. We claim that this is an improbable proposition. Evolution happens in various limited ways, and explains very little about the world and the universe in which we live. We arrived at this from economics. Even the most aggressive free-market theorists, such as Paul Romer — who is on track for a Nobel Prize — identify the entrepreneur, as someone who *reassembles* chemical elements. His great breakthrough was to show that the entrepreneur has a tremendous amount of freedom, because there are so many chemical elements and so many ways they can be combined. In other words, the fundamental thing is matter, and the entrepreneur can rearrange the matter in different ways. But no novelty or innovation or idea-based invention is really acknowledged, even by Romer, who goes beyond the Austrian economists, who are supposed to be real specialists in human action. They see the entrepreneur as an opportunity scout. He looks out there at the material world and sees ways to reconcile price differentials by arbitrage. This is really a residue of Marxism and dialectical materialism. It seems that Darwinian materialism (macro-evolutionism) is the kind of hard science that all the social theorists use to justify their blindness to creativity or ideas or mind. It's a blindness that covers the whole intellectual world in the aftermath of Marx and the other materialist theories that have afflicted this century.

***You point to the "blindness" of the materialists. What would constitute "sight"? The acknowledgement of the existence of intelligence that is independent of matter? God, for instance?***

God requires faith; it is not a matter of science. The science of Intelligent Design accommodates the possibility of God — even points in some crude way to God, if you want to look at the vector of its thought. But it does not define or specify or prove God. Darwinians think they can prove the *absence* of God. And what they do know — as leading physicist and Nobel Laureate Steven Weinberg says — is that the earth and life are *astronomically improbable*. The way he explains it, then, is through infinite, multiple, parallel universes. This must be one of the silliest scientific stratagems in the history of the world [*he laughs*]. No kind of thought is ever so utterly obtuse as to imagine that every electron generates a new universe as it makes its path — which is the way they explain how this incredibly improbable world could exist.

***How do you explain how this "incredibly improbable world could exist"?***

Creation: we see creation in economics; we see creation in computer science. You can know everything there is to know about the physics and chemistry of a microchip, without having the slightest inkling of what function it's performing, let alone what content it is processing. The same goes for network theory. You can know every electron or atom across a fiber-optic network, without having any idea of what contents are being transmitted. In network theory, you have seven layers of abstraction. Those same seven layers also apply, in slightly different form, to a computer system. Both are exhaustively and intelligently designed, with elaborate and extraordinarily complex equipment, which itself is exhaustively designed and not intelligible unless you know the "source code." The theory that governs design in the microchip — invented 28-29 years ago by Carver Mead and Lynn Conway — is called "hierarchical design." It is a top-down design, the crux of which is that it is independent of its material embodiment.

**Is that what you're saying about human biology, as well?**

In biology, you find exactly the same model. The content of the DNA program is completely independent of the DNA chemistry: the sugar-phosphate frames that hold the nucleotides do not in any way affect the content of the program that the genes bear. And this is not a casual part of DNA discovery. In fact, it has been pronounced by Francis Crick as nothing less than the central dogma of biology — that the DNA program can affect, and even determine, proteins through the amino acids that they specify; but the proteins in amino acids cannot affect the DNA. In other words, the word affects the flesh; the flesh does not dictate the word. The same pattern that's in computer science and economics and networks reappears in almost the same way in biology.

**What does any of this have to do with Darwinism — which most of us think of as "the survival of the fittest"?**

Darwinism (macro-evolutionism) is a materialist theory, according to which ideas are mere epiphenomena of material forces. Indeed, Darwin did not understand genetics. He actually imagined that inheritance was conveyed by chemical reactions — that the chemicals blended between the two parents in some way. In information theory, which is really the basis of most of my own analysis, chemical blending can't carry information. The key rule in information theory is that it takes a low entropy — a predictable carrier — to bear a high-entropy message. Now, even DNA can't explain the larger question [of the meaning of life on earth]. For example, we share a high percentage of our DNA with garden slugs.

As for "survival of the fittest" — random mutations and natural selection — it, too, explains very little. What random mutations and natural selection can explain is the way bacteria adjust or respond to antibiotics. This is a demonstrable case which can actually be studied. What it shows is that bacteria change, but *do not improve*. And if a bacterium happens to change, it does so in a way that nullifies the effect of a certain antibiotic. Then it multiplies, according to the rules of natural selection, and you get a bacterium with that change. But that bacterium *doesn't* evolve into some more complex, multi-cellular creature. Because the limited nature of this phenomenon is becoming increasingly understood, all sorts of speculative theories arise that try to retrieve some of the total lack of intelligence in the process. Again, it's just materialism, and it's very boring. All of science is based on the assumption that the *mind is independent of the data*. But, if the mind is a mingle of matter that essentially flows into the phenomenon being appraised, then all of science becomes incoherent; it collapses. We like to quote the great physicist-turned-biologist Max Delbruck, who said: "The attempt of neuroscientists to create a purely material brain reminds me of nothing so much as Baron Munchausen's effort to extract himself from a swamp by pulling ever harder on his own hair."

**You said that God requires faith — that it is not science. If so, what is your gripe with scientists who view the human organism as an entity separate from the soul?**

In my next book, which is called *Analogy*, I argue that what happened with Albert Einstein was that scientists stopped being engineers and began being theologians. They stopped being masters of the crucial equipment with which they conducted their experiments, testing their hypotheses and restricted their propositions to demonstrable phenomena, and they began reifying math. "Multiple parallel universes," for example, is just a reification of a model of electron paths — invented by Richard Feynman — which proved to be a very successful tool for mapping the path of a single electron. The assumption that all the electron paths actually existed and each one generated a universe of its own and transcended to infinite numbers of universes is just *delusional materialism*. It is a desperate tactic to avoid facing the implications of the incredible complexity and particularity of the world in which we live and of our own minds. The effort to reduce consciousness to pure material phenomena is a total failure, but still, it doesn't stop. In other words, the key thing that makes us human and makes science possible and makes the theoretician viable, he denies.

**You say that scientists stopped being masters of the equipment with which they tested hypotheses. Are you implying that science is actually regressing rather than progressing?**

In engineering science, there are tremendous advancements and achievements. But theoretical scientists profiteer on the prestige that is earned by the engineers. Carver Mead, the greatest engineer in Silicon Valley by many estimates, believes that we've had a Dark Age in theoretical science since early this century.

**You mentioned computer source codes. What are they, actually?**

The source code tells, in intelligible language, what functions all the unintelligible array of binary symbols means.

*If you take* Genesis *as an allegory, is the Tree of Knowledge the source code?*

Yes, it sounds like the Tree of Knowledge might be a particularly exalted source code — the divine source code that is beyond our reach. God, whose very name can't be voiced; it's the assertion that total knowledge means usurpation of the Godhead. And that human beings are not capable of such knowledge.

**Maybe that the minute they aim for it, their punishment is mortality. If your computer succeeded in having a personality, it would no longer be a computer, after all.**

Yes, and of course, there's endless science fiction that envisions such computers. Many people project the development of such computers as an extension of Moore's Law, ordaining that every 18 months the capacity of computers essentially doubles. Ray Kurzweil' book, *The Singularity Is Near*, follows this logic that the human mind is nothing but a particularly complex circuitry which, through some set of feedback loops, generated consciousness. My belief is that no matter how many transistors they put in the computer, it won't have consciousness. It will still be a machine that can be manipulated by a programmer or owner.

**Is consciousness the difference between humanity and other life forms? Dogs have consciousness, don't they?**

We have a much richer consciousness that far exceeds that of dogs; it's qualitatively distinct. There's a tendency today to blur the distinction between dogs and human beings, or dolphins and human beings, or chimpanzees and human beings. But there really isn't such a close tie, unless you assume that human beings are essentially animals, and consciousness, intelligence, abstraction, will, aspirations, sentiment and intentionality are all mere epiphenomena.

**In other words, the difference between human beings and animals doesn't lie in degree, but rather in essence.**

Yes. The dolphin and the chimpanzee are *assumed* to have all our capabilities, in slightly or substantially less developed form.

**Throughout this discussion, you haven't really said that Intelligent Design means God.**

I said that intelligent design allows the *possibility* of God. It doesn't *specify* God, or *dictate* God, define or put God in a box, but it does show that the universe is hierarchical. And hierarchy points to a summit. The summit remains enclosed in fog, but this doesn't exclude the possibility that behind the fog is a divinity that we, through our faith, might worship. The hierarchy itself orients us to aspire and to aim for higher levels of being, consciousness, complexity and intelligence, rather than seek to follow our animal natures down into a pit of futility and degradation.

**You don't exclude the possibility of God, because you see the hierarchical structure of our being. Yet you also don't assert that it is God at the summit which remains enclosed in fog either.**

I can talk about that; I'm just not going to say that it's science. It has to do with faith and imagination and aspiration and a sense of the good. A belief in God is essentially a belief that good will prevail, rather than entropy and futility and evil, which is the message of much of 20th-century literature and art.

**Isn't it more complicated than that? Contemporary writers and artists would argue that they are aspiring to the greater good of mankind.**

The greater good they proclaim is pleasure — that the pursuit of pleasure yields pleasure and therefore is good. I believe that pleasure is an epiphenomenon of the pursuit of good, rather than being something that can be directly pursued by the indulgence of appetites.

***But indulgence of appetites does lead to pleasure. Our brains —
whether their material manifestation or their hierarchical — tell
us we're hungry or sexually aroused. And we are compelled to sate
those appetites.***

We eat to be healthy and nourish ourselves, and in that pursuit we
experience pleasure. But gorging and gormandizing are likely to make
us sick — the opposite of pleasure. As for sex: It should have a higher
purpose — love, aspiration, procreation and other crucial dimensions.

***A huge population in the world today worships a higher power, has
great aspirations and commits mass murder in their pursuit.***

What they're worshiping is the devil. People who go around killing and
beheading other people in the name of God are pursuing Satan.

***Your life's work has been eclectic, to put it mildly. What do the
relations between men, women, supply-side economics, microchips
and intelligent design have in common?***

I believe that the universe is hierarchical, with creation at the top — the
idea that there's a Creator and that we, at our best, act in his image.
This top-down model is what all of my work has in common. I sensed
that the basic flaw and failure of feminism was its gradient toward pure
animal passion with no procreative purpose. In economics, I believed
that it was the supply that created the demand. In my examination
of computers and telecom, and subsequently biology, I saw the same
thing. That's really how I came into the Intelligent Design movement
— through the recognition of this same structure that I'd previously
examined in sexuality, economics, information theory, computer science
and network theory.

I'm a religious person. So are the Darwinians religious people: They
believe in an anti-religion of materialism that liberates them to pursue
pleasure any way they wish. It's the highest purpose of their existence.

They thus believe in a random, futilitarian universe where — if they're existentialists — they might imagine that occasionally a heroic human being could assert some purpose above the froth of randomness, but in general, we're all doomed to decay and destruction. That's pretty much the philosophy, and it's debauched a whole century of intellect. I think we're going to transcend it in the 21st century.

Life is very meaningful, and its meaning comes not from its physiology, but from its imagination and aspiration and worship. The fact that I believe these things is crucial to my ability to understand biology.

***If life on earth is indeed governed by a divine hierarchy, what difference does it make whether scientists espouse a materialist view? And isn't Intelligent Design stronger than the "futilitarian" forces you described?***

Human beings have free will. Paradoxically, this means that we aren't at liberty simply to withdraw from the fray and expect good to triumph. We have the burden of climbing that mountain. This combination of *destiny and free will* is the crowning paradox and glory of the human condition. The good does not necessarily triumph in one lifetime. What gives goodness its effect is that it transcends a particular lifetime. By committing to it, you partake of a higher order that surpasses your own life and its limits.

## BEING & LIFE TRUTH KEY POINTS:

- o   Life was *not* created by pure chance; the odds are too great.
- o   The laws of biology, chemistry, and physics determine which biological structures can and cannot evolve.
- o   The double helix genetic codes (DNA), guides all forms of life, from algae to oak trees, from microscopic bacteria, to humans.
- o   All natural life processes proceed by differentiation and integration, such as the human cell after it's fertilized.
- o   The human egg contains the entire Human Genome of a person.

o   Advances in food processes and medical technologies, since 1800, have extended human lives, and the population to seven billion persons.

o   Human life expectancy at birth has increased from about 55 in 1900, to about 79 years by 2010.

o   Promoting health standards, expanding education, opening up to international trade, and supporting older citizens, are all policies that help to offset the negative impact on society of an aging population.

o   During the Cambrian explosion, 530-540 million years ago, entirely new species came into being on planet Earth. It was an "explosion of new species."

o   Darwin's *Origin of the Species theory*—that nature does not make jumps, has been proven false, at the macro-evolution level.

o   Micro-evolution theory, that organisms evolve and adapt, has been proven accurate.

o   Intelligent design and evolution theories are compatible.

o   Intelligent Design directly challenges Darwinism (macro-evolution theory) and other naturalistic approaches to the origin and evolution of life.

o   Life is a wonderful adventure, a journey, a process, a testing ground between the great human moral forces of good and evil.

# II. Societal Truths

*The inferior person makes demands on other people, while persons of honor make demands on themselves.* --Chinese Maxim

## SOCIAL JUSTICE

What is social justice? Some say it is "equitable distribution of wealth." Is it equitable and reasonable to give those who earned their wealth by their intellect, hard work and risk taking to distribute their earnings to those who did not developed their own skills, never took any risks and worked much less? That is *Socialism*. How has socialistic societies worked out so far?

We have freedom, justice and opportunity, but the constitution *does not* give us any guarantees of economic outcomes or success. That depends of each individual's ingenuity, skills, risk taking, and determination. Social Justice is about "equal opportunity," to obtain a good education and develop a set of skills that makes one more marketable in this very competitive society. What is wrong with learning carpentry, plumbing, and electrical trades, among others?

There is no free ride; one has to earn their ticket to economic success.

## Marx & Mobs

Karl Marx and fellow German thinker Friedrich Engels (1848) published "*The Communist Manifesto,*" which introduced their concept of *socialism,* based on conflicts inherent in the Capitalist system. He denounced all religions, and this ideology was adopted by Russia, China, North Korea, Cuba, and Venezuela. Communism/Socialism began with mob rule, violence, toppling statues and governments to establish a new "utopian" world order. One cannot learn from history if it is erased.

More recently, the mayor of Seattle said this is simply a "Summer of Love." In reality, anarchists within these mobs rebelled against police authority, especially criminals who used violent means to overthrow the established order. Liberal Judges added to this chaos by releasing criminals *without* bail. That encouraged more violence and mob rule.

> **The goal of education is to "know and appreciate the goodness of this life, and to know the Wonder of the Lord.**

Endowed with a spiritual soul, and the gift of eternal life, the human person is the only known creature on earth that the Creator has willed for its own sake. The human person *participates* in the light, intelligence, creativity, and power of the Creator's Spirit:

By *reasoning*, humans are capable of understanding the natural order of things established by the Creator.

By *free will*, human persons are capable of directing themselves toward seeking what is true and good.

By *intelligence*, human persons are endowed with *knowledge*, which is an outstanding manifestation of the Divine Wisdom.

By *faith*, one recognizes the revealed message of the Creator, which urges them to do what is good and avoid what is evil.

Because of original sin, man and woman are divided within themselves as individuals and in social groups, in the endless struggle between what is good and evil. Civilized societies, states, and institutions must respect fundamental, God-given rights of every individual person; *it's the basic foundation of civilization.*

> **To be human means to be connected to others and have compassion for others. We are social beings and cannot be complete alone. We cannot empathize with inanimate objects—only with personas. –Author**

## FREEDOM & INDEPENDENCE:

> **The desire for complete and absolute freedom is not good. The birds and the beasts have more freedom than man does—aimlessness is natural to the lower forms of life. Obedience to duty and a sense of responsibility are natural to higher forms of life, humans. --Ralph Waldo Emerson**

Freedom, according to Thomas Aquinas, is for excellence, for virtue, for truth, for goodness, and for happiness. Freedom is a matter of gradually acquiring the ability to choose what is good, and avoiding what is bad; to do what we choose with perfection, with excellence. It's like slowly learning to paint or play a music instrument to perfection, and then one finally sees or hears *wondrous beauty.*

**Perfection is not attainable, but if we chase perfection we can catch excellence. Vince Lombardi**

Our youth today say: "*This is a free country; you can't tell me what to do!*" They may not fully realize that millions of men and women suffered and died for this freedom and independence in America (and elsewhere). Nevertheless, freedom, *without moral responsibility,* is not a good thing, as Emerson says so plainly, above.

John Adams in a speech to the military in 1798 warned his fellow countrymen stating: "We have no government armed with power capable of contending with human passions unbridled by morality and religion . . . *Our Constitution was made only for a moral and religious people. It is wholly inadequate to the government of any other.*" John Adams was a signer of the Declaration of Independence, the Bill of Rights, and he was our second President.

Many 'individualists' demand religious independence. A recent survey showed that 80% of Americans agreed: "*An individual should arrive at his or her own religious beliefs independent of any church or synagogue.*" Yet, if they plan to invest money they seek (should seek) a financial expert. If they are sick they consult a medical specialist. If they want to learn golf they go to a pro. Would one climb a mountain or explore a remote jungle, without an expert guide? Therefore, wouldn't it be sensible to listen to an ordained minister or priest, if one wants to learn about their faith? Should parents simply let their children drift aimlessly until they reach maturity? What will happen to their soul if they never reach that stage of maturity? Parents, by definition, must guide their children in morals, manners, and responsibility, and especially, their eternal spiritual life.

## Intimacy & Cooperation

Men instinctively crave freedom and independence. Women intuitively crave intimacy and cooperation. The challenge for men is to develop their feminine side. In order to become whole a man must learn to listen with his heart, share his feelings and express his emotions. The greatest challenge for women is to develop their masculine side; that is, their assertiveness as a woman. However, there is a big difference between assertiveness and aggressiveness. Assertiveness comes from self-esteem. Aggressiveness originates from anger. Many problems center on the emotions of the woman and man's need for freedom. Until a man understands the importance of his own emotions, he cannot appreciate it in the lives of others. A woman will never appreciate man's need for freedom or a personal life, until she develops one herself.

Human beings are not free in terms of empirical objects. In the scientific world there is only causality and purpose. As ethical subjects, human persons are truly autonomous, or can be, if they act according to universal moral reasoning. Not what is right for me, my family, or my nation, but what is right and fair for *all* peoples, regardless of race, status, or creed? Then, one is obeying not just exterior forces, but the interior forces of his/her own moral reasoning, and then they are *truly free.*

We have freedom to eat and drink all we want, to get hooked on addictive drugs, to lust after someone or something, among many other 'freedoms.' In reality, we become 'slaves' to those appetites, inordinate cravings and consummate desires. There are many things that also bound, trap and confine us, such as sickness, financial obligations, jobs that inhibit our creativity, and all the other barriers to freedom. True freedom is within your mind and spirit. *The truth shall set you free!*

There is a contemporary craze about purity of foods and vitamins, a preoccupation concerning weight, fat, cholesterol, and exercising. While we should be concerned about what goes into our mouth, there is little concern about what comes out. Also, where is the consideration for what feeds our mind and spirit, that which is received by our eyes and ears? There is much that is lovely to see, to hear, to read, and behold in God's universe. So, why are we so indifferent to the violence and the rubbish that constantly assaults and degrades us, frequently masked as news and entertainment? In the name of freedom or free choice, our humanity is violated when we claim that nothing outrages us."

Equality doesn't really exist—*we are all born unequal*—physically, mentally, sexually, economically, environmentally. We have absolutely no control over when, where and why we are born? Equality under the law is an "ideal," which a society should always endeavor to achieve. The reality is that corporations, groups, and individuals with greater wealth, and more resources, are much more powerful and they get superior legal advice. They are "more equal" than those with less resources and money.

None of us are born equal! Some of us are stronger, more intelligent, better looking, have greater talents and are richer. Should those with greater beauty wear masks? Should we repress smarter people by denying them higher education? A millionaire's wealth is not necessarily the cause of a destitute persons' poverty. Surely, fundamental goodness and decency is parceled out unequally at birth.

Great men and women are no longer admired, unless they learn how to disguise their greatness; otherwise they are charged with "elitism." Yet no one seems to be jealous of the superior athlete or entertainer. Must we bring everyone down to the economic and social condition of the lowest standard, a common dominator? There are inherent individual differences between all of us. Thank God we are not all the same; otherwise it would be a very boring world.

All of us, without any exception, will experience or face adversity, liabilities and the burdens of this life. It comes with the basic 'human package.' Fortunate are those who encounter less of these disadvantages in their lifetime.

Today, one can easily identify the underdeveloped or third-world countries which experience suffering and early death by starvation, disease and other calamities, that are part of their everyday struggle to exist. Shouldn't we in the more advanced and privileged western world, count our blessings? Hopefully, the disadvantaged may get to paradise more easily than the privileged.

## SEARCHING FOR MEANING:

> *We are the mineral that blooms, the animal that speaks, the intellect that thinks, and by our love, we bring it all back to our Creator.* **--Ralph Waldo Emerson**

Many people from time to time, especially when they are ill or experiencing grief, think life lacks fundamental meaning. This is usually expressed rhetorically: "What's the point of it all?" Religion and philosophy, art, music, and literature attempt to formulate answers. Literary works help us find meaning in life. But we require that our lives have more than *internal* meaning: we want life to have *transcendental* meaning, a kind of "seal of approval" from outside and beyond, that authenticates our existence with a sense of purpose.

Some suggest the meaninglessness of the human situation by pointing out we have grand objectives and thoughts, yet in fact we are only one kind of primitive primate, scuttling around on a very small blue planet, attached to an ordinary star, in one galaxy among billions. At the very least the emphasis on size in this litany seems misplaced: would people have a more meaningful existence if they and their habitat were larger? The complaint shouldn't be that we are small and the universe is large. This small blue dot called Earth is located in a *very unique position* in our galaxy, the Milky Way.

In *The Privileged Planet*, Gonzalez and Richards wrote: "Simply stated, the conditions allowing for intelligent life on Earth also make our planet strangely well suited for viewing and analyzing the universe. … Even more mysterious than the fact that our planet is so congenial to diverse measurement and discovery is that these same conditions appear to correlate with habitability. This is strange, because there is no obvious reason to assume that the very same properties that allow for our existence would also provide the best overall setting to make discoveries about the world around us. We don't think this is merely coincidental. It cries out for another explanation, an explanation that suggests there is more to the cosmos than we have been willing to entertain or even imagine."

The answer to meaning *does not* lie simply in whether we are the only rational and reflective beings in the universe. If we are the only conscious beings in the universe, then to our way of thinking, that is a mere contingency. Human beings have consciousness, intellect, and free will, which is certainly meaningful. These particular characteristics of human beings means that *we transcend* other forms of life, and the hierarchical nature of the universe itself. Humans have a particular place in the intelligent order of things.

There are two different thoughts here, which were brought together in traditional Christianity: One is that human existence means something because there is a Supreme Being, to whom it means something. The other is there is an intelligent and beautiful order of all things, which is the order of the universe itself, in which humans have an intelligible part to play, a part which places us above all other creatures in virtue of our consciousness, intellect, free will, and spirit. That life can be (is) meaningful, in terms of the order of the universe, is illustrated by the philosophy of Aristotle.

## Philosophy of Aristotle:

> ***Small errors in the beginning, cause big errors latter
> on. --Aristotle***

**Thomas Aquinas:** *Like an arrow aimed at a target, which didn't consider the wind.*

Philosophy for Aristotle was the pursuit of Truth and Wisdom. It's a higher level of knowledge and science that seeks and studies the *first principles* of all things; its Love (*philia*) of Wisdom (*Sophia*) or philosophy. Philosophy relies on everyday experiences, not on experimental methodologies and instrumentation. The history of philosophy, however, is littered with corpses of completely wrong theories; e.g., Kant (1724-1804), Hegel (1770-1831), and Leibniz (1646-1716). (Many of these earlier ideologies are reviewed in this book).

Aristotle's peers believed that Earth sat at the center of the universe, and there was a hierarchy of living things in which humans occupied the highest position, compared to all other creatures, by virtue of intellectual powers and capacity. This structure does not, in itself, tell human beings what is expected of them. The universe as Aristotle imagined it is like a "symphony orchestra," so organized that each person can play its part in universal harmony. However, for those governed by reason and free will, there is no score. The orchestra is playing a piece to which humans can choose to tune into *only* by consciously, freely, and willingly joining in. (When one observes conductors of classical symphonies, they often seem to be "tuned-into" the music of the universe).

## Life's Significance

We have to come to understand the "best life" for human beings is by working it from the inside-out, from our life experiences, in terms of what things make sense to creatures like us. This may seem to leave us in just the situation we would find ourselves in anyway, using our good sense to look for the most fruitful and satisfying life, without the benefit of Aristotle's illustration. But this is not so. Aristotle's orchestra has no score, no conductor—and most importantly—no audience, besides the players (among whom *only* humans understood that they were players). This "grand picture" gives a sense of a larger context within which human life has both significance and meaning.

One can always ask, as skeptics have: "Even if Aristotle's representation is correct, why should one join this cosmic orchestra?" If Aristotle's image of the universe is plausible, it would seem appropriate to adopt our human role as suggested by the cosmic orchestra. We would want to join the orchestra. If the earth were the focal point of the universe, that would be a rather salient fact, not just an astronomical accident. It would suggest that the earth and universe is our *special* home, not simply the place in which we live.

The earth is *perfectly* positioned in our galaxy, the Milky Way, which is within a Galactic Habitable Zone, according to discoveries reported in the *Privileged Planet*. If earth was not exactly where it is, we should realize that life could not exist.

## FINDING MEANING

> ***Scientific truth is marvelous, but moral truth is divine and whoever breathes its air and walks by its light has found the lost paradise -- Horace Mann***

The meaning of life has no need of being validated from *outside* life. Many people derive meaning through the values their *internal* (mental and spiritual) activities have for them. To what extent then do we need a shared social existence for an individual's life to have value, as opposed to it consisting of a purely individual set of inclinations and goals? Some people can give their life value by themselves—through artistic creation, personal relationships, or simply assertion of the will, in selected projects. Many people, however, think a valuable life can't be led in isolation from a substantive set of values *shared* with society at large (e.g., constant messages from cell phones, Facebook, and emails), a question more pressing in modern societies than it has been in the past.

The question is not whether a person's life has meaning, but rather, what conditions are needed for a person to find meaning? This is not only a metaphysical, mental and spiritual question, but also political and social one. While we are the product of our past, we don't have to be prisoners of it. We often carry the "baggage" from the past into the future. Nevertheless, unlike all lower forms of creatures, we can certainly change our baggage if we choose to do so.

In *Ethics for the New Millennium*, The Dalai Lama writes: "We have, in my view, created a society in which people find it harder and harder to show one another basic affection. In place of the sense of community and belonging, which we find such a reassuring feature of the less wealthy (generally rural) societies, we find a high degree of loneliness and alienation. The misery of millions is not a cause for pity. Rather it is a cause for developing compassion. We must also recognize that the failure to act when it is clear that action is required may itself be a negative action.

"The more we develop concern for other's well-being, the easier it becomes to act in others' interest. As we become habituated to the effort required, so the struggle to sustain it lessens. ... We need to restrain those factors that inhibit compassion. We need to cultivate those which are conducive to it. What is conducive to compassion is love, patience, tolerance, forgiveness, humility, and so on. What inhibits compassion is lack of inner restraint which we have identified as the source of all unethical conduct. We find that by transforming our habits and dispositions we can begin to perfect our overall state of heart and mind (*kun long*)—that from which all our actions spring. There are no shortcuts. ... It is self-evident that a generous heart and wholesome actions lead to greater peace. Happiness arises from virtuous causes."

What Differentiates Humans? Archbishop Desmond Tutu, of South Africa, put it extremely well: ***I am me, because you are you. I have gifts you don't have—and you have gifts I don't have. Let us celebrate our diversity.***

We are capable of the most terrible acts, and yet, the greatest noble acts—*that's incredible.* Each and every person has the capacity to change. We are extraordinary creatures, who crave knowledge of our Creator. In the words of St. Augustine, *"Our hearts are restless, until we find our rest in Thee."*

## DESTINY & FREE WILL

> ***Every man and woman has his/her own destiny: the only imperative is to follow it, to accept it, no matter where it may lead. Paradise is everywhere and on every road, if one continues along it far enough, you shall find it. --Ralph Waldo Emerson***

The meandering of nature and of society produces challenges to each person, contingent upon his or her particular setting. How one reacts to those challenges can provide them with spiritual significance. For example, the moral choices of a German today, are much easier made than those of Germans in 1936, during the dictatorship of Hitler. Though humans *cannot* fully control their environment, or ultimate destiny on earth, moral conduct is *completely* in his or her hands.

> ***"There is perpetual movement, displacement, which is circular, spiral, and endless. The real issue of life is not getting on with one's neighbor, or of contributing to the development of one's country, but of discovering one's destiny, of making a life in accord with the deep-centered rhythm of the Cosmos (God). To be able to use the word Cosmos boldly, to use the word soul, to deal in things "spiritually"—and to shun definitions, alibis, proofs, and petty duties." Ralph W. Emerson:***

## Duties of the Family:

> ***There are no illegitimate children—only illegitimate parents. --Leon Sandwich***

Family is the natural society in which husband and wife are called to give themselves in love, and participate together with the Creator, in the gift of life. Authority, stability, and a life of relationships within the family constitute the foundations for freedom, security, and fraternity within any society. The family is where, from early childhood, one learns moral values, begins to honor God, and make good use of freedom. Family life is an initiation into life in the greater society. Following the principle of subsidiary, larger communities and governments should be careful not to usurp the family's prerogatives or interfere with its inner life, without due cause.

Family structures in traditional societies are usually patriarchal, ruled by the father, but today more often matriarchal, ruled by the mother. Whichever is the case, there should be only one ruler in any family, as there is only one captain of a ship. Divorced and/or unmarried single parents are the major cause of disintegration of the family structure (exceptions are noted). This is especially true when the father or mother abandons his or her responsibility to each other and to their children.

A God-centered civilization, that has individual freedom, is family-oriented, teaches its children moral values, demands individual responsibility, and promotes literacy. That kind of free society produces compassionate, productive, responsible individuals, who exemplify *"a cult of life."*

Everything that's good flows from Freedom, Faith and Family. Conversely, a purely secular nation, or fanatical religious society, such as Iran, Pakistan, and Saudi Arabia, often leads to dysfunctional families, deterioration of human values, lack of individual responsibility, and disintegration of the cultures—*"a cult of death."*

Dysfunctional parents produce impaired children. That dysfunctional situation often leads to abused grandchildren. It's an endless cycle, similar to a cancer that spreads, incessantly. Children (and many adults) today, have an "instant gratification," or selfish attitude. Who were their role models? Nevertheless, we have seen numerous examples of fantastic, wonderful children who have grown up in broken or dysfunctional families, under disadvantaged circumstances, and yet, somehow they became responsible adults, even great leaders. Who or what saved them? Let's depict it as the "Three Pillars for Survival:" (1) At least one truly loving parent, or relative; (2) A good education; and (3)

Moral foundation in the faith. If one pillar is broken, the child usually goes under in *any* society.

Some claim that minority prejudice, economic conditions, and the social climate caused these *worst of times*. Yet, a few generations ago other ethnic groups were the "minorities," including: Asians, the Irish, Italians, Germans, Jews, and today it's the Hispanics. These 2nd generation immigrants also experienced significant hardships, like The Great Depression, urban squalor, and appalling discrimination. Yet, legions have succeeded. Let's face it, the *fundamental roots* of our societal crises' are primarily caused by: (1) Abdication of parental responsibility; (2) Faulty education systems; (3) Negative role models; and (4) Most importantly, lack of any spiritual life.

## Duties of Parents:

> ***Children need love, especially when they don't deserve it.* --Harold S. Hulbert**

The richness of conjugal love cannot be reduced solely to the procreation of children, but must extend to their moral education and their spiritual formation. Any two consenting adults can produce children; it happens by the tens-of-thousands, every day, throughout the world. Unfortunately, too many of these kids are born into underdeveloped poor countries, where poverty and disease are widespread, and formal education doesn't exist. The definition of parenting is NOT merely procreation; it's about nurturing, supporting and educating children. Otherwise, it's simply irresponsible sex.

Today, the once venerated family and multi-ethnic cultural communities are rapidly disintegrating. The effects of these trends are obvious everywhere: children lack respect for their parents; moral values have declined; teenage-pregnancy is on the rise; a culture of addictive drugs is upon us; and crime has increased at an alarming rate. Many ethnic families, such as Hispanics, Asians, Muslims and Jews, do pull together to help each other. For instance, an orphaned child will usually be taken in by members of a Hispanic family and brought up as if they were actual blood brothers or sisters.

The role of parents in education is of such great importance that it is almost impossible to provide an adequate substitute. The right and duty of parents to educate their children is *"a primordial and inalienable right."* Parents must regard their progeny as children of God and respect them as human persons. Parents have the first responsibility for the basic education of their children at home. They bear witness to this responsibility first by creating a home environment where security, tenderness, forgiveness, respect, fidelity, and selfless service by all members are the rule.

If all children are born innocent, precious, and loveable, then what caused so many of these "beautiful and wondrous flowers," to become delinquents, drug addicts, sexually permissive, or amoral? Isn't this learned behavior? Of course it is! Did they learn basic moral principles from their parents? How many of these good children had dysfunctional parents, or grew up in a faithless family? Who were their early role models? What kind of friends did they grow up with? Were their childhood experiences secure, positive and supportive, or were they insecure, negative and indifferent?

Consider my analogy from nature: without good earth, without rain and sunshine, and without cultivation, nothing flourishes. Gardens have to be pruned and cultivated, until the roots of flowers have grown deeper and are well established. Innocent children resemble beautiful flowers of every type and variety, and they too require constant nurturing in a loving family, until their roots are fully developed. The nature of a flower is to blossom; and the radiance of its colors and smells can be like God's extraordinary paradise.

**Remember this truism:** *the neglected or abused child of the past, in any country on Earth, will become the primary source of terrorism and misery in the future.*

This author grew up in a "blended family." My mother abandoned her four children (I was less than one year old at the time). Father placed us in a foster home, until he remarried. His new wife had three children from a prior marriage. Our step-mother naturally favored her children. There were many arguments and drunken fights over money, marriage, and manners. This was a dysfunctional family of seven children. What saved me from this family crisis? My cousin, Marietta Gehring, took a special interest in me. She was the art teacher at St. John's school. Marietta took me to her home after school, taught me about art, and told me stories about her brother, Reverend Frederic Gehring, who was called by the Marines, the *"Padre of Guadalcanal,"* during the War in the Pacific. Capt. Rev. Gehring, was the first navy chaplain to receive the Legion of Merit Medal from the President. He also authored a book, *A Child of Miracles,* the story of Patsy Li, during the war in the Far East. These stories inspired me, deepened my faith and trust in the God, and gave me a very positive attitude about life, at the age of seven.

This author, together with my spouse, Miriam, was a volunteer with *Guardian ad Litem* for five years. We handled thirteen challenging cases of mostly clueless and/or dysfunctional parents that abused or neglected each other, and their children. The parents had to complete case plans (parenting training, substance abuse classes, and anger management groups, among other programs) before being reunited with their children. (See *Best Interests of the Children* (2014), by Robert & Miriam Fertig. If the parents lack adequate Christian instruction, how can one expect them to teach their children about Christ? Parents and their children need *special* religious instruction, which must be provided by the church.

The *five principles* that will determine how well you deal with your children's future—that will also affect your eternal life, are:

1. **Attitudes:** Children develop early positive or negative attitudes and behaviors, which depends on the family, the school, the neighborhood, and most importantly, good role models.

2. **Parenting:** At least one loving parent is essential to guide children and to teach good morals, faith, and a sense of responsibility.
3. **Education:** A well-rounded education is essential. BA or BS students will earn about 3-5 times as much as persons with a high-school diploma. However, education is much more than earnings. *Education is the key to happiness!*
4. **Role Models:** It's the duty of parents to control who the child hangs out with especially, after school, within the neighborhood. And they must also control what is watched on the TV and computer networks.
5. **Spirituality:** Without trust in God, your children and you will wander aimlessly throughout life. *Without a spiritual purpose you and they will likely be lost!*

According to a recent Department of Commerce survey, about 17% of the population, age 25 and older lacked a high school diploma; 24% had a college degree, and 8% earned graduate degrees. Interestingly, those without a high school diploma only earned $16,124; those with a high school diploma earned $22,895; the BA/BS degree folks earned $40,478; and the advanced degree group earned $63,229. (All are average salaries). These statistics by themselves should convince parents and teenagers that *education really pays*.

## Duties of Children:

> ***Children have never been good at listening to their elders, but they have never failed to imitate them.* --James Baldwin**

Respect by children, whether minors or adults, for the father and mother, is nourished by the natural affection born of the bond uniting them. It is required of the fifth commandment (Ex 20:12). Respect for parents (filial piety) derives from gratitude toward those who, by the gift of life, their love and work, have brought their children into the world and enabled them to grow in stature, wisdom and grace. Remember that through your parents you were born; *what can you give back to them that compares to their gift of life?*

As long as a child lives at home with their parents, they should obey the parents in all that is reasonably asked when it is for their good or that of the family. But if the child is convinced, in conscience, that it would be morally wrong to obey a particular order, he/she must not do so. Obedience toward parents ceases with the emancipation (defined as reaching legal age and living alone) of the children; not so respect (for parents), which is always owed to them.

Some young adults today, think that they need not respect and obey their parents. *"I'm not a child anymore; I'm an adult, and you can't tell me what to do,"* they claim. Nevertheless, while this young adult lives in their parent's house they must continue to follow reasonable rules and guidelines of the mother and father under their roof, have good manners, and give honor for those who gave them life, no matter how "mature" they think they are.

Another typical expression by some of today's adolescents and young adults is: *"I'm bored! Let's go to the movies, or go shopping at the Mall."* My response is simply this: Boredom is within you; movies, TV, and other activities may provide a temporary diversion but it will not last. The solution is to do something useful, better yet do something for someone else. Avoid thinking about your wants, which usually are not needs. Read a good book. Do work around the home, or better yet, a work of charity. Meditate and pray for guidance, and then, listen to that voice within.

## Duties of Society

Society is an assembly of persons bound together naturally by a principle of unity that goes beyond each of them individually. By means of society, each man and woman is established as "heirs" and receives certain "talents" that enrich his or her identity, whose fruits they should develop. Most humans need to live in a society, where through the exchange and dialogue with others, and mutual service with their brethren, they can develop their full potential. *Love of neighbor is inseparable from love of God!*

Human society cannot be well-ordered or prosperous unless it has some people invested with legitimate authority to preserve its institutions, and who devote themselves to care for the common good of all. Members of a society rightly owe loyalty to the communities of which they are a part, and should respect *just* legal authorities who have charge of the common good. Society should always promote the exercise of good virtues.

> **When the heart is set right, then the personal life is cultivated;**
> **When personal life is cultivated, then family life is regulated; When family life is regulated, then national life is orderly; When national life is orderly, then there is peace in the world.**
> **--Confucius (5th Century BC)**

States have no permanent alliances, only permanent self-interests. The state must be concerned foremost about the security and welfare of its citizens. It should promote the "common good" of the society by creating and enforcing the rule of *just laws*, while always respecting the dignity of each person. Authority of the state does not derive its moral legitimacy from itself. It must act for the common good of all as a "moral force'" based on freedom and responsibility.

The good of the individual person should be the principle, subject, and the end goal of *all* state social institutions. Excessive intervention by the state can (will) threaten many personal freedoms, and must be avoided.

Regimes whose nature is contrary to "natural law," to public order, and to the basic rights of its citizens cannot achieve the common good. Any state that views persons as "means to some end," will engender unjust political and economic structures that can make individual conduct difficult, if not impossible. We've seen many examples of evil states from Nazism and Communism.

## Diversity is good

The Creator, in his wisdom, made men and women *different*. How can anyone disregard these differences? Physically, a woman is built differently from man; her bone and muscle structure, among other attributes, make her distinctive. Sexually, a man and woman are *not equal*. A man cannot give birth, nor nurse a baby, and a woman cannot conceive without the sperm of the man. Together, with their Creator, they maintain the foundation of human society.

These facts make ones' sex very different from race, ethnicity, age and many other criteria upon which crucial distinctions beg to be made in our culture today. The case can be made with regard to race, religion, national origin, but that perspective is simply wrong when it attempts to treat sexual differences as no more important than any other distinction. It is not a distinction that views one sex worth more than the other—it's a difference which cannot be dismissed as inconsequential. *Sameness doesn't exist!*

## MULTICULTURALISM

> *Culture refers primarily to that which we honor and worship in society; behavioral phenomena dependent upon social, and symbolic learning, consisting of shared understanding, communicated from generation to generation, structured according to its own laws.*

# Culture Definition: What Society Considers "Good & Honorable."

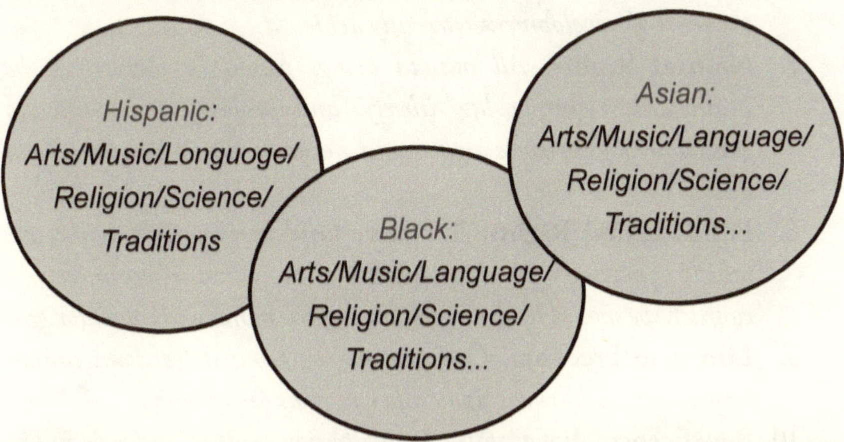


Citizens & Immigrants <u>must</u> learn English, History, Constitution & the Laws

➢ *Fig.3 Culture Definition**

*Culture's Ten Principles* by Robert J. Spitzer, S.J., Ph.D. (abridged): The evolution of culture and civilization has arisen from the development of ten fundamental principles: Three concern evidence and objective truth; three concern ethics; three concern the dignity and treatment of human beings within any civil society; and one concerns personal identity and culture. Ten principles are:

1. **Complete Explanation.** *The best opinion or theory is the one that explains the most data or information;*
2. **Non-Contradiction.** *Valid opinions or theories have no internal contradictions;*
3. **Objective Evidence.** *Non-arbitrary opinions or theories are based on publicly verifiable evidence;*
4. **Non-Maleficence.** *Avoid unnecessary harm; if harm is unavoidable, minimize it. Silver Rule: Do not do unto others what you would not have them do unto you.*

5.  **Consistent Ends and Means.** *The end does not justify the means;*
6.  **Full Human Potential.** *Every human being deserves to be valued according to the full level of human development, not according to the level of development currently achieved;*
7.  **Natural Rights.** *All human beings possess in themselves the inalienable rights of life, liberty, and property ownership; no government gives these rights, and no government can take them away;*
8.  **Fundamental Rights.** *The more fundamental right is the one which is necessary for the possibility of the other; where there is a conflict, we should resolve in the favor of the more fundamental right;*
9.  **Limits to Freedom.** *One person's (or group's) freedoms cannot impose undue burdens upon other persons (or group's).*
10. **Beneficence.** *Aim at optimal contribution to others and society. The Golden Rule: Do unto others, as you would have them do unto you.*

Failure to teach and practice several of these principles will most certainly lead to widespread maltreatment of humans, a decline in culture, and serious abuses of individuals (and groups).

Some may say that it is the legal system, or democracy, or the courts that are the real protectors of all individuals, our culture, and civil society. However, without these ten principles, democracy could vote out the rights of individuals, court systems could legalize every form of indignity and harm, and legal systems would have nothing upon which to base their secular laws.

World history teaches us that unfair court systems, arbitrary persecution of people, discrimination, and maltreatment of people, has always occurred when these ten principles are dismissed. The absence of these principles opens the path for corruption, deceit, injustice, and cultural decline.

> **Our Constitution was made only for a moral and religious people. It is wholly inadequate to the government of any other. -- John Adams**

America is a community, a nation of people having common traditions, institutions, and mutual interests. It is distinguished by its standards of living, honorable conduct, the Constitution, the Bill of Rights, and just laws. Long regarded as "the land of opportunity," this tiny group of religious outcasts from Europe and England, and Spanish explorers, who founded America, hit upon a formula for success that perhaps went beyond what they could have imagined. How else can anyone explain that they established a nation that has become the greatest example of economic growth, global power, religious liberty and free speech, the world has ever known?

> ***Culture is like a tapestry that contains many different threads. Each thread is a thought, a dream, an experience. Some are short threads, of dull pigment; others are long threads, of vivid color. Reality and dreams are in the hands of that expert carpet weaver. He connects different strands of our lives to others. He weaves them together to pattern our distinctive, universal being. We are dependent on His will and skilled hands. In the end, we must affirm: Thy will be done. --Author***

Of the seven billion people in the world (based on UN surveys), Asians represent 60%; Europeans are 20%; Africans are 9%; and 15% come from the Americas. About 70% are non-white. *Anglo-Saxons are the minorities of the world.*

Culture is a much-abused word in Western and American society. *Civilized Culture* does not sanction immoral behavior, substance abuse, violence, and irresponsible sex, nor does it support repulsive language, nor does it sanction gross dress codes (pants that do not cover ones' butt), or some forms of repugnant modern art, and anti-social manners from our youth or *alleged* mature adults.

Culture in a "civilized society" is about customs, language, religion, history, and institutions for promoting the sciences, arts and music, based on *moral values* that we collectively prize. Culture refers to that which we honor and worship in any country. It is the behavior of people in society that is dependent upon social and symbolic learning, consisting of shared understanding, communicated from generation to generation, structured according to the *virtuous rules* for the society, which are based on just laws.

### Black Lives Matter

BLM goals, quoted from website, <u>blacklivesmatter.org</u>:

- "We dismantle the patriarchal practice that requires mothers to work double shifts so that they can mother in private even as they participate in public justice work.

- "We disrupt the Western-prescribed nuclear family structure requirement by supporting each other as extended families and Villages' that collectively care for one another, especially our children, to the degree that mothers, parents, and children are comfortable.

- •"We foster a queer-affirming network. When we gather, we do so with the intention of freeing ourselves from the tight grip of heteronormative thinking."

> ➤ **Fig. 4 Black Lives Matter Defined***

Black Lives Matter as a movement gained more influence and funds following the death of George Floyd in Minneapolis. Protests and riots have taken place worldwide. Many have clearly *exploited* the tragic death of Mr. Floyd for political and financial advantage. One of the major exploiters and agitators is Rev. Sharpton of New York City.

**Mr. Innis National Chairman of Congress of Racial Equality,**

- "[BLM] does nothing to advance racial equality. [Causing] the disruption of the nuclear family is a clear and present danger to the black community."

- "Fatherlessness represents a crisis for all races. Disrupting the family is going to hold black people back."

- Black Lives Matter's "most famous goal," defunding police services, Innis says the black community does not actually want less police.

- "They want less bad police," he emphasized and there are "bad apples" in every profession.

> ➤ **Fig. 5* Chairman Innis on BLM**

The National Chairman of Congress of Racial Equality, Mr. Innis said, "There is a difference between protestors and the leaders who run the Black Lives Matter organization. Founder Alicia Garza says she is a Marxist." Chairperson Innis also said that defunding the police is "just at the beginning" of what the BLM organization wants. "These agenda items [show] a Marxist mentality that…does nothing for the black community."

- "It does nothing to advance racial equality. [Causing] the disruption of the nuclear family is a clear and present danger to the black community."
- Fatherlessness represents a crisis for all races. The civil rights leader said that disrupting the family is "going to hold black people back."
- Regarding Black Lives Matter's "most famous goal," defunding police services, Innis said that the black community does not actually want less police.
- "They want less bad police," he emphasized, and noted correctly that there are "bad apples" in every profession.

> - Census Bureau Statistics

- 13.4% of the population in 2019, were "classified black;" 18.5% are classified "Hispanic/Latino" (excluding 12-million undocumented residents).

- Hispanics (brown-skin people from Mexico, Puerto Rico, Cuba) have surpassed Blacks, by growing nearly 30% per year.

- Black families accounted for 38 percent of reported abortions, (abortions per 1,000 women aged 15-44 years) is 3.8 times higher than all other groups.

> ➢ **Fig. 6* Census Statistics**

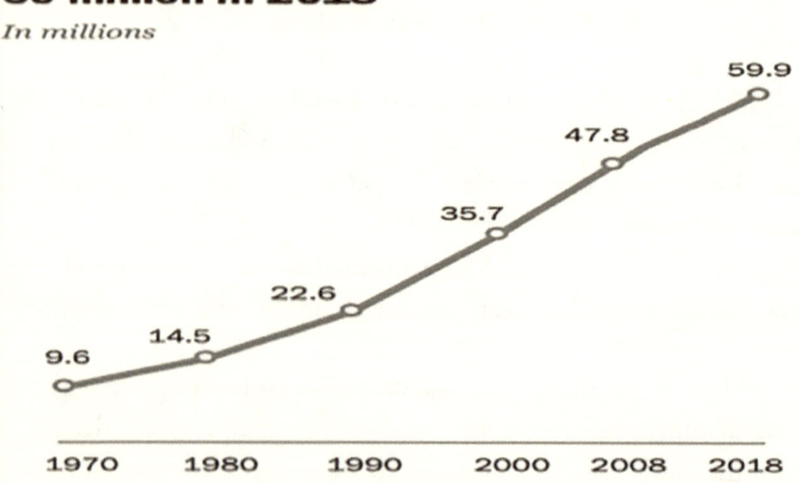


> ➢ **Fig. 7* Hispanic Growth**

- Hispanics (brown-skin people from Mexico, Puerto Rico, Cuba, etc.) are growing by about 30% per year. Black people are 13 percent of the U.S. population, yet they accounted for 38 percent of all abortions.

- The Black abortion rate (abortions per 1,000 women aged 15–44 years) is 3.8 times higher than all others.

BLM substitutes Marx's Communist class conflict for *conflict* between blackness and whiteness. The black vs. white dichotomy creates a *permanent enemy class*. The president of New York Black Lives Matter, Hawk Newsome said, "If this country doesn't give us what we want, then we will burn down this system and replace it. All right? I could be speaking figuratively. I could be speaking literally. It's a matter of interpretation," Newsome said this during an interview on Fox News "The Story" with Martha MacCallum.

Have NOT Asians, Irish, Hispanics, Jews, Muslims, experienced racism, and economic hardship? Why are they not shouting: "Brown Lives Matter," "Jewish Lives Matter"? The truth is that, *All Lives Matter!*

BLM receives millions of dollars from Corporate, Political, and Catholics Charities. A selective list of financial supporters includes:

- Airbnb – $500,000 to BLM and the NAACP
- Democracy Alliance – a Soros-linked group, added BLM to its annual $500 million donor list
- Ford Foundation and Borealis Philanthropy – Left-wing groups that established a $100 million donor fund.
- George Soros' Open Society Foundation – $33 million and the Catholic Church (without approval from parishioners).

Everyone is a slave to something: We are slaves to our jobs, which some of us do not enjoy; We are slaves to our families, which we willing accept; We are slaves to bad habits, which can only be replaced by good habits. Many are slaves to drugs, which are destroying our youth.

***We are ALL slaves to sin, and seek the Mercy and Love of Christ, which is the only act that can remove our "shackles."***

**Dominant Cultures:** Although the evolution of culture seems to have a higher potential for reversible movements, the available record of global cultural evolution indicates that there has been a more or less consistent development in the direction of higher complexity. There is a significant function for dominant types—those culture-types which tend to spread at the expense of others. The dominant culture tends to overwhelm the others, causing members to develop greater resemblance to the dominant type, but also often creating hybrid developments that are new cultural dominants.

**Asian Cultures:** As a group, they represent about 17 million or nearly 6% of the U.S. population. In general, Asians seem to act ethically (exceptions obviously exist). Why is this so? From early childhood, they learn morality and respect for the family. To steal or to perform immoral acts is a "disgrace," for the individual *and* the entire family. "Exceptional-ism" is another trait of proud Asians. Why do corporations, employ Asian foreigners to handle intricate online computer problems and other complex services, from far away countries, such as India and the Philippines? Obviously, it is because of lower costs, but also significant is large populations of self-motivated, skilled work forces, that offer firms *quality of service*.

**African-American Culture:** This culture represent about 14% or nearly 45 million of America's population. In *Runaway Slave*, Rev. C.L. Bryant, in this documentary, where he is the star of the film, interviews African-American politicians, and holds meetings with community activists, and discovers the little known "other" history of the Civil Rights Movement.

Rev. Bryant: exposes the NAACP as a mouthpiece of the Democratic Party, and the NAACP' leaders as the ultimate 'race hustlers' who perpetuate—and profit—from a '*victim mentality*' that hurts the African-American community." The theme of Runaway Slave is compelling: while the African-American community has triumphed over the scourge of *physical slavery*, many still suffer from a *mental slavery*—to government [dependency]. What emerges from this posit is an authentic and honest discussion of race in America, a discussion Americans need to have together.

"There is a 50-year-old lie that has caused an entire people to become harlots to the political idea that government knows what is best," declares Bryant. Research has shown that about 72% of African-American children have only one active parent, typically the mother. *That is an appalling statistic!* We believe most of these families have collapsed because of government policies that encourages one-parent families. When fathers cannot cope with being real fathers to their children, government welfare takes over. That is a creeping and deleterious form of government dependency.

**Hispanic Culture:** Hispanics or Latinos have been part of the American culture centuries before the Pilgrims arrived. Spanish-speaking people represent 17% of the U. S. population, or over 50 million people. Hispanics are the fastest growing population (over 28% per year). Unlike Asians and Anglo-Saxons, Hispanics are perhaps more "impulse driven;" that is, they are particularly emotional about family, religion, and historical cultural traditions.

Their inability to speak and read English is a major factor in their lack of assimilation, especially Latinos (Mexican-Americans). Education is the solution to future adaptation for this proud culture. Hispanics should also be more politically involved to address issues prevalent in their communities. It is interesting to note how many Cubans succeeded after coming to America with limited resources and poor English skills. Perhaps they "over-compensated" for the many hardships they had endured in Cuba, and were more educated and they became politically active.

**Islamic Culture:** Muslims represent only about 1% of the American population, or 3.3 million people, but they are growing rapidly. Most are good conservative families, who instruct their children, from a very early age, to be moral and obedient to the parents and God's teachings. Islamic cultures in *some* Muslim countries have *harsh* treatment for offenders. If you steal, you will lose a hand or your arm. Commit adultery, or show that you are openly gay, and you will lose your head. Islam does *not* accept American's Bill of Rights; this fundamental law is foreign to their culture, faith and *Sharia* laws.

Most Muslims live peacefully together with Christians, Jews and other cultures and religions, in America. On the other hand, there are *extreme fundamentalists* who are still living in the 7th century, who want to establish separate societies based on *Sharia* law, which is *totally incompatible* with American laws. Islam is more than a religion—*it is a way of life*. Spiritual beliefs and specific rules form equal parts of the Muslim faith, and no distinction exists between doctrine and laws, or the separation of church and state. No thought, act, contract, or relationship is beyond its scope. **Christ's injunction to "*Render to Caesar the things that are Caesar's and to God the things that are God*," is alien to Islamic belief.**

We should always have tolerance and respect for all cultures and religions, as long as they adhere to the *just* laws of the country. Some *fanatical* Muslim promote polygamy, arranged marriages, wife beatings, ritual circumcision of young girls, and also "honor killings." (The UN estimates that over 5,000 women worldwide are victims of 'honor killings' each year).


## CULTURE & TRUTH:

Source: *Reflections on Fides et Ratio* by former Cardinal Ratzinger, Prefect of the Congregation for the Doctrine of the Faith, and former Pope Benedict XVI.

**Indigenous Cultures:** Whoever poses the question of truth today…is necessarily directed to the problem of cultures and their mutual openness. Christianity's claim to universality of truth is often countered in our day with the argument of the relativity of cultures. It is maintained that in fact the Christian missionary effort did not disseminate a truth, which is the same for all people, but instead subjugated indigenous cultures to the particular culture of Europe, thus damaging the richness of those cultures, which have evolved among a variety of peoples. The Christian missionary effort thus appears as another of the great European sins, as the original form of colonialism and thus as the spiritual despoiling of other peoples.

**Evangelization Blunders:** To this argument we must reply first of all by noting that in the history of evangelization there were certainly mistakes: about this no one would disagree. Moreover, that the cultural multiplicity of humanity must find a place in the Church, as the common home of all people, is today recognized without exception. But in the radical critique of the Christian missionary effort from the standpoint of cultures there is something deeper at work: it is the question of whether there can be a communion of cultures within the truth that unites them, the question of whether truth can be expressed for all people beyond cultural forms? ...

**Communion of Cultures:** Cultures are predisposed to the experience of encounter and reciprocal enrichment. As man's inner openness to God leaves its mark on a culture to the extent to which that culture is great and pure, so there is written in such cultures themselves an inner openness for the revelation of God.

**Euro-Centrism Inheritance:** When the pope insists upon the inalienability of an acquired cultural inheritance, one which has become a vehicle for the common truth of God and man, the question naturally arises as to whether this does not amount to the canonization (glorification) of a Euro-centrism in the Christian faith, a Euro-centrism which would not seem capable of being superseded later by the possibility that a new patrimony (inheritance) could enter—and in fact has entered—into the permanent identity of the faith. ...

**Israel's Self-Transcendence:** Former Cardinal Ratzinger continues: The Bible is not simply the expression of the culture of the people of Israel but rather manifests a constant conflict with the completely natural desire of the people of Israel to be only themselves, *to shut themselves in their own culture.* Faith in God and their yes to the will of God are wrested from them against their own ideas and wishes.

**Cultural Identity and Religious Desires:** God places Himself against certain expressions of the religiosity and religious culture of Israel … (For example) From the anger of God and of Moses against the worship of the golden calf at Sinai, to the late post-exilic prophets, Israel must constantly be drawn away from elements of its own cultural identity and religious desires; that is, it must leave the worship of its own nationality, the worship of "blood and land," in order to submit to God, who is completely other, a God who is not of Israel's own making, the God who created the heavens and the earth, and who is God of *all the peoples* (emphasis mine).

**Self-Transcendence of Culture**: Israel's faith requires a continual self-transcendence, an overcoming of its own culture, in order to open itself and enter into the expansiveness of a truth common to all. … In a sense, when St. Paul departs from the (earlier Jewish) law, a departure based on his encounter with the risen Lord, this fundamental trajectory of the Old Testament is bought to its logical conclusion: it expresses fully the "universalization" of the faith of Israel, released from the particularity of an ethnic structure. Now all peoples are invited to join this process of self-transcendence of their own particularity, the process that first began in Israel. …

**Everything (of God) Belongs to All:** Faith in Jesus Christ is of its nature a continual opening of the self: it is God breaking into the world of human beings and the response of human beings breaking out toward God, who at the same time leads them to one another. Everything particular now belongs to everyone, and everything which belongs to another becomes also our own. (See: *Origins* Vol. 28, No. 36, Feb. 25, 1999, for the complete text from the Cardinal).

## Monopolized Minorities:

Unfortunately, in growing *socialistic and materialistic* American society today, the pendulum is swinging in the opposite direction. A large majority wish to lay claim upon, or attempt to monopolize minorities, or those who are disadvantaged. Scandalous judicial decisions are being rendered on a regular basis, based on claims of "disadvantaged." Murderers, sex perverts, rapists and other criminals, along with their unscrupulous lawyers and liberal judges, are on a daily basis making a mockery of justice. There are advantaged and disadvantaged in all societies. However, the "disadvantaged criminal offenders" are today judged as "victims," and set free, while the sufferers of these horrendous crimes become victims, once again, by liberal courts.

**State of Mind:** A person's state of mind (and formed conscience) determines one's fate in life. You become what you 'think' you will 'become.' Again, this is evident in all societies. If you 'think' you can, you 'can.' If you think you 'can't,' you 'can't.' In either case you are right. If you think or feel you are disadvantaged, try to define or identify why you think so. Then do what you need to do to correct your situation, lawfully. No one else has the most to gain. No one else has the motivation required to improve your situation. Just thinking about it is not going to make it happen. Do you have the motivation? We are not guaranteed that 'all will be better tomorrow.' Only your effort and 'action,' and determined burning passion will make it happen!

## INDIVIDUAL & SOCIETAL TRUTH KEY POINTS:

o   There is "clear and convincing evidence" that unlike most of the known universe, humans are thinking creatures, with free will, consciousness, unlimited imagination, and eternal souls (spirit).

o   Human beings have dignity, and their existence have meaning because, unlike many undistinguished powers of nature, they are living, thinking creatures, and more importantly, they have an eternal spirit.

o   Diversity in nature is good, not evil. The Creator, in his wisdom, made men and women different. How can anyone disregard these differences?

o   Families and states have a duty and responsibility for the security, welfare, and education of all citizens.

o   Multi-culturalism is good, if people assimilate, and respect American human rights and just laws.

o   Love is doing what is *good* for the one you love, even if it sometimes hurts. *That is what real love is all about!!*

o   We must all take responsibility for all our acts in this life.

o   Humans are rarely satisfied or content with life. They are always seeking something more. All our dreams and aspirations are always looking ahead to what will be, or what may come. We must somehow transcend ourselves.

o   Without a purpose, life is motion without meaning, without direction, without reason.

o   Joy of love and grief are all part of this "human package." No person has ever avoided grief on his/her journey of life!

o   When our minds are focused it is like a light that's highly-focused, a laser beam, and it can cut through everything.

o   By *reasoning*, humanity is capable of understanding the natural order of things.

o   By *free will*, human persons are capable of directing themselves toward seeking what is true and good.

o   By *intelligence,* we are endowed with knowledge, which is believed to be an outstanding manifestation of the Divine Wisdom.

o   By *faith,* one recognizes the revealed message of the Creator, which urges them to do what is good and avoid what is evil.

# III. Philosophical Truths

*Bad philosophical theories have had lethal consequences, such as Fascism, Nazism, Materialism, Nihilism, Communism, and in the 21ˢᵗ century, we have Atheistic-Humanism, Scientific-Materialism, Secular-Progressive, and Socialism remains with us.* —Author

Philosophy is "Love of Wisdom." It's thinking about thinking. Within philosophy, *Metaphysics* is concerned with the structure of reality: What is the meaning of life? Does God exist? How does one event cause another to happen? How can we know something really exists (Being or Ontology)? What is the essence of an object? *Epistemology* is about the nature of knowledge: Are there different kinds of knowledge? What is the most reliable source of all knowledge?

During the 16th through 19th centuries, the more important philosophers that determined our Worldviews and Ideologies were:

1596-1650 Rene Descartes *Discourse on Method, "I think, therefore I am."*
1623-1662 Blaise Pascal: *An Apology for the Christian Religion.*
1632-1677 Baruch de Spinoza: *"Hero of Modernity and Secularism."*
1632-1704 John Locke: *Empiricism and Naturalism (Agnosticism).*
1685-1753 George Berkeley: *Epistemological Idealism.*
1694-1746 Francis Hutcheson: *Enlightenment, and Utilitarianism*
1711-1776 David Hume: *Epistemological Idealism.*
1712-1778 Rousseau: *"Father of Romanticism."*
1724-1804 Emmanuel Kant: *Codified Philosophical Idealism.*
1770-1831 Hagel: Metaphysical Idealism: *"The real is what's rational."*

1806-1873 John Stuart Mill: *Utilitarian, known as Empiricist.*
1813-1855 Soren Kierkegaard: *God is transcendent and unfathomable.*

## EMPIRICISM & NATURALISM:

***Empiricism thesis is that all knowledge of the world and meaningful claims about it is only derived from experience. Naturalism is a philosophy that rejects all spiritual and supernatural explanations of the universe.***

Empiricism, in opposition to rationalism, denies that there are "universal truths" and that there are objective necessary connections in the real world. Empiricism is a philosophical position that embraces a hypothesis of knowledge or epistemology, and a method of discourse.

Empiricism and its metaphysical counterpart, Naturalism, are dominant schools of thought in modern times. Modern philosophical literature and science consists of development, criticism, and defense of claims. Naturalism is a philosophy that rejects all spiritual and supernatural explanations of the universe, and "believes "that the sciences are the *only* basis for what can be known. Unfortunately, many naturalists will not consider any possible alternative reasons for human life, such as Intelligent Design by a Creator, even though macro-evolution (not micro-evolution) has not been proven.

The distinction between thinking about something and experiencing it, should be obvious. Thought, when true, may be about past, present, future, or nonexistent things; while experience, if true in what it claims, involves encountering its object. Empiricists claim that the *only* meaningful statements are those where the truth-value is subject to actual or conceivable verification. This does not fully describe empiricism, for what counts as an experiential encounter with reality is controversial. This is the central issue which experts are divided.

Rationalists have claimed that reason is not simply the capacity for abstract thought about things, which must be tested by experience, but also a capacity for a unique kind of experience, an "intellectual intuition," which is a conceptual encounter with "universal truths" and their relationships. Empiricists have insisted that experience, the way of testing truth-claims, is totally restricted to sensory perception and self-knowledge of one's own mental activities.

In commonsense terms, sensory perception normally involves a physical encounter with its object. There is a causal relationship between the object and the sensory organs of perception. No other mode of experience is related to an object in this way. In the case of self-knowledge, it is undeniable that if one clearly sees something, one knows that one sees it; and if one clearly desires something, one knows that one desires it. The conclusions from conceiving experience in the restricted manner of the empiricist are: Reality as humans experience it consists of concrete particular things and events (whether sense-data or physical objects) and their contingent properties and relations, according to our experiences of them, and all general non-analytic truths are known by inductive generalization and consequently are always subject to being overthrown or modified by further experiences.

We say things are good or bad, right or wrong; about people having rights and obligations; about what ought to be, and how things should be, and the like. It is not obvious that either sensory experience or self-knowledge *alone* can validate value-claims; or that what is meant by value-terms can be found in either mode of experience. Rationalism has been invoked to account for knowledge of value-requirements.

## ENLIGHTENMENT:

> ***The essence of Enlightenment was that the state does not have the right to legislate or promote any particular version of the "good life."***

Enlightenment was primarily that states cannot legislate morality; the separation of church and state (which is *not* in the Constitution); individuals have the right to decide what constitutes their own happiness, as long as it does not violate the rights of others; the state may not unduly infringe on our private personal lives; among other "rights." In other words, separation of the individual morality the "I," from the collective morality of the "We." Humans are predisposed by nature to moral action. Virtue consists in the degree and extent to which they advance the welfare of others. The enticement to perform virtuous acts lies in the *beauty of its form,* rather than in the benefits that accrue from it.

Philosophers and writers who preceded and succeeded the Enlightenment era, such as Kant, Milton, Voltaire, Spinoza, among others, did not generally reject the idea of a Creator or God. They rejected any belief in a "tyrannical God," who threatened humanity with damnation and fire, as well as Scripture and Church doctrines which they considered "mysterious," that seemed to contradict human reasoning.

Baruch de Spinoza (1632-77), a Dutch Jew of Spanish ancestry, became a Gentile Rationalist or "free thinker." Today, many people regard Spinoza as the "hero of Modernity and Secularism," He published a Theological-Political Treatise, postulating that God was merely the principle of all eternal and immutable laws of the universe, which was (actually) a fundamental denial of *Transcendence*; that is, a Personal God. The Jewish leaders in the synagogue of Amsterdam excommunicated him.

The founder of Enlightenment was actually Francis Hutcheson (1694-1746). Although of Scotch ancestry, he spent the greater part of his life in Dublin, where he wrote the works on which his fame as a philosopher rests. In 1729 he accepted the Chair of Moral Philosophy at Glasgow University, which he held until his death in 1746. It was during this latter period, devoted largely to lecturing that he awakened students to an active appreciation of philosophy.

## UTILITARIANISM:

> *Utilitarianism is doctrine that actions are right, judged by its consequences, if they are useful in so far as they promote happiness for the benefit of the majority.*

As an exponent of the "moral sense" school, Hutcheson was closely associated in thought with both Shaftesbury and Joseph Butler. Hutcheson differs from Butler in conceding no virtue to the principle of self-love directly. Hutcheson took over the concept of the moral sense—a term incidental in Shaftesbury's exposition of virtue—and made it the central idea of an elaborate moral system. His influence was felt in Britain, France, and Germany. He anticipated the *Utilitarian* school in his use of the phrase, "the greatest happiness of the greatest number." Hutcheson trained Adam Smith and influenced David Hume, Thomas Reid, and Thomas Brown. Hutcheson's most important works include: *Inquiry concerning Beauty, Order, Harmony, and Design* and *Inquiry concerning Moral Good and Evil* (1725); *Essay on the Nature and Conduct of the Passions and Affections and Illustrations upon the Moral Sense* (1728); and *System of Moral Philosophy* (1755).

The Age of Enlightenment of the 17th and 18th centuries presented new, *very serious threats* to Christian theism, because of the skeptical Deism of John Locke in England. Although Lessing in Germany brought Christianity in tune with the rationalist scientific and philosophic views of the time, it had little to do with the traditional personal God of infinite justice and wisdom. Most of the churches, whether Catholic, Eastern, or Protestant, were closely tied to the state. The Toleration Act in England (1689) weakened this church-state system. Later came Romanticism and the French Revolution (1789-99), which was anticlerical, in part anti-Christian, and the Napoleon Wars (1804-14) badly weakened political structures that dominated many of the churches. Emmanuelle Kant (1724-1804) in his *Critique of Practical Reason* (1788), wrote that dialogical reasoning (morals, not science), point clearly to a spiritual knowledge of God.

## MODERNITY:

> ***Modernity or modernism is contemporary ideology that often devalues the supernatural and religious aspects, altogether.***

Modernity marked the 19th century's attitude toward Christianity. Several of its characteristic movements further challenged the faith. In some Catholic regions the growing revolutionary forces were mostly anticlerical, even in Spain. The Industrial Revolution weakened all structures of society traditionally associated with the Church. New social theories, notably *Marxist Socialism*, were clearly anti-Christian and won adherents among the intellectuals and the laborers in the burgeoning industries. Scientific discoveries and theories such as Darwinism, and the application of historical methodology to the Bible, *appeared* to make the faith untenable to many "educated" minds. Atheistic writers such as Nietzsche openly attacked Christianity. We all know what followed these extreme ideas: World Wars I, II, and the Communist (atheistic) Cold Wars.

## AGE OF REASON

> ***There is sufficient light for those who desire to see, and there is sufficient darkness for those of a contrary disposition.* –Blaise Pascal (17th century genius and skeptic)**

At the dawn of the 17th century, the Western world was experiencing one of the most profound paradigm shifts in scientific and philosophic intellectual history. With the overthrow of the ancient Ptolemaic geocentric cosmology, Copernicus and Galileo had prevailed in astronomy by demonstrating the theory of heliocentric. Francis Bacon had laid the groundwork for a new scientific epistemology (i.e., *scientific method*), and Rene Descartes, impressed by strict mathematical deductive logic, rejected the a priori assumptions of the medieval scholastic philosophers and instead set forth a new methodological process of arriving at philosophic truth. Essentially, Descartes' method emphasized a *subjective* approach, beginning with his classic dictum: *"Cogito, ergo sum" ("I think, therefore I am")*, thus rejecting the pre-suppositional acceptance of certain *objective* theistic assertions.

## SKEPTICISM:

### *This is the theory that certain knowledge is impossible.*

Although theism had not yet been denied, this new shift in methodology would clearly predict the ascent of *reason*, which would culminate during the era of the Enlightenment, or *Age of Reason*, in the eighteenth century. (Also, Darwinism by that time *significantly* supported this "age of skepticism.") Thus, it was at the threshold of this new era, marked by the Copernican revolution and Cartesian epistemology, that the spirit of skepticism and freethinking would be born - and a fire had been kindled which would eventually explode into a "war of worldviews," a war that we even witness today, i.e., the war between theism *(revelation and reason)* and philosophical naturalism *(reason alone)*.

## BLAISE PASCAL

**Converting Skeptics:** A summary based on *Pascal* by Bill Tsamis:

In 1646, Blaise Pascal would begin a spiritual journey that would possess his mind and occupy his soul until his tragic death at the young age of thirty-nine. During this short period in his life, "Pascal the mathematician and physicist" would become "Pascal the apologist and philosopher." Though he never abandoned his scientific experiments, he nevertheless consecrated his work to the glory of God, and began to focus his mind on philosophical and theological pursuits.

When Pascal's father had severely injured his leg, two profoundly religious men came to care for the ailing Etienne. Pascal would be deeply impressed by the degree of Christian charity and spirituality that these two men evoked. Since they were *Jansenists*, a movement within Roman Catholicism that was based on the teachings of Cornelius Jansenius (1585-1638), Bishop of Ypres, author of the controversial work *Augustinus*, it seemed natural for Pascal to be drawn toward the Jansenism school of thought. Jansenism resurrected the Pelagian controversy, a theological debate in the ancient church (ca. 400) between Augustine and Pelagius over the issues of grace, free will, and original sin.

In contrast to the Jesuit teaching, that grace is effective when the recipient assents and cooperates with God through free will, Jansenism taught that grace is wholly unmerited and therefore granted to the recipient by God through *predestination*. Consequently, the ideas proposed by Jansenism were in the tradition of Augustinian thought, and not unlike those of John Calvin. These propositions were declared *heretical* by Pope Innocent X in 1653, but the firestorm of controversy would continue to rage on for some time. In the midst of this theological conflict, Blaise Pascal would enter the arena as a philosophical thinker and polemicist par excellence.

In 1654, Pascal experienced a profound spiritual awakening and conversion that he described in terms of mystical illumination. Prior to that fateful night, Pascal had taken the Roman Catholic ritual quite seriously, especially since he experienced the profound religiosity of the two *Jansenism* brethren who cared for his father in 1646. Nevertheless, Pascal was plagued by spiritual distress and despair - he still felt as if he hadn't yet experienced *true* communion with God.

Consequently, at the height of his struggle, while he was yearning and hungering for a deep interpersonal relationship with the God who seemed to evade him, or the "hidden God" as he later referred to the Supreme Being, Pascal's spirit was filled with immense grace and glory, as the "hidden God" determined to reveal Himself to the earnest seeker through a profound spiritual experience. Later, Pascal would relate his mystical experience with the following words: *"FIRE – [the] God of Abraham, God of Isaac, God of Jacob, not of the philosophers and scholars. Certitude, heartfelt joy, peace. God of Jesus Christ. My God and thy God. Thy God shall be my God"* (This text is from what is called the *Memorial*, a piece of parchment which was sewn into the lining of Pascal's coat).

It was at this point that Pascal dedicated himself entirely to God and sought to serve the Divine Master with austerity and rigor. With the same degree of penetrating ingenuity that he had applied to his mathematic and scientific pursuits, Pascal now immersed himself in the study of Scripture and the Church Fathers.

As the great thinker was unwittingly entering into the final phase of his life (1657-62), Pascal took it upon himself to prepare *An Apology for the Christian Religion*, a work which would be written with the intent of *converting skeptics* and freethinkers. With his years of experience among the intelligentsia of his time, and with his penetrative ingenuity, Pascal was certainly proven for such a monumental work. However, fate would have it that the great Pascal would be *cut down* in his prime at the young age of thirty-nine, and the world would be left with about a thousand of his maxims, aphorisms, philosophical insights, and notes, later to be compiled into a work called *Pensees* (lit. *"Thoughts"*).

Why was Pascal's thoughts so unique, and why has his perspective transcended the centuries? Ironically, Pascal's philosophic insight differed greatly from the thinkers of his time. For instance, whereas Descartes, who was also a mathematician of great repute, *reasoned* that mathematical principles could serve as the paradigm for inferring philosophic knowledge, Pascal regarded Descartes' exaltation of mathematical sovereignty as overly ambitious and useless with regard to philosophical and theological applications.

The philosophical genius of Pascal was that throughout his career as a mathematician and physicist, he had plunged the very depths of *reason* to such a degree that only a handful of thinkers in the course of human civilization could be ranked with him. Because he deeply penetrated the very depths of reason to a point which was beyond the common reach of man, he recognized the *limitations of reason*. He had journeyed to its very perimeter, and consequently knew that there was no traversing beyond that point. Before him stood an unsurpassable chasm; and though he realized that the truth regarding *ultimate reality* waited on the other side, he knew that not he, nor anyone else, could pass over the unsurpassable chasm. As a consequence, he dismissed the Omni-competence of *reason,* and instead recognized the finitude of man's potential intellect.

## *We know what we are, but know not what we may be.*
## William Shakespeare

In one of Pascal's famous quotes from *Pensees*, he humbly concedes the finitude of his own reason - and ironically it is reason herself, which he has met *face to face*, who instructs him as to her limitations. In his honest encounter with *uncertainty*, he wrote:

"I do not know who put me into the world, nor what the world is, or what I am myself. I am terribly ignorant about everything. I don't know what my body is, or my senses, or my soul, or even that part of me which thinks what I am saying, which reflects about everything and about itself, and does not know itself any better than it knows anything else. I see the terrifying spaces of the universe hemming me in, and I find myself attached to one corner of this vast expanse without knowing why I have been put in this place rather than that . . . All I know is that I must soon die, but what I know least about is this very death which I cannot evade. Just as I do not know whence I come, so I do not know whether I am going. All I can know is that when I leave this world I shall fall forever into nothingness or into the hands of a wrathful God, but I do not know which of these two states is to be my eternal lot." –Blaise Pascal

This spirit of uncertainty regarding the Omni-competence of reason, contrary to modern positivistic and naturalistic notions, is actually indicative of the humility of other great thinkers such as Socrates , who has served as the paradigmatic thinker for intellectual modesty and careful epistemology ever since the Greek classical era (ca. 400 BC). Thus, echoing Socrates, Pascal recognized his own limitations (despite his magnificent academic achievements which were based on *reason alone*, and in so doing, he anticipated the thought of Soren Kierkegaard (1813-55).

Kierkegaard was reluctant to build an ambitious rationalistic system, and like Pascal, he perfectly understood the *apparent ambiguity* of God, and the importance of *faith* in the Christian life: "I contemplate the order of nature in finding God, and I see omnipotence and wisdom; but I also see much else that disturbs my mind and excites anxiety. The sum of all this is an objective uncertainty."

Nevertheless, despite these realizations of the *ambiguity of God*, both Pascal and Kierkegaard, rather than seeing uncertainty as a weak link in an apologetic system, perceived such ambiguities as *"that which must be,"* especially if we stand by the assertion that God is wholly transcendent and unfathomable (Rom 11:33; Is 55:8-9), apart from His own determined *self-revelation*.

Notwithstanding our discussion of Pascal's concept of God's *ambiguity*, the great thinker did in fact integrate an undeniable existential principle into his system which was, at the same time, both similar and dissimilar to the assertion of Descartes. Whereas Descartes argued that *self-existence* ("Cogito, ergo sum") was the key pillar upon which man must erect all subsequent knowledge, Pascal argued that it was in fact "the *end* of self-existence" (i.e., the consequence of *death*) with which man must concern himself primarily and ultimately.

For Pascal, knowledge and acclaim in life was futile, if man disregarded this essential existential problem: "Nothing is so important to man as his state: nothing more fearful than eternity. Thus the fact that there exist men who are indifferent to the loss of their being and peril of an eternity of wretchedness is against nature. With everything else they are quite different. They fear the most trifling things, foresee and feel them; and the same man who spends so many days and nights in fury and despair at losing some office or at some-imaginary affront to his honor is the very one who knows that he is going to lose everything through death, but feels neither anxiety nor emotion. It is a monstrous thing to see one and the same heart once so sensitive to minor things and so strangely insensitive to the greatest. An inevitable death, which [as a consequence] threatens us at every moment, must infallibly in a few years face us with the inescapable and appalling alternative of being annihilated or wretched for all eternity." (See *Pensees pages 427, 432)*

## Pascal's Wager:

For Pascal, then, the shadow of death loomed large, and the idea of facing eternity without knowing one's destiny was simply a burden too wearisome to bear—the stakes were simply too high. Thus, Pascal articulated his famous *Wager-argument*, which essentially set forth the idea that the *Christian* has nothing to lose (even if one is mistaken), while the *atheist* has everything to lose (if he is mistaken).

The most *reasonable* position, then, would be for one to place his *wager* on the *existence of God*, since there is nothing to lose one way or the other. And the sensual pleasures he might sacrifice in his devotion to God, would simply be reciprocated by the peace of mind, joy, and harmonious living which would be the product of his devotional life.

Pascal did not offer his *Wager-argument* as a conventional proof of the existence of God, but rather as a challenge to those skeptics and atheists who were unconvinced by the traditional arguments and thus remained comfortably in a state of *"suspended judgment."* As for Pascal, he placed his *wager* on the existence of God, and he found his perfect hope in the person of Jesus Christ.

> ***Acknowledge the truth of religion in its very obscurity… for it is not true that everything reveals God, and it is not true that everything conceals God. But it is true at once that He hides from those who tempt Him, and that He reveals Himself to those who seek Him. (Pensees 439, 444).***

Pascal *Pensees* Reference Sources:

John A. Mackay's "Forward" in Emille Cailliet, The Clue to Pascal (Philadelphia: Westminster Press), 1943. Frederick Copleston, S.J., A History of Philosophy - Vol. 4, Modern Philosophy from Descartes to Leibniz (New York: Doubleday), 1963, Ibid. Antony Flew, "Rene Descartes" in A Dictionary of Philosophy (New York: St Martin's Press), 1979. Plato, Plato's Apology, trans. by Benjamin Jowett (New York: Simon and Schuster), 1928. Soren Kierkegaard, "Concluding

Unscientific Postscript," quoted by Copleston in A History of Philosophy - Vol. 7. Copleston, A History of Philosophy - Vol. 4.

## DEISM & RATIONALISM:

> ***Deists viewed God primarily as the Creator of the universe and held that the universe exhibits unvarying laws, which govern it. These laws are reflected in human morals, and conformity or nonconformity to them results automatically in rewards and punishments here and beyond the grave.***

Deism stressed what it called "natural religion" or rationalists, which insisted that it was supported by reason quite apart from revelation. Deists denied the possibility of miracles, including those described in the Scriptures. They honored Jesus, but only for his "noble life and ethical principles," not as the Christ conceived by the Holy Spirit and a member of the Trinity. A minority of the rationalists became Unitarians, who rejected the Nicene Creed and similar statements of basic Christian doctrine.

## IDEALISM:

> ***The idea is the intellectual knowledge of the mind. It's a reverse theory of reality; our knowledge begins with thoughts rather than the true being of all things.***

Idealism is the philosophical theory that the universe is an expression of the mind. Epistemological Idealism is a form of the theory developed in England by George Berkeley (1685-1753), David Hume (1711-76), and John Stuart Mill (1806-73), a Utilitarian, building upon the foundation laid by John Locke (1632-1704), known as an Empiricist (or Agnostic). Metaphysical Idealism was the doctrine of Hegel; i.e., *"The real is what's rational."*

Descartes and Kant, together, represent *a significant turning point* in the so-called age of "Enlightenment." Ironically, many "mental lights" went out, during and after that age of enlightenment, because truth and realism became overwhelmed by idealism and skeptics, which *as a consequence*, believe that any and all ideas from the past, or anybody's future ideas, are all "relative." (Relativism is a significant negative force in our 21$^{st}$ century, as well).

As a result, objective truths (the "It"), moral and ethical standards (the "We") and individual moral values (the "I") today are considered by many to be *relative*. Moreover, to say that there is "no such thing as truth," is to say words without meaning; *it's proclaiming the very thing you want to deny.* It proclaims as truth that there is no such thing as truth. Any statement that "there are no absolute truths," is an absolute truth statement itself, which is logically false!

"Immanuel Kant codified philosophical Idealism thinking; i.e., one cannot know the object itself, which unfortunately remains the position of much of academia even in the 21$^{st}$ century. The *foundational principles* of Kant's philosophical system are *wrong*. Kant's theory demanded that Euclidean geometry was the only type of geometry that the mind could conceive—whereas Gauss (1777-1855), discovered non-Euclidean geometry, which we use and depend on today." Source: *The Universe Next Door* by James W. Sire

Ken Wilber, in *The Marriage Of Sense and Soul*, wrote in his chapter on The *Rise Of Idealism*: "This idea—cosmic and human history is most profoundly the evolution and development of Spirit—occurred immediately in the wake of Kant, and was one of the great announcements of the Idealists. This was during that extraordinary period when the Big Three (I, We and It) had been clearly differentiated (about the end of the 18$^{th}$ century), but before their massive dissociation and eventual collapse (end of the 19$^{th}$ century). As such, this was truly a fertile period for the value spheres (I of individualism and art; I and We of morality; and the IT of the sciences, to enrich one another..."

It all began with Immanuel Kant, who wrote a *Critique of Pure Reason and Critique of Practical Reason* (1781). He maintained that we can never know (being) 'the thing in itself,' only the appearance or phenomenon that results when the thing in itself is acted on by the categories of the human mind. German Idealism began, in a sense, with the notion that the world is not merely perceived but constructed. Not naïve empiricism, but mental idealism, has a hand in the perception of the world.

## Epistemological Idealism:

This is the central theory of Locke. He resolved from his study of perception that one never directly senses any physical thing; the qualities that one perceives are all effects in the mind produced by the action of things upon them. As regard to sensed qualities such as color and sound, odor and taste, he saw no reason to believe that there was anything resembling them in physical substance. Conversely, he believed that percepts of size, shape, and movement enabled us to infer through resemblance what sort of things and events gave rise to them. Berkeley denied this part of the theory. The belief in a physical nature arose, he thought, from assigning an external existence to qualities which, when examined, proved in every case to be resoluble into sensations and therefore to exist only in minds. *"Esse est percipi—to be is to be perceived."*

## SOLIPSISM:

*Nothing whatever exists except one's sensations and images.*

Berkeley disagreed with this conclusion. There must be an independent cause for perceptions, he thought. However, since the notion of material things had been shown to be illusory, the only reasonable alternative seemed to be a mind similar to our own, but exceedingly more permanent and comprehensive, in which the order of nature remained as an enduring order of ideas. In Hume subjective idealism is carried to the extreme. Hume agreed with Berkeley that all knowledge comes from sense experience. But he concluded that not only physical things, but ourselves as well, including God, are to be regarded as nothing more than sequences of experience. All that we can know to exist is our own impressions and images.

## RELATIONSHIPS:

> ***The nature of anything depends on its relations, and for that reason it cannot be fully known until these relations are explored.***

"Absolute idealists" generally agree that their philosophical system involves certain consequences. It indicates that truth lies in the connection of a belief with experiences as a whole. It signifies determinism in the sense that nothing happens by chance. It implies that everything in our finite experience is an "appearance," whose nature will be seen to be different in the context of extended knowledge. It infers that the good life is to be found in self-realization, i.e., in fuller approximation to that absolute which is already partially expressed in every person. Therefore, it would replace the traditional notion of a personal deity by the idea of a God who is absolute and super-personal.

Ken Wilber adds the following to this topic: Absolute Spirit is the fundamental reality. But in order to create the world, the Absolute manifests itself, or goes out of itself—in a sense, the Absolute forgets itself and empties itself into creation (although never really ceasing to be itself). Thus the world is created as a 'falling away' from Spirit, as a 'self-alienation' of Spirit, although the fall is never anything but a play of Spirit itself.

Having 'fallen' into the manifest and material world, Spirit begins the process of returning to itself, and this process of the return of the Spirit to the Spirit is simply development or evolution itself...

When the Spirit first goes out of itself to create the manifest universe, the result is Nature, which Schelling calls 'slumbering Spirit' and Hegel calls 'God in its otherness.' Nature is a direct manifestation of Spirit, and thus Nature is sacred to the core; but it is slumbering Spirit, simply because Nature is not yet self-reflexively aware. It is the lowest form of Spirit, but a form of Spirit nonetheless. It is Spirit in its objective manifestation, what Plato had called 'a visible God.'

In the second major stage of development, Spirit evolves from objective Nature to subjective Mind. Thus, Spirit has now developed from subconscious to self-conscious, and thus begins to reflect on its own existence. Where Nature was objective Spirit, Mind is subjective Spirit, and thus we see increasingly more conscious forms of Spirit's own self-actualization and return to itself.

But at this point the subject and the object, or Mind and Nature, cannot just differentiate but *dissociate*, and thus this stage is often marked by a rampant dualism—a 'spiritual pathology,' according to Schelling, the 'unhappy consciousness,' as Hegel put it. This unhappiness is not present in the previous stage of Nature, but only because Nature is slumbering; yet with the self-conscious awakening of the Mind these painful divisions become all too obvious...

Here the Idealists—especially Fichte and Hegel—veered sharply away from the Romantics, who by and large wanted to heal the painful unhappy consciousness by a 'return to Nature.' But this return the Idealists pointed out is based on a series of confusions... Fichte and Hegel rail against the Romantic regression to sentiments, feeling, anti-rationalism, and organic immersion, pointing out, quite correctly, that the Romantics were headed in precisely the wrong direction...

Romantics often ended up glorifying anything that was non-rational, including states that were frankly regressive, narcissistic, in-dissociated, and de-differentiated, all of which thoroughly erased not just the disasters of Modernity but the dignities as well...

"That these Idealists (Fichte, Hegel) were witness to this *regressive nightmare* as it actually unfolded makes their polemics all the more cogent—and applicable to similar slides now widely occurring under the guise of a 'New Age' and a 'Scientology.'"

## ROMANTICISM:

> ***Romanticism was creative rather than critical,
> concrete rather than abstract, biological rather than
> mathematical. The Enlightenment age theories cleared
> the ground and planted the seed. Romanticism made
> it come forth.***

To understand Romanticism as a philosophy (in contrast to a historical perspective), during 1770-1850, one must first ignore the ordinary use of the word "romantic." The true meaning lies in the origin of the several words. The noun "romance" indicates a story written in the vernacular—hence simplistic in style, popular in appeal, and characterized by a mixture of factual details and adventure.

Important signs of *genuine Romanticism* are a preference for simplicity and naturalness, a love of plain feelings and truth to commonplace reality, especially as found in natural scenes—in a word, the rejection of anything artificial that inevitably developed in the urban centers of so-called advanced civilization.

Rousseau was the first to break openly with earlier doctrines of the age of Enlightenment which repudiates the ideal of elegant upper-class leisure and preaches modern bourgeois. He defines the principles of democratic society and representative government. He makes religious feeling once again a legitimate emotion. He reforms prose style, anticipates the theory of musical drama, and revolutionizes the aims and methods of education.

He delves into the recesses of the self through his *Confessions and Makes of Nature*, not indeed a primitive state of ignorance to which we should turn back, but an ideal norm ahead of us toward which all our explorations of heart and mind should tend. In Rousseau, then, the new conception of humanity and the good life achieved comprehensive expression, which is why he is known (and attacked) as "the father of Romanticism."

## AGE OF REASON CLIMAX:

The French Revolution is at once the climax of the Age of Reason and the source of the problems and tendencies of Romanticism. Its date, 1789, conveniently divides the pre-Romanticism from the full flowering of the new culture. The French Revolution made a clean sweep of old modes of thought—not only monarchical and feudal, but also "Enlightened" and "Classical" modes.

If one can speak of "Renaissance Man," one can speak of "Romanticist." People of these two distant centuries—the 16th and the 19th—have many points in common: strong passions and heroic characters, determined to create a new order out of the ruins of the old; productiveness in all the arts; failures and tragedies; and both periods were marked by intense individualism and diversity.

The Enlightenment period was critical, destructive, while Romanticism was creative, innovating, and exploratory. Enlightenment presumed the universal applicability of a few simple principles of reason. The philosophers of the earlier period were, on the whole, rationalists, like Descartes and Newton. It was in the name of "universal reason" that they undermined the old regime, which was to them a conglomeration of irrationalities.

In contrast, Romanticists found the 17th and 18th century view too simplistic and abstract; they were impressed by the diversities that existed in the world and looked for substance to supplement and complement abstract truths. Romanticists generally agreed that the world was not simple, uniform, and rational, but complex, diverse, and often irrational. This explains the great renewal of interest in history. Unlike physics or geometry, history is the record of concrete events and persons, each unique in a time and place.

History led to the study of individual nations, which, as Burke pointed out, has a continuous life through the great chain of births. This view, in turn, caused cultural nationalism to replace cosmopolitan attitudes and dynastic loyalties of the 18th century.

The German Herder and the Italian Mazzini are good examples of the new nationalism. It was cultural in the sense that it viewed each nation as a unique entity contributing its special achievements to a common European culture. There was as yet no thought of superiority attached to these differences, and no imperialism. Europe was simply conceived of as a "bouquet made up of many, distinctly different flowers."

## REBIRTH OF FAITH:

Romanticist's return to favor during this timeframe coincided with a powerful religious revival. In England, the Methodist and the Anglican (Oxford) movements; in Germany, the Protestant and Catholic Churches—all experienced a rebirth of faith.

Faith was now held indispensable to building the new order—whatever it might be; and the quality of the faith, its sincerity and scope mattered more than dogmatic details. At the same time the intellectual passion of scientists such as Erasmus, Darwin, Lamarck, Dalton, (among others) proved to be as intense and fruitful as the conscious traditionalism of a poet such as Coleridge.

The subject matter of "classical culture" was not discarded; rather it was transformed in its feeling and character, given a new lease on life, and set within a larger pattern of interests which included all known history and all modern nations.

In the 19th century, all branches of Christianity displayed a strikingly *Rebirth of Faith* and geographic expansion on a global scale, unprecedented in history, which planted Christianity in many regions.

In the Universal Church, the revival included the strengthening of the papacy. As the century progressed able men of high moral character occupied the papal throne. In practice, the papacy exercised more power within the Church than at any previous time. Late in the 19th century, Pope Leo XIII, in his encyclical *Rerum novarum* (1891), gave to the Church a statement of principles for meeting the social and economic problems of that age. Pope Leo also encouraged the study of St. Thomas Aquinas as a means of dealing with intellectual challenges of the day. Old monastic orders were renewed and strengthened, and more new monastic congregations arose than in any other century. *Ironically*, most of the new monastic movements had begun in anti-cleric France. More Catholic missionaries have also set out from France than from all the rest of the Roman Catholic nations. (Paradoxically, France became the center of anticlericalism and agnostic questioning of the faith).

In the East, the decline of Turkish power, and the emergence of Greece, Bulgaria, Romania, and Serbia from Islamic control, freed the churches in these lands from centuries of subservience to a Muslim government. In Russia, fresh currents in devotional life, and in theology, were seen in the Orthodox Church.

Protestantism also displayed fresh vitality. On the continent of Europe, Pietism (personal piety, rather than ritual practices) in the 18th century, and a German revival of the Lutheran movement took place, which changed from its earlier focus on the ritual to a more personal piety.

Orthodoxy, in Anglo-Saxon lands, and Evangelicalism, which counted among its pioneers John Wesley (1703-1791), brought new life to Christianity. As a *consequence*, the Protestant Conscience helped abolish slavery in the British Isles and in the United States, and placed on the statute books of Britain, laws to curb some of the ills associated with the Industrial Revolution. Able minds struggled to bring Theology abreast of the intellectual and more reasoned currents.

## RECONCILING THE IRRECONCILABLE:

*The Romantic Spirit cherished experience and tradition; emotion and reason; religion and science; form and substance; the real and the ideal; individuals and groups; order and freedom; civilization and nature.*

Our 21st century culture is eager to achieve this reconciliation. Like Romanticism, it starts from humanity and accepts the contradictions within it. **People are both great and helpless, destined for glory and wretchedness, endowed with reason and driven by irrational life forces.** They cannot give up or withdraw from their earthly effort, for as Pascal in the 17th century and modern Existentialists have pointed out, they are engaged in the struggle before they know there is one. Hence the Romantic *valuation of qualities* that may see them through this difficult task: energy, daring, capacity for experience, courage, intellect, and imagination.

To many historic Romanticists, regardless of church, party, or nationality, the great embodiment of these powers was Napoleon. He was the man who starting from nothing and had become statesman and conqueror—*the self-made man* in an era of "careers open to talent." He was the prototype of the man of genius. What preoccupied the literary minds of the period was how to ascertain and represent the actual conditions of people in society. Unlike the 18th century philosophers, they did not frame allegories or systems with which to criticize existing abuses. They protested directly and dramatically in poems, pamphlets, or realistic novels.


## EVOLUTION THEORY

No less than in literature and social criticism, the Romantic period was highly productive in terms of the sciences. It is the age that saw the rise of chemistry and the unification of the theories of physical energy. But even more important, it is the age of the "biological revolution."

While the 17th and 18th centuries were shaped intellectually by mathematics and astronomy (ideas that originated from Galileo, Descartes, Newton), the 19th century was shaped by subdivisions of biology—zoology, anthropology, psychology—and all of them were affected by Darwin's Evolution theory.

In the Romantic Age, the *idea of evolution* was not limited to its biological intent. Every branch of social science and philosophy was affected by the idea that *"all things are in flux,"* that becoming is more important than being; in short, change is universal and has significant meaning.

Whereas the Enlightenment sought order and stability by finding permanent truths, Romanticists sought what might be called *"truths in motion."* When they studied history it was to find the origins of their society and to discover the laws of its becoming. Social reformers prefaced their purpose with an account of how humankind had evolved from primitive beginnings to the present state of civilization.

This method of persuasion was employed by Augusta Comte, the founder of "*Sociology*," and by Fourier and Saint-Simon, founders of "*Socialism*," and by Hegel, the evolutionary logician and philosopher of history, to whom Karl Marx was later indebted for much of his own revolutionary doctrine (he also supported Darwin's Evolution theory).

Together with Evolution and its applications, the Romantic age produced a vast amount of research in the science of humans. Late 18th century travelers had brought back information about the newly explored South Seas as well as the newly-discovered continent of Australia. The early 19th century sought to organize this information into a new science, known sometimes as Ethnology (science of peoples) and sometimes as Anthropology (science of human beings).

These sciences and/or pseudo-sciences dealt with the mind from the outside. But another tradition was started by Rousseau in his *Confessions*. He made use of introspection as a means of finding out what humans are really like. The observations of poets, novelists, and autobiographers, supplemented by physicians and travelers, soon laid bare some of the unsuspected sources of human actions.

The *unconscious* or unreasoning part of human nature, which ceaselessly wills and desires, was seen at work not only in individual but in social behavior, not only in art and law and morality, but also in religion. The development of this *awareness*, from Rousseau through the poets to Schopenhauer, Von Hartmann, Nietzsche, Dostoyevsky, and Freud is perhaps the most fundamental contribution of the Romantic search, and it is (perhaps) sufficient refutation of the view that Romanticism sought merely to pit "the heart" against "the head." What it did was to demonstrate that *neither the heart nor the head was independent of the other,* and the whole was more complex and powerful than had been suspected.

Raised to maturity by a great political upheaval that brought every idea and institution into question, the Romantic found that rationalism of the 18th century would not work. Rationalism, however, succeeded excellently in mathematics and physics—abstract sciences. But living things had *irrationality* at the core of their being and must be studied with this important difference in mind. The way to study them was through history, sociology, religion, biology, anthropology, and art. The old idea of progress was thus deepened and enlarged into the *overarching theory of Evolution.*

## NATURE AND SCIENCE:

Perhaps the best example of this Romantic attempt at synthesis is to be found in the life and works of Goethe. Born in Germany in 1749, he grew up at the height of the philosophy of the *Enlightenment.* Influenced by Rousseau and Shakespeare; he reacted against it and became the teacher of the new Literary Renaissance in Germany. Passionately fond of ancient art and literature, he also produced in his drama Faust (based on late medieval legends), a prototype of the *Romanticist* who seeks concrete experiences to form his own morality and regain peace in a personal religion. Poet, dramatist, critic, and philosopher, Goethe was also a scientist. He applied the doctrine of Evolution with great brilliancy and correctness to botany in his *Metamorphosis of Plants,* and to the philosophical uses of poets and thinkers in his *Essay on Nature.*

### Cause-and-Effect:

Goethe, Hegel, and other Romantics were determined to show the role of "becoming" or evolutionary development in life. But the age was rich in philosophers, and this is to say that they differed. What united an age are not the solutions it proposes, but the problems it takes up, because it feels that they are inescapable. The two problems with which the Romanticist philosophers grappled were *Nature and Science* (which we are still dealing with in the 21st century). It is easy to see that the question "How do we come to know the world of nature?" leads directly to the question "What is the certainty of science?" In the rationalist period, David Hume had demonstrated the inability of the human mind to know *external truths* and had reduced the validity of the cause-and-effect principle to a mere habit. Hume's position was the final step of rational destruction; *it was reason undermining itself.*

## Critique of Judgment:

The philosophers of the next generation, of whom Immanuel Kant was the principal, had the characteristic Romantic task of building on the ruins of the past. Kant's solution to Hume's difficulty was to distinguish between *phenomena*, which were the ordinary changeable, uncertain perceptions of humans, and things-in-themselves, which formed the unchanging but unknowable structure of the universe.

The fact (false belief) that reason could not know things-in-themselves (being) was therefore no cause for despair, or even for skepticism. People could always study phenomena, for they are known, said Kant, according to uniform patterns common to all human minds, the patterns of Time and Space. These are called "Categories" and all experience falls into them. No phenomenon (no being), no experience exists apart from the activity of a human mind, which knows whether a fact comes before or after another, whether it is like or unlike, and so on.

Consequently, the ways of Science, which consist in measuring time, matter and space, in isolating causes, and in classifying things were vindicated by the Kant's philosophy. In his *Critique of Judgment*, Kant also argued that mechanisms can explain everything in the world but two: beauty and organisms.

## American Romanticism:

If any proof were needed of the logic and unity of Romanticism as a general movement of mind in Western culture, it could be found in American Romanticism. Without direct influence from Germany or England, the two generations embracing Emerson, Thoreau, Theodore Parker, Bronson Alcott, Margaret Fuller, Hawthorne, Poe, Whitman, and Melville. They went through similar struggles to reach their several philosophies of life.

Like their European counterparts, they were moved by a religious and poetic instinct, which rejected abstraction and empty dogmas, as they sought in nature the secret of their being, a strengthening of their moral impulses, and a refuge from the unthinking herd materialists. Lastly, they saw humankind as a single entity, embarked on an enterprise greater than it knew and not to be expressed through the ordinary channels of class, or national policy.

Romanticism was an inclusive voyage of discovery and it is no surprise that Emerson, Carlyle, Coleridge, Wordsworth, Schiller, Goethe, and the rest should be as much concerned with philosophy as with science, as much worried by social problems as by religious. For all of them life was a total thing. It might be broken up for convenient study, but it did not exist in separate parts as specialties. "We murder to dissect," as Wordsworth said, meaning not that he was an enemy to science, but that any branch of study, precisely because it was a branch, could not be the whole tree of life. The symbol of the tree was in fact the one chosen by Goethe to express his sense of the gap that exists between experience, felt at first-hand, and the abstract statement made about it. (Note that Darwin also used the "tree" idea to express his *false* macro-evolutionary theory).

## MATERIALISM:

> ***Materialism is where the primary object of one's mortal life is to accumulate material goods and sensory gratification, often at the expense of others, which can result in the loss of one's soul and loss of eternal happiness.***

Materialism or Modernity strives to destroy the objective validity of all religious beliefs, making it (modernism) the product of the human soul, not any supernatural revelations from God. This heresy, which denies the divinity of Christ and rejects the authority of His Church, is particularly treacherous because it usurps Christian premises to which it attributes new and false meanings.

All sciences are essentially "value-free." They tell us what is, not what should be or ought to be. For example, biological cells are neither good nor bad. The solar system, galaxies and the universe isn't good or bad. Electrons, protons and other elements of physics are neither good nor evil particles. Since God made all things, they are all good. *The search for objective truths, not values, is the primary role of the sciences.* The role of religion is the search for both the objective and subjective meaning of things, the "why?" It's concerned with finding the meaning of life and moral values (good and bad), wisdom—and theology—which is the science of God.

It shouldn't be a matter of one or the other. For example, science shouldn't invent weapons that are not controlled by moral standards, and religion shouldn't limit scientific progress. Value-free science and value-full religion *must coexist.* We need to find a way to integrated both in the 21$^{st}$ century. For this marriage of Science and Scripture to be consummated, it must have the free will and full consent of both parties.

## Secularism:

> ***A secular society that has no end beyond its own satisfaction is a monstrosity—a cancerous growth which will ultimately destroy itself.* --Christopher Dawson**

What's confronting institutionalized religion today is an empty postmodern secularity that has tainted mainline churches and society at large. It expresses itself in a shallow life dedicated to the search for material pleasure. Frequently this attitude is not so much articulated as it is lived. It is a response even of those who, because of the habits of a lifetime, still relate to religious institutions at a nominal level, even though they find no sustenance there. Membership in such an institution does not finally affect their life, and ultimately it is so divergent to their being that they will not pass on to their children a living religious heritage. No seeds of renewal will be found for the church in those who either consciously or unconsciously takes up citizenship in this secular city.

Religion in too many communities has become peripheral, or marginalized in Western society. It's for Sunday mornings only. The church that does not face this dilemma seriously either does not understand the problem or does not know how to address it. Such a church drifts aimlessly, replacing faith with fellowship, avoiding the tough issues of life, standing for less and less for fear that another part of its congregation might be offended and depart, knowing full well that the church's drawing power is declining day-by-day. There is no future for (this kind of) Christianity unless the *'essence of Christian truths'* can be extracted from the framework of the ancient past. There is no better place to pose the issue in all its searing power than by opening readers in a new way to the *Gospel according to Mark*. For this is the issue by which this Gospel confronts a modern-day reader (which was written in Rome during the time of Emperor Nero, when corruption existed almost everywhere, as it is today in Europe, and in the rapidly evolving socialistic America).

## GOD-CENTERED SOCIETY:

A God-centered civilized society is *usually* family-oriented, teaches its children early moral values, demands individual responsibility, and promotes literacy. That kind of society generally produces caring, productive, responsible individuals, who exemplify a cult of life. Like a pyramid, faith in God is at the pinnacle, followed by respect for parents, moral values, and a sense of responsibility for ones' acts, and everything else that's good flows from faith and family.

Conversely, an agnostic and secular society can often lead to disintegrating or dysfunctional families, the deterioration in moral values, and lack of individual irresponsibility. Secular American culture has tried everything; that is, except teaching that morality, individual responsibility, and the human conscience, have a vital role to play in our lives. A faithless society is clearly a culture of death.

Materialism results partly from capitalism and partly from socialistic atheism; that is, since God doesn't exist—'why not party and make the most of this relatively short life.' Materialism also flows from the *false illusion that humans can control their life, environment, and ultimate destiny.* No human has the power to 'create' in the proper sense of the word; i.e., to produce and give being to that which in no way possessed it (to call into existence 'something out of nothing).'

Our fantastic technology cannot create a living bug, nor control the forces of nature, such as hurricanes, floods, droughts, or earthquakes (although we think we can). Yet we have the ability to totally destroy the entire living world, which God entrusted to us.

## NIHILISM & MODERNISM:

> *Traditional values and beliefs are considered unfounded. Existence is senseless and useless. A doctrine that denies objective grounds for truth, especially moral truths.*

A summary of an article by Phillip Johnson on *Nihilism and the End of Law*: Modernism is the condition that begins when humans think (or misunderstand) that "God is dead," and they therefore have to decide all the big questions for themselves. Modernism at times produces an exhilarating sense of liberation: *we can do whatever we like, since there is no unimpeachable authority to prevent us.* Modernism at other times is downright scary: How can we persuade other people that what they want to do is actually barred by unchallengeable, moral absolutes?

## UNNATURAL LAWS:

Yale Law Professor Arthur Leff expressed the *bewilderment of an agnostic culture* (emphasis mine) that yearns for enduring values in a brilliant lecture delivered at Duke University in 1979. The published lecture titled *"Unspeakable Ethics, Unnatural Law"* is frequently quoted in law review articles, but it is little known outside the world of legal scholarship. In my view, it happens to be one of the best statements of the modernist impasse.

As Professor Leff put it: I want to believe—and so do you—in a complete, transcendent, and immanent set of propositions about right and wrong, findable rules that authoritatively and unambiguously direct us how to live righteously. I also want to believe—and so do you—in no such thing, but rather that we are wholly free, not only to choose for ourselves what we ought to do, but to decide for ourselves, individually and as a species, what we ought to be. What we want, Heaven help us, is simultaneously to be perfectly ruled and perfectly free, that is, at the same time to discover the right and the good and to create it.

The heart of the problem, according to Leff, is that any normative statement implies the existence of an authoritative evaluator. But with God out of the picture, every human becomes a "godlet" with as much authority to set standards as any other godlet or combination of godlets. For example, if a human moralist says, "Thou shalt not commit adultery," he invites "the formal intellectual equivalent of what is known in barrooms and schoolyards as 'the grand sez who?'" Persons who want to commit adultery, or who sympathize with those who do, can offer the crushing rejoinder: What gives *you* the authority to prescribe what is good for *me*?

## Unevaluated Evaluator:

Putting it that way makes clear that if we are looking for an evaluation, we must actually be looking for an *evaluator*: some machine for the generation of judgments on states of affairs. If the evaluation is to be beyond question, then the evaluator and its evaluative processes must be similarly insulated. If it is to fulfill its role, the evaluator must be the un-judged judge, the un-ruled legislator, the premise maker who rests on no premises, the uncreated creator of values. . . . We are never going to get anywhere (assuming for the moment that there is somewhere to get) in ethical or legal theory unless we finally face the fact that, in the Psalmist's words, there is no one like unto the Lord. . . . The so called death of God turns out not to have been just *His* funeral; it also seems to have affected the total elimination of any coherent, or even more-than-momentarily convincing, ethical or legal system dependent upon finally authoritative, extra-systematic premises.

Leff pointed out that it is not we who define God's utterances as unquestionably true, in the manner that we define a triangle as a three-sided plane figure. In a God-based system, God is not an idea in the human mind but a separate and controlling reality. If human reason aspires to be the judge of God's statements, it makes itself the unevaluated evaluator, which is to say it takes God's place. In Leff's words, our relation to God's moral order is the triangle's relationship to the order of Euclidean plane geometry, not the mathematician's. We are defined, constituted as beings whose adultery is wrong, bad, and awful. Thus, committing adultery in such a system is 'naturally' bad only because the system is supernaturally constructed.

## NATURAL LAWS:

In the philosophic tradition of Thomas Aquinas, "natural law" is distinguished from divine law because its commands are accessible to human reason even in the absence of divine revelation. To a (mono) theist like Aquinas, the reality of a moral law was not in question. The question was how much of that law we could know from natural reason (or academic philosophy), and how much we could know only from Scripture or the Church. This two level system of reason and revelation made it possible for Aquinas to fuse the pre-Christian philosophy of Aristotle with the revelation-based doctrines of the Church.

To a modernist, who by definition relies only upon human authority, natural law in the Thomas Aquinas sense is no longer supportable because it would have to rest upon the unacceptable premise that nature was supernaturally created. There are still plenty of people around who would like to argue that a moral code can be discerned from nature, but the modernist understanding of nature undermines their efforts.

Even the term "natural law" is an anachronism. The majority of educated Americans believe that nature is the amoral scene of Darwinian struggle. Occasional attempts are made to derive social norms from nature so conceived, but they are not likely to succeed. It is true that a variety of widely accepted norms, including the keeping of certain promises, the abhorrence of unjustified killing of human beings, and perhaps even the sanctity of property rights, promote the adaptation of the human species to its environment. But so does genocide.

In other words, a certain amount of social cooperation is natural, in the Darwinian sense, because it tends to promote the survival of a tribe or kinship group. Murderous violence against outsiders is equally natural, because it promotes the spreading of one group's genes by eliminating competing genes. In fact, Darwinian natural selection is *defined* as a process by which superior varieties exterminate their inferiors, whether by attacking them directly or by competing more effectively for limited resources. [Darwinism was used by Hitler to justify killing millions of Jews]. It is therefore no wonder that equating what is natural with what is good—i.e., trying to derive "ought" from is—is dismissed these days as the "naturalistic fallacy." (Also, remember former President Clinton's infamous "is" defense during his Impeachment hearings).

Modernists therefore see no merit in natural law propositions about, say, sexual morality. For example, even if one grants that homosexual intercourse or abortion is in a sense less natural than heterosexual intercourse or childbirth (because it does not further reproduction), it does not follow that "unnatural" means wrong, or even undesirable. It is equally unnatural for humans to fly in airplanes, since we are not born with wings. Rejection of the naturalistic fallacy does not necessarily mean that modernists discard natural law altogether, however. As Vice President Biden indicates, modernists are much more comfortable with the idea of natural rights than with natural obligations. Because the individual human subject—Leff's godlet—is the modernist starting point, it seems reasonable to place a heavy burden of justification upon anyone who seeks to restrain the liberty of that subject. This burden of justification is what Leff whimsically called "The Grand Sez Who."

## Imposing Obligations:

The assertion of rights cannot for long be separated from the imposition of duties, however. If we give X a right to do as she wants, and she wants to get an abortion, we must soon face the question of protecting her from Y, who wants to protect the rights of unborn child. If majority opinion in the legislature favors some restrictions upon abortion, and there is no specific language in the Constitution on the subject, then "pro-choice" forces have to invoke something very much like a natural law duty to get their way. "Thou shalt not interfere with a woman's right to choose abortion; indeed, thou must help to pay for abortions through tax money; more than that, thou shalt not legislate that the woman contemplating abortion must be fully informed about the potential adoptive parents who desperately want to provide a loving home for her unborn child." Sez who?

The modernist impasse, in other words, does not stymie as long as all we are doing is proclaiming liberties. The problem for modernists is how to justify imposing obligations. Homosexuals have a right to be homosexuals, of course, but do employers who disapprove have an obligation to hire them? The poor have a right to public assistance, of course, but do the more fortunate and productive citizens have a right to refuse to pay when they think the tax burden has become unreasonable? The rights of all citizens must be protected, of course, but who are the citizens? What about infants, the unborn, foreigners, and animals? Who or what has the authority to tell us whom we ought to admit to the sphere of protection?

Most of Leff's lecture consisted of a review of all the unsuccessful attempts to establish an objective moral order on a foundation of human construction, i.e., *to put something else in God's place as the unevaluated evaluator* (emphasis mine). The asserted non-supernatural sources of moral authority are many and varied, and each is only temporarily convincing. They include: the command of the sovereign; the majority of the voters; the principle of utility; the Supreme Court's varying interpretations of the Constitution's great but ambiguous phrases; the subtle implications of platitudinous shared values like "equality" or "autonomy"; and even a hypothetical social contract that abstract persons might adopt in the imaginary "original position" described by John Rawls. Every alternative rests ultimately on human authority, because that is what remains when God is removed from the picture. But human authority always becomes inadequate as soon as people learn to challenge its pretensions. Every system fails the test of "the grand sez who."

Leff's lecture made a powerful impression upon a generation of legal scholars because he stated the nature of the impasse so convincingly. Most modernist thinking consists of attempts to evade the impasse with superficial resolutions. *Scientific socialism can usher in a secularized Kingdom of Heaven by giving economic power to the proletariat* (emphasis mine). Criminal tendencies in individuals can be greatly reduced by providing education, psychiatric treatment, and economic opportunity. Public education can produce rational, self-controlled citizens, who can govern themselves through liberal political institutions and free markets. Scientific technology can provide abundance and health, and even eventually improve the human species itself by genetic engineering. Above all, we can still know what the good *is*, however difficult it may be to achieve it. Modernist philosophy teaches that when we lost God, we lost only a projection of the best that was in ourselves; what was real in that projection therefore remains, and only the illusion is gone.

Arthur Leff had a deeper understanding of what the death of God ultimately means for man. He saw modern intellectual history as a long, losing war against the nihilism implicit in modernism's rejection of the unevaluated evaluator who is the only conceivable source for ultimate premises. Leff rejected the nihilism implicit in modernism, but he also rejected the supernaturalism that he had identified as the only escape from nihilism. Here is how he concluded his 1979 lecture:

"All I can say is this: it looks as if we are all we have. Given what we know about ourselves, and each other, this is an extraordinarily unappetizing prospect; looking around the world, it appears that if all men are brothers, the ruling model is Cain and Abel. Neither reason, nor love, nor even terror, seems to have worked to make us "good," and worse than that, there is no reason why anything should. Only if ethics were something unspeakable by us could law be unnatural, and therefore unchallengeable. As things stand now, everything is up for grabs. Nevertheless, napalming babies is bad. Starving the poor is wicked. Buying and selling each other is depraved. Those who stood up and died resisting Hitler, Stalin, Amin, and Pol Pot—and General Custer too—have earned salvation. Those who acquiesced deserve to be damned. There is in the world such a thing as evil. All together now: Sez who? God help us. "

What Leff said is fascinating, but what he failed to say is more fascinating still. If there is no ultimate evaluator, then there is no real distinction between good and evil. It follows that if evil is nonetheless *real*, then atheism—i.e., the idea of the nonexistence of that evaluator or standard of evaluation—is not only an extraordinarily unappetizing prospect, it is also *fundamentally untrue* (emphasis mine). Because the reality of evil implies the reality of the evaluator who alone has the authority to establish the standard by which evil can deserve to be damned. When impeccable logic leads to self-contradiction, there must be a faulty premise. In this case the premise is that because God is dead, "it looks as if we are all we have." Why not reexamine the premise? Why not at least explain *why* you refuse to reexamine the premise?

## Circular Reasoning:

The most interesting aspect of any argument is not what it explicitly states, but what it implicitly assumes. A rationalistic culture teaches us to think that truth is the product of a process of logical reasoning. When we are dealing with intermediate or detailed truths, which rest on more fundamental premises, this model is correct. The model breaks down, however, when we try to apply it to the fundamental premises themselves. This is because logic is a way of getting to conclusions from premises. By its very nature, a logical argument cannot justify the premises upon which it rests. When these premises are questioned, they have to be justified by a different logical argument, which rests upon different premises.

We may follow this process forever, and we will never encounter anything but another logical argument, which will itself be based upon premises. But then what is the ultimate premise, the Archimedean fulcrum on which intellect can sit and judge all the rest? If we try to answer that question by employing logic we lapse into the absurdity of circular reasoning. Reasoning has to start *somewhere.* Any attempt to justify the ultimate starting point necessarily fails, because it only establishes a different starting point. Hence, the really important step in any argument is apt to be the unexplained, unjustified, and often unstated starting point.

## Cain and Abel Model:

The primary answer is that modernist thinking *assumes* the validity of Darwinian evolution, which (they think) explains the origin of humans and other living systems by an entirely mechanistic process that excludes in principle any role for a Creator. In the words of the Neo-Darwinist authority George Gaylord Simpson, the meaning of "evolution" is that "man is the result of a purposeless and natural process that did not have him in mind." For modernist intellectuals, belief in evolution in precisely this sense is equated with having a scientific outlook, which is to say, with being a modernist. The price for denying "science" is to be excluded from modernist discourse altogether. That is why "it looks as if we are all we have," even if the model for "we" is Cain and Abel.

## Scientific Naturalism:

In Philip Johnson's *Darwin on Trial* he explained that Darwinian Theory finds its basis in the philosophy of scientific naturalism rather than in an unprejudiced examination of the evidence. In other words, the theory that is itself the most important supporting pillar for the modernist system is itself supported by that very system, in a classic example of circular reasoning. If that analysis is correct, then scientific naturalism itself is the product of a faith commitment rather than an irresistible inference from the facts provided by scientific investigation. In that event, the modernist impasse may be a problem of the mind that has sold itself into captivity. Can a way out of this captivity be found in "religion"?

## Progressive Liberalism:

R. Kent Greenawalt, University Professor at Columbia University, is a distinguished legal philosopher who has tried to justify a mild theism without directly challenging the modernist definition of rationality, In Greenawalt's words: "With some uncertainty and tentativeness, I hold religious convictions; but I find myself in a pervasively secular discipline."

In the 1986 Cooley Lectures at the University of Michigan Law School, Greenawalt defends a limited role for religious convictions in a jurisprudential culture whose ruling paradigm, called "liberalism," is roughly identical to what I have been calling modernism.

Some legal philosophers say that liberalism implies the exclusion of religious considerations from public life. Their reasoning is that public decisions should be made on the basis of principles and arguments accessible to all persons. This basic principle implies that common sense and science must supply all the essential factual knowledge and those standards of ethics and justice must come from secular philosophies that rest upon uncontroversial assumptions. For example, Cornell University philosophy professor David Lyons declares that to reject the idea of "a naturalistic and public conception of political morality . . . is to deny the essential spirit of democracy." In the same spirit, Yale Law School's Bruce Ackerman writes disparagingly of those who want to restrict abortions "on the basis of some conversation with the spirit world." According to this influential version of liberalism, people who want to make public policy on the basis of some private knowledge of God are fundamentally undemocratic, because they refuse to share a common base of discourse with their fellow citizens.

Responding to this "religion is for private life only" position, Greenawalt argues that in some circumstances citizens of a liberal, modernist state may rely upon their personal religious values in casting votes or framing arguments. Some religious citizens may have difficulty understanding why the argument even has to be made. All they have to do, after all, is invoke "the grand sez who" and then vote and argue as they like.

Greenawalt concedes that citizens of a secular liberal state have a *legal* right to vote their religious convictions, but he is more concerned with when and whether they ought to exercise self-restraint in the interests of good citizenship. Model citizens do not do everything they are legally entitled to do. They do not, for example, advocate the legal subjugation of one race by another or the establishment of a particular religion, even though such advocacy is constitutionally protected. Good citizens also decide how they will vote on rational grounds, as far as they are able. But according to modernist liberalism, religious beliefs are inherently non-rational. Does it follow that model citizens should leave their religious convictions at home (where they are relatively harmless), and base their votes and arguments concerning public questions on secular considerations only?

## Secular Rationality

Professor Greenawalt concedes that, "legislation must be justified in terms of secular objectives." Nonetheless, "when people reasonably think that rational analysis and an acceptable rational secular morality cannot resolve critical questions of fact, fundamental questions of value, or the weighing of competing harms, they (may) appropriately rely on religious convictions that help them answer these questions." He assumes the modernist position that only secular reasoning can be completely rational, because he thinks that "a critical non-rational element" is always present in religious belief. The presence of such a non-rational element does not disqualify religious values from consideration in lawmaking, however. Because "rational secular morality" cannot conclusively decide such important value questions as how highly we should rate the preservation of fetal life, or how generously we should provide for the poor, legislators and judges as well as ordinary voters may with good conscience rely on their personal religious convictions to resolve such questions.

By implication, Greenawalt accepts the crucial modernist assumption that there exists a common secular rationality capable of resolving some important public issues without relying upon controversial and un-provable (i.e., non-rational) assumptions. Otherwise, the conceded distinction between "religious" and "rational secular" thinking would collapse. This is an extremely important concession: giving modernists the power to define rationality ensures that, even if "religion" is allowed a modest place in public discussion, God will continue to be effectively excluded.

The reason lies in the very basis of modernist metaphysics. "Religious belief" is a real category to modernists; so is belief in fairies. All religions are equal—equally imaginary, that is. To modernists "God" is an idea in people's heads, not a reality outside of human subjectivity. As long as modernists make the rules, every godlet can undermine every theistic proposition at will by invoking the grand sez who. The culture will still be left to choose between an intolerable nihilism and continuing to chase the illusion of liberal rationalism.

At times Greenawalt seems to accept that illusion, but at other times he shows an awareness that it is an illusion. Here is how he explains his own understanding of rationality: "I confess to considerable uncertainty about where rationality ends; but among rational convictions we include those that are apparent to anyone with ordinary rational faculties or that can be demonstrated or persuasively argued on rational grounds. Beliefs that humans have greater ethical capacities than leaves, and that love is more productive of happiness than hate, can be rationally established. An irrational conviction is contrary to what can be established on rational grounds. A non-rational conviction is a conviction that is not irrational but that reaches beyond what rational grounds can settle. "

When a philosopher defines his central concept only in terms of itself (rational propositions are those that appeal to rational people or that can be supported on rational grounds) it is a sure sign of confusion. Moreover, a secular rationalism that can't resolve anything more controversial than humans have more ethical capacity than leaves is useless. The point modernist rationalism has to establish, or assume, is that a common secular rationality exists which is capable in principle of resolving the issues that actually divide people. Examining the most famous recent example of such a system, the rights-based liberalism of John Rawls, Greenawalt clearly recognizes that this basic modernist assumption is false.

Recognizing that citizens in liberal societies have variant religious beliefs and ideas of good [ness], Rawls begins with premises that are widely shared by people who disagree on many fundamental questions. From these premises, he aspires to draw principles of justice whose acceptance allows political decisions to be made without reference to the fundamental religious and metaphysical beliefs that divide citizens. ... Contrary to what Rawls supposes, he does not provide a theoretical basis for thinking that this ambition is either realizable or desirable.

But why then does Greenawalt build his defense of religious opinion on the assumption that this ambition is both realizable and desirable? The probable answer is that in these lectures he was addressing an audience of modernist liberal rationalists, and wanted to persuade them that even their own philosophical system had to concede at least some room for non-rational opinions on public questions, and therefore for religious opinion. Moreover, Greenawalt is a generous-minded person who understands that it is desirable to conduct public discussion on as ecumenical a basis as possible. However confused his notion of rationality may have been, his intention was to persuade his adversaries by meeting them on their own metaphysical territory.

## Standards of Rationality:

Up to a point, this way of arguing is itself an act of good liberal citizenship. If a society is to be governed on the basis of consent rather than force, it is important that the laws make sense to as many citizens as possible. To that end, we should try to justify the laws on the least controversial basis that is available. That is why nowadays we defend Sunday closing laws (if at all) by the secular purpose of encouraging a general day of rest and recreation rather than the original purpose of honoring the Lord's Day or maximizing church attendance. In a more general sense, the courtesy we owe to fellow citizens argues for framing public questions in language that invites everyone to participate in the discussion on comfortable terms. It would be insensitive as well as ineffective, for example, for Christians to exhort their Jewish, Muslim, or agnostic neighbors about what Jesus would want us to do. On the other hand, Christians (or religious people in general) shouldn't be excluded from the political conversation either, as they would be if only agnostic opinions could count. Greenawalt's moderate and nuanced position about the proper role of religion in secular political discourse rightly addresses these questions of political good manners.

But good manners is one thing; giving away the authority to define rationality is something else altogether. Good citizens treat their neighbors' deeply held convictions with respect *not* because they are necessarily rational, but because they are deeply held. Standards for defining rationality are as controversial as any other assumptions. What Greenawalt accepts as "rationality" is actually the irrational assumption that we can get along very well without employing any controversial assumptions about the nature of ultimate reality. This assumption is the idol of rationalism, the faith commitment that holds the tribe together. We should perhaps treat the idol gently, because it is still very dear to many admirable people, but we should not bow down and worship it. For any genuine theist, ultimate reality must be God—not the unanchored, self-validating human mind.

## Refutation of Faith:

Theists (belief in One God, Superior Being) may be entering a time of great opportunity for affirming that understanding of reality, because the modernist idol's substance is dissolving a little more every day. In the twenty-first century, philosophy's task will be to rebuild a positive response to the human predicament that starts with the cause of that predicament, man's alienation from God. Before it can undertake the positive task, however, it must complete the critique of atheistic rationalism. On the scientific side, theists need to continue to expose the vulnerable philosophical assumptions that provide the only real support for the Darwinian theory of evolution. On the ethical and cultural side, they need to help the public as a whole to understand that the nihilism permeating contemporary life is the inevitable consequence of apostasy. King Lear's words provide the appropriate epitaph for modernism: *"Nothing will come of nothing."*

Secularized intellectuals have long been complacent in their *apostasy* (defined as: revolt; renunciation of religious faith). That is because they were sure they weren't missing anything important in consigning God to the ashcan of history. They were happy to replace the Creator with a mindless evolutionary process that left humans free and responsible only to themselves. They complacently assumed that when their own reasoning power was removed from its grounding in the only ultimate reality, it could float, unsupported, on nothing at all. As modernist rationalism gives way in universities to its own natural child—postmodernist nihilism—modernists are learning very slowly what a bargain they have made. It *isn't* a bargain a society can live with indefinitely.


## COMMUNISM:

> **What is a communist (or extreme socialist)? One who hath yearnings for equal division of unequal earnings? --Ebenezer Elliott**

Communism is basically a radical theory of government in which *all* material goods are owned by the atheistic state. Voluntary communism also exists where the individual members *willingly* give up their natural rights to private property for the good of the organization or when the rules of the group, which they joined of their own free will, required it, such as in some religious orders, where vows of poverty, obedience and chastity exist.

Compulsory communism such as existed in the former USSR until 1989, and currently exists in China, Cuba, and North Korea, is *involuntary*. This faulty philosophy of government is based on *class warfare*, atheistic materialism, the rejection of personal property, and complete denial of human rights. Communism preys especially on underdeveloped, poverty-ridden states by "promising a fairer distribution of material wealth to its followers," as some leading politicians have recently emphasized and promoted in America and South America.

Karl Marx, in 1867 wrote *Das Kapital*, that the only true source of economic value was human labor, which created material goods or wealth. Capitalism took most of the profits of labor, and gave the laborers only a small subsistence in return. Hegel joined Marx, with his theory that the state exists "merely to protect property for the masses."

In such an "ideal" communism setting, religion has no place, since according to its supporters it sanctioned private property and its philosophy is heaven-centric, whereas the sufferings of this world are willingly accepted for the greater reward of God and heaven. All religions are "the opiate of the people," and distract them from their serious social problems. Therefore, it must be completely eradicated by force, if necessary, they claim.

## PHILOSOPHICAL TRUTHS KEY POINTS:

o *Mono-Theism: Jewish, Christian, Islam: Personal God of the Bible, and Koran. God is revealed by His Word (Revelations in the Bible), works, and prophets.*

o *Deism/Skepticism (16th & 17th centuries): God is only the first cause in nature in a closed universe. God is not imminent (not existing in, and extending into the created universe). He is not personal, and not sovereign. Reason is sufficient to know God, not Revelation. There is no evil, no sin.*

o *Idealism (17th & 18th centuries): Knowledge starts with thoughts rather than things or objects. Material things do not exist independently but are merely constructs of the mind. The pursuit of perfection is an attainable goal. It supports Moral Relativism (morality is flexible and depends on different cultures and changes in society).*

o *Enlightenment & Rationalism (18th century): Emphasizes reason and science in philosophy, in the study of human culture and the natural world.*

o *Nihilism (20th century): All traditional values and beliefs are unfounded. Existence is senseless and useless. No objective truths exist, especially morality. Revolutionary reform is needed, using terrorism and other methods of force.*

o *Communism/Marxism (20th and 21st centuries): Man is a supreme being. God doesn't exist; he is merely a false projection of human ideals. Forced division of all wealth, controlled by the people, for the benefit of the masses. Class struggle is essential for any major social change.*

o *Existentialism (20th and 21st centuries): Denies that the universe has any intrinsic meaning or purpose. Individuals must assume ultimate responsibility for his/her acts of free will, with/without certain knowledge of right or wrong. We are merely beings in time and space, and must shape our own destinies, accordingly.*

o *Naturalism (19th, 20th and 21st centuries): Rejects all spiritual and supernatural explanations for creation and the universe. Nature and natural causes, and science are the sole basis of what we can know. No gods. No spirits. No free will. Everything is deterministic.*

o *Pantheistic Monism (many centuries ago): Gods are present in everything. We worship the multiple deities of different creeds, cults, or peoples indifferently. Reality is a unified whole; only one single kind of ultimate substance or principle exists. Typical forms are Hinduism, Yogi, and Buddhism (Zen).*

o *New Age (20th & 21st centuries): Popular movement since 1980s based on Eastern ancient concepts such as mysticism, holism (the whole system), metaphysical, nature, and spirits, that claims to lead to higher consciousness. "We can all become gods."*

# IV. Scientific Truths



Philosophers led us to Astronomy, which steered us to Physics and Mathematics, which caused us to think about creation. A few of these earlier great thinkers were:

- Aristotle: Truth and Wisdom (335 BCE).
- Copernicus: Earth revolves around the Sun (1473-1543).
- Galileo: Telescope, and Physics (1564-1642).
- Kepler: Laws of Planetary Motion (1571-1630).
- Descartes: Discourse on Scientific Methods (1596-1650).
- Isaac Newton: Laws of Gravity (1665).

Johannes Kepler in the *Third Planetary Motion Law*, said the square of the orbital period of a planet is proportional to the cube of its mean distance from the sun, which became the foundation for Newton's General Physical laws of Motion and Gravity, which in turn became the basis for Einstein's General Theory of Relativity, 200 years later. Astronomy thus gave birth to Physics. It took one thousand years—from Aristotle to Ptolemy, from Copernicus to Kepler and Galileo—to establish the geometry of our Solar System, the Milky Way.

One can understand by their intellect that a hierarchy of sciences and knowledge exists, which includes the ordering of all things from the highest to the lowest level. Each successive level transcends and includes its predecessors, such as:

- Spiritual and Mystical level.
- Philosophical level.
- Rational and Psychological level.
- Biological level: plants, creatures, humanity (DNA).
- Physical level: earth, stars galaxies, universe (energy, matter, space, and time).

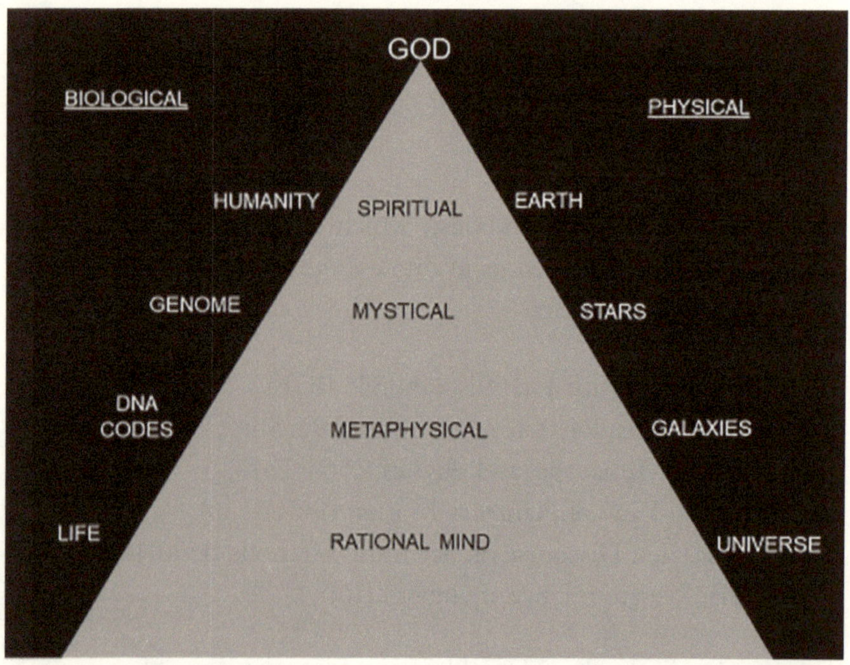


> **Fig. * Biological, physical, mental realm. Created by Author.**

The Mental aspect includes the rational mind, metaphysical, mystical, and spiritual levels. The Biological level includes all living things, and DNA codes that regulate them, as well as the human genome. The Physical includes the universe, galaxies, stars, and earth. Philosophy is knowledge and reflection of all things; that is, what is common to all of them, and how they differ. It's the study of "being as being," a system of causes and effects. It's the highest level of abstraction, and concerns material *and* immaterial dimensions.

Higher nested levels control, synthesize, and embrace all lower levels. For example, the human body includes the physiological level, and matter in its makeup, yet it adds the five senses, emotions, and movement, which are not found in the inanimate world of matter. The human mind or psychological level, controls emotions, yet it also provides higher cognitive faculties as well; that is, reasoning and understanding which is lacking in most of the animal world.

Empirical Science (the "IT" or physiological level) concerns itself with objects, and therefore lacks any consciousness, awareness, intentions, feelings, introspective, contemplation, intuition, values and meanings. Atoms are parts of molecules, which are parts of cells, which are parts of organisms. Mathematics is a vital part of empirical science, which deals with logical patterns seen with the "mind's eye."

While we may further divide these levels or spheres into additional groupings, such as matter divided into atomic and subatomic; life separated into microorganisms; and the rational part of the mind divided into conscience and subconscious groupings, this is essentially the basic hierarchical framework of *all* sciences in the universe and our world. This structure has enabled civilization to establish specific disciplines of knowledge that concern themselves with one or more of these primary levels. Each of these bodies of knowledge have also developed their own particular laws, hypothesis, languages and methodologies in their search for truth.

## SIX "COSMIC" DAYS OF CREATION:

***Let there be light, and there was light.* Genesis 1:3**

When I was a child of seven, I asked my religious teacher, an older nun: "What was God doing before He created the universe?"

She answered: "He was creating hell for children like you, who ask such ridiculous questions."

While humiliated by her response, I was determined to find the truth, which was discovered two decades later. The answer is, since the Creator is outside of time and space, there is "no before."

The "Big Bang" is when time, space, matter, dark matter, and light (energy) began. Edwin Hubble established that galaxies are moving away from one another, according to the "red shift," at rates of speed proportional to the distance between them. The resulting expansion of the universe has been verified by different and independent experiments. The further we look back in time, using the Hubble telescope, the closer the galaxies are. Also, the universe becomes denser, hotter, and more luminescent, until we reach a point approximately 13.75 billion years ago, when the temperature and density attain enormous values, which is Big Bang theory.

<table>
<tr><td colspan="2">

**Six "Cosmic" Days of Creation:**
Source: "The Science of God" by Gerald L. Schroeder
(Beginning and end times in billions of years in the past):

</td></tr>
<tr><td>**Time Line**</td><td>**Inorganic *Exterior* Objective Truths:**</td></tr>
<tr><td>14.75 – 7.75</td><td>Big Bang: Clouds of Hot Gases & Elementary Particles Universe: Time, Matter (Atoms), Energy', Gravity, Space</td></tr>
<tr><td>7.75 – 3.75</td><td>Galaxies Formed (rapidly move apart from each other)</td></tr>
<tr><td>3.75 – 1.75</td><td>Earth, Moon, Water, Early Life (bacteria, algae), Atmosphere, Ozone Layer, Electromagnetic Shield</td></tr>
<tr><td></td><td>**Organic *Interior* Objective Truths:**</td></tr>
<tr><td>1.75 – 0.75</td><td>Era of Bacteria and Development of Ecosystems</td></tr>
<tr><td>0.75 – 0.55</td><td>Multi-cell Organisms and Initial Species were Created</td></tr>
<tr><td>0.65 – 0.63</td><td>Massive Extinction of Dinosaurs & Most Creatures</td></tr>
<tr><td>0.55 – 0.54</td><td>Destruction of Species (from Comets/Asteroids?)</td></tr>
<tr><td>0.54 – 0.53</td><td>Cambrian Explosion: (50 New Body Plans Created), Plants & Creatures show Evidence of Intelligent Design</td></tr>
<tr><td>0.53 – 0.25</td><td>Microevolution of all Species of Plants & Animals</td></tr>
</table>

➤ **Fig *. "*The Science of God*" by Schroeder. Author chart**

This author believes the energy and matter of the universe was *not* created from "nothing"—matter was created from enormous energy produced from the "Word of God." (Physicists today can produce elementary matter from light energy in the lab). Let's examine time:

**Day One** (Gen. 1: 1-5): An explosion of enormous energy was created, causing matter to be *created* (according to Einstein's law E=MC squared), where gases and particles came together to form the basic elements. The universe began as a homogenous mass of elementary particles: electrons, photons, quarks, neutrinos, gravitons, and other fundamental particles.

**Day Two** (Gen. 1: 6-8): Elementary particles assembled to form new structures, which developed into more complex molecules and compounds, which became the primary elements required to form galaxies. Galaxies, such as our Milky Way contain billions of stars, and solar systems within galaxies that include suns, moons, planets, and earth.

**Day Three** (Gen. 1: 9-13): Oceans and dryland appear (Gen.1: 9-13) with atmosphere, basic organisms like algae, and the vitally important protective electromagnetic shield, the ozone layer, ecosystems, and many different plants.

**Day Four** (Gen. 1: 14-19): The Sun, Moon, and Stars become visible in the heavens. Photosynthesis produces oxygen-rich atmosphere.

**Day Five** (Gen. 1: 20-23): The first species of animals swarm abundantly in the waters, followed by reptiles and winged animals.

**Day Six** (Gen. 1: 24-31): Animals, and mammals were made.

During this timeframe, many organisms became extinct, such as the dinosaurs that suddenly disappeared 65-million years ago. Comets and asteroids hit the earth causing various upheavals and ice ages (about every 200,000 years, on average).

Humans were "made,"—*not created*—from the soil (all living creatures contain nearly similar DNA codes or "blueprint"). Hundreds of thousands of years later, hominids evolved, such as Neanderthals, followed by more intelligent Homo sapiens, about 100,000 years ago. At some stage of this evolution, Adam and Eve were "created;" that is, they received an *eternal spiritual soul.*

Note: Gerald L. Schroeder's source for his Genesis interpretation was Nahmanides (Moses B. Naḥman, also known as Naḥamani and RaMBaN – an acronym of Rabbi Moses Ben Naḥman; 1194–1270), Spanish rabbi and scholar, and one of the leading -authors of Talmudic literature in the Middle Ages. Spanish rabbis regarded him as their great teacher and referred to him as *ha-rav ha-ne'eman* ("the trustworthy rabbi").

> **Fig 3. Milky Way, Solar System & Earth provided by NASA**

## Age of the Universe:

Some Christians presented evidence that the Earth is young, only about 6,000 years old. After carefully reviewing this data and various reports from their "experts," this author continues to believe in the "Old Earth and Universe" theory. Nonetheless, whether it's old or young universe, one must conclude that: the universe was created; and it was designed by an All Powerful and Intelligent Being. (See *The Privileged Planet* by Gonzalez and Richards, Regency, 2004).

The million-million-factor difference between our local perception of time and Genesis Cosmic time is an average for the six days of creation. As Schroeder discussed in *The Science of God*, it derives from the million-million-fold stretching of light waves as the universe expanded. Genesis used the absolute cardinal form, for day one, because it was viewing time from the beginning of time, a perspective from which there was no other time for comparison. As Nahmanides wrote, "when matter forms time grabs hold." Centuries later, science finally came to match the biblical account of Genesis.

> ***Every living thing in nature is ever in the middle of being born and dying. Everything in the universe evolves towards higher order. Atoms of hydrogen, by fusion, become more complex and form higher order atoms of greater weight and complexity; combinations of molecules create more complex compounds of higher order. Humanity is a universe within itself: we experience the same cycles as stars—birth, growth, maturity, death, and rebirth. --Author***

## EQUATIONS THAT CHANGED THE WORLD

Fundamental equations were discovered that had a significant impact on the world, and technologies that enriched humanity:

1. Newton's Gravitational Law: (G force = Constant *M*m/d squared), where G is Gravity; M is Mass 1; m is Mass 2; and d is Distance.
2. Claudius's Law of Energy Conservation: (All Energy is always a constant > 0)
3. Maxwell's Electromagnetic Field Law. Amount Elect. = Rate of increase/ decrease of Magnetic Field.
4. Einstein's Special Relativity Law: (E=M*C squared), and (Energy/C squared = Mass), where E is Energy; M is Mass; and C is the Speed of Light.

5.  Bernoulli's Law of Hydrodynamics: (P+p*1/2 V squared = Constant) where P is Pressure, and V is Volume.

Other fundamental laws (equations and constants) concerning nature and the universe include: Mechanics (Hamilton); Quantum Mechanics (Schrodinger); General Relativity (Einstein); and Statistical Mechanics (Boltzmann), among others. Today, many of the above theories and laws are typical graduate physics experiments done by our students at leading universities.

> ***The harmony of natural law reveals a beauty and intelligence of such superiority that compared with it, all the systematic thinking and acting of human beings is an utterly insignificant reflection.* --Albert Einstein**

Four of the primary forces of physics that control the agglomeration of sub-atomic particles, atoms, molecules and structures of the universe are:

1.  Nuclear or the "strong force," unites all atomic nuclei;
2.  Electromagnetic force, controls the adherence of all atoms;
3.  Gravity force, affects movements of all celestial objects; and
4.  Weak force controls radioactive decay.

Why do these four forces exist? How do we know they are unchanging? Why do they have *exact* mathematical properties? We don't know all the answers to these questions, except that they are *all supremely adjusted intelligent forces.* For example, if the nuclear force had been slightly stronger, all the photons of the universe would have quickly gathered into heavy nuclei, and there would have been no hydrogen to assure the longevity of stars, and consequently to form the 70% of total water on this earth.

Professor Roger Penrose, of Oxford, one of the -Author of the "Big Bang" theory, finds the laws of nature "fine-tuned for life". This balance of Nature's Laws are so perfect and so unlikely to have occurred by chance that he avers an intelligent "Creator" must have chosen them. It is as if we were written into the equation of the universe at its beginning, or in the words of the physicist Paul Davies, *"Built into the scheme of things in a very basic way."*

**Supernovas:** Einstein asserted that the mass of any physical object and the energy it contains is in fact interchangeable (E=MC squared). *A beautiful and simple formula!* One can never destroy matter, only convert it into another form, energy; i.e., energy (E), equals mass (M), times the speed of light (C) squared. When atoms are smashed in atomic reactors they give off enormous energy. In essence, matter is nothing more than another form of light energy. Our bodies couldn't exist without carbon, iron, oxygen, water (interestingly, about 70% of our body and the earth is water), and all the other complex elements, much of which comes from exploding stars—Supernova. We are in essence composed of "animated stardust." (See Vij Sodera's book *"One Small Speck to Man"*).

➢ **Fig 4. Supernova (exploding star) provided by NASA.**

All life forms use the same coding system. We all had a common beginning billions of years ago. A signal, a light was turned on inorganic earth causing it to become alive, in every nook and cranny. An infinite variety of life forms have been produced in nature, yet they are all amazingly united. They are formed from the same basic stuff. All life forms use the same intelligent genetic coding system; give rise to identical amino acids, creating similar proteins. All life forms are also particularly interdependent.

**Time is Not Constant!** If anything in life seems constant, it is the flow of time and constancy of space. This *misperception* of time results from a view of reality as seen from Earth. Time is *not* a constant. Einstein's Relativity is firmly established: the flow of time at any location where there is high-gravity or high-velocity is *slower* than locations with a lower gravity or lower velocity. There exists universal time, and earth based time. The clock of Genesis, the *"cosmic clock,"* started with the creation of the universe and continued until the creation *and* evolution of humankind. We invented clocks based on the rotation of the earth and relationship to the sun.

> ***Really, we create nothing; we merely plagiarize nature, and our plagiarism has not the perfection of the original. When we succeed, it is because, on some imperceptibly small point, our logic has turned out to be in conformity with the logic that goes prodigiously beyond us. At every stage we are exploiting the really creative power of the vital; we are ingeniously making use of the genius.* --Ralph Waldo Emerson**

**Immutable laws:** Recent advancements in Astrophysics and Cosmology have enabled us to bring these questions to the forefront of contemporary thinking. We know that the fundamental laws of physics *cannot* change, in space or in time. In the context of his "Big Bang" theory, Fred Hoyle said, "An explosion in a junkyard does not lead to sundry bits of metal being assembled into a useful working machine," and "the more physicists have learned about the universe, the more it looks like a put-up job (an *intentional* plan)."

Hoyle discovered one of the most celebrated examples of fine-tuning (for life) in physics (see: *On Nuclear Reactions Occurring in Very Hot Stars, Astrophysical Journal* Supplement 1, 1954): As a result of these four astounding "coincidences" (a bit too complex to be fully reviewed in this book), exploding stars produce carbon and oxygen in comparable amounts, which is absolutely essential for all life.

What is astonishing about these laws is, the intelligent formulas and numerical values (constants) are *"extremely well adjusted."* Physicist and cosmologist Brandon Carter (1973) wrote: *"The most minuscule change in the fundamental constants would completely eliminate the possibility of life."*

Any minor tinkering with the values of physics—gravity, electromagnetism, nuclear strong force, and nuclear weak force—would cause the universe to consist entirely of helium, without protons or atoms, without any stars, or a universe that would collapse back upon itself. Carter believes that *"Life had to be, in effect, 'pre-planned' from the very origin of the cosmos."*

Mathematical simulations *prove* that if these values were slightly different, the universe would never have emerged from its initial chaos. No complex intelligent structures would have ever emerged, not even a simple molecule.

## UNIVERSAL FORCES:

Before examining the interaction of "forces," clear definitions are required:

1. Strong Nuclear force is what binds particles (photons and neutrons) together in atomic nucleus.
2. Electromagnetic force is that which exists between all charged particles.
3. Gravitational force is, for example, that which produces stars from parcels of gas clouds, causing fusion, resulting in light and heat.

4. Weak Nuclear force is what governs the conversion process of protons to neutrons and vice versa, etc., so that when stars explode (supernova) they produce the heavier metal-enriched elements that are *essential for all life.*

For example, if the nuclear force was slightly stronger all of the protons would have quickly gathered into heavier nuclei and there would have been no hydrogen left to assure the longevity of the sun and stars, or to form water for the earth. Instead these forces were just intense enough to produce some heavy atoms (carbon, iron, oxygen, etc.) that are required by all known living organisms, and not so intense as to completely eliminate living creatures—*just the right dose.* One could say that some kind of "consciousness" was implicit in the universe from the very first instance of the Big Bang. It is inscribed in the laws of physics.

Some examples, taken from Patrick Glynn's book on: *God: the Evidence* (Prima Publisher, 1999) cites that gravity is roughly 1039 times weaker than electromagnetism. If gravity had been 1033 times weaker than electromagnetism, stars would be a billion times less massive and would burn a million times faster. Nuclear weak force is 1028 times the strength of gravity. Had the weak force been slightly weaker, all the hydrogen in the universe would have been turned to helium, making water impossible. A stronger nuclear strong force by as little as 2% would have prevented the formation of protons, yielding a universe without atoms. Decreasing it by 5% would have given us a universe without stars. If the difference in the mass between a proton and a neutron were not exactly as it is—roughly twice the mass of an electron—neutrons would have become protons. Say goodbye to chemistry as we know it—and to all life.

The nature of water—so vital to life—is something of a mystery, a point noticed by one of the forerunners of *anthropic* reasoning in the 19th century, Harvard biologist Lawrence Henderson. Unique among the molecules, water is lighter in its solid than liquid form. Ice floats, if it did not, the oceans would freeze from the bottom up, and earth would now be covered with solid ice. This property is traceable to the unique properties of hydrogen.

**Astonishing Coincidences:** The synthesis of carbon—the vital core of all organic molecules—on a significant scale involve what scientists view as "astonishing" coincidence in the ratio of the strong force to electromagnetism. The ratio makes it possible for carbon-12 to reach an excited state of exactly 7.65 million electron volts, the temperature typical at the center of stars, which creates a resonance involving helium-4, beryllium-8, and carbon-12—allowing the necessary binding to take place during a tiny window of opportunity of less than a few picoseconds. The list goes on. A comprehensive compilation of these "coincidences" can be found in John Leslie's book *Universes*. See also *Our Universes* by Barrow and Tipler (Columbia Univ. Press, 1991) Wilkinson on *Cosmic Coincidences* (Bantam, 1989); Fred Hoyle, *The Origin of the Universe and the Origin of Religion* (Moyer Bell); and especially *The Privileged Planet* by Gonzalez and Richards (Roguery, 2004).

## Beauty and Harmony:

> *The best and most beautiful things in the world cannot be seen or even touched - they must be felt with the heart.* **Helen Keller**

The universe is like a living organism that is constantly expanding and evolving—on a grand scale. New stars are born as old stars die, and some give birth to planets. Supernova, the larger exploding stars produce heavier, more complex atoms like iron, oxygen and especially carbon, the stuff that all living things are made of. Comets with a rich harvest of molecules and water sow their seeds of higher elements and hydrocarbons as they travel throughout interstellar space.

The order and harmony of the universe is the *consequence* of the immense diversity of its being and from the complex relationship which exists within it. Man discovers them progressively as Laws of the Universe. This wondrous beauty and intelligent order should inspire deep respect of man's intellect for such marvelous truths.

In astrophysics one can actually "see the past" with modern instruments like the Hubble telescope. The speed of light is a *scientifically established constant* that travels 300,000 kilometers (186,000 miles) per second. Light from the Sun, which is 93 million miles away, reaches us in eight minutes. Light from the closest star takes four years. Light from Vega takes eight years to arrive. The galaxy Andromeda, visible by the naked eye, is an image that's two million years old. If intelligent people existed within Andromeda were to look back at Earth today, what they would see would be the light from Earth that existed in prehistoric times. The light from the most distant galaxies and quasars are about 12 to 14 billion light-years away from us. We see them *not* as they now exist, but in the distant past, as they were billions of years ago.

> **It is during our darkest moments that we must focus to see the light.** Aristotle

## EINSTEIN'S BLUNDER:

Using his law of General Relativity, Einstein developed a series of equations describing the condition of the universe. They showed something seemingly illogical, that the universe was not static—*it is very dynamic.*

Vesto Slipher of Lowell Observatory in Flagstaff, Arizona, had already reported astronomical measurements that suggested the universe was expanding. Slipher's data rested totally on Einstein's own laws of Relativity. However, Einstein's mind-set for the concept of an eternal, *static* universe was too strong.

Einstein realized that if day-by-day the universe was expanding, getting even larger, then what about yesterday, a year ago, and backward until billions of years ago, there was only a single point, a point that marked the beginning.

Einstein could have followed his own discoveries and predicted the most important statement ever made relative to man and the universe: *there was a creation.* And if there was a creation, there must have been a creator. Einstein blew it! He couldn't give up his hard held opinion in favor of objective truth.

The important lesson: desired axioms die very hard even in the face of contradictory evidence. The scientific fact is that if the earth was slightly closer or farther away from the sun, life as we know it couldn't possibly exist because it would be much too hot or too cold, respectively, as is the case for Venus and Mars.

*All life forms are interdependent! Creatures and humans exist in dependence on each other, to complete each other, in the service of each other. Trees are dependent on the atmosphere, and birds and bugs to exist. Birds make homes there, consume its fruit, and transport its seeds. Bugs, in turn, spread the pollen and produce fungus, essential nourishment for the roots of the tree. A complex web of interdependency exists in all nature—one with the other, and all collectively. ---Author*

➤ **Fig. 5 Earth. Image by NASA (public domain).**

> ➤ **Fig. 6 Twin Earth orbiting a star in the Milky Way.
> Illustration by NASA.**

Kepler 452b (illustrated by NASA) has been dubbed Earth 2.0 - is six billion years old, has a 385 day year, and orbits its star at the same distance as earth. It is 1,400 light-years away in the constellation Cygnus. It is believed to be rocky, with active volcanoes, and is so like Earth that NASA believes it is possible that life once inhabited the planet. But because it is 1.5 billion years older, scientists say it gives a 'peek into a crystal ball showing a possible future for Earth as it reaches a point where it is no longer habitable.

The increasing energy from its aging sun might be heating the surface and evaporating any oceans. The water vapor would be lost from the planet forever. Kepler 452b could be experiencing now what the Earth may undergo a billion years from now, as the Sun ages and grows brighter. It is 60 percent larger in diameter than Earth and is considered a super-Earth-size planet. It is six billion years old.

That means a considerable opportunity existed for life to arise on its surface and in its oceans, should all the necessary conditions for life have appeared on this planet.

> ***"This is the closest thing that we have to another planet like the Earth. And the Earth follows nearly in the footsteps of its older cousin and will be there in 1.5 billion years' time."-- NASA.***

The 21$^{st}$ century has produced significant shifts in energy sources, with gradual declines in fossil fuel usage, such as coal and oil, replaced by more efficient fuels like natural gas and nuclear. Technological advances in biotechnologies will cause a greater usage of biofuels, and efficient voltaic cells. Hydrogen based fuel cells may also find greater usage in this century.

## NATURAL DISASTERS:

Earthquakes, especially volcanoes, cause significant disruptions in the atmosphere, death and destruction. Yet, they are also *vitally important* to support all forms of life. Hot gases and molten lava flowing from inside the Earth causes mantle convection, crust movements that builds mountains, sub-ducts older seafloors, *recycles carbon dioxide*, all of which makes Earth more or less inhabitable. Major earthquakes cycle organic and inorganic substances, and regulate the exchange of carbon molecules between the land, sea, and the atmosphere, thereby inducing photosynthesis within plants and phytoplankton close to the sea surface, which takes carbon dioxide from the air, feeding organic matter and provides oxygen nurturing all life. The molten metal core spinning inside the Earth also produces a strong magnetic field, called the magnetosphere, that shields the Earth from powerful Solar winds and Cosmic Rays, that otherwise would destroy all life.

## The Great Flood:

At each stage of human development, the Creator withheld His control to a greater or lesser extent, which allowed the world to develop according to the Laws of the Universe that were created at the beginning, and the moral responsibility and free will implanted in the human soul. A limited experiment was underway. In this universe each member of mankind chooses his or her own path. When we failed, re-tuning redirected humanity. Perhaps the greatest re-tuning of all was the story of the Noah's flood:

> ***And the Eternal saw the wickedness of man was great upon the land. And the Eternal repented that he had made man upon the land. And the Eternal said I will wipe out man whom I have created from the face of the soil, from man to beast to creeping animals and to winged animals of the heavens, for I repent that I have made them.* --Genesis 7:20***

There was clearly a huge flood during Noah's time, but some scientific experts believed it was *regional*, while others firmly believe it was worldwide. There is fossil and geological evidence of a flood. However, various Ice Ages might have caused earlier floods, and many of these formations, including the creation of the Grand Canyon.

From Noah's perspective, the flood would have appeared to be worldwide, and he wrote this story. The author asks the following questions:

- Why animals had to die since they are not morally evil?
- Would forty days and nights be enough time to flood the entire world, including the tops of the highest mountains?
- What would the resulting ecology be like without plants?
- How could Noah's family of eight, and all the animals in the Ark, live after all vegetation was destroyed?
- How could a dove bring Noah an olive branch back when all the olive trees were destroyed by the flood?

- What happened to the Ark? (Noah probably used most of it as shelter, to stay warm, and to cook food).
- Why would the Lord cause global flooding, when men continue to do *countless works of evil,* centuries after this great flood? And, why do we continue to have floods?

**Alternative Viewpoint**: Two senior scientists from Columbia University have proposed an alternative theory. They agree that a massive transfer of water had occurred about 5600 BCE - over seven and a half millennia ago. They wrote: "Ten cubic miles of water poured through each day, two hundred times what flows over Niagara Falls." "The Bosporus flume roared and surged at full spate for at least three hundred days." 60,000 square miles of land were inundated. The Black Sea shoreline significantly expanded to the north and east. The lake's its water level was raised many hundreds of feet. It changed from a fresh-water landlocked lake into a salt water lake connected to the world's oceans.

They have drawn on the findings of experts in agriculture, archaeology, genetics, geology, language, development of textiles and pottery. They postulate that this deluge had catastrophic effects on the people living on or near the shores of the Black Sea. It triggered mass migrations across Europe and into the Near East, Middle East and Egypt.

## MAN-MADE DISASTERS:

Worldwide deaths caused by man-made events include:

2019-2022: Pandemic (Communist China): 2-5 million deaths

1980-2015: Abortions (elected & forced): 500 million deaths.

1945-1989: Communism and "Cold War": 150 million deaths.

1939-1945: World War II: 50-100 million deaths.

1914-1918: World War I: 20-65 million deaths.

1851-1864: Taiping Rebellion in China: 20-80 million deaths.

1860-1864: American Civil War: 620,000-700,000 deaths.

1207-1472: Mongol conquests: 30-60 million deaths.

Other man-made causes of deaths include the Rwandan genocide; terrorism, primarily in the Middle East, including the Iraq-Iran War. Atheistic Communism, during the "cold war" undeniably caused more total deaths in USSR, China, Cuba, Cambodia, Vietnam, and Korea, than any combination of "hot wars."

The next war will result in at least an **order-of-magnitude of more deaths** than past wars, due to Weapons of Mass Destruction (WMD), which give these evil powers the technology (nuclear, chemical and bacteria) and the missile delivery leverage of mass destruction to cause far greater devastation. The most probable evil leaders of such destruction will be (in order of probability): North Korea; Iran and Syria; China; and Russia; and/or their proxies.

## CLIMATE CHANGE:

No other creatures have the power to save or destroy the earth (and each other) except the human species. Some claim we are destroying the planet through pollution of air, and deforestation, which is destroying the ozone layer, and creating "greenhouse" effect that *may* ultimately cause the polar icecaps to melt, *consequently* resulting in drastic changes in weather patterns. However, we really *cannot* control much of our environment. For example, we can't control hurricanes, tsunamis,' earthquakes, volcanoes, among other natural forces. Moreover, China, India, and South America are major users of fossil fuels, and these developing countries are unwilling to alter their energy sources.

Is the earth experiencing an ice-age, *or* global warming, and is it due to man-made or natural forces? Can we really control these forces? Will more people die from a mini-ice age, than from earth warming? Does that mean we should do nothing? Before we potentially spend trillions of dollars, we should try to better understand the science of nature and explore *all* alternatives.

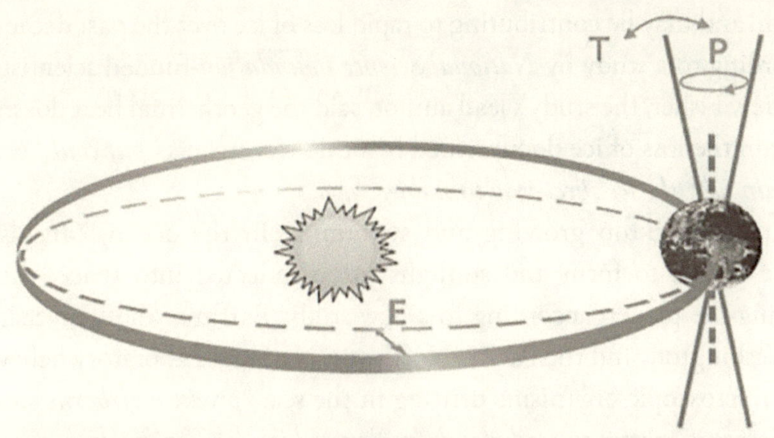

Milankovitch Cycles. *Schematic of the Earth's orbital changes (Milankovitch cycles) that drive the ice age cycles. 'T' denotes changes in the tilt (or obliquity) of the Earth's axis, 'E' denotes changes in the eccentricity of the orbit (due to variations in the minor axis of the ellipse), and 'P' denotes precession, that is, changes in the direction of the axis tilt at a given point of the orbit. Source: Rahmstorf and Schellnhuber (2006).*

➤ **Fig. 1* Milankovitch Cycles.**
**Source Rahmstorf & Schellnhuber. Illustrated by the Author.**

These natural Milankovitch cycles increase and decrease the amount of solar energy forcing imposed within our climate system and that actually causes the temperature to rise and fall with calculable regularity. The more time the earth or spends closer to the sun (at perihelion), the more energy it receives consequently causes warming. The more time it spends farther form the sun (at aphelion), the less energy it receives and the earth cools.

**Disadvantages of Global Warming:** Higher sea levels leading to flooding in lower regions; more deaths from people living in lower regions; changes in agricultural production; flooding in dry regions.

**Advantages of Global Warming:** Prevents a mini-ice-age (which occurred 10,000 years ago); more rain fall in many regions; longer growing seasons and less food shortages; less energy consumption.

The melting of the Antarctic ice sheet might be caused, at least in part, from geothermal heat that is escaping from deep within the

Earth, and may be contributing to rapid loss of ice over the past decade, according to a study by *National Science Foundation*-funded scientists. Andrew Fisher, the study's lead author, said the geothermal heat doesn't explain the loss of ice documented by other researchers "*but could help explain why the ice sheet is so unstable.*"

Tiny plankton growing and swimming in the ocean, can also cause clouds to form and sunlight to be reflected into space, thus cooling the planet, according to a new study. Baffin at the University of Washington, and the Pacific Northwest National Laboratory believe that microscopic organisms drifting in the sea: "*produce airborne gases and organic matter to seed cloud droplets, which lead to brighter clouds that reflect more sunlight.*"

Their research was published in the open-access journal *Science Advances*. The scientists said that the area they studied – the Southern Ocean covering latitudes between 35 and 55 degrees south – had revealed interesting findings about the Earth's climate. Results suggested that, averaged over a year, the increased brightness reflected about 4 watts of solar energy per square meter, according to the University of Washington.

Daniel McCoy, co-lead author of the US government-funded study, and doctoral student in atmospheric sciences at the university, said: The clouds over the Southern Ocean reflect significantly more sunlight in the summertime than they would without these huge plankton blooms. In the summer, we get about double the concentration of cloud droplets as we would if it were a biologically dead ocean. The Baffin chose to study the Southern Ocean because marine life in other parts of the globe are "swamped out by aerosols from forests or pollution." For this reason, it would be much harder for them to measure similar processes in the Northern Hemisphere.

They used NASA satellite data to measure cloud droplets in the skies. "The dimethyl sulfide produced by the phytoplankton gets transported up into higher levels of the atmosphere and then gets chemically transformed and produces aerosols further downwind, and that tends to happen more in the northern part of the domain we studied," said Pacific Northwest National Lab scientist Susannah Burrows, co-lead author of the study. "In the southern part of the domain there is more effect from the organics, because that's where the big phytoplankton blooms happen."

Energy Sources:

Estimated sources of energy during the centuries:

Pre-16th century:50-60% animal power; 40-50% biomass.

Mid-19th century: 20% animal power; 30% biomass; 50% coal.

<20th Century: 10% animal; 20% biomass; 45% coal; 25% oil.

>20th Century: 15% biomass; 30% coal; 50% oil; 5% nuclear.

Power Generation 2016 (WSJ 10/27/16):
Solar 1.5%; Wind 7%; Hydro 7.5%; Nuclear 9%;
Coal 26%; Nat. Gas; 42%; Other 7%

> **Fig. 7 Energy sources, illustrated by the author.**

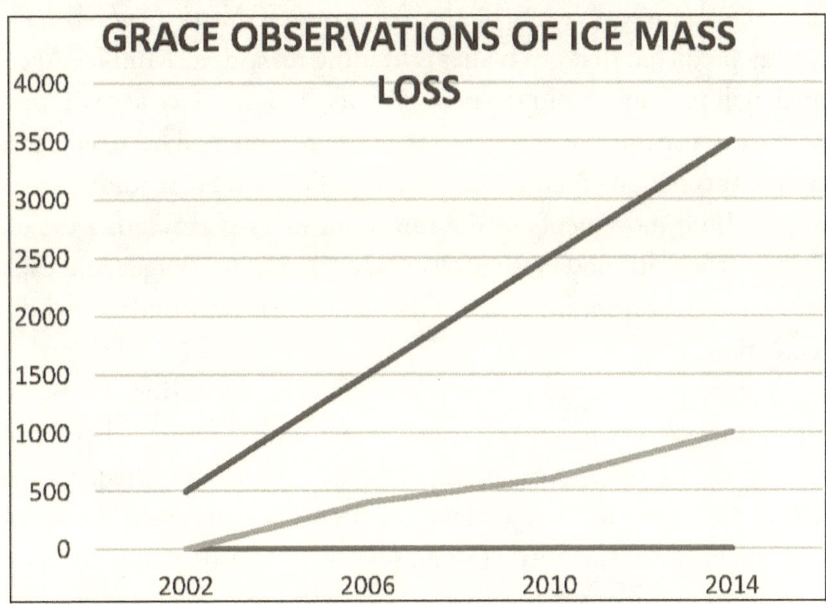


> **Fig. 2 * NASA's Gravity Recovery and Climate Experiment (GRACE). The loss of ice mass from Earth's polar ice sheets. Illustrated by the Author.**

Greenland is subjected to rapidly warming temperatures of the Arctic. The result is that, for now at least — as you can see above — it is losing ice mass considerably faster than Antarctica is, to the tune of several hundred billion metric tons per year— but spread around the world, it's only equivalent to 0.74 millimeters of average sea-level rise per year (that's the figure in the center of the graph). Thus, adding together Greenland and Antarctica's contributions right now, gives you a millimeter of annual sea level rise, roughly — and the remaining two millimeters comes from the expansion of ocean water as it warms, and from melting glaciers around the world.

One might ask: Should the world spend trillions of dollars to try to change uncontrollable events? Would trillions of dollars be better spent on educating people, and moving millions (people in Bangladesh, and low sea-level populations) to safer regions?

## Mini Ice Age

Current solar research out of the *University of North Umbria,* have recently predicted that our planet is heading towards a "Mini Ice Age," which will probably hit in the next 15 years. This mini ice age will find the northern hemisphere facing far harsher winters. The researchers say that this period could freeze the River Thames. Solar studies show that the fluid movements in the sun result in 11-year weather cycles. The first time this observation was made was 172 years ago. And each cycle is different from the last, but they still don't really understand the fluctuation.

"We found magnetic wave components appearing in pairs, originating in two different layers in the Sun's interior. They both have a frequency of approximately 11 years, although this frequency is slightly different, and they are offset in time. Over the cycle, the waves fluctuate between the northern and southern hemispheres of the Sun. Combining both waves together and comparing to real data for the current solar cycle, we found that our predictions showed an accuracy of 97%," said Professor Valentina Zharkova.

Zharkova goes on to say, "In cycle 26, the two waves exactly mirror each other – peaking at the same time but in opposite hemispheres of the Sun. Their interaction will be disruptive, or they will nearly cancel each other. We predict that this will lead to the properties of a 'Maunder minimum' [the period between 1645 and 1715, in which the northern hemisphere faced a similar cooling]."

Finally, Zharkova notes, "Effectively, when the waves are approximately in phase, they can show strong interaction, or resonance, and we have strong solar activity. When they are out of phase, we have solar minimums. When there is full phase separation, we have the conditions last seen during the Maunder minimum, 370 years ago."

It's now widely admitted that global warming, as measured by temperatures around the world, stopped at the turn of the century. Many observers have been expecting it to resume, perhaps starting this year – but a new report from the UK Met Office says that in fact the so-called "hiatus" may carry on for some time yet. The Met Office climatologists say that the long-awaited El Nino is finally brewing in the Pacific, which ought to heat the world up noticeably. The Pacific Decadal Oscillation, another mechanism active in the Pacific, also looks set to warm things up.

Unfortunately for those desperate to see a return to a warming world (for instance at the Met Office's Hadley Centre for Climate Science and Services, dependent on global warming for its raison d'être), there's a third powerful mechanism in play: the Atlantic Multi-decadal Oscillation, or AMO, which varies up and down on long timescales. The AMO has actually been heating the world up since the mid-1990s, but now it looks set to swing into a negative phase and cool the planet off, probably for a long time, as AMO phases typically last several decades.

The Met Office has this to say about the AMO: "The current warm phase is now 20 years long and historical precedent suggests a return to relatively cool conditions could occur within a few years ... Observational and model estimates further suggest AMO shifts have an effect on global mean, near-surface temperatures of about 0.1°C. A rapid AMO decline could therefore maintain the current slowdown in global warming..."

**Disadvantages of a Mini Ice Age:** Lower sea levels; death for people living in colder regions; greater energy consumption; decease in agricultural production and starvation; less rain and more deserts.

> *Each generation exercises power over its successors. And each, insofar as it modifies the environment bequeathed to it and rebels against tradition, resists and limits the power of its predecessors. Each new power won by man is a power over man as well. Each advance leaves him weaker as well as stronger. In every victory, besides being the general who triumphs, he is also the prisoner who follows the triumphal car.* --C. S. Lewis

## Uncertainty Principle:

Quantum theory by Niels Bohr cannot be ignored. It shows that things are indeed "fuzzy," "murky," "chaotic." This new physics provides the most convincing scientific evidence that *consciousness* plays an essential role in the nature of physical reality. Quantum theory is a practical branch of physics that has given us the electron microscope, lasers, transistors, superconductors and nuclear power. It explained the structure of the atom, electrical conduction, chemical bonding, and many other important scientific phenomena.

This basic *Uncertainty Principle*, co-founded by Heisenberg, extends to all atomic and subatomic phenomena, and requires a radical revision of our commonsense beliefs to explain it. It says you *cannot* know where an atom or electron is located and also know how it is moving, at one and the same time. You can ask where it is, and get a sensible answer. Or you can ask how it is moving, and get a sensible answer. But there is no answer to a question, "where is it *and* how is it moving, *and* how fast is it going?"

In the absence of observation, the atom is a kind of "ghost," and only materializes when you decide what to look for. One can look for its location, or observe its motion, but you can't detect or observe both. Quantum theory is difficult to understand. For a more through discussion see *Other Worlds* by Paul Davis (Touchstone Books).

Many of the perplexing features of quantum theory can be understood in terms of "wave-particle" duality; i.e., light (a photon) acts like a particle and sometimes as a wave. This is suggestive of the spirit-mind-body of theology. How can the mind be thoughts and also electrical neural impulses? How can a novel be both a story and a collection of words? The wave is not a physical substance, but a wave of knowledge. The wave is also a wave of probability. The wave thus "encapsulates" the inherent uncertainty, unpredictability of the quantum factor. Thus, the universe is not a collection of separate but coupled objects; it is *a network of interacting relationships.*

## Chaos & Chance

> ***Chance favors only the mind that is prepared.*** **Louis Pasteur**

Chance is an intersection of two independent lines of causality. It is the absence of any explanation; e.g., "that happened by chance." Absolute chance is completely irrational: being derived from non-being is *absurd!* The essence of "chaos" is the global nature of certain laws of periodicity and rhythm—laws which most eerily manifest themselves in the ability of non-organic substances such as water molecules, cloud formations (and even stock market trends) to organize themselves in complex patterns of repetition, without any apparent (known) outside cause.

According to one authority on Chaos Theory, Polkinghorne, Ph.D., these discoveries have restored the force of the theological "Argument from Design." As Harvard paleontologist Stephen Jay Gould (a leading evolutionist) has pointed out, only the most stubborn Darwinist, would still insist the universe is entirely the product of blind chance and random mutations.

For in "Chaos" we can now read some of the recipes of global self-organization for ourselves, and simply marvel at what Dr. Polkinghorne calls, the obvious "fine-tuning" in Nature that has allowed intelligent beings like us to exist. From chaos, from disorder, there developed order, "the symphony of life." Randomness doesn't cut it when it comes to generating meaningful order out of chaos—direction is required—*always.*

Chaos theory, primarily built upon the mathematical work of Mitchell Feigenbaum and Benoit Mandelbrot, also reinforces the age-old Judeo-Christian belief that humans are not just "machines made of flesh," but deeply complex beings whose exact natures can never be exhaustively known. Another interesting point of Polkinghorne's observations are the growing acceptance among scientists coming to terms with the synthesis of "chance and necessity." Both of these he suggests carry out "within a cloudy unpredictable process," the designs of a Creator who—unlike the geometry of Newton, content to merely start the machine in motion at one end of the temporal continuum—actually and consistently sustains the being of the universe at all points of space-time.

> ***Some of the most important conditions and events of our human life are as dependent on what might be called "intentional accidents," as deliberate intent or goal-directed action. For everything in the universe that comes under our understanding and control, we see at once how much more is far beyond us. The mystery of the universe is forever unfolding before us— if we have the vision to see its beauty, its power, its wonderment. --Author***

## CHANGED BELIEFS:

> **God, give us grace to accept with serenity the things that cannot be changed, courage to change the things which should be changed and the wisdom to distinguish the one from the other. --Reinhold Niebuhr**

Scientists firmly believed in a "Steady State" Universe. Now they believe in "Big Bang" theory. They believed in Darwinism, or more accurately, that all life started by random chance. But the lack of fossil evidence clearly refutes this theory. Science originally believed in Determinism. Today they believe in Quantum Mechanics, which confirms that identical causes don't always produce identical results.

If anything in the scientific world seemed constant, it was the flow of time. This perception, or rather *misperception* of time, resulted from a reality limited to earth. Einstein's theory of Relativity has now become law; i.e., the flow of time at any location with high gravity (G) or high velocity (V) is actually slower than at another location with lower G or V. There is earth based time, and cosmic time, human facts, and u*niversal truths*.

## Anthropic Principle:

> **The physical, chemical, and biological laws of the universe and nature are so amazingly fine-tuned that they could not have possibly occurred by chance. --Brandon Carter**

In 1973, the most distinguished astronomers and physicists arrived in Communist Poland, to celebrate the 500th birthday of Copernicus. Of the many scientific papers presented, only one astonished the gathered group and the entire world ever since. The speaker was Brandon Carter, astrophysicist and cosmologist from Cambridge University. The technical title of his paper was, *"Large Number Coincidences and the Anthropic Principle in Cosmology."*

Basically, the Anthropic Principle indicates that all the known and seemingly arbitrary and unrelated constants of physics were "extremely fine-tuned," from the very beginning of the universe, for the creation of human beings. Examples of these essential constants include: Gravitational, Planck constant, Speed of light, Mass of Elementary Particles, Electromagnetic Force, among fifty-nine others. These seemingly unrelated fundamental constants have one thing in common—they are precisely the values needed to have a universe capable of producing life.

The Anthropic Principle completely shattered the *opposite belief* held by many scientists, such as Copernicus, Newton, Darwin, and noted atheists, such as Russell, Marx, among many others. The earlier *erroneous* "scientific" belief was that the universe was simply blindly mechanistic, highly random, completely impersonal, and therefore, human life came about by "random chance." In other words, the new scientific evidence is that the earth and universe we inhabit appears to be *expressly designed* for the emergence of human beings and life, by an Intelligent Being.


## SCIENTIFIC TRUTHS KEY POINTS:

o The evidence is *beyond a reasonable doubt,* that the universe was *created,* as in Genesis 1.1-13: *"In the beginning God created the heavens [universe] and the earth..."*

o Time, space, matter, energy, and all living things, were *not* created in six earth days; they were created in *six cosmic days,* which is billions of years.

o Order exists in the universe, based on the well-established natural, and immutable laws, and the scientific constants, now finally known by scientists.

o The major sources of energy has continued to change from fossil fuels to more efficient and cleaner natural gas, nuclear and solar cell technologies.

o We can't control natural disasters, such as hurricanes, and volcanos.

o Man-made wars have caused millions of deaths, and religious sectarian battles in the Middle East, continues to kill tens of thousands each year.

o The greatest man-made disaster and cause of death was during the atheistic communism era (the so called "cold war").

o China's "one child law," and other worldwide abortions, have resulted in the death of hundreds of millions of innocent victims.

o There is a hierarchy of knowledge, universal laws, and known equations that dramatically changed our world. All material things are changeable (matter into energy, hydrogen and oxygen into water, etc.).

o Everything in the universe passes through multiple evolutionary cycles of birth, growth, adolescence, maturity, death, and rebirth.

o The "Anthropic Principle" shows that all constants of physics are "extremely fine-tuned" from the very beginning of the universe, for the creation of life.

o New scientific evidence is that the earth we inhabit appears to be *expressly designed* for the emergence of human beings and life, by an intelligent creator.

**The heavens declare the glory of God; the skies proclaim the work of His hands. Day after day they pour forth speech; night after night they display knowledge. There is no speech or language where their voice is not heard.** --Psalm 19, King David

# V. Moral Truths

*If we have full employment and great economic growth—if we have cities of gold and alabaster—but our children have not learned to walk in goodness, justice, and mercy, then the American experiment, no matter how gilded, will have failed. --William Bennett*

In Western society many people claim that "everything is relative!" No one should impose his/her moral standards on another! This modern idea is considered fundamental, or self-evident in today's culture. They insist that no moral or ethical standards exist. "Who are you to tell me what's right or wrong? You're being judgmental."

How could anyone organize a civilized cultural society without standards? Moral relativism is illogical, impractical, and amoral. Ignoring the human conscience, reasoning, and free will, to choose between what is right or wrong, ultimately results in "might makes right." The USSR, Cuba, North Korea are examples of such societies, "where might makes it right." Who wants to live in such a society?

## Standards of Behavior:
*What's self-evident is to do what's good and avoid what's evil.*

There are degrees of goodness and evil, and Western society has established standards of human behavior and laws that govern how one should act. The foundation of these laws is the Ten Commandments, and what Christ taught us by His Gospel.

Ethics is a branch of philosophy, which concerns the laws of right conduct. Ethics is about human acts (I and We) from the standpoint of natural reason, and seeks to establish the criterion of good and evil.

Morality is individual (I) acts, which are good or evil in relation to what they should be, as in keeping with or in violating God's laws. To live as if only I mattered, to abuse, to exploit and treat others as objects, is unethical. To willingly hurt another, to cheat, to mislead, to humiliate, to insult or degrade, is to commit an immoral act.

Ken Wilber writes in *The Marriage of Sense and Soul*: Ethics is described in "We" language. It is part of the inter-subjective domain, the domain of collective interaction and social awareness, the domain of justness, goodness, reciprocity, and mutual understanding.

Pollster Daniel Yankelovich reported that "public distress about the state of our social morality has reached nearly universal proportions: 87% of the (U.S) public fears that something is fundamentally wrong with America's moral condition."

As the novelist John Updike put it: *The fact that … we still live well cannot ease the pain of feeling that we no longer live nobly.*

## Morality and Laws:

> ***Right and wrong assumes we agree on moral standards
> or rules of fair play.***

Moral perfection is the "ideal," in the sense that we cannot fully achieve it. Three states exist: moral, immoral (not moral), and amoral (one who doesn't accept any moral laws).

"Free will" makes us "moral subjects." Human acts, or acts that are freely chosen, based on judgment of our conscience, can be morally evaluated: they are either good or evil. The morality of human acts depends on three fundamental elements: The object(s) chosen; the intentions; and circumstances of that action;

The object chosen is a good or evil toward which the will deliberately directs itself (the "matter" of the human action).

Objective norms of morality express the rational order of good and evil attested to by our conscience. The intention resides in the acting subject because it lies at the voluntary source of the action and determines it by its end. Circumstances, including *consequences*, are secondary elements of our moral actions. They contribute to increasing or diminishing the moral goodness or evil of human acts, and the agent's responsibility. It is therefore a serious error to judge the morality of human acts by considering only the intention that inspired them or circumstances (environmental, social pressure, duress, etc.).

There are acts, in and of themselves, independent of intentions that are *always illicit* by reason of their object, such as blasphemy, perjury, murder, and adultery. Except in very special situations, usually during times of war, one may *not* do an evil act so that a greater good may result from it. The end does not justify the means, *except a just during war*, after all other efforts have failed.

## Ethics & Bio-Ethics

> ***Ethics is a branch of philosophy dealing with human values and conduct; the rightness or wrongness of specific actions and goodness or badness of the motives related to such practices.***

Bio-Ethics is concerned with medical decisions, procedures, treatments and practices. The guiding principles are patient "autonomy," such as their right to make informed choices, and make these decisions based on their values and religious beliefs.

Doctors, nurses and guardians must follow two ethical principles: *Beneficence*—helping others further their legitimate (legal) interests; and *Non- Maleficence*—in treatment, above all do no harm. Justice and truth-telling are required so that the "competent" patient (or surrogate) can make informed decisions.

Morality and ethics are *not* modes of conduct arising from constraints by laws. Morality and ethics arises from love. To deceive, to offend, to hurt intentionally, is clearly immoral. To live as if 'only I matter,' to exploit others, is unethical. Morality and ethical conduct are not just academic matters to be debated and legislated. Practices that in the past were once customary in the Old Testament, and Islam Koran—slavery, polygamy, stoning for adultery, killing a child who curse a parent, are today not just immoral, *it is clearly illegal.*

## Moral Theology:

> ***Moral theology was emphasized by the revelations in the Gospel; in particular, Christ's Sermon on the Mount, and the tradition of the Church, as in the lives and teachings of great saints.***

The Sermon on the Mount was a poetic message of mercy. A lustful thought is not the same as adultery. Anger does not have the same penalty as murder. Jesus was not so unyielding about success and perfection, but the willingness to rise when one has fallen.

With the Scholastics, especially St. Thomas Aquinas (1227-1274), moral theology became an essential part of apologetics, and was developed systematically, influenced immensely by Greek moral philosophy. Distinctions were made between formal and material Sin (the former being deliberate sinfulness, whereas the latter was "sin" done in ignorance), and between mortal and lesser sins (mortal being deadly serious, though repentance is possible). To this belong such classifications as the Seven Deadly Sins: Pride, Covetousness, Lust, Envy, Gluttony, Anger, and Sloth. Seven Christian Virtues: Faith, Hope, Charity, Prudence, Justice, Temperance, and Fortitude. Seven Corporal Works of Mercy: feeding the hungry, giving drink to the thirsty, clothing the naked, caring for strangers, visiting the sick, ministering to prisoners, and burying the dead.

## SECULARISM:

> **Secular laws should be based on morality—the foundation of all laws.**

The Supreme Court, since the early 1900s, has functioned as an "elite" group of intellectuals, who think they have supreme power to over-rule the other two branches of government. Since this small elitist group of nine judges, are appointed for *life* (even when they might become senile), the other branches are no longer "equal."

This kind of "secularism" and government control has gone to the extreme in communist states, and in many countries of the European Union, and Canada (e.g., it is illegal to publicly object to homosexual acts and gay marriage in Canada and Sweden. A pastor was actually jailed in Sweden for his sermon).

In America, some Circuit Court judges and the Supreme Court have "dictated" what the government can and cannot do. For example, in this secular welfare state, public money may not be given to faith-based institutions, unless they avoid all religious activities. Yet public money is given for abortions.

The Founding Fathers of our Constitution, except perhaps Jefferson and Monroe, actually agreed that America is based on the fundamental concept that: *[This] 'Nation was established under God.*

The courts, in the author's view, have gone too far in this so-called 'separation of church and state,' which is actually *not* in our Constitution.

## Sex & Chastity:

> **Chastity is the most unpopular of the Christian virtues. The Christian attitude does not mean that there is anything wrong about sexual pleasure, any more than about the pleasure of eating. --C. S. Lewis**

Sex in itself cannot be moral or immoral any more than gravitation or nutrition. The sexual behavior of human beings can be moral or immoral. Like economic, or political … filial behavior, it is sometimes good and sometimes bad. Sexuality affects all aspects of the human person in the unity of body and soul. It especially concerns the capacity to love and to procreate, and forming bonds of communion with others.

Every man and woman, should acknowledge and accept his/her sexual identity or sexual orientation. Physical, moral, spiritual differences exist (and they can be complementary), and are oriented towards the good of marriage and the flourishing of family life. Each of the two sexes is an image of the power and tenderness of God, with equal dignity, though in a different way. The union of man and woman in marriage is a way of imitating, in the flesh, the Creator's generosity and fecundity (fruitfulness): "Therefore, a man leaves his father and his mother and cleaves to his wife, and they become one flesh." (Gen. 2:24). All human generations have proceeded from this union, of one man and one woman.

**Defense of Marriage Act**: DOMA was considered unconstitutional by Supreme Court Judges, as a result, same-sex marriages became the "law of the land." This *judicial activism* transformed (redefined) marriage between one man and one woman, going back thousands of years, from early Biblical times. Moreover, this ruling by nine human judges, which now promotes "gender neutrality," will impact many legal areas, such as probate laws, estate titles, contracts, social security, and legal ownership documents (past and future).

## Birth Control:

There are many *developed* countries, such as Japan, Russia, and the European Union (EU) that have population growth rates that are *declining*, while the older population is growing, and will soon pass-on. This imbalance will seriously impact economics, employment, crime rates, political systems, and government ability to cope with change. For example, in France and the UK, as well as much of the EU, Moslem birth rates are far greater than Christian births. Moslems citizens will likely have a greater political base in future generations.

*The Economist* (November, 2009) devoted its front cover story to *"Falling fertility—how the population problem is* [allegedly] *solving itself."* It concluded, among other things, that rising world populations are forecasted to *only* reach approximately nine billion by 2050, instead of earlier forecasts. According to the UN, World fertility rates of *half* the world will decline to about 2.1 or below, by 2045-50, from nearly 5.0 in the 1950-55.

The fertility rate concerns children that an *average* woman is *likely* to have during her childbearing years, typically between ages 15-49. It is not the same as birth rate, which is the *actual* number of children born in a year, as a share of the total population. Since child mortality is higher in poorer developing countries, the replacement fertility rate is higher there.

The U.S. has an estimated fertility level of less than 2.0, and a GDP of about $50,000 per person, inflation adjusted. Developing countries have a slightly higher fertility level (all figures are *approximate*), and have GDPs as follows: Iran ($12k), Brazil ($8k), China (less than $5k), Indonesia ($3.5k), as compared to India's nearly 3.0 fertility rate and $2.5k GDP. Undeveloped countries, like parts of India and most of Africa, have a *far higher* population growth versus GDP.

Considering the above statistics, and problems for many *undeveloped* countries, the author's argument for contraception are:

(1) According to the Bible (Genesis 2:28-30), God gave man (and woman) dominion over nature and all creatures. By definition, that should include his or her reproductive nature. Moreover, because of our God given intelligence and reasoning powers we are superior to all animals that simply reproduce continually and aimlessly.

(2) Through use of this God given intelligence, we have developed the capability to replace human organs, limbs, and otherwise use medical technology to *delay* death. Why shouldn't we also

use our intelligence to *delay* life, using methods that do *not* include destruction of any form of human life (egg, fetus)?

(3) The Church *appears* to be inconsistent in permitting the regulation of birth by periodic abstinence or "rhythm," while condemning the use of artificial contraceptives. What's the difference between having sex when the spouse is infertile, versus using a pill or other *nondestructive* contraceptive measures? Isn't the result the same? Abstinence seems to be unnatural since it inhibits not only conception, but more importantly, the natural expression of love and affection between married couples. The sacrament of marriage does not exist *primarily* to produce children.

(4) Contraception is *totally different* from abortion. Contraception delays conception, or actually delays our cooperation in God's Creation. Abortion destroys created human life. The Church approves the use of artificial means to *extend life*. Logical reasoning would suggest that the Church should likewise approve the use of artificial means to temporarily *delay life*.

(5) If some families are destitute, should they bring more children into a world, when they cannot feed, clothe, and educate them? Should we give birth to children, and then let them die of starvation (as is happening in too many undeveloped countries)? Procreation for procreation's sake seems to be irrational in a world that cannot feed most of its six billion plus inhabitants, many of which are living worst off than wild animals. Where is the "human dignity" and "respect for life," in this kind of inhuman existence?

(6) How will the Church teach the faith and basic morals to adults and children who have no access to this basic education? Moreover, if tens-of-millions of people have no access to the media or basic education, then they will never learn about this anti-birth control doctrine, and they will not follow it anyway.

(7) Contraceptive measures, such as condoms, have been proven effective against the spread of contagious diseases such as HIV/

AIDS. The prohibition against such preventive measures would likely result in millions of premature deaths. CNN reported that ten million orphans now exist in Africa, primarily because millions of parents died of AIDS. These are clearly innocent victims. Again, where is the "human dignity" in this doctrine? It should also be noted that studies by the UN have shown that 50% of the millions of worldwide HIV carriers are young people, below the age of 25 years.

(8) Many (most?) American and European Bishops agree, as is evident by the following (see below) special papal committee votes, that some form of contraceptive measures are reasonable and are *not evil*, for the health and wellbeing of the family.

**Of Human Life:** During Vatican II, Pope Paul VI convened a Birth Control Commission in 1964. At its final meeting in 1966, the full commission voted 52 to 4 to *drop the ban on artificial birth control in marriage.* One of the many reasons for this change reportedly was that earlier generation peasants and farmers had a stake in large families; sons and daughters meant extra hands. Frequent pregnancies offset much higher rates of child mortality. This situation is now nonexistent in developed countries, and significantly reduced in many developing countries.

This "drop the ban" proposal was later reviewed by sixteen cardinals/ bishops who voted 9 to 3 (with others abstaining) that contraception was *intrinsically not evil.* Two years later, Pope Paul VI shocked everyone by his *"Humanae Vitae"* doctrine, *disapproving any and all forms of contraception.* Nevertheless, the Vatican admitted that the Pope's Doctrine on this subject did *not* represent "infallible teaching." As a practical matter, *Humanae Vitae* is probably a stillborn letter in many Western Churches, including Catholics.

Christians generally agree that some form of contraception (which does not destroy the fertilized egg) is acceptable for the well-being of the family. However, the Church still teaches: "Called to give life, spouses share in the creative power and fatherhood of God. Periodic continence, that is, the methods of birth regulation based on self-observation and the use of infertile periods is in conformity with the objective criteria of morality. In contrast, "every action which, whether in anticipation of the conjugal act, or in its accomplishment, or in the development of its natural consequences, purposes, whether as an end or as a means, to render procreation impossible" is intrinsically evil.

Church teaching in the case of war is: *the end can justify the means,* when the objective is the "greater good of society" (See topic on War). It is also true that many of today's youths and adults just want unrestrained sex. On the other hand, the reality is that the worldwide AIDS epidemic is a 'microbe war,' where over 25 million have died so far, and additional millions have been infected. Many will continue to die without reasonable preventive measures and education.

Should we let tens-of-millions die, in order to teach them a Christian lesson? The fact is that condoms do protect people and a contrary conclusion is faulty, if not totally false. In the final analysis, couples must consult their formed conscience, their "inner voice," on this extremely difficult issue. As St. Augustine taught: "In fide, unitas; in dubiss, libertas; in omnibus, caritas" (In faith, unity; in doubtful matters, liberty; in all things, love).

## Abortion:

> ***Abortion is killing and removal from the uterus an embryo or fetus before it has attained viability, before the unborn infant with appropriate life support, has become capable of surviving and eventually maintaining an independent life outside the uterus. Induced abortions are those initiated voluntarily at any point in gestation. --Author***

Science has *not* been able to objectively refute that life begins at conception, and the embryo is a living person with a soul. This fundamental moral law, the 'right to life,' has existed for thousands of years, and was specifically emphasized by our Founding Fathers: '… [*The*] *right to life, liberty and pursuit of happiness.*' The Supreme Court concerns itself with interpretation of Constitutional law, based on fallible judges, and is not supreme to God's laws. Sequencers confirm that the fertilized egg contains 100% of the human genome.

Worldwide, the total number of pregnancies terminated each year by abortion is not accurately known. China has the worst record, with about 400-500 million (forced) abortions, so far. Nevertheless, the total number of "legal" abortions in America is estimated to be *cumulatively* about 60 million.

The World Health Organization estimates the number of *clandestine* abortions at approximately 20 million—of which about 70,000 also resulted in the mother's death. In the early 1990's, in countries where abortion is legal, rates ranged from a low of 5 per 1000 women (ages 15-44) in the Netherlands, to a high of 192 per 1000 in Romania, where government sponsored abortion was the primary means of birth control during communist rule. The rate in the United States was 26 per 1000 in 1992, and it climbed to 1.5 million by 1997, and leveled off to about 1.3 million more recently.

Development of the human embryo requires approximately 270 days. During this time, the original single cell multiplies to over 200 billion cells and the size of the embryo increases from microscopic size to about 15-20 inches in length. Human embryonic development consists of three basic stages:

The first stage begins with the fertilization of the ovum, or egg. It concludes at the end of the 14-15 days of life, when the developing embryo burrows into the uterine wall and begins to obtain nutrition from the mother.

The second stage extends from the third through the eighth weeks, at which time all the major organs begin to form and the embryo becomes recognizable as a human person.

The third stage of growth extends from the third month until birth, which is normally the ninth month. Recently, because of new technology, many premature babies have been born during the sixth through eighth months. In this final stage, systems of organs complete their specialized development, and the fetus becomes equipped to live on its own, outside the mother's womb.

## Roe vs. Wade:

> ***The Bible, not the Supreme Court, is one of the earliest sources of ideas and natural laws essential for civilization. … The sanctity of life, dignity of the individual, personal and communal responsibility, peace as an ideal, love as the foundation of justice. ---Author***

The *Roe vs. Wade* Supreme Court decision (1973) approved abortions in the U.S., under certain conditions. This decision was made *without any evidence.* At the time, DNA Sequencers were not available, which ten years later proved that a fertilized egg contains the total human genome. *The absence of evidence is not evidence!*

An unborn fetus is "technically" not a complete person. Therefore, abortion is not murder claimed the proponents of "free choice." They argue that all women have the "Constitutional right" to control their bodies, and have abortions for any reasonable situation, such as economics, concern about the mother's safety, or the unborn child's health, among many other circumstances.

Some advocates believe that this 'right' should be extended to allow them to terminate any pregnancy, any time, for any reason. (In the great majority of cases, according to official medical records, abortion is a means of birth control, a means to terminate unwanted pregnancies).

**Actual Reasons Given for Abortions**
Source: Wm. Robert Johnson, Survey Aug. 2012

| % Abortions | Reasons Given 2008/2009 |
|---|---|
| 1.85 | Rape |

| 0.16 | Physical Health of mother |
| 0.14 | Emotional/psychological health of mother |
| 8.08 | Socio-economic |
| 89.02 | Elective |

97% of abortions are elective, including 8% economic reasons.

There is no such thing as "safe abortions." There is a broad consensus in America that "abortion on demand" is morally repugnant. With millions of people representing all faiths, these -Author (among many others) believe that abortion destroys not only the child in the womb but also creates untold conflict in the lives of millions of women. Abortion cheapens human life, tears families apart, and contributes to the violence that plagues our culture. Whether legal or not, abortion is lethal for the child and destructive of the mother, and of society.

The United States is doing the world no favor by exporting this *false ideology*, which claims that any type of union, permanent or temporary, is as good as the traditional family. There is mounting evidence that being part of an intact, traditional family or extended family, helps children grow into emotionally well-adjusted and productive citizens. While it is true that many single parents do an admirable job of raising their children, nonetheless, we owe it to the children of our country, and of the world, to encourage stable, intact, two-parent families.

Naturally all women (and men) have a right to vote, a right to equal justice, and a right to control their bodies, which God created and gave them as stewards. Adults must take moral and legal responsibility for all of their acts.

*Rights for rights sake, is foolish without moral responsibility!*

You have a right to drive an automobile, *after* you obtain a license that shows you have driving skills. That doesn't mean you have a right to drive carelessly and hurt or kill others. Adults have a right to drink alcohol, but *no right* to abuse or mistreat others by drunkenness. If consenting adults claim they have a right to unprotected sex, they must also take responsibility for sexual diseases they may pass on to others. And if by this procreative act, a human offspring happens to result, they must be morally responsible for the child's care and welfare. *'Rights' are not one-way or one-sided privileges.*

More healthy embryos are destroyed each year in the America, than deaths from all other causes combined. That is a terrible shame on this country. Pro-Choice advocates should consider this logic: What if their parents decided to terminate them, a few months before they were born? Then, they wouldn't have any 'rights' at all, especially the God-given right to eternal life.

We are stewards, not owners of the gift of life (and this earth) that God has entrusted to us. The gift of life is not ours to dispose of, to terminate, as if it were merely some kind of inanimate disposable commodity. We are the only known warm-blooded creatures on earth that kills its own offspring, in cold-blood, before it is born.

The unborn is a helpless, defenseless victim who will never have a chance in a court of law to argue its case, despite society's law condemning such acts. When one kills a pregnant woman, they are judged guilty of *two murders* in most courts. (Abortions also has a major impact on the economy by reducing ratio of young persons in our Social Security system by tens-of-millions).

## Compromise:

In order to defuse this emotional moral issue, and establish a consensus, as to when a human life actually begins, one could first ask: *when does life end?* When a person is brain dead; when no brain waves exist, are declared legally dead, even if the heart is still pumping blood. Therefore, to untangle this difficult and emotional issue, we should at a minimum, accept this definition for the life of the human fetus. Scientists generally agree that the fetus does not have a functioning brain until after the first four weeks. If we can agree on this definition, then federal laws could be established to restrict abortions before the first full month, unless the life of the mother is clearly at risk. This 'reasonable compromise,' would save millions of humans that cannot otherwise defend themselves.

As a Christian, Muslim, Jew, or any member of *a civilized society,* one must take a stand against racism, rape, murder, and other acts of physical or psychological violence. That's because these acts involve someone—*a victim.* Racism, rape, murder is not a "choice," that someone makes in a vacuum—it clearly involves victims. The issue is not one of "private morality" but civil rights—keeping the innocent from becoming victims. *If there's a victim involved—it's undoubtedly a civil rights abuse.*

Isn't this a matter of private morality—like deciding which church to attend, or which Christian teaching to follow? Is there really a helpless victim involved in abortion? There are some who say that there is not—that the fetus is merely a mass of tissue, without a soul, and in any case part of the woman's body. *Where's the proof?* If this were true, then no one would oppose abortion any more than they would oppose heart replacement, or kidney transplants, or appendectomies. But this is obviously not the case.

Developments in the science of fertilized eggs and embryo technology have given us greater opportunities than ever to learn about the pre-born: By the 18th day after conception, the baby's circulatory system is different from the mother, and its heart has begun to beat (See *Time-Life*, Growth Life Sciences Library, 1965). Brain waves are also detectable by the 40th day (See *Life or Death by EEG*, AMA). By the 60th day or about eight weeks, a woman discovers she's pregnant. *All* human body functions and systems by then exist (See *The Prenatal Origin of Behavior*, Univ. of Kansas Press, 1952).

Isn't it barbaric that some people find human organs worth saving—but not the entire human? The pre-born is unmistakably human, definitely alive, and unquestionably distinct from the mother, by about the 40th day. In the film, *The Silent Scream* Bernard Nathanson, M.D. (American Portrait Films, 1984), an actual first-trimester abortion is seen via ultrasound. The baby can be seen repeatedly moving to dodge the abortionist's instrument of death, and her heart rate doubles. As the baby is dismembered, her mouth opens in a "silent scream." Clearly, abortion is violence against helpless unborn children—and one that should be vehemently oppose. *This is infanticide!*

## RIGHT TO CHOOSE:

*It's not about choosing; it's about what is chosen!* ---Author

We can choose many things—our careers, where we live, our partners, and whether or not to engage in sexual intercourse, and/or have a child. Nevertheless, we have no right to make choices that violate the basic human rights of living humans, and helpless pre-born persons. If you choose to have unprotected sex, then you must also accept responsibility for motherhood and fatherhood, when your sex partner becomes pregnant.

Abortion is an act of violence, which victimizes a defenseless human being, and therefore, is not a valid choice. Some Christians say they are personally opposed to abortion, and wouldn't do it themselves, but they can't do anything about someone else taking innocent life. *That's a cop-out!* Did you really do all that's reasonably possible to stop such an immoral act? We need to work for new state and federal laws that protect the lives of all human beings, especially those that can't defend themselves, the pre-born. We need to crusade for non-violent solutions for teenagers, women with problem pregnancies, and poor families that have economic and other hardships. Many Christian Churches are willing to provide adoption services for the unwanted child. We need to take action, not just talk about the immorality of abortion. Why do endangered species, such as some birds, fish, and turtles have more legal protection in America than an unborn human child? What about *endangered human species?*

## Adultery:

*Momentary pleasures afforded by an adulterous liaison are far out-weighted by the risk of the likely negative effect of our actions on ourselves and others (especially children).* --The Dalai Lama

Consensual sexual relations between a married person and another adult, who is not his or her spouse is clearly *adultery*. It is a sin against both chastity and justice. Adultery does not always require sexual intercourse, as other intimate acts can morally be considered adulterous. As the Bible teaches, if you lust after another, *it is sin.*

Throughout history, Christians, Jews and Islamic societies have taught that sex is *fundamentally a moral activity*, and one should not therefore be indifferent towards it. The wonder and power of sex has many complex and profound repercussions as related in the Bible stories of the infidelities of Kings David, Solomon and Herod. Adultery can be, and has been, a serious threat to the stability of all human affairs. Acts of infidelity frequently lead to destructive passions, such as jealousy, irrationality, and make one vulnerable to bribery or blackmail.

Who has not known individuals, friends, or relations who actually ruined their lives by yielding briefly to such temptations? A very brief moment of sexual self-gratification can, and often does, cause one to destroy a long-term marriage, family relations, and one's eternal soul. In marriage, each spouse is entrusted with the care of the body and soul of the other. That special power is unlike any other human relationship. An extramarital affair violates the solemn vow; it is a betrayal of the person one has promised to honor. There are victims—the spouse, children, extended family relations and mutual friendships. More importantly, adultery is a mortal (grave) sin against the laws of God. Thus this act, if not confessed, destroys the eternal soul.

Many in the mass media believe that adultery is "so common," that it should be excused (such as President Clinton's admitted adulterous affair with a young White House intern). Most people believe "consensual sexual affairs between two adults, is a private matter," which the media concludes. The truth is a comprehensive study of sexual patterns by the National Opinion Research Center (NORC) of the University of Chicago shows that 21% of men and 11% of women have committed adultery sometime in their years of married life. This survey also indicates that only a small percentage of those who committed adultery are actually repeat offenders.

## Euthanasia:

**The American Declaration of Independence proclaims our inalienable right to "life, liberty and the pursuit of happiness." If our right to life itself is diminished in value, the other rights really have no meaning.**

Euthanasia is Greek for "easy or happy death," popularly known as a "mercy death," implying measures deliberately taken by a physician to curtail pain and suffering, in agonizing terminal and definitely fatal chronic conditions. This is supposedly a merciful infliction of death. This action has been extended to include such action in incurable diseases, particularly those in which the patient endures torment and extreme pain.

On the other hand, euthanasia enters the field of *eugenics* in the form of *infanticide*, which aims to improve the race by the elimination of children born with irreparable defects, or other anomalies. The idea is not new. In ancient Sparta, the militaristic nation regarded marriage as a means of furnishing vigorous soldiers. Weak infants were exterminated.

The practice of *euthanasia is illegal,* but is recognized in a few states. In the United States, euthanasia has considerable support in many "cultured and professional" groups, including some physicians, jurists, social workers, and attorneys. The *Hemlock Society,* for example, aims to change state laws to allow physicians to provide drug overdoses or lethal injections to terminally ill patients. They insist that the right to choose prevails over all other considerations. Opposition is equally vigorous and finds support within these same ranks. All Christian leaders are opposed to euthanasia. Objections to the practice may be dismissed by advocates of euthanasia as emotional and unscientific, but there remains the logical objection that legalized mercy killing may be resorted to by unscrupulous and nefarious persons. A condition regarded as incurable at one time, may later respond to medical therapy.

Intentional euthanasia, whatever its form or motive, is considered *murder* by the Church. It is gravely contrary to the dignity of the human person and to the respect due to the living God. The Church *does allow* artificial life support systems to be discontinued when there is no hope for the person, and does permit the use of drugs, but only to ease severe pain.

Life is the *most basic gift* of a loving Creator—life is a gift, not absolute dominion. We are stewards, not owners of the life entrusted to us. It is not ours to dispose of. "Euthanasia and willful suicide" are "offenses against life itself." They "debase the perpetrators more than the victims and militate against the honor of the Creator." Moreover, we have no right to ask for this act of killing, for ourselves or for those entrusted in our care, nor can any authority legitimately recommend or permit such an action. We are dealing here with a *violation of the divine law*, an offense against the dignity of the human person, a crime against life, and an attack against humanity.

Legalizing euthanasia (and abortion-on-demand) also violates International human rights and equality. To destroy the boundary between healing and killing would mark a radical departure from longstanding legal and medical traditions of our country, posing a threat of unforeseeable magnitude to the most vulnerable members of our society. The California legislature approved a bill to legalize physician-assisted suicide for terminally ill patients.

Governor Jerry Brown (former Catholic seminarian) approved this bill. The new law allows mentally competent patients to request a prescription that would end their lives if two doctors agree the patients have only six months to live. It was the subject of much debate, as supporters argued that the measure would allow people in the last stages of terminal illness to die peacefully, while advocates for seniors and the disabled argued it could make people vulnerable to greedy relatives who wished to avoid taking care of them or inherit their money.

## Suicide:

> *Everyone is responsible for their life before God.*
> *He is the Master of all life. We are obliged to accept*
> *life gratefully and preserve it for His honor. We are*
> *stewards, not owners of the life He has entrusted to us.*
> *It is not ours to dispose of.* ---**Author**

Christ was human in every way, *except in sin*. Hence, Christ sympathizes with our human weaknesses and will help us during times of great trial (Hebrew 2:17-18; 4:14-16, 1 Cor. 10:13). He directly experienced anguish, temptation, despair, fear, great disappointment. In the end, He died on the cross, alone, abandoned by the disciples, except John, Mary Madelyn, and His blessed Mother.

Suicide contradicts the natural inclination of the human being to preserve and perpetuate his/her life. It is gravely contrary to the just love of self. It likewise offends love of neighbor because it unjustly breaks the ties of solidarity with family, nation and other human societies to which we continue to have obligations. Suicide is contrary to the love of the living God. Grave psychological disturbances, mental anguish, or grave fear, as well as critical suffering, or torture can significantly diminish the responsibility of the person committing suicide. God, in His divine mercy and love shall judge the person responsible for such a momentous deed, accordingly His perfect justice.

## Capital Punishment:

> *No follower of Christ should encourage vengeance. We*
> *may not be able to "love our enemies," as Christ did,*
> *but we shouldn't intentionally kill them.*

In recent times, many have accepted the death penalty. In certain cases, Christians cannot advocate capital punishment if they claim to believe in Christ, who condemned violence and vengeance. Christ is the prime example of the absolutely innocent person, wrongly condemned and executed. Christ took no revenge against his enemies. In fact, he said with His dying breath, *"Father, forgive them for they know not what they do."*

Preserving the "common good of society" requires rendering the aggressor unable to inflict harm. The traditional teaching of the Church has acknowledged as well-founded the right and duty of legitimate public authority to punish malefactors by means of penalties commensurate with the gravity of the crime, this includes cases of extreme gravity, such as allowed for reasons of mass crimes whereby those holding authority have the right to repel by armed force aggressors against the community in their charge.

Legitimate defense can be not only a right—it's a grave duty for someone responsible for another's life, as for the common good of the family or of the state. Love towards oneself remains a fundamental principle of morality. Therefore, it is legitimate to insist on respect for one's own right to life. Someone who defends his life against grave peril to his life or his family is not guilty of murder even if he is forced to deal his aggressor a lethal blow.

**St. Thomas Aquinas wrote:** ***"The act of self-defense can have a double effect: the preservation of one's own life; and the killing of the aggressor... The one is intended, the other is not."***

## Self Defense:

> *In peace sons bury their fathers; in war, fathers bury their sons.* **-Herodotus**

The fifth commandment forbids the intentional destruction of human life. All citizens and governments are obliged to work to avoid wars. However, people and governments cannot be denied the right of self-defense, once all peace efforts have failed.

The decision for war must be based on *all* of the following:

(1) That potential or actual damage inflicted by the aggressor on the community must be considered grave, certain and long lasting.
(2) All other means for avoiding war is considered impractical or ineffective.
(3) There must be some prospect of a successful outcome, and the expected war should not create even greater evil.

The Church and human reasoning assert the permanent validity of moral laws during armed conflicts. Non-combatants, wounded soldiers, and prisoners must be respected and treated humanely. Blind obedience to authority does not suffice to excuse those who carry out immoral acts or commands. Obedience to God's Universal laws and our Human Conscience must be considered the higher authority. The greater good of the society may permit *"the end to justify the means,"* during times of grave wars; e.g., assassination of evil leaders and promoters of wars of terrorism.

Bishop Fulton J. Sheen wrote: "Peace, or contentment, harmony, and serenity, are similar words—but it has a true and a false sense. True peace is a gift of God; false peace is of our own making. True peace flourishes in an increasing friendship with God; false peace is spawned in forgetfulness of God and exaltation of the self. True peace deepens in sorrow. False peace is shattered by reverses. True peace has no wants; false peace is restless and covetous. True peace has a lowly estimate of self; false peace lives in fear of being found inferior. True peace is firm trust in God despite its own sins. False peace shrinks from the thought of God because it will not put an end to present sins."

## War & Peace:

***War is mainly a catalogue of blunders.* --Winston Churchill.**

Lessons Learned from History:
- If you wish for peace, you must prepare for war.
- What's really important is to see the real trends.

- Easy decisions are always made at the lower level.
- Every war produces injustices and brutality.
- Lack of evidence is not evidence (e.g., WMD).

During the last three thousand years of recorded history less than ten percent were years of peace. The remaining 90% were war years. Most of those battles in the past were over religious disagreements: Moslems opposing Jews. Irish Catholics fighting Irish Protestants. Moslems against Hindus,' etc., etc. Why is this so? In past history (and indeed today) many believed they are the *"chosen ones."* Mine is the true religion, and all the others are "infidels" and must be eliminated. Consider, for example, the early Crusades, Religious Wars, and Catholic *and* Protestant Inquisitions. Jesus taught: "love thy neighbor, brotherhood, forgiveness, and justice for all." Men and women—not God—create such terrible evil in the world (with Satan's help), by their free choice. It was their willingness to go to war to justify, defend and impose their religious choice, and to impose their *Ideology* on others.

## Research:

***Knowledge given to us by God cannot be denied. One cannot inhibit this God-given genius of men and women, and progress. ---Author***

Good *and* bad things can result from DNA research. For example, recent research has discovered that Sickle Cell disease mostly occurs in Africans and East Indians, where both parents have the mutated gene. If only one parent has the gene, the disease doesn't materialize as a disease in the offspring. However, the single Sickle Cell gene protects the child against a malaria disease which in most instances exists in jungles of Africa and India. Since malaria kills over six million people per year, the Sickle Cell mutation is a way for the human biological system to survive. This same gene mutation is also at work in Cystic Fibrosis, where the single mutated gene protects against diarrhea and dehydration. This dual gene, from both parents, may ultimately kill the child. Mutated genes of this kind kill some, so that many may live. On the extreme negative side of DNA or gene science is the possibility of creating human clones to use as slaves or soldiers in war, among other immoral possibilities. Science and researchers *cannot* ignore their moral responsibility.

## IMPACT OF MODERNITY:

According to Max Weber and Jurgen Habermas, et al., and the *Marriage of Sense and Soul* by Ken Wilber, the differentiation of the cultural value spheres, in essence means the separation of the individuals, morals, and the sciences. Modernity is the dissolution of what is *morally* good (the "I" and "WE"), from scientific *objective* truths ("IT"), from subjective sense of beauty by individuals ("I"). Historians generally agree that its roots (of dissolution) began during the Renaissance, flourished in the West after the so-called Enlightenment, and reached new highs during modernity, throughout the troubled 20th century, and particularly during the chaos of the *immoral* Vietnam War, beginning in the mid-1960's.

> ***Many people, believing that science has 'disproved' religion, make the further assumption that because there appears to be no final evidence for any spiritual authority, morality itself must be a matter of individual preference.* -- The Dalai Lama***

Some would claim modernity is negative because it marked the "Death of God," according to some philosophers. It changed society's emphasis to Materialism and Secularism. It demolished qualitative distinctions by substituting quantity for quality. It produced oppressive capitalism and communism. Modernity they claim was the cause of the loss of moral values and real meaning in our lives. On the positive side, modernity has produced democracies; created the idea of equality, freedom, and justice, regardless of race, creed, and/or gender; and enabled modern physics, astronomy, biology, chemistry, and medicine to flourish, while postulating "universal rights" for humankind.

According to *Science & Creation* by Stanley Jaki: *modern science was, in fact, taught and practiced by the Catholic culture of the middle-ages.* The key elements that grew from Catholic teachings were:

1. Our world and universe exists independent of us, and is orderly.
2. Humans can [partly] understand our world.
3. We should observe and work with nature, and experimentation was encouraged.
   (See *Victory of Reason* by Rodney Stark).

Lynn White, renowned historian in her book, *The Dynamo & the Virgin Reconsidered*, says about Catholic monks, during the middle-ages: "… for the first time the practical and the theological were embodied in the same individuals …

"The monk was the first intellectual to get dirt under his fingernails … in his very person he destroyed the old artificial barrier between empirical and the speculative … and thus helped create a social atmosphere favorable to scientific and technological development."—Lynn White

In contrast, the religious culture of Islam by about the middle-ages, decided it was *not* okay to analyze the world in rational terms. The use of human reason was against the Moslem culture. According to Islam, God is Sovereign in a sense that excludes secondary causes. They believe that Allah's activity is completely inscrutable to man. Unfortunately, this kind of thinking has had a significant impact on the Moslem people of today. Source: *A History of the Modern World*, by R. R. Palmer and J. Colton.

> ***Any society that believes that reason threatens its foundations will suppress reason.* St. Thomas Aquinas, Doctor of Church Doctrine.**

Modernity attempts to reduce everything in the universe to merely matter, quantity and energy, while eliminating any notion of the "Great Nest of Being," and the hierarchy of creation—matter and energy; life and biology; human mind, soul, spirit; and God, the First Cause and Creator of all. God is not merely some "Supreme Being," the highest being of all, heading a hierarchy of lesser beings. God's essence is *incomprehensible.*

As a result, these "value spheres" didn't just separate—they actually *exploded apart*—into isolation and total detachment. The scientific and secular materialism became dominant, thus classifying all other value spheres as "illusory or non-scientific," while, in general, avoiding consideration of morality and ethics in numerous technological advancements (e.g., cloning of creatures like sheep).

## Relativism:

> ***Relativism is also known as post-enlightenment thinking, post-modernism. It proclaims that there are no grounds for our values, and no solid proof or argument exists establishing that any one thing is better or more valid than another.***

This "Contextualize" thesis is that the meaning of a term is contingent upon the use that is made in a language ("meaning *is* use"). For example, what one community holds to be true, beautiful, and good is only so according to the criteria by which that community defines it. The criteria are always *intra-* rather than *inter-*cultural. There are no meta-criteria that can establish intrinsic or basic truths, absolute beauty, or the universal good. All criteria, according to this line of reasoning, are *contextual.*

## Beauty & Truth:

> ***Some claim that beauty and truth, in whatever form (fine arts, dance, music, and sciences) is always "relative." "It's in the eye of the beholder."***

> ***There are only two mistakes one can make along the road to truth; not going all the way, and not starting.***
> **Buddha**

We argue that "standards" of beauty, and objective truths must exist. Furthermore, we can observe what they are, for example: the beauty and truth of intelligent designed laws of the earth, nature and the universe. Objective truths are also required in most of our court systems. Judges will not (should not) accept subjective evidence or hearsay; "where are your objective facts," they typically demand.

Beauty is *both* objective and subjective. Consider my instances:

(1) A rose is perfectly formed, its soft color is marvelous to see, its smell is enchanting, and it harmonizes with the garden, or vessel in which we place it.

(2) A dancer has form, style, balance, and rhythm in tune with the music.

(3) A woman (or man) whom we judge to be "beautiful" will have style, good form (face and hair is perfect), the body is well formed and balanced, and he or she knows how to dress with complementary colors and style.

(4) Even an old person, ninety years of age, can be beautiful: their facial wrinkles show the character that was formed from long interesting experiences in their life. The twinkle in his or her eye demonstrates the inner most expression of feelings. His or her humility and intelligence shows their education and the good manners, established over many decades.

(5) All of us can appreciate beautiful sunrises or sunsets, a mountain covered with snow, contrasted with the valley or grasslands. This "perception" of beauty depends on our attitude or frame of mind, our education, and most importantly, with whom we share it with at the time.

(6) One must also appreciate the wondrous intelligent design of the universe, of the earth, and of all creatures, especially human beings. We also know clearly what ugliness is when we encounter it, in whatever form it's presented to us.

Music and art is more subjective and difficult to define because it depends on (not totally) the observer's culture, education and experiences.

If one does not know what truth, goodness, and harmony are, how can they appreciate them when they are observed or heard? We have to teach children to see, to hear, to observe, to understand, and most importantly, to comprehend the fine attributes of the sciences and the arts. Truth and beauty are *not* relative! We all need to appreciate, or should appreciate, the natural beauty of the sciences and arts in whatever form they are presented to us. Only then can we say: *That is truly beautiful!*

St. Augustine defined beauty perfectly in his *Confessions*:

"Late have I loved you, beauty so old and so new: late have I loved you. And see, you were within and I was in the external world and sought you there, and in my unlovely state I plunged into those lovely created thing which you made. You were with me, and I was not with you. The lovely things kept me far from you, though [if] they did not have their existence in you, they had no existence at all. You called and cried aloud and shattered my deafness. You were radiant and resplendent, you put to flight my blindness. You were fragrant, and I drew in my breath and now pant after you. I tasted, and I feel hunger and thirst for you. You touched me, and I am set on fire to attain the peace which is yours."

## Death of Outrage:

> ***Prosperity actually depends upon good morals. When lying, cheating, manipulation, lack of moral discipline, and personal irresponsibility become commonplace, then national economies will decline.* William Bennett**

A society that produces street predators and white-collar criminals has to pay for prison cells. A society in which drug use is rampant must pay for drug treatment centers. The breakup of families means many more foster homes and lower high school graduation rates. ... Just as there are enormous financial benefits to moral health, there are enormous financial costs to moral collapse. Bennett continues, Religious congregations dismiss pastors for unethical or inappropriate private behavior, regardless of the quality of their sermons. In law enforcement, a good police commissioner will rid his department of a bigoted cop, regardless of how sterling the officer's arrest record. In the world of the military, the code of military justice demands rigid standards of personal conduct, no matter how great a soldier's prowess on the battlefield.

What Bennett was suggesting in his book is this: Should we expect lower moral standards from anyone, including our U.S. presidents?

The attempt to use God's forgiveness as a pretext to excuse moral wrong is a dangerous (and old) heresy known as *antinomianism*—literally 'against the law.' Essentially it rejects the moral law as a relevant part of Christian experience. The thought that Christ's death at Golgotha, would justify licentiousness has long been considered contemptible by saints and scholars throughout the ages.

Those who constantly invoke the sentiment of 'who are we to judge?' should consider the anarchy that would ensue if we adhered to this sentiment in, say, our courtrooms. Shouldn't judges judge? What would happen if those sitting on a jury decided to be 'nonjudgmental' about rapists and sex harassers, embezzlers and tax cheats? Without being 'judgmental,' Americans would never have put an end to slavery, outlawed child labor, emancipated women, or ushered in the civil rights movement.

Forgiveness cannot be granted without admission of guilt, without an apology, without repentance. Forgiveness has become, in some societies, a synonym for lax standards and tolerance for (and acceptance of) all kinds of misbehavior. We violate God's cannons of justice when we invoke forgiveness casually, trivially, promiscuously. We reap what we sow—even when there is contrition. Remember: God forgave David for his infidelity with Bathsheba and for the death of her husband, Uriah, but terrible tragedy still visited David's life—including the death of his infant son. If we do not confront the soft *relativism* that is now disguised as a virtue, we will find ourselves morally and intellectually disarmed (and society will pay the consequences).

***Finally, morality and ethics are not modes of conduct or behavior arising from compulsion or constraint or from fear of the law: right conduct arises from love of God and neighbor.***

## MORAL TRUTHS KEY POINTS:

o   Sexuality affects all aspects of the human person in the unity of body and soul. It especially concerns affectivity, the capacity to love and to procreate.

o   Everyone, man and woman, should acknowledge and accept his/her sexual identity or sexual orientation.

o   Sexual orientation is something we are born with, and not primarily 'acquired' from our social environment.

o   Many *developed* countries, such as Japan, Russia, and much of the European Union (EU) that have population growth rates that are *declining*, while the older population is growing, and will naturally pass-on, over the next few decades.

o   This demographics imbalance will seriously impact economic growth, employment, crime rates, political systems, and government ability to cope with these changes.

o   Science has *not* been able to objectively refute that life begins at conception, and the embryo is a living person with a soul.

o   This fundamental moral law, the 'right to life,' has existed for thousands of years, and was specifically emphasized by our Founding Fathers: '… [The] right to life, liberty and pursuit of happiness.'

o   The Supreme Court concerns itself with interpretation of Constitutional law, based on fallible judges, and is not supreme to God's laws.

o   Sequencers confirm that the fertilized egg contains 100% of the human genome.

- o Consensual sexual relations between a married person and another adult, who is not his or her spouse is clearly *adultery*. It is a sin against both chastity and justice.
- o The American Declaration of Independence proclaims our inalienable right to "life, liberty and the pursuit of happiness." If our right to life itself is diminished in value, the other rights really have no meaning.
- o Legitimate defense is not only a right—it's a grave duty for those responsible for another's life, and the common good of the family or of the state.
- o One cannot inhibit genius, and technological progress.
- o Modernity is negative because it marked the "Death of God," according to some philosophers. It changed society's emphasis to Materialism and Secularism. It demolished qualitative distinctions by substituting quantity for quality.
- o Truth and beauty are *not* relative!

# VI. Faith & Reason

*Conflicts between Science and the Bible arise from either a lack of scientific knowledge or defective understanding of the Bible.* --Moses Maimonides

*Begin with the folly of faith and you will obtain knowledge. This folly is wisdom; this folly is the path of truth.* --Blaise Pascal.

Rene Descartes in his *Discourse on Method*, found the evidence for God in human consciousness: *The idea of 'perfection' couldn't exist if we didn't also have an idea of 'imperfection,* he wrote. Reason involves understanding, arguments, judgments, and finally our reasoned conclusion:

First, our mind must understand and agree on the terms used (definitions); and they must be intelligible and unambiguous. Second, we must accept the premise as true, if it corresponds to our current knowledge of reality. Third, the arguments must be correct. If the judged conclusion(s) follow undeniably from the premises. If all the terms used are clearly understood. If all the premises are valid. If all the arguments are logically correct, then the conclusion must be true.

For example: If one asserts that religious faith must remain private, and never become a matter of secular public policy or discourse, they must define religion. Religion is actually a set of beliefs that explains the Purpose of life? Why does life and humanity exist? It includes a set of faith-based assumptions about the nature of the universe and man's place within it.

Our most fundamental ideological, philosophical and theological convictions, are based on beliefs that are difficult to justify to those who do not share them.

Past and present ideological convictions include: nationalism, fascism, socialism, communism, atheism, progressive-rationalism, and secularism. It is impossible to leave these convictions behind, when we attempt to reason together. Proponents of such ideological views do the very thing they forbid others to do—they cannot leave their religious beliefs behind. *Faith and Reason are Compatible!*

All science begins with "faith or trust" in an idea, to eventually be proven true or false by experimentation. Theology and Science can never be at odds, since God is the author of all creation and every law that governs it. Science and theology is about discovering the Creator. One may never fully understand and comprehend *all* of creation and its laws. If the God exists, then His creation and laws cannot be in conflict. If any theory is proven false in science, then it must be equally false in theology as well.

Reason is a friend of faith; it's a journey towards truth, and the ultimate truth is Love Itself. Good reasoning and valid arguments may not bring one to faith, but bad reasoning and invalid arguments will keep one away from faith. Love is greater than faith. You cannot love that which you do not know. The more we love someone, the more we want to know them. *Reason and faith are true lovers!*

Unfortunately, many of our youth today (and immature adults) say: "Your conclusion seems to be reasonable, but I still don't accept your 'perception' of what's true." They claim all truths are 'relative.' In other words, they insist on following what is false. They will not admit that you're right, no matter how thoroughly you reasoned with them; it becomes a matter of personal pride. *"You're not going to win, even if what you say might be true!"* They decide what's true by their emotions, instead of reason. What can one do in this case? You can only do your best in your dialogue, and then pray for them, and finally leave it to God. *He's ultimately in charge!*

Faith in a proper sense means *trusting* the word of another, when you have no other proof. Belief or trust is clearly *not* certain knowledge; it's *probable* knowledge. Secular trust today is based mostly on the authority of another; it is based on opinions, and fads; that is, "so and so said, or wrote it about it, therefore it must be true."

Science and theology should welcome all questions; it's an essential part of knowledge. The human mind was created so that we may think and question everything. Scientists often learn that they must scrap past theories, methods and processes, and start anew from first principles, and think of new theories, in order to discover truth. Science begins with faith or trust in something not yet proven.

In one of his latest encyclicals, *Fides et Ratio*, the late Pope John Paul II, wrote: "In every human heart there are questions which transcend all differences of culture, nationality, race or religion:

*Who am I? Where do I come from, and where am I going? Why is there evil in the world? What will there be after this life?*"

He continues, "The fundamental harmony between the knowledge of faith and knowledge of philosophy is once again confirmed. Faith asks that its object be understood with the help of reason; and at the summit of its searching, reason acknowledges that it cannot do without what faith presents."

## Faith & Good Works:

**The certainty that divine light gives is greater than that which the light of natural human reason gives. -- St. Thomas Aquinas**

**Faith is a perspective about reality—the refusal to avow the meaninglessness or opacity of the universe.**

## Justification by Faith:

Many Christians believe that when they are "born again," they are "justified," and thus they have an "automatic ticket to heaven." The blood of Christ has saved us, *forever,* they claim based primarily on justification by Christ, as Paul wrote in Rom. 2:13 and in Gal. 2: 15-21. *That's a very significant presumption.* One might ask: who validated their ticket to heaven? These Christians should consider Bible quotations that *directly refute* this justification by faith *alone* presumption: (See Mt 16:27, Mt 19:17, Luke 10:26-28, 2 Cor. 5:10, 11:15, and 1 Pet 1:17). Especially, see John 5:29: "… they that have done good unto the resurrection of life; and they that have done evil, unto the resurrection of damnation." One should also consider Romans 2:6, 13: "Who will render to each one according to his deeds. For the hearers of the law are just in the sight of God, but the doers of the law will be justified."

The reality is that we are constantly tempted and tested and true love is greater than hope and faith alone. Therefore, if an opportunity presents itself to do a good deed for love of neighbor, and one chooses to ignore that opportunity, or do nothing, they have failed the test of true love of Christ. As James 2: 14-17 says: "What will it profit, my brethren, if a man says he has faith, but does not have works? Can the faith save him? ... So faith too, unless it has works is dead in itself."

The truth is that before we die all of us are capable of sin, and Rev. 21:27 says nothing unclean shall enter heaven. There are also degrees of sin (1 John 5:16-17). Some evangelicals' don't agree. They say that all sin is the same. Why then do we have laws against misdemeanors and felonies in our civil and federal court systems, and very different penalties for each offense?

Consider Jesus statement in Matt. 24:13: "*but he who stands firm to the end will be saved,*" that clearly shows that *both* faith and good works are required. More specifically, in the story of the Rich Man (Matt. 19:16-26), Jesus commends the man for his faith and obedience to God's laws. But, Jesus calls him to a higher level of obedience; that is, giving his riches to the poor in order to attain the kingdom of God. He fails this opportunity, this challenging test. (See *Not by Faith Alone,* by Robert A. Sungenis, from Queenship Publishing) for a much deeper insight on this vital issue.

## CHRISTIAN TRADITIONS:

Scripture and tradition are inextricably linked: as "two fonts of the one spring of the fountain of Revelation." Christian Tradition should never contradict Scripture, but rather complements and explains it better. The early Christians leaders preached orally because they didn't have copies of the Bible, most of which was not completed at that time (Matt. 15:3-6, Mark 7:8-13, 4:33, 6:34; John 16:12, 20:30, 21:35). The Bible is not all-inclusive! *It is not a static book*! We can and do learn new insights every time we read it. It is imprudent for Christians to disregard what God has taught so many, throughout these centuries.

Evangelical fundamentalist Christians claim the Bible is the "sole rule of faith" (Sola Scriptura). Everything that one requires to be saved is in Scripture, and nothing should be added or subtracted. They see the Bible as a static document set in stone. However, Sola Scriptura is *not* found in the Bible. Many others see the Bible as the 'living word of God.' The Holy Spirit of God continues working throughout the history of mankind and Christ's Church. John 20:31 tells us that the Gospels help us to believe that Jesus is the Messiah. It does not say Scripture is all that's needed for our salvation (John 21:25). One must realize that Christians before the 4th century, didn't have any accepted Gospel Cannon, and most people couldn't read or write anyway. They all depended on oral communication and traditions of the early Church fathers.

Finally, Paul says in 1 Tim 2:2, "… stand fast, and hold the traditions which you have learned, whether by word or by our Epistle." In addition, Christ said to His apostles, "He who listens to you, listens to me; he who despises you, despises me." (Luke 10:16). And, Jesus Christ said: "Go, therefore, making disciples of all nations." (Mt 28:19). We are reminded by 2 Peter 1:20 that: "no prophecy in Scripture is the subject of private interpretation."

**The Illustrated Jesus through the Centuries** by Jaroslav Pelikan (Yale Univ. Press):

In the decades between the time of the ministry of Jesus and the composition of various Gospels, the memory of what Jesus had said and done, circulated in the form of an oral tradition. The apostle Paul, writing to the congregation at Corinth, about A.D. 55 (twenty years plus after the life of Jesus on earth), reminded them that during his visit a few years before, he had orally "delivered to you as of first importance what I also received" still earlier. Thus perhaps in the forties, concerning the death and resurrection of Jesus (1 Cor. 15:1-7) and the institution of the Lord's Supper (1 Cor. 11:23-26).

Chronologically there was the tradition of the Catholic Church many years before there was any New Testament or a single book of the NT. Many Evangelists ignore this historical fact. As W. Somerset Maugham wrote: *"Tradition is a guide and not a jailer."*

By the time the materials of the oral tradition found their way into written form, they had passed through the life and experience of the (early) Church, which laid claim to the presence of the Holy Spirit of God. It was to the action of that Holy Spirit that Christians would attribute to the composition of the books of the "New Testament," as they began to call it, and before that of the "Old Testament," as they began to describe the Hebrew Bible. Since the apostles believed that the second coming of Jesus might occur during their lifetime, little need existed to write what Jesus taught until it was clear He would not appear during the current generation.

## Sola Scriptura:

Scripture is a 'standard of truth'—even the preeminent one—but not in a sense that rules out the binding authority of authentic Apostolic Tradition and Church teaching. The Bible doesn't teach that Scripture is materially sufficient. In other words, on this view, every true doctrine can be found in the Bible, if only implicitly and indirectly by deduction. But no biblical passage teaches that Scripture is the formal authority or rule of faith in isolation from the Church and Tradition. *Sola scriptura* can't be deduced from implicit passages.

"Word" in Holy Scripture often refers to a proclaimed, oral teaching of prophets or apostles. What the prophets spoke was the Word of God, regardless of whether or not their utterances were recorded later as written Scripture. So for example, we read in Jeremiah: 'For twenty-three years . . . the word of the Lord has come to me and I have spoken to you again and again . . . But you did not listen to me,' declares the Lord. . . . Therefore the Lord Almighty says this: 'Because you have not listened to my words.' (Jer. 25:3, 7-8). When the phrases 'word of God' or 'Word of the Lord' appears in Acts and the Epistles, they refer to *oral preaching*, not to Scripture. For example: 'When you received the Word of God which you heard from us, you accepted it not as the word of men but as what it really is, the Word of God'" (See 1 Thess. 2:13; see also 2 Tim 3:16).

**Tradition Is Infallible and Binding:** If Paul wasn't assuming that, he would have been commanding his followers to adhere to a mistaken doctrine. He writes: "If any one refuses to obey what we say in this letter, note that man, and have nothing to do with him, that he may be ashamed." (2 Thess. 3:14). Take note of those who create dissensions and difficulties, in opposition to the doctrine which you have been taught; avoid them." (Rom. 16:17).

Christians who accept *Sola Scriptura* as their rule of faith appeal to the Bible. If they are asked why one should believe in their teaching rather than another, each will appeal to 'the Bible's clear teaching.' They act as if they have no tradition that guides their own interpretation. This is similar to people on two sides of a constitutional debate both saying, 'We go by what the Constitution says, whereas you don't.' The Constitution, like the Bible, is not sufficient in and of itself to resolve differing interpretations. Judges and courts are necessary, and their decrees are legally binding. Supreme Court rulings cannot be overturned except by future rulings or by Congress. There must be always a final appeal to someone, or another creditable source, that settles the matter. ---Author

## History of the NT (AD)

10-160: Apostolic Fathers early development of the NT;

160-250: Canon of NT discussed by Irenaeus with Origen;

206: Gospels accepted. Revelations by John finally accepted;

250-365: Epistles and Revelation *disputed* in the Eastern Church;

325: Council of Nicaea queries James, 2 Peter, 2 John, 3 John, Jude;

325-339: Council of Carthage. Athanasius first list 27 books of the NT;

328: Church Cannon is closed (approved by all the Church leaders).

> ***Like Scripture, the American Constitution is only useful in practice by the courts and the nine judges who interpret it. Who is the final authority for today's thousands of different Christian Churches? How does one arrive safely on a difficult journey, without a compass, when the ship has so many competing captains? -Author***

## Skeptical Students:

A significant number of students that enter college as Christian believers, graduate as skeptics or unbelievers. Loss of faith is caused by peer-pressure, the secular environment, and most significantly, by skeptical teachers or negative role models. Students often encounter two extreme views that leave them confused and skeptical: radical fundamentalists in the hometown churches, and progressive humanism from secular professors at college. One preaches 'hell and damnation,' and the other teaches them about their absolute right to 'freedom of expression.' Guess who wins that contest?

Peer-pressure is a much stronger force than teacher influences alone, but the invitation to total freedom of expression, while away from home for the first time is too much to resist: 'Mom and dad can no longer tell me what to do, or what not to do. I'm free at last. I'm free to do my own thing; to experiment with drugs, sex, booze and whatever.'

Fanatical fundamental evangelical ministers, or zealot priests, can do more damage to early youthful believers than all of the other factors combined. They typically start by citing the absolute authority of Sacred Scripture; that human reasoning cannot be trusted, and certainly will never lead you to God. They stress that the 'Word' is the infallible book of God; every word is exactly as He revealed it; you must accept all, without questioning.

This dogmatic approach by numerous preachers may convince less educated children and adults over the short-term, but they are *building this belief on a bed of sand*. Sooner or later educated students will see how irrational the hometown preacher was. This dogmatic method is a total turn-off for many of our college bound youth.

On the other hand, those college students that have received a solid foundation in the Christian faith during their early years, by both loving parents and preachers, that are receptive to all questions, will survive their challenging college experience. Actually, they may even be better qualified to help some of their skeptic peers.

In *The Hidden Jesus* by Donald Spoto, he wrote: "Christian faith is, in fact, fundamentally not a matter of the past but of the present. It is an experience of, and a relationship with, someone alive, someone whose existence in the economy of earthly life, the life in and of the flesh—in other words, bodily life as we know it—ceased almost two thousand years ago. Faith proclaims, in light of a mysterious but certain experience, that Jesus of Nazareth is completely transformed, forever altered."

In the OT, faith is rarely mentioned. The word "trust" is used frequently, and verbs like "believe" and "rely" are used to express the right attitude towards God. The classic example is Abraham, whose faith was reckoned as "righteousness" (Gen. 15:6). At the heart of the Christian message is the story of the Cross; Christ's dying to bring salvation. Faith is based on trust, where a believer receives God's good gift of salvation (Acts 16:30-31) and lives in that awareness thereafter (Gal. 2:20; cf. Heb. 11:1).

Faith is the assurance of things hoped for, the conviction of things not seen. (Heb. 11:1) The best examples of faith are Abraham, as revealed in Letter to the Hebrews, and the Virgin Mary: By faith, Abraham obeyed when he was called to go out to a place; and he went out. By faith, he lived as a stranger and pilgrim in the promise land. By faith, Sarah was given to receive the son that was promised. By faith, Abraham offered his only son in sacrifice to God, as *a supreme test* of his faith in the Lord.

By faith, the Blessed Mary welcomes the tidings brought by the Angel Gabriel, believing that *"with God nothing will be impossible"* and so giving her assent: *"Behold I am the handmaid of the Lord; let it be (done) to me according to your word."* (Luke 1:37-38). Unlike most of the apostles, Mary's faith never wavered. She never ceased to believe in the fulfillment of God's word throughout the difficult ordeal of her life. Thus the Church *venerates* Mary as the purest realization of true faith, along with St. Paul.

Faith also depends on grace, a gift of God, a supernatural virtue infused by Him. In faith, the human intellect and will cooperate with divine grace. Faith is certain. It is more certain than all human knowledge because it is founded on the very word of God who cannot lie. To be sure, revealed truths can seem obscure to human reasoning and experience. Though faith is above reason, there can never be any real discrepancy between faith and reason. The act of faith is of its very nature a free act. Therefore, nobody should be forced to embrace the faith, against his/her God-given free will.

Is faith alone sufficient for salvation? Faith is necessary, essential, but not sufficient for salvation. The Lord himself affirms: 'He who believes and is baptized will be saved; but he who does not believe will be condemned' (Mk 16:16). Faith apart from good works is dead, when it is deprived of hope and love. Faith alone does NOT fully unite the believer to Christ and does not make them a living member of His Body. We have faith in many secular professionals in our daily life—doctors, lawyers, teachers, pilots, engineers, political leaders, and stock brokers—shouldn't we therefore have even greater faith in our Creator and Savior, Jesus Christ?

> **Faith is the confidence that a person may "come boldly to the throne of grace," obtain mercy and find grace to help in time of need (Heb. 4:16). Faith is "the substance of things hoped for, the evidence and assurance of things not seen." –Hebrews 11:2-40**

The perception that religion requires faith alone is a serious misconception. Christianity is not just about accepting Creeds—it's about action—*a living faith,* as Abraham demonstrated when he offered his only son to God. The key expression is: If you got the root, show me the fruit. Religion requires trust, and such belief is built on knowledge. For knowledge, we live in an extremely opportune time. The discoveries of the last decades in astronomy, high-energy physics, DNA (codes of life), Intelligent Design (ID), and paleontology, have revolutionized our understanding of our cosmic genesis. They have taken us to the threshold of time, and to the beginnings of all life.

C. S. Lewis said: *"Relying on God has to begin all over again every day, as if nothing had yet been done."* It is the work of a lifetime; an approach toward reality that has to begin daily, for faith, as Paul in the Letter to the Hebrews wrote, *(Faith) is of things unseen—of things imperishable, beyond decay and death.*

"Blessed are those who have not seen and yet have come to believe," Jesus said to his disciple Thomas, who required proof of his Master's triumph over death, proof of His resurrection. "Faith is, then, like a lens through which I gaze out at reality and inward at the life of God quietly breathing within me and making my own breath possible. It is essentially a perspective that refuses to deny that there is ultimate meaning, order and purpose. The meaning, order and purpose may often be unclear; they may appear to shift and change, and they may be articulated differently.

In the final analysis, faith is an attitude about reality that is deeper and more realistic than denial, for it takes with absolute gravity the provisional nature of all human knowing. One who denies the existence of anything transcendent is locked into the poverty of narrow perceptions; those who are open to transcendence are freed from the constraints of that poverty. They are susceptible to surprise. They can be found, and so they find. Source: *The Hidden Jesus* by Donald Spoto

Spoto sums up faith with these poetic words: The object of faith is a place into which one may step, a room one may enter, a power on which one may lean, a love to which one may commit. And faith itself? It is the act of meeting this reality, of building one's life around it. In this regard, one does not really believe in the Bible, but in God Whom it attests. One does not believe in tradition, but in God Who's sustaining love it witnesses. One does not believe in the Church, but in God Whom the Church proclaims. Hence, biblical texts; the writings of saints, mystics and theologians; the formulas of the Church's creeds and doctrines—all of these express in human language the straining and striving toward intimacy by which is meant, in the simplest language, the experience of and the concomitant desire for God. Despite all uncertainties, insecurities and questions, the believer clings fast to God. After all, you can long for and hope for only what you already know, however partially, and have glimpsed, however imperfectly.

## TRADITION AND SCRIPTURE:

Is there any single interpretation of the Bible? Can we know the full truth of what God intended to communicate to us? Is *Sola Scriptura* (the Bible alone) a good method for determining Christian orthodoxy? Do we only trust *our opinions* of what the Bible teaches, 1,200 different languages? Have we reduced Christianity to a pluralistic, intellectual exercise, as opposed to a unified orthodox faith? If this is so, are we saying that the Bible is unreliable, that it does not contain a specific and comprehensive message from God, and that it is not the Sacred Book of a particular Faith?

Why are there are so many disagreements about what the Bible actually teaches? Do we really believe God would make such a great miscalculation? Would God establish a covenant with all mankind through His Son's precious blood, and then put mankind in a situation where they could never agree as to what God really requires of them?

## LIBERATION THEOLOGY

**Vatican II: Focus on "Liberation Theology"**

**Idol worship allowed by the Pope in Catholic Church**

**Same-Sex Marriage is not condemned.**

**Divorcees allowed to receive Holy Communion**

**Homosexually by priests/bishops is acceptable**

**Borders are bad! We are not a Nation without borders**

**U.S. Revitalization need before preaching elsewhere.**

> ➢ Fig. 3* Vatican II Focus on Liberation Theology

Declining U.S. Catholic Statistics:

1958: Sunday Mass Attendance 74%; 2000: 25% attended

1965: 58,000 Priests; 2002: 45,000 Priests.
1965: 49,000 Seminarians;2002: 4,700 Seminarians

1965: 126,000 Adult Baptisms; 2002: 80,000 Adult Baptisms

1965: 352,000 Catholic Marriages: 2002: 256,000 Marriages.
1965: 338 Annulments; 2002: 50,000 Annulments

1965: 1,575 Ordinations to Priesthood; 2002: 450 Ordinations

1965: 180,000 Religious Sisters; 75,000 Sisters (Ave. age 68)

> ➢ Fig. 4* Declining Catholic Trends

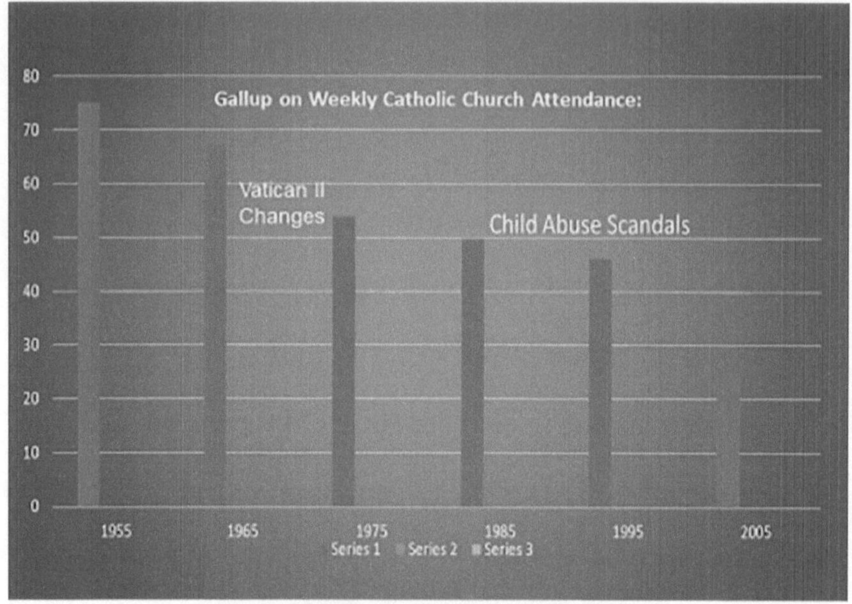


> ➤ **Fig 5* Declining Catholic Trends**

Catholic Christians *cannot* allow "secular radicalism" to invade the Church, such as Black Lives Matter, or "Antifa." The Catholic Church needs stronger participation in the secular political process. (Without ever saying who to vote for).

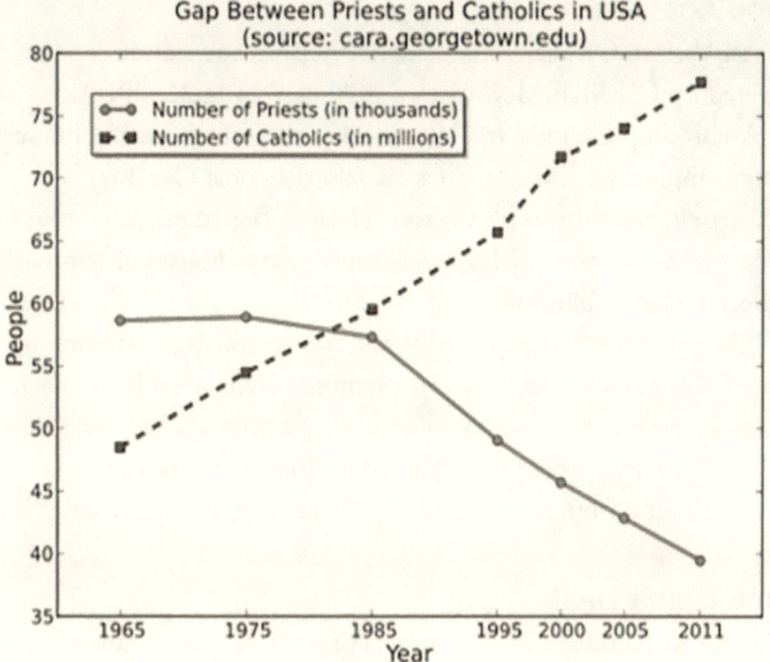



> ➤ **Fig *6** Catholic population vs priests**

## New Catholic Schism

Under the leadership of German Cardinal Reinhard Marx of Munich, the Church in Germany is pursuing a *radical* 'binding synod path' that seeks to dislodge settled Church teaching.

The German Church is pushing a plan in close partnership with the Central Committee of German Catholics, a lay group demanding:

- The ordination of women,
- An end to clerical celibacy,
- The blessing of same-sex unions, and
- Rethinking all Catholic teachings on sexuality.

Next door, the Polish Catholic Church remains traditional and conservative in its teaching, going back to pre-Vatican II practices, which is also in conflict with Pope Francis.

## Pope Accused

Former Vatican Official, retired Archbishop Vigano claims Pope Francis Covered up Cardinal McCarrick Sex Abuses (Aug 26, 2018)

Archbishop Carlo Maria Vigano, wrote a letter accusing Francis of being complicit in covering up accusations against Cardinal Theodore McCarrick. Archbishop Vigano claims Benedict XVI, Francis' predecessor, disciplined McCarrick for his many abuses of seminarians and priests [and children].

"Pope Francis has repeatedly asked for total transparency in the Church," Vigano writes. "He must honestly state when he first learned about the crimes committed by McCarrick, who abused his authority with seminarians and priests [and children]. In any case, the Pope learned about it from me on June 23, 2013 and continued to cover him."

## Pope China Deal

In 2019, Cardinal Parolin, Secretary of State under Pope Francis, signed a "secret" agreement giving control over the appointment of *all* Bishops to the Communists (the United Front of China), under Bishop Fong. They also agreed *not* to permit minor children in Catholic churches or schools.

## Pope Idols:

- Pope participated in services at St. Peter's, where Amazonians and their pagan idols were presented.
- At the end of Synod works, Francis spoke on the pagan idols being displayed at Synod events and *permanently* at altars at the church of Santa Maria, near the Vatican.
- Francis claimed there had not been "idolatry" in worship and display of the pagan idols. He said the pagan idols will be brought to Saint Peter's basilica for the closing ceremony of the Synod.

## Pope Racism Agenda:

Pope Francis and the Vatican have seized on George Floyd's killing and suggested a coordinated messaging strategy aimed at the National Catholic Church that Francis has criticized for its *political and ideological partisanship.*

It was a clear effort to *call out some conservative Catholics* for whom the abortion issue is paramount, while other "life" issues dear to Francis — racism, immigration, the death penalty and poverty — play second fiddle at the ballot box.

## BLM Criticized

July 7, 2020: South African Cardinal Wilfrid Fox Napier (a black man) strongly criticized the Black Lives Matter movement for its "dismantling" of civilizations and cultures.

Napier is archbishop of Durban on the South African coast, tweeted that a " brief study of the founding statement of 'Black Lives Matter' indicates the movement is being hijacked by the interests & parties committed to dismantling the very values, structure & institutions which have over the centuries undergird the best civilizations & cultures!"

"Another crucial test of the authenticity of the Black Lives Matter movement will be its stance vis a vis Planned Parenthood and the Abortion Industry!"

The Illinois Right to Life, Parenthood is a danger to the black community. (*Planned Parenthood founder Margaret Sanger was a racist).*

"According to the U.S. Center for Disease Control (CDC), there have been over 15.5 million abortions performed on African Americans. These Black lives lost to abortion *outnumber* the deaths of Black people due to AIDS, violent crimes, accidents, cancer, and heart disease *combined*."

Bishop Joseph Strickland of Tyler, Texas, also criticized the movement. He talked about the platform of the Black Lives Matter movement, which contains several positions Catholics can in no way support.

"Please educate yourself on this!" He then pointed out that Black Lives Matter's statement of belief mentions two points: "that are contrary to FAITH": Opposing the nuclear family, and Opposing God's plan for sex as a union of male & female. This is DANGEROUS!" Strickland emphatically conclude."

## Funds for Radicals:

CCHD is the official anti-poverty program of the US Conference of Catholic Bishops (USCCB).

WASHINGTON, D.C., July 15, 2020 (Source: LifeSiteNews) — At least eight organizations funded by the Catholic Campaign for Human Development (CCHD) are publicly advocating for the defunding and complete abolition of police departments. Several states which heeded this call have witnessed a dramatic increase in violent crimes.

# Specific Catholic Solutions:

1. Catechism Update Sessions for Parents.

2. More Effective Outreach for Hispanic Families.

3. Civic Support & More Spanish Masses.

4. Deacons Learn Spanish to "Fill the Gaps."

5. Must Teach English & American History.

6. Provide Seminars on the Deception of Socialism.

7. Coach Teens on the Real Meaning of the Bible

8. Focus on Fathers to get Children to Mass.

9. We All Need a "Transcendental Purpose" in Life.

> **Fig 7* Catholic Solutions**

**Proverbs 4:13** *"I guide you in the way of wisdom, and lead you along straight paths… Hold on to [my] instruction, do not let it go; guard it well, for it is your life."*

To be a true follower of Jesus Christ we must live in conformity to His original teaching.

- Catholics need to participate in the secular world and bring traditional Christian values into the discussion.
- It is critical that church leadership take positions on policy issues such as Black Lives Matter, and Radical Liberalism.
- Antifa," is an anti-fascist movement that engages in militant protests and does not shrink from violence. These extreme left members are self-proclaimed "anti-capitalists," and "enemies of the right."

When good people remain silent, evil always triumphs!

Taking a stand against mob violence, *will increase* Christian leadership in the community and bring that influence into the daily lives of all parishioners. ***The church is at a crossroads in its history.***

**Christ's longest prayer in the Gospels was:** ***"Father, I pray that they may be one, even as You and I are One...."***

Does the Bible present us with a comprehensive message or not? And, if it does, can we know it or not? Shouldn't we listen to what early Church Fathers taught about the Bible? If we cannot all share this "knowledge" of what God desires to teach us in the Bible, then we cannot believe in God, Who desires us to be one, unified people (John 17:20-22, 1 Peter 2:9-10), but rather in a God who scatters us, and who does not desire for us to know His truth (1 Tim 2:4).

Some oppose the Catholic Church and Papacy so strongly, that they apparently detest Christian unity. If one disagrees with "Universal Church" teachings, what does one have to give in exchange? God unifies *all* people in love and in truth.

Humans are clearly fallible, and they often disagree with one another on many issues. But God is not so (Isaiah 55:11): *"... my word that goes out from my mouth: it will not return to me empty, but will accomplish what I desire and achieve the purpose for which I sent it."*

So, whom do we trust to interpret the Bible? And how can we know they are trustworthy? What should be our objective standard for interpreting the original apostolic documents, so that we arrive at Christian orthodoxy?

Name any "ancient Christian" who one considers "orthodox." One can perhaps say "Paul," or "Clement of Rome," among others. But some people interpret Paul in different ways, and we must therefore document that some post-apostolic persons interpret Paul the same way we do. Of course, people also disagree about how to interpret the writings of those post-apostolic men. So, we may end in circular logic, and get nowhere!

Both the Scriptures *and* the writings of the early Church Fathers are open to someone's interpretation of them. What is to be the *objective standard*? Since people disagree over what the early Church Fathers taught, do we have to appeal to some even earlier or later source to interpret the church fathers for us? Isn't it absurd to keep appealing to some other source to interpret the apostles' writings for us when we can just read the documents ourselves? *Not at all!* We are *not* experts of Greek and Hebrew, nor do we belong to the era which produced the New Testament. The Church Fathers did, however. That gives them a distinct and significant advantage over us coming along 2000 years later, after the fact of the actual history, and of His Revelations.

The Church Fathers belonged to city-churches which were established by the Apostles themselves. These city-churches possessed customs and traditional understandings which were inherited directly from the Apostles, and which were part of the living experience of those churches (2 Thess. 2:15). Thus, their understanding is superior to ours. Thus, their understanding shouldn't be ignored when considering an "objective standard" for interpreting Scripture.

When the Scriptures say that everyone *must* be Baptized, and we ask if this includes infants, we can turn to each and every one of the Apostolic City-Churches and show that they did indeed baptize infants and young children (2 Thess. 2:15). And, if you object to this, explain why Martin Luther (a believer in *Sola Scriptura*) disagreed when it came to the nature of Baptism? Some teach that it's symbolic, and Luther taught that it was regenerative. So, which does the Bible teach? What makes this interpretation of the Bible any better than Martin Luther? *What is the objective standard for interpreting the Bible?*

According to Tertullian, writing in 199 A.D., "Clement was ordained by St. Peter (*De Praescript.*, xxxii), and St. Jerome tells us that most of the Latin [people] held that Clement was the immediate successor of the Apostle (*De viris illustr.* xv). St. Jerome himself in several other places follows this opinion, but he correctly states that Clement was the *fourth pope*. Clement believed in doctrines, like (a) The Eucharist as Sacrifice, (b) Apostolic succession, and (c) Salvation by *both* faith and good works."

St. Clement taught: "The Apostles received the Gospel for us from the Lord Jesus Christ; and Jesus Christ was sent by God. Christ, therefore, is from God, and the Apostles are from Christ. Both of these *orderly arrangements*, then, are by God's will" (1 Clement). So, Clement sets up a pattern of authoritative succession: God, Jesus, and the Apostles. Then, in the very next line, he says: "Through countryside and city they preached; and they appointed their earliest converts, testing them by the Spirit, *to be the bishops and deacons of FUTURE BELIEVERS.*" What is he teaching here? He sets up the pattern (i.e., God sent Jesus and Jesus sent the Apostles). He THEN says that the Apostles appointed men to be the bishops and deacons of FUTURE BELIEVERS. What does that presuppose? It presupposes that the APOSTLES were the bishops and deacons (servants) of the FIRST BELIEVERS. Therefore, the men whom they appointed SUCCEEDED to their ministries.

**Pope Clement wrote:** "Our Apostles knew through our Lord Jesus Christ that there would be strife for the office of bishop. For this reason, therefore, having received perfect foreknowledge, they appointed those who have already been mentioned, and afterwards added the further provision that, if they should die, other approved men should succeed to their ministry" (1 Clement 44:1-2). "Ye therefore, who laid the foundation of this sedition, *submit yourselves to the presbyters*, and receive correction so as to repent, bending the knees of your hearts. *Learn to be subject, laying aside the proud and arrogant self-confidence of your tongue*" (1 Clement 57).

## CHURCH DOCTRINE:

*Doctrines are not God: they are only a kind of map. But the map is based on the experience of hundreds of people who really were in touch with God. ...If you want to get any further, you must use the map. ...Neither will you get anywhere by looking at maps without going*

> *to sea. Nor will you be very safe if you go to sea without*
> *a map.--C. S. Lewis*

## Banning Mass

According to Cannon Law 213, Bishops do *not* have authority to ban Catholic Mass and the Sacraments. The Church has *never* closed its doors to Christians who need the sacraments in its 2,000-year history. Even during World Wars, and epidemics or pandemics, priests and bishops served the people's needs. (Saint Pope John Paul II, when he was a priest, held secret masses, during the Communist era).

The responsibility to minister to the faithful is entrusted to the priest and bishop's care, in celebrating the Mass and administrating the Sacraments. This *trumps* any order by a superior or secular civil authorities. It is Divine Law.

Bishops must take up their cross--*and carry it.*

Bishops could have planned for Easter Sunday Masses in 2020. There were *practical solutions* to deal with the pandemic. In Florida (and other states), Governors never banned Christian services.

Government is responsible for protecting us physically against our enemies. Bishops are responsible for saving souls—*that is the **primary mission of ALL Bishops!***

**Canon 213 states: "The Christian faithful have the right to receive assistance from the sacred pastors out of the spiritual goods of the Church, especially the word of God and the sacraments."**

## Idols in St. Peter's:

> *Fig 8* * Pictures of Pope with Idols in Church

> *Fig 9* * Pictures of Pope with Idols in Church

## Archbishop Accuses

Archbishop Carlo Maria Vigano, then-Apostolic Nuncio to United States, listens at the United States Conference of Catholic Bishops' annual meeting.

> ➤ *Fig 10* Archbishop Vigano**

Former Vatican Official Claims Pope Francis Covered Up Cardinal McCarrick Sex Abuses

- Former Vatican diplomat Archbishop Carlo Maria Vigano, wrote a letter accusing Francis of being complicit in covering up accusations against Cardinal Theodore McCarrick.

- Archbishop Vigano claims Benedict XVI, Francis' predecessor, disciplined McCarrick for his many abuses of seminarians and priests.

> ➤ *Fig11 * Archbishop Vigano**

## Pope's American Racism Agenda

Pope Francis and the Vatican have seized on George Floyd's killing and suggested a coordinated messaging strategy aimed at the <u>National Catholic Church that Francis has criticized for its *political and ideological partisanship*</u>.

It was a clear effort to *call out some conservative Catholics* for whom the abortion issue is paramount, while other "life" issues dear to Francis — racism, immigration, the death penalty and poverty — play second fiddle at the ballot box.

> ➤ *Fig 12* Pope's Racism Agenda*

Early fathers of the Church, such as St. Clement of Rome and St. Ignatius of Antioch, adhered closely to Scripture and Apostolic preaching without much development of doctrine. In the second and third centuries, two types of apologists arose, traditionalists like Tatiana who rejected philosophy, and others like St. Justin Martyr, who were willing to use Greek speculation in the interests of the faith. Fortunately for the latter, which were in danger of absorption by the dualistic, Hellenized Gnostic heresy, St. Irenaeus urged all to the need of remaining faithful to Church *Traditions, the living depositary of revealed truth.*"

The *high points* of later controversies coincided with the first seven Ecumenical Councils, which profited from both the Alexandrian and Antioch schools in defining the principal dogmas on the *Holy Trinity* and the Person of Christ. Among the Fathers, perhaps no one contributed more to theological development than St. Augustine. He synthesized four centuries of tradition which preceded him, clarified, in many cases solved the most vexing dogmatic questions, and coordinated the ensemble of sacred knowledge which Aquinas and the Scholastics later organized into a system of Christian thought.

In the 8th and 9th centuries, the Carolingian school under Alcuin and Rabanus Maurus began the fusion of sacred and profane culture that became so characteristic of the Middle-Ages.

The "Father of Scholastic Theology" was St. Anselm (1033-1109), archbishop of Canterbury, who was not satisfied with gathering the statements of the fathers on various questions but introduced and stressed the dialectic method. Abelard exploited this rationalistic method to an extreme, which St. Bernard of Clairvaux (1091-1153) balanced along Augustinian lines by placing the faith above rational dialectic. Peter Lombard (1100-1160) carried on the Anselmian tradition. His comprehensive and lucidly arranged *Books of Sentences* were the basic text in all theological schools up to the 17th century.

The 13th century focused on synthesis, which produced the *Summa Theologiae* of Thomas Aquinas, of whom H. Richard Niebuhr says that "he combined without confusing, philosophy and theology, state and church, civic and Christian virtues, natural and divine laws, Christ and culture. Out of these various elements (Aquinas) built a great structure of theoretical and practical wisdom."

Preceding Thomas were speculative writers like Hugh of St. Victor and Alexander of Hales, on whom Aquinas depended at least for his external structure. Following Aquinas was a period of decline, when theology often degenerated into formalism and pomposity, and brought on the discredit of the sacred sciences, which typified so much of the Renaissance.

Under the force of the Reformation and the Council of Trent, theology entered a new phase of orientation. The Protestant emphasis on the Bible and rejection of the Roman primacy, stimulated Catholic theologians to investigate more closely the sources of revelation in Scripture *and* Tradition, to establish the grounds for a rational apologetic in support of the Catholic claims. The first need was met by developing a system of positive theology, whereby the truths professed by Catholic Christianity were sought in the deposit of faith. The Jesuits, led by St. Robert Bellarmine (1542-1621), became the primary advocates of this system, and laid the foundation for fundamental theology, which seeks to prove from history and philosophy the credibility of the religion.

The speculative side of the science began a new era, occasioned by the challenges of Protestantism on almost every position of the Catholic Church. During the twenty years of the Council of Trent (1545-1565), the combined intelligence of Catholicism focused its efforts on defining the "Nature of Grace," the "Sacrifice of the Mass," the "Priesthood," the "Sacramental System" and "Ecclesiastical Authority." Their framework was mainly the *Summa* of St. Thomas, with analysis in all the major schools of thought.

## Early Church Leaders

The Fathers of the Church were the great ancient Christian spiritual thinkers and gifted writers who expounded the faith on the basis of Scripture *and* Tradition. Through these scholars the Church came to terms with the philosophy and culture of the Greco-Roman world, partly by absorption of its sound elements, partly by renunciation of its errors.

In the West the Venerable Bede (died in 735 AD) is sometimes considered the last of the Fathers; but the patristic spirit, Biblical, devotional, and in a general sense Platonic, continued till the rise of Aristotelian scholasticism in the 12th century.

In the East there was no such sharp break, at least not until the end of the Byzantine Empire, after which modern Western influences affected Greek and Russian theology. The massive collection of the Abbé Migne in 383 volumes, *Patrologiae cursus completus*, comprises Latin writers through Innocent III (1216 AD) and Greek writers until the fall of Constantinople (1453 AD).

After the Apostolic Fathers came Justin Martyr and the other apologists, who stated the claims of Christianity in terms of the best thought of the era. Between 180 and 260 AD the foundations of *Greek Theology* were laid by the Alexandria Platonists, Bishops Clement (4th pope) and Origen. In Latin Christian thought the ethical and dogmatic writings of the two great Carthaginians, Tertullian and Cyprian, have a similar importance. After the Council of Nicaea (325 AD) the need for Christian teaching and the exigencies of controversy brought forth an outstanding series of Christian writers.

In the East, the work of Athanasius was followed by the more systematic writing of the Cappadocian's—Basil of Caesarea, his brother Gregory of Nyssa, and their friend Gregory of Nazianzus—and the magnificent preaching of John Chrysostom. Divergent schools of Christology were developed by the Antiochene Theodore of Mopsuestia and the Alexandrine Cyril. The opposing Nestorian and Monophysite heresies looked back to these teachers, respectively, while later Fathers developed the middle way laid down by the Council of Chalcedon (451 AD). Leontius of Byzantium is important in the sixth century, Maximus the Confessor in the seventh, John of Damascus in the eighth.

In the West, classical Latin theology began with Hilary, Ambrose, and Jerome, the translator of the Vulgate Bible. Later developments, all built on the massive work of Augustine (died 430 AD), the great teacher of *salvation by grace* in the fellowship of the Church. Two popes end the traditional series of ancient Latin doctors of the Church—Leo the Great (461 AD), doctor of the *Incarnation*, and Gregory the Great (604 AD) with his pastoral and mystical writings.

## Doctors of the Church:

***Doctor of the Church is bestowed on learned, saintly theologians in the Christian Church. Persons so designated are judged to be great teachers of Christian Doctrine.***

The Eastern Church honors as "Universal Doctors" St. Basil the Great, St. Gregory of Nazianzus, and St. John Chrysostom. The Roman Catholic Church includes St. Athanasius, St. Ambrose, St. Augustine, St. Gregory the Great, and St. Jerome. These are the traditional Greek and Latin doctors of the Church. Since the middle ages, the Roman Catholic Church has conferred this title on about 25 other persons.

Nonetheless, Saint Augustine of Hippo (354-430), and St. Thomas Aquinas (1224-1275), are credited with creating the essential theological foundation for the Church, and Emperor Constantine (285-337) established the political foundation for Christianity. The Holy Spirit of God inspired all.

## Mysticism:

> ***The mystical voyage depends not at all on its being mystical—that is, on it being a departure—but on its motives, skill and constancy of the voyage, and on the grace of God. Departures are all alike; it is the landfall that crowns the voyage.* --C. S. Lewis**

Mysticism implies a relation to mystery, from *mysterium* in Latin, and originally comes from the Greek meaning: *"to keep your mouth shut."* It's a transformation from the world of noise to that of silence, so that one may concentrate on God. So long as we clog our minds with petty ideas based on mere sense perception, it is impossible to discern the Transcendent elements of the divine sphere, God's Creation. In ecstasy, some mystics had a vision of their own liberated and enlightened self— touched indirectly by God.

Different souls have different growth cycles and pathways to God. Mysticism is a religious tendency and desire of the soul toward an intimate union with God. God, enabling them to feel His presence, gives some souls true mystical contemplation.

The mystic's knowledge of God is greater than that acquired through faith and reasoned intellect alone, but less than the final knowledge of the Beatific Vision. Some examples include: Saints Anthony of Padua, Augustine of Hippo, Francis of Assisi, Francis Xavier, Catherine of Siena, Ignatius of Loyola, Jerome, Joan of Arc, John of God and John of the Cross, Peter and Paul, Teresa of Avila, Therese of Lisieux, Vincent de Paul, Julian of Norwich, and Hildegard of Bingen.

## Mediation:

> *Silence also hath a way, words and prayers to convey.*
> *Perhaps in time I shall learn to live in that deep,*
> *consistent and undistracted center of being, where the*
> *will does not intrude, and the sense of time passing has*
> *no power over the imagination.* **–Ralph W. Emerson**

The role of Blessed Mary and the early Martyrs had its effect on the prayer of the Church, as did the emphasis placed by St. Bernard of Clairvaux and St. Francis of Assisi on the role of Christ's humanity. The Eucharist, medieval Mysticism the Protestant Reformation movement, the use of popular devotions, and the contribution of Ignatius of Loyola (1491-1556) founder of the Jesuits, and Francis de Sales, Pierre de Bérulle, among others affected prayer. Modern tendencies include an increased interest in the psychological prerequisites of prayer, simplifications of methods, as in St. Therèsa of Lisieux (1873-97), of the Child Jesus, who wrote *The Story of a Soul*, and the accommodation of public and liturgical prayer to the conditions of contemporary life.

We should always remember what the *primary purpose* of prayer is offering to God our sincere homage and adoration, i.e., recognition of God's supremacy and our complete dependency. Thanksgiving, or gratitude for our God giving us life and our soul. Atonement and confession of our sins, and sorrow for offending God, and appeal to Him for all that contributes to our perfection.

Since we cannot visualize what God looks like, and can only know indirectly who God is by His many works, it can be difficult to pray to God. The mind is limited, imperfect, and thus has to focus on "a person." How can one imagine "absolute truth," and "endless mercy"? How can one "see" what "perfect love" looks like? We need to find symbolic ways of representing God, which in the final analysis, cannot be really represented in human terms.

> *During the day, when we see something beautiful—an*
> *innocent child, a snow covered mountain, a special*

> *seascape, or fantastic sunset—we think about how much greater must be the Creator of such beauty. When we hear majestic music, such as Mozart, Bach or some wondrous human voice singing, we marvel about the God that created such geniuses and human vocal instruments that invigorate our mind and spirit.* ---Author

## DOCTRINES & DOGMAS:

> **My doctrine is not mine**, Jesus said, *but His that sent me.* --John 7:16

The Greek word, *dogmas*, refers to the teaching of Jesus (Matt. 7:28) and later the teaching of his followers. The word was used for Christian doctrine (Acts 2:42), to which believers are to be wholeheartedly committed (Rom. 6:17). It is important to "continue" in the doctrine (II John 1:9) and to be able both to teach it and to refute those who oppose it (Titus 1:9). Dogma is a doctrine related *only to faith and morals* that is taught by the pope and bishops. However, the Church is not merely a legalistic corporation, with laws that have no life in them.

Development of Doctrine: Increased in understanding by means of teaching of the Holy Spirit, by prayer, by study and reflection. (Eph. 4:13-16; Gal. 4:4) For example: The Divinity of Christ was not defined until the Council of Nicaea in 325 AD. The dogma about the two natures of Christ (God and man) was not defined until the council of Chalcielon in 451 AD. The New Testament Canon wasn't finalized until 397 AD. Also, the definition Original Sin was slowly developed. St. Augustine had a major impact on its explanation.

### The Resurrection:

All the saints that died for Christ were fools; today's two billion Christians are wasting their time praying; the Bible and the 2,100 year history of the Church is all a work of fiction—if Jesus did not rise on Easter Sunday (see *Resurrection*). It's a *historical fact* that Pontius Pilate was Governor of Judea during 26 to 36 AD, and to be crucified was a Roman (not Jewish) common form of punishment at that time. The inscription that was placed over Jesus head was recently found by archeologists, and it names Him: "King of the Jew" (INRI). All of the Apostles, except John, were frightened after the death of Jesus, and then they boldly proclaimed Him the Son of God, after the Resurrection. Blessed Mary, Mother of Jesus Christ, Mary Magdalene and eleven apostles saw and talked to the risen Christ. St. Thomas didn't believe, until he put his hand into Jesus' side and touched His wounds. Over five hundred people later conversed with and ate with the risen Christ (much of which has been documented by the Church). Finally, eleven of the apostles suffered and died because they totally believed in the risen Christ.

## CHRISTIAN PRINCIPLES:

> *People will not die for what is false, but only for what is true. Eleven of the twelve apostles died a martyr's death because they firmly believed in the risen Christ. Doctrine is not a matter of inventing new beliefs; it's about explaining existing beliefs. The Church constantly moves forward toward the fullness of God's Divine Truths.* **--Author**

Gregory the Great said: "With the progress of the times the knowledge of the spiritual fathers increased; for, in the science of God, Moses was more instructed than Abraham, the prophets more than Moses, the apostles more than prophets." In 2 Tim 3:14, the disciple says: "It is for thee to hold fast to doctrine handed on to thee, the charge committed to thee."

## Communion of Saints:

We address public judges as "your honor," and are commanded by God to honor our mothers and fathers, and Christian teachers (1 Tim. 5:17), and fellow Christians (1 Cor. 12:12-26), and all governing authorities. Saints are not only believed to be alive [spiritually], and thoroughly able to influence and assist us, as Revelations clearly testifies. The veneration of saints can be found in Paul, where the apostle exhorts his followers to "imitate" him (1 Cor. 4:16; Phil. 3:17; Thess. 3:7-9). Also to "honor the heroes of the faith" (Hew. 6:12, and chapter 11). Relics also have a biblical basis: The bones of Elisha were so spiritually powerfully that they caused a dead man to come back to life (2 Kings 13:20-21). St. Peter's shadow healed a sick man (Acts 5:15-16). Also, see Acts 19:11-12, regarding relics touched by Paul.

## Development of Doctrine:

John H. Newman resolved the most pressing difficulty in his mind regarding acceptance of the Church of Rome (when he was about to convert from the Anglican Church): had Rome adhered to or swayed from primitive (original) Christianity? He concluded that "of all existing systems, the present communion of Rome is the nearest approximation in fact to the Church of the (original) fathers."

Newman, moreover, presented not only a conclusion, he documented it with the results of a serious study in which he contrasted the teachings of Roman Catholicism in the 19th century with those of the early Christian Church. The fact and the necessity of development comprise only a part of Newman's efforts in this treatise; for the process by which religious ideas genuinely develop forms an even greater selection of his study. In the course of time, an idea may not become a development; it may become "a corruption." Development denotes life; "corruption, on the contrary, is the breaking up of life, preparing for its termination." Newman distinguishes *seven tests*, to judge development or corruption of (any Christian Church) doctrine:

1. **Preservation of Type:** This the first test offered, and it is based on the analogy of physical growth. Animals remain within a species throughout their lives. Birds cannot become fish; the child does not degenerate into a brute. Continuity of species is maintained. Ideas also developed with subsequent thought and reflection; they take on new meaning in a crucible of experience. As Christians reflected upon and sought to apply Christ's doctrine to their everyday lives, their faith took on new dimensions without undergoing radical change. Newman details the history of the church in the first six centuries with the entire problems attendant upon an organization seeking the fullest possible growth in order to fulfill the aims of its Founder (Christ). When viewed "in its age" or "in its youth," the organization has maintained identity. In her grown and development, "such a religion brought it to the Church is not unlike the Christianity of the fifth or sixth centuries."

2. **Doctrines Evolve from Principles:** The sciences of mathematics and physics, by analogy, have developed basic permanent principals from which, in the course of study and experimentation, much new knowledge has been derived. Although principles are largely general or abstract, their application leads to discovery of many new facts. As a second test, continuity of principles causes religious doctrine to grow and develop: Christ enunciated the basic common principles. His church enlarges upon them as they are applied to future generations. The Church of Rome, faithful to Christ's principles, as the primacy of faith over reason, the preference of the mystical to the literal interpretation of Scripture, the necessity to defend and to transmit the defined doctrine—has stood firm, especially against heresies; has maintained the principles and has put them in vigorous operation.

3. **Power of Assimilation:** Life grows by absorbing or assimilating into its own substance external materials, as is done in a matter of food. In the intellectual order, many an idea has resulted from

a similar process. In seeking to attract converts, yet desiring to have them feel "at home" in a newly adopted religious faith, the Church has frequently employed many customs and usage of (earlier) pagan rites, such as incense, candles, festival days. Rather than obliterate, the church has "Christianized" them.

4. **Logical Sequence:** The fourth test, logical sequence, is development simply by affirming any progress of the mind from one judgment to another. If the original teaching is correct, doctrines logically deduced from it represent logical conclusions. To demonstrate this test in the churches history, Newman confines himself to examples of doctrine, which considers sin after baptism. The necessity of remitting sin after baptism and of rendering possible reconciliation with God was given serious thought in the early Church. In her desire to fulfill Christ's hope for the salvation of sinners and to carry out its authority of "binding and loosing," the church adopted systems of penance and satisfaction for sin.

5. **Anticipation of its Future:** Considers an idea that has life (and) has the power to develop under favorable circumstances with the passage of time. The development of a doctrine, therefore, may be vague and slow; but the workings of logical minds will eventually bring a doctrine to its fullest development. Such would be the case, Newman asserts, with doctrines relating to relics, to the Cult of Saints and Angels, and to the Blessed Virgin.

6. **Conservative Action upon its Past:** The words of Christ, "I have not come to destroy, but to fulfill," provide the basis for the sixth test. Heresies, he points out, have made it necessary for the church to reaffirm previously declared doctrine, as for example, in the Incarnation, the Trinity, and the Blessed Virgin; but it did so with the purpose of clarification and of placing a proper emphasis on various aspects of the specific doctrine.

7. **Chronic Vigor:** Duration or longstanding characterizes the faithful development of an idea. Heresies or corruption of doctrine, as are the peculiarities of any country, customs

of a race, or the temporary response to the changing tides of opinion; they cannot maintain their vigor with the passage of time and with divergent cultures. An examination of doctrine in themselves and in comparison with other religious faiths leads him to conclude: after violent exertion men are exhausted and fall asleep; they awake the same as before, refreshed by the temporary cessation of their activity; and such has been the slumber and the restoration of the Church. She pauses in her course, and almost suspends her functions; she rises again, and she is herself once more; all things are in their place and ready for action. Doctrine is where it was, and usage, and precedence, and principal, and policy; there may be changes, but they are consolidations or adaptations; all is unequivocal and determinate, with an identity which there is no disputing.

## What is Sin?

***The really tragic thing is the loss of the sense of sin, which is the loss of a true sense of God. Views on what is right and wrong should not change with time, or the culture of any particular age or society.***

One must have free will and control over an evil act before it can be considered *actual sin*. Sin is not merely a human development flaw, or psychological weakness, some mistake, or the necessary consequence of an inadequate social structure. Sin is an abuse of the freedom (free will) that God gives to all created humans and angels so that they are capable of loving Him and one another. The evil of grave or mortal sin is the rejection of God and opposition to His teachings. In general, sin is anything that fails to conform to the law of God. Sin is conveyed by a variety of expressions like missing the mark, or rebelling against God, or going astray, or transgressing, and stumbling.

Basically, "sin is the transgression of the law" (1 John 3:4), referring to an inward attitude as well as to the breaking of the written commandments of God given to Moses. All people commit sin (I Kings 8:46; Rom. 3:23). To deny that we have sinned is to make God a liar (I John 1:10); all His dealings with humanity are on the basis that we are all sinners. But the blood of Jesus cleanses all from sin (I John 1:7).

Sin is an offense against reason, truth, and right conscious. Sin is a failure in genuine love for God and neighbor, caused by perverse attachment to certain possessions (objects or persons). It wounds the nature of man and injures human solidarity. It has been defined as "an utterance, a deed, or a desire contrary to the eternal law." St. Augustine, in *Contra Faustrum*, said: "Sin is thus love of oneself even to the contempt of God."

Sins can be distinguished according to their objects, as can every human act; or according to the virtues they oppose, by excess or defect; or according to commandments they violate. They can also be classed according to whether they concern God, neighbor, or oneself; they can be divided into spiritual and carnal sins, or again as sins in thought, word, deed, or omission. The root of sin is in the heart of man, in his free will, according to the teaching of the Lord: *"For out of the heart come evil thoughts, murder, adultery, fornication, theft, false witness, slander. These are what defile a man. But in the heart also resides charity, the source of good and pure works, which sin wounds."*

For sin to be mortal three conditions must together be met: The object of the sin must be a *grave matter*, committed with *full knowledge*, and *deliberate consent* (personal choice). Sin is an utterance, a deed, or a desire contrary to reason and the eternal law of God. The type and gravity of the sin depends on its object. Grave sins are defined by the Ten Commandments God gave to Moses, and also includes: anger, blasphemy, envy, hatred, malice, murder, neglect of Sabbath obligations, sins against faith, hope, and charity, and disrespect for mother and father.

Sins of the flesh include: adultery, carousing, drunkenness, envy, fornication, idolatry, impurity, licentiousness, slander, sorcery, theft, and false witness. Unintentional ignorance can diminish or even remove the immutability of any grave offense. No one is considered to be completely ignorant of the principles of moral law, which is written in the conscience of everyone.

## Original Sin:

*An analogy of Original Sin is that of a spiritual gene defect in parents (Adam and Eve) that is transmitted to their descendants. Thus all offspring inherited this primeval abnormality, as is the case in the biological gene transmission. --Author*

Satan, the first good and former preeminent angel, created by God, through his *free choice*, radically and irrevocably rejected God and His reign, thus creating serious (mortal) sin (see Isaiah). There is no repentance for angels after their fall, just as there is no repentance for humans after death. The gravest of these works by Satan was the untruthful deceitful seduction that led Adam and Eve to disobey God. It's a great mystery that providence should permit (allow) diabolical activity, but we can know that in everything God works for good with those who love Him (Rom 8:28).

Each day we see the horrible toll that humanity is capable of exacting against itself. The denial that we are capable of evil is the surest sign of evil's existence. It is too easy to blame it all on Satan. We cannot excuse ourselves by always claiming: the devil made me do it! Nonetheless, you will find that the closer you come to God the more Satan battles to jeopardize your relationship with Him. The "Evil One" is very powerful—you cannot fight him by yourself. The grace of God is absolutely essential to support you in this endless mortal battle on earth.

## Greatest Sin:

*If I am a proud man, then, as long as there is one man in the whole world more powerful, or richer, or cleverer than I, he is my rival and my enemy. ... Pride is the*

> ***chief cause of misery in every nation and every family
> since the world began. (Pride) is purely spiritual:
> consequently it is far more subtle and deadly. For pride
> is spiritual cancer: it eats up the very possibility of love,
> or contentment, or even common sense. --C. S. Lewis***

A very important difference exists between the sin of Satan and the Original sin of Adam and Eve: The great sin of Satan was based on arrogance, conceit, and self-love or pride, which is unforgivable. However, the Original sin of man and woman was disobedience and involved seduction and temptation by Satan, which was nevertheless grievous sin. God, knowing the circumstances of this sin of Adam and Eve, in His *perfect justice and mercy*, made the Immaculate Conception, Mary, full of grace, the "Second Eve," and sent His only begotten Son as the "Second Adam." Blessed Mary, by her absolute faith in God, freely accepted her solemn and venerable role. Jesus Christ redeemed us by His victory over sin, thereby giving humanity once again, another most *wonderful* opportunity, for salvation and eternal happiness with God.

By our first parents' sin, the devil has acquired significant domination over man, which makes our life a constant battle, although man still retains free will to choose good or evil. The reason Christ suffered and experienced death is that God loved us so much, that in order to destroy the works of the devil, and save us from original sin, and demonstrate that our resurrection is real, He sent His only son (John 3:16).

As the Apostle said: "Then as one man's trespass led to condemnation for all men, so one man's (Christ) act of righteousness leads to acquittal and life for all men." The new Adam (Christ) makes amends superabundantly by His death, for the disobedience of the first Adam. St. Thomas Aquinas wrote: "There is nothing to prevent human nature's being raised up to something greater, even after sin; God permits evil in order to draw forth some greater good."

Saint Augustine of Hippo was one of the greatest sinners, before he was baptized, and after became one of the greatest saints of the Church. His mother Monica prayed for his conversion for nineteen years. We all, without exception, have the potential to become saints—or devils. Someone once said: The greatest tragedy in life is not dying a saint.

## Greatest Virtue:

*Charity is the only gift that is a portion of thyself.* --Ralph W. Emerson

A work of charity can be false; that is, a selfish act, to "feel good." A real work of charity is to serve, to know, and to love another human being. Perfect Charity is what Christ did for all humanity—each and every individual person—on His Cross: He also gave comfort to the daughters of Jerusalem; He gave assurance to the penitent thief; He gave His mother into the care of John; He forgave the Jews and soldiers that killed Him; Finally, He gave up His Spirit to His Father.

St. Paul spoke of charity when he wrote in I Corinthians: Though I speak with the tongues of men and of angels, and have not charity, I am become as sounding brass, or a tinkling cymbal. And though I have the gift of prophecy, and understand all mysteries, and all knowledge; and though I have all faith, so that I could remove mountains, and have not charity, I am nothing. And though I bestow all my goods to feed the poor, and though I give my body to be burned, and have not charity, it profits me nothing. Charity never fails: but whether there be prophesies, they shall fail; whether there are tongues, they shall cease; whether there be knowledge, it shall vanish away. For we know in part, and we prophesy in part. But when that which is perfect is come, then that which is in part shall be done away. When I was a child, I spoke as a child, I understood as a child, I thought as a child: but when I became a man, I put away childish things. For now we see through a glass, darkly; but then face to face: now I know in part; but then shall I know even as also I am known. And now abideth faith, hope, charity, these three; but the greatest of these is charity.

## Grace:

*Left to our own inclination, preference, appetite, we would probably choose evil.*

In *The Imitation of Christ*, Thomas a 'Kempis wrote: "If you knew the whole Bible by heart, and all the teachings of philosophers, how could this help you, without the grace and love of God?"

According to St. Augustine, grace is an "interior master," that perfects human nature, which includes free will as a significant part of its essence. On the other hand, true freedom is *not* merely indeterminism, or freedom *from* all influences, but rather self-determination, self-realization, self-perfection; freedom *for* the realization of our end and destiny. Grace and free will are two sides of the same coin. Grace is a gift from God. St. Augustine declared: The preparation of man for the reception of grace is already a work of grace. This latter is needed to arouse and sustain our collaboration in justification through faith, and in sanctification through charity. God brings to completion in us what He has begun, since He who completes His work by cooperating with our will began by working so that we might will it.

There are two kinds of grace, *actual* and *sanctifying* grace. Actual grace is that transient gift with support from God that enlightens the mind and strengthens the will to do what is good (such as acts of charity), and avoid evil. Grace is a gift from God; it is receiving His favor; it is the power that makes salvation possible. Orthodox Christian theology asserts that all people deserve punishment due to original sin, but through the sacrifice of Jesus Christ on the Cross, those who trust in Him and are baptized in Christ receive the grace of salvation, which cannot be otherwise earned. Catholics, Lutherans and Episcopalians believe that *sanctifying grace* is also obtained through the sacraments: Baptism, Confirmation, Holy Eucharist, Confession (Reconciliation with God), Extreme Unction (blessing of the dying), Holy Orders, and Matrimony. Many Christians also believe that God gives us grace "wherever He wills," and that reading Scriptures can awaken faith, which enables anyone to receive grace.

However, we must be willingly to cooperate with the grace given by God. For example, many saints have performed great acts of charity because of the graces received. A possible analogy is where someone gives you a gift, and you naturally have the choice to accept it with thanks, or you may throw it away. Thus grace can be discarded or destroyed by grave (mortal) sin. Any person who dies in "a state of grace," is saved. St. Peter wrote, "(with grace) we become partakers of the divine nature."

Grace is "God's favor," which no one can earn. The Greek words for joy and grace are related; *grace causes joy*. In Christian understanding, nothing brings joy like the Good News Gospels of what God has done in Christ to bring us salvation. "For by grace are you saved through faith; and not of yourselves: it is the gift of God" (Eph. 2:8-9). God's grace brings about qualities of conduct in the believer (II Cor. 9:8; 12:9; Eph. 4:7). Grace came to be used as a prayer ("grace to you") in Christian greeting at the beginning and end of the New Testament Letters (II Cor. 1:2; 13-14).

Grace is participation in the life of God. Grace allows us to respond to God's call to become His adopted sons and daughters, partakers of His Divine Nature and eternal life. Baptism allows the Holy Spirit into souls to heal them of original sin and to sanctify them. It allows Christians to participate in the grace of Christ. This vocation to eternal life is supernatural. It depends entirely on God's gratuitous initiative, for He alone can reveal and give Himself. It surpasses the power of human intellect and will, and that of every creature. God the Father, Jesus insisted, embraces all who desire Him, and even, in a mysterious way, those who do not. Regardless of race, gender, or any other characteristic, *every person is the target of God's grace.*

No one should claim that they committed grave crimes or grave sins, because God didn't give them sufficient grace. Grace precedes, prepares, and elicits the free response of man and woman. It calls for us to cooperate with grace in freedom. Each day and night we are in constant dialogue within ourselves. Our mind and conscience and free will work that way: it's constantly thinking about past, present or future events, and carefully weighing alternative choices. It is as if we have two minds within one body: the good and the evil sides of us. It's a delicate balancing act as to which way one finally decides.

Augustine asserts: Indeed we also work, but we are only collaborating with God who works, for His mercy has gone before us. It has gone before us so that we may be healed, and follows us so that once healed, we may be given life. It goes before us so that we may be called, and follows us so that we may be glorified. It goes before us so that we may live devoutly, and follows us so that we may always live with God: for without Him we can do nothing. God's free initiative demands man's free response, for God has created man in His image by conferring on him, along with freedom, the power to know Him and love Him. The soul only enters freely into the communion of love. God immediately touches and directly moves the heart of man. He has placed in man a longing for the truth and goodness that only He can satisfy.

"The promises of 'eternal life' respond, beyond all hope, to this desire: If at the end of your good works, You rested on the seventh day, it was to foretell by the voice of Your book that at the end of our works, which are indeed 'very good' since You have given them to us, we shall also rest in You on the Sabbath of eternal life."

## Marriage:

> **The Bible says that marriage was instituted by God and is a permanent bond (Gen. 2: 18-24; Matt 19: 56). It states that: sex between two consenting males is a sin against nature (Rom 1: 26-27). Adultery is a grave (mortal) sin (Matt 5: 32).**

The marriage covenant (a vow), by which a *man and woman* form with each other an intimate communion of life and love, has been founded and endowed with its own special laws by the Creator. By its very nature it is ordered for the good of the couple, as well as to the generation and education of the children. Christ raised marriage between the baptized to the dignity of a Sacrament. Unity, indissolubility, and willingness or openness to fertility, are essential to any sacramental marriage. (Gen 2:24)

On June 19, 2015 our nation took a great blow. In an unprecedented display of judicial activism, five Supreme Court Justices imposed their will on the American people. On this day the Supreme Court declared that all 50 states *must redefine marriage.* Nothing in the Constitution requires the Court to interject itself into our democratic debate among citizens about marriage policy. This was not the Supreme Court's decision to make.

Some Christians attend pre-Cana classes (required by all Catholics), to learn the purpose of the Beautiful and Holy Sacrament of Marriage, and the moral obligations of the couples before and after marriage—and then, ignore everything they learned and promised, and have sex before they are married. Thus, they cheapen the relationship before starting out in life together. More importantly, they commit this grave sin of fornication (unless they confessed it before being married) against God.

Same sex unions and polygamy is *incompatible and unnatural* with the unity of marriage between one man and woman. The refusal of fertility between healthy couples turns married life away from its "supreme gift," the child. Today, too many couples (assuming they are physically, mentally and psychologically ready to have children) are essentially selfish by refusing to have children because they don't want to "interrupt a career" or take on the responsibility required. In Northern Europe today, about 80% of all children are born out of wedlock. How can unmarried couples really bond together for life, and effectively teach their children Christian principles?

The Christian home is the place where children receive the first proclamation of the faith. For this reason the family home is called "the domestic church," a community of grace, prayer, and a school of human virtues, and of true Christian charity.

One shouldn't consent to the bond of marriage with preconditions, as if it is simply some kind of legalistic business contract. Preconditions such as property right agreements, to not have children, among other specific elements, are unnatural and selfish because it focuses on me, instead of us. It puts limits on total sharing between the partners in the union of marriage. Research shows that the major factors leading to divorce are financial, emotional, sexual, incompatibility, among other reasons.

Marriage is a contract between two parties, where both give their solemn vows of matrimony and fidelity. In the recent past (which still exists in some cultures today, such as India and Moslem countries) marriage is arranged by the parents based on family relationships as well as for financial gain. True love, if it didn't exist at first, sometimes develops over time, especially after the parties have children—that 'wonderful glue' that binds them together.

Too many of today's young adults are afraid of any commitments. As a result, they frequently have sex before marriage (if they ever get married). They don't fully realize that such acts of 'fornication' are grave sins.

## Divorce:

Divorce was originally permitted under Greek, Roman, Jewish, Islamic laws, and the Eastern Orthodox Church. Talmudic law allowed Jewish men and women to obtain divorces on grounds of adultery and desertion. Early Roman law permitted divorce by mutual consent. The Roman Catholic Church departed from the practice of ancient societies and other religions in prohibiting divorce. In medieval Europe, the Catholic Church regarded marriage as a "sacred contract" that could only be broken by the death of one of the partners, which still remains true today.

Under church law, there were only two ways to escape from a miserable or abusive marriage: A judicial separation, in which a church court might allow a husband and wife to live apart, without remarrying during the other's lifetime, or an annulment on grounds that the marriage violated church rules, such as those prohibiting the marriage of close kin. Annulment means that a valid marriage based on free choice, blessed by God, *never really existed.* For example, if one of the parties was not baptized, and/or was forced to marry under duress, and/or one spouse refuses to have children, then annulment will likely be approved by the Church.

The medieval Church absolute ban on divorce was broken during the Protestant Reformation, when nearly all Protestant rulers legalized divorce with remarriage in cases of adultery or another serious rupture of the marital bond, such as willful desertion. Protestant Reformers found biblical justification for divorce with remarriage (in Romans 7:2 and Deuteronomy 22:20-21), and denounced the Catholic practice of judicial separation, claiming that it encouraged adultery and resulted in illegitimate children.

Protestant theologians viewed marriage as a contractual relationship that could be dissolved if one of the spouses violated any fundamental marital duties. Many Protestant thinkers rejected the Catholic doctrine that "marriage existed for the sole purpose of bearing children" (*corrected* in the new Catechism of the Catholic Church). They argued that a Christian marriage should provide mutual support, sexual pleasure, companionship, and the bearing of children. According to the staunchest Protestant proponents of legal divorce, like the English poet John Milton, divorce should therefore be allowed on grounds of incompatibility.

In England, where divorce remained largely illegal, despite the infamous King Henry VIII case, the most common way for poor people to end an unhappy marriage was desertion. The normal way of ending an unhappy marriage among the middle and upper classes was by a deed of private separation, an agreement drawn up by attorneys dividing the family's property and setting out the custody support for any children. The very rich and powerful might petition Parliament for a private act of divorce, but only after they had obtained a judicial separation from an Ecclesiastical court with bishops as judges.

By the mid 1990's, *over half of all marriages* in the United States and more than a third of those in Great Britain would end in divorce—double the rate of the early 1960's and triple that of the early 1950's. A principal reason for this increase was a shift in the family's economic roles. In the past, the family was not merely a natural unit; it was an interdependent economic system that required the cooperation of both husband and wife, as on the family farm. By the mid-20th century most middle-class and upper-class families had one wage earner, the husband, and large numbers of women married without acquiring the skills required to enable them to support themselves should the need arise. This changed during the 1960's and 1970's, when increasing numbers of women began earning college degrees and established themselves in professions, giving them the economic leverage to be self-supporting, and leave unhappy marriages.

A major shift in cultural values has also contributed to the increased frequency of divorce. During the 20th century, the expectations of personal, emotional, and sexual fulfillment that spouses brought to marriage have risen, and cohabitation and out-of-wedlock births were more socially acceptable in many countries. Divorce among Catholics in the U.S. has increased to about 26%, according to the National Opinion Research Center (NORC) General Social Survey. Divorce rates in America increased to 1,150,000 or 4.3 per 1000 population. That's half the total number of marriages (2,344,000). About 75% of all divorced Americans ultimately remarry.

## Heaven & Hell:

> *It's not a place to which we go—it is a state of being we enter. It's another dimension—a spiritual universe where we can see and know The Creator, in all His wonder and glory.* ---**Author**

Heaven is the abode of God (I Kings 8:30) and of the angels (Mark 13:32); believers will be there in due course (I Pet. 1:4). The New Testament uses striking imagery to bring out the wonder and loveliness of heaven (Rev. 21:21). Heaven means eternal joy in the presence of God. It is Christ-centric. It is where we experience the splendor, glory and magnificence of the Son within the Holy Trinity.

Heaven is not merely the absence of pain, tears and death. It can only be imagined and defined in human terms, using vague metaphors. Imagine perceiving Absolute Beauty, Infinite Power and the Wonder of Perfect Love, which is God. Think of heaven as the prospect of knowing the ultimate meaning of the entire work of, and reason for creation, and of the purpose of salvation. Understanding the marvelous ways by which Divine Providence led everything to its final end—*all in perfect peace and harmony.*

Hell already exists here on earth. Just consider the great evil of terrorism, the killing of the unborn (especially late-term abortions), and the immense suffering on this planet. Hell may be an eternal fire, but the truly painful attribute of hell will be isolation from God.

Cain's punishment for murdering Abel was the withdrawal of God's presence: "Cain said: My punishment is greater than I can bear. …From they face I shall be hid." (Gen. 4:13, 14). Jesus Christ warned people much more about Hell (90 times), than of Heaven.

## Happiness & Joy:

> *One of the hardest lessons to learn is that we don't have the power to make anyone happy, or to save them spiritually.* ---**Author**

While there may be someone who can provide words of comfort at the right time, that person cannot rescue us. No matter how much we love or care for another, *we can't do it for them.* They must ultimately help themselves. Happiness is a fleeting, temporary human condition on this earth, like eating a good meal, or having sex. Joy is within the mind and soul; and is much deeper and longer lasting. Real joy can only be found through sacrifice and suffering. Have you ever met anyone who did not experience grieve or suffering? Suffering and death comes with the total human package, called life. Each of us must pick up and shoulder our cross.

## Beatitude:

> *Though we travel the world to find the beautiful, we must carry it with us or we find it not. He whom has learned to see the beautiful in due order and succession, when he comes toward the end, will perceive a universe of wondrous beauty; not growing and decaying, not waxing and waning; nor fair from one point of view and foul from another; but beauty absolute, separate, simple, and everlasting (God).* -Ralph W. Emerson:

The Gospels uses several expressions to characterize the Beatitude to which God calls man and woman: the coming of the kingdom of God (MT 4: 17); the vision of God, "Blessed are the pure in heart, for they shall see God." (MT 5: 8): and "… entering into the joy of the Lord." (MT 25: 21-23). Beatitude makes us "partakers of the divine nature" and eternal life (2 Peter 1: 4). True happiness is not found in riches or well-being, in human fame or power, or in any human achievement—however beneficial it may be—such as science, technology, and arts, or indeed in any creature, but in God alone, the source of every goodness, and of "Love Itself."

## Education:

> *The most gifted minds, when they are ill-educated, can become pre-eminently evil.* --Ralph W. Emerson.

> *Give a man a fish and you feed him for a day. Teach a man to fish and you feed him for a lifetime.* --Chinese **Proverb**

Democracy cannot function in a poorly educated and ill-informed society. While many of the demonic expressions of Atheistic Humanism were defeated in World War II and the Cold War, lots of 'intellectual and moral toxins' still remain. For example, the less educated Moslem masses in Palestine elected terrorist leaders to run the country in 2006. Lebanon Muslims voted for Hezbollah (a terrorist group) to be part of that government. What's the result so far? Chaos for them! Europe and the Americas are not immune from these poison toxins of socialism and dictatorships. Consider some of the characters that were actually elected to high office in Russia (ex-KBG chief Putin), Spain (an extreme Socialist), Venezuela (Chavez, a communist). In America we almost elected Gore, who spoke in Egypt against American interests. We almost elected many other unqualified, corrupt, and what one might consider, some really weird characters.

The Dalai Lama says: If we wish to bring about a more compassionate—and therefore fairer society—it is essential that we educate our children to be responsible, caring human beings. The human mind ('lo') is both the source, and properly directed, the solution to all our problems. … When we bring up our children to have knowledge without compassion, their attitude toward others is likely to be a mixture of envy of those in positions above them, aggressive competitiveness toward their peers, and scorn for those less fortunate. This leads to a propensity toward greed, presumption, excess, and, very quickly, to loss of happiness. Education is much more than a matter of imparting the knowledge and skills by which narrow goals are achieved. It is also about opening the child's eyes to the needs and rights of others.

The preamble to the *Declaration of Independence* referred to 'Nature and Natures' God, and ends 'with a firm reliance on the protection of Divine Providence.' God is in our Constitution, and the Congress begins each day with a prayer. The U.S. dollar says, 'In God We Trust.' Yet, our public education system which began as Christian schools has become secular if not anti-Christian, where group prayers are no longer permitted.

According to a recent *Gallop Poll* of over 1,000 Americans, about 45% Catholics and 48% Protestants said they attend religious services weekly. Yet, if you look around during Sunday services in almost any place of worship, you will find fewer teenagers or young adults in attendance. In *Young Adult Catholics*, author Dean Hoge says, that

[only] about 30% of today's young adults remain religiously active during their teenage years and by age 20 plus. What happens to the other 70%? More than half continue to *think* of themselves as Christians but become 'religiously inactive,' and *nearly half never return to any church*. This lack of faith and interest in anything spiritual happens when they leave home and enter the secular world of work or college. The other 30% usually come back when they are about 25 years or older, and/or get married and have children.

You don't plant flowers in your garden, and then hope that the soil is rich enough and it will rain. You cultivate the garden and water the flowers, until the roots have fully developed. Children resemble beautiful flowers, of every type and variety, and they need nourishment in the faith, until their roots have been fully established. It is not sufficient to give our children a few dozen hours of religious instruction, and then let them fade-away, in the glare and competition of today's media-intensive world. Academic skills alone are not sufficient—the whole child must be educated. Most students are ignorant about the Bible; are taught five days a week that God is a myth; and are not equipped to defend their faith against the poison of macro-evolutionism; and are vulnerable from liberal professors and peers when they enter college, away from home.

If there has been no agreement on what to teach young people about their religion, it's not the fault of the children. Significantly, it's the young people who are (in many cases) more informed about their religion—recent Christian college graduates—are also among the most committed to the church and among the least disposed to accept the rote dictates of any authority. Part of the solution is for the government to give families a choice in selecting schools, and a tax break to pay for it. Many are for Pro-Choice. Why not 'Pro-Education' as well?


## Religions:

> *Religion is the sum-total of revealed truths, teachings and laws (Doctrines and Dogmas), which regulate the Divine worship of God.*

Christianity is not merely a body of doctrines and dogmas—but a personal experience of Jesus Christ. The study of God is poetry for the heart, mind and spirit. Religion is a moral virtue that inspires one to give to God the worship that is *His due*. Since God is the Supreme Creator and Ruler of the universe and provider of all that is good, it is *our duty* to honor, obey, love and thank God.

By Revelation in the Gospels, *and* human reasoning, we can know God and His Creation. During our short lifetime we must continually search and 'seek the truth' about God.

Ultimately the whole purpose of religion is [to glorify God, and] to facilitate love, compassion, patience, tolerance, humility, forgiveness. If we neglect these, changing our religion will be of no help. ... Such a believer is no better off than a patient with some fatal illness who merely reads a medical treatise but fails to undertake the treatment prescribed. This then is my true religion, my simple faith of love and compassion. In this sense, there is no need for temple or church, or mosque or synagogue, no need for complicated philosophy, doctrines, or dogma. Our own heart, our own mind, is the temple. The doctrine is compassion and love for others and respect for their rights and dignity, no matter who or what they are: ultimately these are all we need.

Christians, Jews and Moslems should teach the same message of love, compassion, forgiveness, spirituality, and mutual respect. *They clearly don't!* Many Christians believe that since John's Gospel says: the way to the Father is through the Son; it's the only way! In other words, all non-Christian religions are worthless. We believe what John really means is: *Jesus Christ shall be the final judge of all.* Thus, we should accept that there are multiple paths to truth. It's like climbing a mountain that has many dangerous turns and chasms. One needs an experienced guide to reach the peak at the top, safely. Of course, the best guide of all is the Gospels of Jesus Christ.

## Faith & Reason Key Points:

- o Faith is a daily process, *a journey of wonder!*
- o Faith is forceful, and is filled at times with questions. The questions are about reality, the desire to understand our universe much deeper, and the Creator Himself.
- o Scripture and tradition are inextricably linked: as two fonts of the one spring of the fountain of Revelation.
- o Christian Tradition should never contradict Scripture, but rather it complements and explains it better.
- o Doctrine is not a matter of inventing new beliefs; it's about explaining (existing) beliefs.
- o Doctrines of the Church are a kind of map, based on the experience of theology authorities, some of whom were in touch with God.
- o The Fathers of the Church were the great Christian spiritual thinkers and gifted writers who expounded the faith on the basis of Scripture *and* Tradition.
- o Mysticism originally comes from the Greek meaning: *"to keep your mouth shut."*
- o Mysticism is a transformation from the world of noise to that of silence, so that one may concentrate on God.
- o So long as we clog our minds with petty ideas based on mere sense perception, it is impossible to discern the Transcendent elements of the divine sphere, God's Creation.
- o Eleven of the twelve apostles died a martyr's death because they firmly believed in the risen Christ.
- o Views on what is right and wrong (morality) should not change with time, circumstance, or the culture of any particular age, or society.
- o Real works of charity is to serve, to know, and to love another human person.
- o If you knew the whole Bible by heart, and all the teachings of philosophers, how could this help you, without the grace and love of God?

o   Marriage is a covenant (a vow), by which a *man and woman* form with each other an intimate communion of life and love. By its very nature it is ordered for the good of the couple, as well as to the generation and education of the children.

o   Heaven is eternal joy in the presence of God. It is Christ-centric.

o   Christians, Jews and Moslems should teach the same message of love, compassion, forgiveness, spirituality, and mutual respect.

# VII. Theological Truths

*Theology is the Science of God. It is derived from the Greek words, Theos (God) and logos (study).*

Theology was used in the third century BC to describe a reasoned analysis of the deity. Plato in the *Republic* and Aristotle in his *Metaphysics,* called Homer, Hesiod, and Orpheus theologians, because they determined the genealogies and attributes of the gods.

## Early History (BCE):

2,500 Canaanite tribes occupy Palestine.

2,100 Abraham is Father of the Jews, and (later) the Christians

1,700 Famine causes Hebrews relocation to Egypt.

1,200 Moses frees Hebrews from slavery in Egypt.

1,100 Hebrews established the Kingdom of Israel in Palestine.

1,000 King David succeeded by King Solomon.

900 Assyrians in control of Judea.

750 Rome established by Romulus & Remus.

586 Temple in Jerusalem destroyed by Nebuchadnezzar II.

540 Persian Empire conquers Babylonia, Palestine, Egypt.

510 Roman Republic founded.

387 Plato establishes Academy in Athens.

335 Aristotle establishes Academy in Athens.

334 Alexander the Great controls most of the Near-East.

200 Dead Sea Scrolls first produced.

150 Rome expands after Third Punic War.

49 Civil War in Rome (46-49).

46 Julian calendar established (365 days per year).
44 Julius Caesar assassinated.
37 Herod King of Judea.
27 Octavian is Roman Emperor Augustus.
3-4 Jesus Christ is born.
30AD Death and Resurrection of Jesus Christ.

With the accession of Christianity, *theology* came to mean what its etymology suggested, and was defined by St. Augustine as "reasoning or discourse about the divinity." St. Thomas Aquinas (1225-1274) defended theology as a science, because it investigates the contents of belief by means of reason, enlightened by faith, in order to acquire a deeper understanding of revelation. By the end of the 13th century, theology was applied to the whole body of revealed truth and gradually replaced its rival synonyms.

There are four major divisions of theology:

1.  Dogmatic (eternal truths),
2.  Ascetic (explicit truths),
3.  Moral (virtuous truths),
4.  Mystical (obscure truths).

We may identify four areas of theology further as:

1.  Biblical (Scripture studies);
2.  Historical (history of the church);
3.  Systematic (beliefs and ethics); and
4.  Practical (preaching, teaching, and worshiping).

In *The Divine Mystery of God*, St. Augustine wrote: "Oh Lord my God, how deep is the abyss of your secret being, and how far away from understanding are the consequences of my sins. Help me. Cleanse my eyes and let me rejoice in your light. Surely my Lord, if there was a mind of such knowledge and fore-knowledge that all things past and all future things were clearly known to it, as a familiar song is known to me, such a mind would be marvelous beyond all measure. Everyone seeing it would be silent in awe. A mind that knew everything that was and will be. To such a mind nothing would be hidden of ages past or yet to come.

"You my Lord are the Creator of souls and mind's, and the creator of the universe. Far more marvelously, far more mysterious do you know things ... In the beginning you knew the heavens and the earth, without any element of change of your knowledge. And in the same way, in the beginning you created the heavens and the earth, without any element of change of your action. Let him who understands it and him who does not, praise you together. For you my Lord, are the highest, and the humble of heart are where you dwell. You lift up those who are cast down, and they do not fall that cling to you at that high ledge. Oh God through thy today's pass all tomorrow's, and become all yesterday's. But to you, neither has been or shall be, have any meaning. There is no tomorrow and there is no yesterday, for to you, all things simply are."

## Personal Choice:

Pascal was the 17th century genius, philosopher, mathematician, mechanical computer inventor, and author. He was also the "first modern" to concede that, in this new scientific and industrial age, *belief in God could only be a matter of personal choice.* Faith, he insisted, was not a rational assent based on common sense. It was a gamble. It was impossible to prove that God exists, but equally impossible for human reason to disprove His existence: *"We are incapable of knowing either what (God) is or whether He is ... Reason cannot decide the question. Infinite chaos separates us. At the far end of this infinite distance a coin is being spun which will come down heads or tails. How will you wager?"*

In 1654, Pascal had a mystical religious experience one night that lasted about two hours, which revealed to him that his faith had been too remote and academic. Pascal's presumable pessimism in this wager question must be countered by his firm belief that once the wager is made, God reveals Himself to anyone who seeks Him. Pascal writes that God would say: *"You would not seek me, if you had not already found me."*

Faith by definition is not an intellectual certainty; it's a leap into darkness, and that experience brings forth enlightenment to those who are willing to accept such a wager. In other words, one has to surrender completely to God. See *Pascal's Pensees* (his thoughts), his critical arguments against extremism at that time, which was published in 1669. The key point is this: *What do you have to lose?*

> **God is a mystery beyond words: If you thought you understood God, it would not be God. God told Moses, "I Am, Who I Am."**

God cannot be summed up in one word or a human expression since the Divine Reality is inexhaustible. We cannot experience God objectively or scientifically alone—but we can experience Him personally. **The Revelation God makes within each of us is personal.**

Every life is linked at every stage to the lives of its genetic predecessors, from Adam and Eve to the present, and is also linked to every other life—by virtue of the unity of the universe. Humans invented the metaphor of "past, present, and future" to cope with our need to measure and communicate our experiences on earth. We understand fragments of our experiences by measuring them in time and space. Past experiences are understood by reflection from memory. Belief, hope, and intuition anticipate the future.

> **God 'sees' everything as the present. Past events that seem dead to us are still alive and current to Him, as if they just happened, in His Universal Present.**

In *The Hidden Jesus*, Donald Spoto writes: "For God, with God, there is no time. God does not 'see' the past, 'observe' the present, or 'know' the future, as if He were in a cosmic movie theater as the sole spectator, watching all time un-spool before Him—but knows the whole plot and each line of dialogue in advance."

## CREATOR SIX PROVES:

> **Thomas Aquinas wrote in Summa Theologica: The
> nature of each thing is shown by its operation. Now
> the proper operation of man is to understand; since he
> (she) surpasses all other animals. ...**

Man must therefore derive his species from that which is the principle of this operation. But the species of anything is derived from its form. It follows, therefore, that the intellectual principle is the proper form of man (woman). A soul is a spiritual being. As such it cannot be too dependent upon matter (or energy, which is the other form of matter). Since that is true, it follows that it [soul] need not be destroyed with the destruction of the body. (It has been proven that matter cannot be destroyed; it is simply converted into energy). Since it is not subject to dissolution, the soul is said to be intrinsically and naturally immortal.

In the *Summa Theologica*, St. Thomas Aquinas in the 13th century concluded that mortals *can* attempt to postulate the qualities of God, and "reasonable proofs," which summarized as follows:

1. **Change:** We cannot deny that there is change everywhere in the universe. Change is the process of reducing something (being) from potentiality to actuality. Nothing can change itself; it's the *principle of causality*. There has to be a prime mover, the cause of all change. The first mover must be *immutable* (unchangeable), otherwise it would need (another) prime mover to change.

2. **Efficient cause:** The cause rather than its effect, which is motion. Everything that happens proceeds from a cause; this is undeniable. We don't know the details a priori of the cause or structure of the world and universe, but we know that every change has a cause. Nothing can be the efficient cause of itself. Thus, we must ultimately come to *"The Cause"* that is uncaused, which is responsible for all the other causes we see operating.

3. **Necessity:** There must exist something the existence of which is necessarily is caused by another. We cannot but postulate the existence of some *Being* having of itself its own necessity … causing in others their necessity.

4. **Goodness:** Our world and universe contains various degrees of goodness, and evil. Nothing in our natural human experience is considered "perfect goodness." Any person lacking in some good, that only share in goodness, that are not perfect goodness in itself, do not contain their reason for goodness in themselves. Any lack of goodness implies a reference to another, a comparison to someone outside of itself. Therefore, we must come to one, who is Perfect Goodness, Total Being, Absolute Intelligibility, having every possible Perfection.

5. **Order and Intelligence:** Everything in the universe and world has order; and follows the Natural Laws and [astonishing] constants that govern it. Order is the potency [force] toward action. Potentiality exists only in reference to actuality. Things cannot act for an end, unless there is an intelligence guiding them [towards that end].

6. **Transcendent Being:** Things and humans cannot be foreordained; i.e., ordained before they happen, unless somewhere they are ordained to happen. Thus, we must come to a *Transcendent Being* who is directing and providing the foreordination of all things, but not subject to the causality of an end.

God is Supreme Being, Pure Goodness, Pure Act, the Uncaused Cause, Necessary Being, Infinite Intellect, Transcendent, and Divine Love, who gave His only begotten Son for our salvation. Each of these individual arguments should be suitable and sufficient to demonstrate His existence and qualities. In addition, the Gospels demonstrates the existence of our very personal God.

## Who Is God?

> ***Who is God is the wrong question! It is not so much what God is, as what God does. You cannot perceive God directly; you can see God's aftereffects. Jewish theology is not about the nature of God; it's about the will of God.* --Rabbi Harold Kushner**

We have to ascent to a reality within ourselves, into the deepest recesses of our mind and soul to experience God. Knowledge of the divine is fundamentally *intuitive*, and not possible by our reasoning processes *alone*. Our soul must recollect the simplicity it has forgotten and return to its true self. God does not force Himself on us. Yet, He will come to meet and guide us by His grace, if we ask Him through prayer. (Rom. 1:20)

We can know God Directly: by our Faith and Trust in His revealed Word, the Gospels. Indirectly, by His Good and Wondrous works, on earth and in the universe. Internally, by our Consciousness, that makes us cognizant of our inner self. And by our Conscience, that inner light that always tells us morally what is good or evil.

Without God there are no truths, there is no reason for the existence of the universe, no explanation for why we exist, no morality, no justice, no mercy, no compassion, and finally, no love. God is spirit, and can take on any form He desires. Since we cannot know God's essence we can clearly say what God *is not*:

He is not an object that has shape, dimension, or measurable.
He is not any other-being, or "three separate Gods."
He is not living in Paradise, filled with human expressions.
He is not a tyrant, forcing us to do anything, against our will.
He is not playing dice with the universe, said Albert Einstein.
He is not the exclusive God of any person, race, tribe, or nation.

Astronomer Hugh Ross explains in *Imagining the Designer*, "that it is impossible to impose any limit on either the power or intelligence of a Transcendent Creator. ...Think for a minute of being outside of time [and space] and the limitations of gravity and other natural forces. Our natural laws would have no power over Him, since He would be in complete control of them. And, being outside time, He would know everything: past-present-future."

> ***Since God is everywhere, within and outside our known universe, He is nowhere in particular, because to be somewhere, He would have to not be somewhere else, which is not possible for God not to be. --Author.***

> ***The Spirit of God is like a "Universal Sea" that is continually ebbing and flowing, sustaining all life. Humans are 'sponges' (biological receptors with antenna) in this mighty sea. The Spirit of God is not somewhere—He is everywhere—He is the Wondrous Sea. We only have to open our hearts (unclog our sponges), to tune-into God, to know His unlimited love, to absorb more of His grace. If we have faith in the ebb and flow of this Mighty Sea, and trust where the current takes us, we will then experience God. --Author***

God is *not* amenable to scientific verification, because He is not a measurable 'object.' Can sincere seekers of truth determine why poetry, art, music, and love make us blissful? Would scientific researchers want to live *without* these *subjective truths*?' Look at the wonder of humanity, of nature, of the universe, with its billions of galaxies and stars, and fantastic order. How much greater must be its Creator.

In his book *Super force*, Paul Davies, one of the leading theoretical physicists in the world, writes: ***"The laws that enable the universe to come into being spontaneously seem themselves to be the product of exceedingly ingenious design. If physics is the product of design, the universe must have a purpose, and the evidence of modern physics suggests strongly to me that the purpose included us."***

A person, group, exclusive creed, or religious belief cannot limit Omnipresent and Omnipotent God. He is not exclusive—but inclusive. All paths to God may be valid, provided they are based on love for the One Eternal God. Catholics, Protestants, Jews and Muslims *do not have a monopoly on God.* This is not about preaching 'Universalism.' God does not desire orthodox prayers, or rituals alone. He wants our burning love. The truest path to God is the teachings of Jesus Christ in the Gospels.

## Scripture on God:

Acts 10:37-43: That word, (I say), you know, which was published throughout all Judea, and began from Galilee, after the baptism which John preached. How God anointed Jesus of Nazareth with the Holy Ghost (Spirit) and with power: who went about doing good, healing all that were oppressed of the devil; for God was with him. And we are witnesses of all things which he did both in the land of the Jews, and in Jerusalem, whom they slew and hanged on a tree. Him God raised up on the third day, and showed him openly; not to all the people, but unto witnesses chosen before of God, (even) to us, who did eat and drink with him after he rose from the dead. And he commanded us to preach unto the people, and to testify that it is he which was ordained of God (to be) the Judge of quick and dead.

> ***According to St. Augustine, God created the universe without any movement [or effort]: "Let there be light."***

All creatures move to maintain life which requires them to (1) search for food, (2) locate water, (3) avoid predators and danger, and (4) find mates in order to breed and reproduce. What if we could obtain these four needs, without much movement? When humans are *not* actively seeking these four essentials of life, thinking becomes their *primary activity.* Thinking and contemplating does not require movement. Movement and effort is a distraction which disrupts thinking.

In a more perfect world, where one does not have to avoid danger, can easily obtain food and water and sex partners, more creativity would likely take place. Throughout history, those persons and societies which were well-off, and could afford servants to handle most of their needs, gave us some of the best works of literature, revolutionary ideas and inventions to serve humanity.

The key question is: How can one minimize unnecessary movement and distractions, and thereby enjoy more creativity and perhaps a more meaningful life? First, one has to change their daily habits, by avoiding most audio/video pollution. This can be partly accomplished by shunning unnecessary cellphone calls, and limiting TV programming, that is senseless or worthless. One must also control their daily activities; and don't let insignificant, valueless events control them; and spend more of their precious time reading good books, and thinking about how one might have a more productive, meaningful, and spiritual life.

## What is Love?

> *An object of love and thought moves others, without being moved. It produces motion by being loved, and what it moves, moves all things in the universe. --R. W. Emerson*

There are four kinds of love, defined by C. S. Lewis, in *The Four Loves*:

1. **Affection** includes love of home and village or city, where one grew up. It includes love of man for his dog and other creatures; love of nature, and love of the universe and all of God's Creation.
2. **Friendship** is the least jealous of loves. Two friends are pleased to be joined by a third or fourth friend.
3. **Eros** is sexual pleasure between a man and woman. Eros is about the beloved. Without Eros none of us would have been born. However, sexuality may happen without Eros.
4. **Charity** is unselfish love, which gives of itself without expecting anything in return. Charity is when a person gives his life for

another, as was the perfect example of Jesus Christ suffering and dying on the cross to save us sinners.

Within these loves, there are three significant activities:

**Gift-Love** is the Divine Love of God. The Father gives all to the Son; the Son gives Himself fully to the Father and Holy Spirit. The Son gives Himself to the world, and gives the world (in Himself) back to the Father and Holy Spirit. Gift-love wants to give comfort, protection and joy to others, willingly, benevolently.

**Need-Love** expresses our fragile human condition. We are born helpless and need love from our parents. The infant child especially needs the love of the mother (gift love). As we mature we need love from others, physically, emotionally, and intellectually. This is the love that sighs, "I cannot live without him or her." This love cries to God from our poverty, and longs to serve Him.

**Appreciative Love** is when we rejoice and give thanks for the Gift-Love that is received. It is gratitude for the love our parents gave us, and it is also love of family. It is love of the deeds that our ancestors did to establish this country, its freedoms, and those who died to protect them; it includes love of the nation.

> *Need-love cries to God from our poverty; Gift-love longs to serve, or even to suffer for God; Appreciative-love says: 'We give thanks to thee for thy great glory.' Need-love of woman [says] 'I cannot live without her'; Gift-love longs to give her happiness, comfort, protection—if possible, wealth; Appreciative-love holds its breath and is silent, rejoices that such wonder should exist even if it [is] not for him, will not be wholly dejected by losing her, would rather have it so than never to have seen her at all.* **C. S. Lewis**

> *Why do we experience bliss when we're in love? Because we feel whole once again. With true love, one finds peace and tranquility: the music is more melodious; food tastes better; the aroma of flowers is everywhere; sunrises and sunsets are more beautiful. These basic things in life are perceived so differently— when there's true love. Love always implies free will, and with love comes freedom, and with freedom comes responsibility. When you are in love, you eventually come to the realization that you want something much more, besides one another—quite a different kind of love --God's Love. --Author*

We are much more than the sum of the parts of our bodies? Our true essence is something greater than any X-ray scan can detect? The love that's inside each of us is a vital part of us, although you cannot see it, or feel it, nor sense it, unless you're willing to share it with someone. Yet, it's more real than anything you can see or touch in the universe. To love is to will what's good for another. Only goodness should be loved. Love demands indissolubility, fidelity, faithfulness in definitive mutual giving.

## Love of Neighbor:

> *It is immortals, whom we joke with, work with, marry, snub, and exploit—immortal horrors or everlasting splendors. --C. S. Lewis*

The language used in the Jewish Torah (Leviticus 19:18), and Gospels (Matthew 5:43-48), the 'Golden Rule,' raises serious and complex questions. The verse ends with the admonition, "And you shall love your neighbor as yourself."

Is it love of neighbor who is a Jew, Moslem or a Christian? Is it love of countryman, or all human beings? What is meant by 'love' in this context? How can anyone be commanded to love? What is meant by 'as yourself?' Is it possible to love anyone to the degree that one loves oneself? What if one doesn't love oneself? Whose life comes first in any life and death situation, saving yourself and family, or someone else?

These are very interesting and complex questions. Maybe this is an 'ideal' that should not be taken literally. How can God expect us to love a child molester, a mass-murderer, or a terrorist, who kills the innocent? Should we accept Hillel's (Shabbat 31a) negative interpretation of the verse, "What is hateful unto you do not do to your neighbor," to be correct? If one cannot love a neighbor, they should at least do nothing to them that they would not like done to themselves. Also, God clearly cannot expect us to love Satan, or what is obviously evil, but rather, only love what is good.

## Forgiveness:

> *Those who hate you don't win unless you hate them—*
> *and then you destroy yourself.* **–President Richard Nixon**

Many people think that forgiving our enemies, means pretending or acting like they are not so bad after all, when it is quite clear that *they are very bad indeed.* Christianity teaches us to hate the sin, but not the sinner. How can you hate what someone did, and not hate the person? The answer is that there is one person to whom you have been doing this to, all your life—namely, yourself. However much you might hate your own conceit, pride, or selfishness, among other "bad acts," you continue to love yourself.

> *Ask yourself this question: whatever evil someone did to you, is it really deserving of eternal punishment in hell? We think the answer is maybe, sometimes; it all depends on the specifics of the evil act. If someone who hurts you and repents, but doesn't ask for forgiveness, do you forgive them? Perhaps! Leave it to Christ to judge them. The practical truth is that hate damages one, mentally, physically and spiritually.* **–Author**

Christian theology stresses the importance of love because God has revealed that He is Love (1 John 4:8, 16). Love is both what God is and what he has done. God always acts in love. Human love is a transitive reality, and requires a subject. In the Bible, love is described as personal and selfless, desiring the best for other Christians. Such as God's love in sending His Son to die on the cross to save all sinners (Rom. 5:8; John 3:16; I John 4:10). Christians are to be known by their love God and others (John 13:34-35). Their love is not to be like the love of the world (Luke 6:32, 35). Love is best seen in the will, in action, by what we do, in our compassion and commitment to those around us. Jesus said that only two commands are needed to govern our lives: love of God and love of neighbor. If you love your neighbor, all the other commandments are thus observed.

Christ's message was not about exclusion—but of *inclusion* of all people in the coming kingdom of God. This message, however, carried many moral implications: repentance was essential, that God cherishes repentant sinners. That the world of military empires must give way to a world of peace. This was not too different from the message of former Hebrew prophets, but it was preached with *a sense of urgency*. Jesus' extraordinary daring, in moving from the prophetic and teaching role to that of Messiah, sealed his fate but showed his total commitment to *action—not just words*.

There is a great deal, especially in the Synoptic Gospels (three similar books by three different -Author), to enable us to see Jesus as a thoroughly Jewish teacher. Both the similarity to the Jewish dream and the unique elements of his teaching as seen in Jesus' emphasis upon what he called: "the kingdom of God." Jesus declared that the kingdom was now at hand and that it was both present and future. He taught that men should "seek it first," before food or clothing, but that a change of perspective akin to that of a "new birth" was imperative. The kingdom was not man's achievement. It is God's gift. Yet men were to strive to accept this gift and enter it.

The very name "Jesus Christ" current among his earliest followers shows that he did eventually (though not at first) claim to be the

Messiah, as indeed the Gospels state unequivocally in the incident of the *Salutation* (Mark 9). By claiming this name, he meant to convey what his hearers understood by it: otherwise, he would have been misleading them. The other, which Jesus often used himself, was "Son of Man." Some have seen in it a reference to the Book of Daniel in which one "like a son of man" came "with the clouds of heaven. ... And to him was given dominion and glory and kingdom, that all peoples, nations, and languages should serve him; ...an everlasting dominion which shall not pass away." Others have believed that Jesus meant to identify himself with men, as being one of them, to serve them. One of the New Testament writers declared: "he had to be made like his brethren in every respect; for because he himself has suffered and has been tempted, he is able to help those who are tempted."

The New Testament accounts affirm that Jesus was God. Yet the three Synoptic Gospels never put this statement into Jesus' own mouth. On the contrary, he makes several statements inconsistent with such a view, for example, "Why do you ask me about what is good? There is [only] one who is good. If you would enter life, keep the commandments" (Matthew 19:17).

Only the Gospel of John, in which Jesus has been divested of all Jewish and Pharisaic characteristics, portrays him as *openly claiming Divinity*. The opening verses of the Gospel of John identify Jesus with the Word or *Logos*, a term much used in Greek philosophy and in Philo to express the power of God by which he created an ordered universe. What is unique is the assertion that: *"The Word of God became flesh and dwelt among us, full of grace and truth."* This means that the man Jesus was the *Incarnation* of the creative power of God, by which the universe came into being.

Somewhat similarly, in what is called *The Epistle to the Hebrews,* written about 90 AD, the statement is made that God "has spoken to us by a Son, whom he appointed the heir of all things, through whom also he created the world. He reflects the glory of God and bears the very stamp of his nature, upholding the universe by the Word of His power. When He had made purification for (our) sins, he sat down at the right hand of the Majesty on high."

What is probably an earlier letter, that of Paul to the Philippians, declares that: "Christ Jesus, who, though he was in the form of God, did not count equality with God a thing to be grasped, but emptied himself, taking the form of a servant, being born in the likeness of men. And being found in human form he humbled himself and became obedient unto death, even death on a cross."

In the New Testament Jesus is also called "the lamb," a reference to the lambs slain in the Temple in Jerusalem on behalf of men's sins. He is also called the "high priest," mediating between God and men, "the Son of God," "the Alpha and Omega (first and last)." The total picture is that Jesus is a Divine sacrifice, whose death enables men to escape from the human condition and find salvation.

## Why Christ Died

Obviously, this is a great mystery, which by definition, humans cannot fully understand the Divine Mercy and Love of God, which consists of *a perfect union* between and within the Holy Trinity. (See Deut. 24:29 and Isaiah 55:8-9).

St. Paul says, Christ Jesus put aside His "divinity" to show us (ultimate) *human* love. Christ demonstrates "perfect human love," wherein a person gives his/her life for others. St. Paul further reminds us that Christ *not only* laid down His life for those He loved, Christ also gave His life for *all* [future] sinners. Still, no person or religious group took His life from Him. Jesus Christ was always in total control, and gave His life *willingly* for all humanity (Jews, Christians, Moslems, Hindus, atheists and agnostics).

It was the high priests, the Sadducees that conspired to kill Jesus Christ, *not* the common Jewish people, and *not* the Father. The Sadducees provoked the Romans into killing Christ because they were afraid of losing their political power over the Jewish people.

Jesus Christ accepted death—by His *free will*—and died to abolish original sin, for those who trusted in Him, to *confirm* His Fathers' immense love for us, and to demonstrate that eternal life exists. The only requirement was "trust." How many Jews and Gentiles accepted His offer of forgiveness? How many Christians will accept His gift in the 21st century? Christ's final words were: ***"Father, forgive them for they know not what they do."***

## Resurrection of Christ:

> ***Resurrection is the raising and transformation of a person who has died. Resuscitation, in contrast, is the bringing back people to this life after they have left it; the raising of the son of the widow of Nain (Luke 7:11-15), and Lazarus (1 John 11), who would ultimately die once again.***

## Evidence of the Resurrection:

Again, from *The Usefulness of Chaos* by John Farrell: What about the resurrection of the carpenter from Nazareth? Isn't this completely beyond the pale of science? Not if we are careful to weigh the evidence, which can be found in the pages of the Gospels: "The primary evidence must come from the New Testament," he said, "and in particular from the gospels. In assessing that evidence, I wish to be scrupulous and take advantage of critical historical inquiry. A realistic assessment of that past will recognize there is no automatic or algorithmic procedure to which it can be reduced. Judgments are called for, just as they are in science itself."

During the last century, many biblical scholars began to doubt the historicity of Jesus' Resurrection, primarily on the seemingly conflicting accounts in all four of the canonical gospels: Who really saw him first? When? And was he even buried in the tomb described in the gospels? On careful consideration, however, this kind of computer analysis approach to the historicity of the gospels hardly seems enough reason to deny the accounts of the First Easter.

In the century of relativity and quantum theory, can we still hang on to the shirttails of David Hume's old skepticism and doubt the occurrence of a miracle merely because it seems to violate natural laws? For if we are to claim the resurrection stories are legendary, we are faced with very startling anomalies. "In the perplexing variety of these stories there is one element unexplained and consistent. And it is this: that it was difficult to recognize the risen Jesus . . . this would be a strange message to recur in stories that were merely made up. It seems likely to us, on the contrary, that this difficulty in recognizing the risen lord is the kernel of a genuine historical reminiscence. For this is not the retelling of a story of a resuscitated corpse."

Women serving as first eyewitnesses would have actually caused embarrassment for the early church because of the low social status of women, at that time. Accordingly, the author of Mark's Gospel would have never included this unless they really were the first witnesses. Still, about five hundred eyewitnesses reported that they saw the risen Christ, besides the eleven apostles, Mary, the mother of Jesus, and Mary Magdalene. Finally, all the apostles, except John, were martyred for their belief in the Resurrection of Christ. These men and women would never have suffered torture and horrifying death for what they knew was false. *They willingly died for their belief in the certain truth of the Risen Christ.*

**Without the Resurrection of Christ, there would be no salvation, no Christianity. Faith—without action, without Love—is meaningless (Rom 10:9). [For] Satan also knows God and His Son, Jesus Christ.**

## FUNDAMENTALISM:

**Fanatical fundamentalism and the literal interpretation of the Christian Bible, and the Islamic Koran, is inappropriate, makes Christianity and Islam teachings vulnerable to future scientific knowledge, and thus unnecessarily confuses many of those who would otherwise be faithful.**

As early as 415 AD, St. Augustine warned, the Church against such Biblical Literalism, which is quoted, in part, as follows: Usually, even a non-Christian knows something about the earth, the heavens (universe, etc.)., and the other elements of the world, ... and this knowledge he holds to as being certain from reason and experience. Now, it is a disgraceful and dangerous thing for an infidel to hear a Christian, presumably giving the meaning of Holy Scripture, *talking nonsense* on these topics; and we should take all means to prevent such an embarrassing situation, in which people show the vast ignorance in a Christian and laugh it to scorn.

The shame is not so much that an ignorant individual is derided, but that people outside the household of faith think our sacred writers held such opinions, and to the great loss of those for whose salvation we toil, the writers of Scripture are criticized and rejected as unlearned men. ... *Reckless and incompetent expounders of Holy Scripture bring untold trouble and sorrow on their wiser brethren when they are caught* ... For then, to defend their utterly foolish and obviously untrue statements, they will try to call upon Holy Scripture for proof and even recite from memory many passages which they think support their position, although they understand neither what they say not the things about which they make assertion.

Everything in this universe, each and every living creature and person, is part of God's beautiful, good and wondrous creation. God seeks all, especially those who are currently lost, *without exception*. Why then do some preachers claim that they are 'damned,' who never heard about Christ? Will all Jews and Moslems go to hell because they are not Christians? Will two-thirds of the world, who never knew about Christ and His Gospels, or multitudes of righteous people that lived thousands of years *before* Abraham, Moses, Muhammad, and the Incarnation of Jesus Christ, be forever damned? They are misguided and unwise ministers that set themselves up as God's judges.

## DIALOGUE ON FUNDAMENTALISM:

A sincere teacher of Scripture, and this author had a dialogue about his views on the "truth of the Bible," which follows. I'm asking the questions; fundamentalist answers are given in bold italics:

Q: Do you believe the Bible represents the "exact words" of God?

***A: Yes! From beginning to end, every word is written exactly as told by His divinely inspired writers.***

Q: While we agree that much of the Bible represents the "words of God," and most of the Gospels are divinely inspired, don't you think that a few errors may have occurred over the centuries, when these documents were translated into different languages and copied by different scribes?

***A: No! God would not allow writers, translators and scribes to make errors.***

Q: What about the Genesis story which claims that the universe, the earth, and Adam and Eve were all created in six days. Do you believe that's six earth days, based on our earth based and human invented clocks?

***A: Absolutely! That's the way it actually happened.***

Q: Since scientific evidence, according to many experts indicates the universe is about 14 billion years old, and the earth is 4.5 billion years old, and dinosaurs existed millions of years ago, do you still believe this story is factual?

***A: Yes. Most of these scientists are atheists and they feed us lots of lies.***

Q: How about the Bible scholars in many of the universities, are they all liars?

***A: Most of these so-called experts are extreme liberals who work for Satan.***

Q: What about our God-given brain, intellect and ability to reason? Should we believe something that doesn't agree with our reasoning, with our commonsense?

***A: You cannot fit God within the limits of your narrow reasoning powers. You either believe totally, or you don't? The Bible is the exact words of God.***

Q: Finally, which of the thirty English versions of the many translations of the Bible are without error?

A: ***No answer!***

At this point the dialogue was pointless, because we really didn't have any reasonable basis for further discussion. He believes that all 47 Scripture writers were infallible because they were divinely inspired. That assumption means that these -Author, centuries ago, lacked free will, lacked the possibility to err, or were superhuman. However naive this man may be, we must respect that he sincerely believes in Christ's teachings, and he performs many good works of love for the poor and disadvantaged. We must also refer to the words of 2 Tim 3:16. Nevertheless, it is human misinterpretation of Scripture that too often leads us to be misguided in teaching God's Word.

Clearly practices that were once normal, or expected for the people of the Bible (OT), thousands of years ago, today are either illegal, and in some cases, immoral; e.g., slavery, teenage marriages and polygamy. Actually, the Bible *properly understood*, should be a handmaiden of science (and vice versa). Knowing the scientific details of the universe, the "what" and the "how," is a far cry from discovering its purpose, the "why."

> **Moses insisted three times on the day of his death,** *that one must read the Bible as a poem, as text having within it subtext harboring multiple meanings.* **–Deut. 31:19, 32:44**

## Battles for God:

At the other end of this spectrum on *extreme fundamentalism*, counter-views will be always found, such as in *A History of God*, by Karen Armstrong. She wrote: *"A passionate and committed atheism can be more religious than a weary or inadequate theism. And one may remember that Karl Marx, one of the originators of communism, saw religion as '... the opium of the people, which made this suffering bearable.'"*

Armstrong's book: *The Battle for God: a History of Fundamentalism* casts Christianity (as well as Jewish and Moslem beliefs) as examples of *fanatical* fundamentalism. Karen Armstrong, we think makes a *significant* error when she claims: *"... most people on earth do not believe in any God, goddess or religion of any sort."*

Since over two billion claim to be Christians, nearly one and a half billion are of the Islam faith (which together is more than half the world's population), not including all the other major religions, her conclusion is obviously false. Moreover, secularism (civil governments and laws) and religion *do* peacefully coexist in many of today's Western societies—known as pluralism.

She also talks about a *"theology of rage and violence." "The Great War (1914-1918) ... showed the lethal and self-destructive tendency of the modern spirit."* One must correctly define and understand the meaning of these words that she uses: What does she mean by "modern spirit?" Spirituality should mean attachment to *only good* religious values. *Theology* is about the study of God.

Furthermore, she states: Many in the West whose education had been entirely rational (where does one get such a rational education?), were *not* equipped for the mythical, mystical, and cultic rituals that had evoked a sense of transcendent value in the past. There was no going back. .. In the early 20th century, people were trying to find new ways to be religious. .. Like any truly creative enterprise, the search for the *modern faith* was supremely difficult. What's her definition of "modern faith?"

Finally, genuine Christians, Jews and Moslems (among other religions) typically teach about love, not anger, rage and violence.

## Religious Bigotry:

> ***We must always fight against all forms of narrow-minded religious bigotry, wherever and whenever it appears, and not forget Christ's 2nd greatest command: 'Love they neighbor.' A central idea in Jewish Scripture is that they are the special chosen people of God.***

It is perhaps understandable that any group or race of people, so designated as the "chosen people," would have a great sense of pride and self-esteem. Yet, when the Son of God was among them, they denied him. He was their hoped for Messiah, as the Old Testament *had prophesized.*

Jesus was causing problems, a real troublemaker, in their view, and they threw Him out of their Synagogues. Jewish *leaders* killed Jesus Christ because He deviated from their long held beliefs. He dared to modify the laws of Moses. He was upsetting ancient traditions. He lived among the outcasts of Jewish society. He was a serious threat to their power and a danger to the status quo (He still is a threat to society, today).

Nearly all Jews still believe that they are the "chosen people," with a very long history of over 4,000 years, which is legitimate (God does not break His Covenants, even though they broke their Covenant with Him, *many times*). While He chose them, most Jews unfortunately *didn't choose* Christ as their Messiah.

The great danger of this 'chosen view' idea is that it becomes easy to believe that all others are 'not chosen.' Some fundamentalist Christians, Jews and Moslems seem to be very arrogant in believing that all other peoples—Gentiles, Hindus, Christians, and strangers, are 'infidels, rejected by God.' Should such ethnic discrimination and prejudice go unchallenged? Have they forgotten the words of one of the greatest Christian, Jewish (and Muslim) prophets, John the Baptist? *'Don't claim you are descendants of Abraham. God can turn these rocks into sons of Abraham, if He so chooses.'*

Judaism, unlike Christianity, can't convert anyone. By its own Jewish law, it can't evangelize; because they are *the only chosen ones.* The problem is that they also believe that they need not prove themselves; they think that salvation is assured for all Jews. Some Protestants also believe that *'once save, always saved.'* Salvation is, so to speak, 'is in the bag.' That's a tragic misinterpretation of the Bible. What about obedience to God's Ten Commandments?

The greatest sins of the world have *always* been related to pride and are religious in nature; e.g., about 80-90% of all the wars of history have been over religious beliefs: Hindus vs. Moslems (India), Protestants vs. Catholics (Northern Ireland), Moslems vs. Moslems (Iraqi-Iran war), and Darwinism's 'Master Race' idea expounded by Nazis during World War II, where 50-100 million died. Many religious sects claim: We are the chosen ones; they are the infidels, the outsiders. Whereas Jesus taught: *love thy neighbor, mercy, forgiveness, and justice for all.*

Why was the "chosen people of God," allowed to be defeated by the Babylonians? Why was the Jewish Temple in Jerusalem destroyed—twice? Some *extreme* Jewish leaders claim it was because their forebears married non-Jewish spouses, and these "alien influences" polluted and corrupted God's elect. However, the principal king in the history of Israel, King David, was *not* a full-blooded Jew. His great-grandmother was a Moabite, named Ruth (see the Old Testament *Book on Ruth*).

## Jewish Holocaust:

Many Jews and Rabbis ponder these questions. Where was God during the Holocaust? Why didn't God respond to their prayers for help? Perhaps the God of mercy, love and justice was distressed by their sins of pride and prejudice; e.g., laws of 'ethnic purity,' under Ezra and Nehemiah (still practiced by some Jewish leaders), which when muddled, became the malicious Nazi laws of anti-Semitism, in the twentieth century?

This author believe the really important lesson is this: God cannot and will not be owned by Jews, Moslems, or Christians—He's a God of *inclusion*—not exclusion. He desires *all* to be saved, if they trust and follow Him. We have trust in doctors, financial experts, accountants, and many other "experts." *Why not, Trust in Christ?*

Many Jews (and Christians) have great difficulty understanding how God could 'permit' atrocities such as the Holocaust (any major disaster) to happen? They feel that either God is not omnipotent or doesn't care, and therefore, is not a loving God. Some have concluded that the former must be true. They don't realize that humans, through their own free will, create ALL evil—*not God.*

Evil is privation of goodness, a lack of something that should be there. Blindness and deafness are *not morally evil*; it's the lack of sight and hearing, respectively. Saying something is less good doesn't necessarily mean that it is evil. Evil *requires* four elements: (1) Knowledge, (2) Free will, (3) Moral judgment, (4) Intention to act, even if the act is not executed.

When Hitler rose to power, most Germans voted for him. They believed he was 'Savior' of the country. Many of the German people looked the other way. They ignored the early signs of depravity and allowed Hitler's evil to flourish (as was the case for Stalin in the USSR, Mao in China, La Duce in Italy, among other evil tyrants).

The cause of the Holocaust *cannot* be blamed on God. It was caused by groups and individual evil persons, which was the *free choice* of many men and women:

1. Hitler created the 'final solution' by his free will;
2. German people ignored Hitler's early evil acts;
3. Allies ignored intelligence reports of unspeakable deeds;
4. Free press decided not to report known mass executions;
5. Many Jews living in Germany, among other countries, ignored obvious early warnings, and failed to flee to safe havens.

All of these decisions were based on 'free choice.' God respects the free will He gave us, and will not interfere with our free will.

In the 1917 Apparition of Blessed Mary, at Fatima (observed by three children and about 10,000 people), God warned people of the world by the words of His Blessed Mother, that another evil and world war would occur, if they did not repent and pray for forgiveness and peace. The secrets of Fatima were:

1. Vision of Hell, seen by the three children at Fatima;
2. Prediction of WWII, and persecution of the Church; and Russia's conversion, which finally happened in 1989.
3. The third secret was the *predicted* attempt on the life of the Pope, which actually happened to Pope John Paul II.

Nearly two decades after World War II, the Church asked forgiveness for its "anti-Semitic Sins." Pope John XXIII wrote a prayer for forgiveness on behalf of all Christians, in 1962, which follows:

"O God, we are conscious that many centuries of blindness have blinded our eyes so that we no longer see the beauty of Thy Chosen people, nor recognize in their faces the features of our own privileged brethren. We realize that the mark of Cain [is] upon our foreheads. Across the centuries, our brother Abel has laid in the blood which we drew or which we caused to be shed by forgetting Thy love. Forgive us for the curse we falsely attached to their name as Jews. Forgive us for crucifying Thee a second time in their flesh. We know not what we did." In 1995, Pope John Paul II said that Christians ought to pledge, as he did when visiting Auschwitz, *"Never again anti-Semitism!"*

## Historical Atheism:

> ***My argument against God was that the universe seemed so cruel and unjust. But how had I got this idea of "just and unjust"? --C. S. Lewis, a former atheist.***

Atheism is the rejection of all belief in a Supernatural Being. It rejects all religions in their belief there is one God who created the universe and has sovereignty over His creation. Atheism has existed from the beginning of recorded history. In America, 23% claimed to be atheists or agnostic, and 73% claimed to be Christians, according to recent Pew Research surveys.

In ancient history, the Greeks called Jews "atheists" because they refused to worship their pagan gods. When the Roman authorities persecuted the Christians, they were accused of "atheism" because their perception of divinity offended the Roman ethos. By failing to give traditional gods their due, people feared that Christians would endanger the state and overturn the fragile order.

Jewish philosopher Philo of Alexandria (ca. 30 BCE-45 CE), a devout Jew, made a quintessential distinction between God's divine essence, which is unknowable or incomprehensible, and His activities, which is discernible by His creative powers in the universe. St. Basil (Epistle 234.1) wrote that "We know God only by His operations (*Energeia*) but we do not undertake to approach His essence."

The Christian doctrine of the Incarnation of God in Jesus Christ, and the Blessed Trinity, has been and still is considered *blasphemous* by both Jews and Muslims. Christian dogma is that all human beings are basically sinful and dependent on God for mercy and redemption. Basic to this religion is the principle that human beings can only make sense of their lives by accepting God's ordinances or laws. Atheism rejects this concept, as well as much of the morality that goes with it. Atheists are convinced that people can make perfectly good sense of their lives as moral beings, without belief in supernatural entities.

Atheism includes Practical Materialism, which restricts its needs and aspirations to time, matter and space. (Einstein, however, proved that time and space is not constant, by his law of Relativity).

Atheistic-Humanism considers man to be "an end in himself and sole maker, with supreme control of his own history." This atheistic-humanism is a deliberate rejection of God in the name of "authentic human liberation."

What Biblical cultures once perceived as the liberation from earlier Roman and Greek pagan gods, the proponents of atheistic-humanism perceive as bondage. They believe that freedom cannot coexist with the God of the Jews, Christians, or Islam. (In fact it has coexisted for many centuries).

> *All of our historical beliefs, most of our geographical beliefs, many of our beliefs about matters that concern us in daily life, are accepted on the authority of other human beings, whether we are Christians, Atheists, or Scientists, ... --C. S. Lewis*

Unlike atheists, agnostics believe that the human mind "cannot know" whether there is a God, an ultimate cause, or anything beyond material phenomena. Another form of contemporary atheism looks for the liberation of man through economic and social emancipation. It holds that religion, by its very nature, thwarts such emancipation by raising man's hopes in a future life, thus both deceiving him and discouraging him from working for a better life on earth.

If we deny God's existence, we implicitly deny the *basic truths* that science rests upon, for all things ultimately lead inexorably to His existence. If the One Being Himself is not our goal, then to the degree He is not our end, an element of disorder, of irrationality, of "nothingness," is involved in our purpose, and we are bound to create havoc for ourselves and for many others.

Within a cultural social society, this lack of reasoning or belief (trust) in God's existence may ultimately lead to a situation where people become mere means for the ends of the powerful. They are deprived of their dignity as human beings; as 'might makes right' (examples are the former USSR, China, North Korea, and Cuba).

## Key Atheistic Authors:

Socrates and his students (See *Xenophon* by Christopher Bruell, and *The City of Man* by Leo Strauss, University of Chicago Press, 1964). David Hume (1711-76), according to *A Short History of Western Atheism* (Pemberton, 1971), argued that given infinite time, nature by chance alone, eventually hit on the order we see around us. Eddington modified

Hume's belief by claiming that: given infinite time, a monkey with a typewriter would eventually type the works of Shakespeare. Charles Darwin's *The Origin of Species* (1859) claims that all living creatures, including human beings, have evolved (he was Agnostic, however). Sigmund Freud claimed that all religion was psychopathic. Bertrand Russell's *Religion & Science* (Oxford University Press, 1935). Also, Karl Marx (1850's), author of *Das Capital,* co-founders of the Communist system. Friedrich Nietzsche, who finally claimed in 1885 that, "God is Dead." In addition, Hobbes, Voltaire, Rousseau, Goethe, Shaw, Sartre, and Skinner were unbelievers.

Randomness doesn't create order; that's an assumption, not an objective scientific fact. It's a gross fallacy to suppose that *quantity* can eventually provide *quality.* The atheistic orientation of the Marxist-Leninist Communist ideology of dictators, such as Stalin, Mao, etc., sanctioned human cruelties and death on a scale never even partly equaled by the Inquisitions and Crusades, during their darkest periods, or all religious wars combined. The facts are that millions were slaughtered during the atheistic communist "Cold War."

There is an interesting correlation between atheism and moral and political catastrophe in our times. Some reasons for atheism today are:

1.  Extreme fundamentalists, who depend on a literal interpretation of Scripture, with over emphasis on fear of God;
2.  False Christians, those sanctimonious hypocrites that go to church on Sunday, and forget everything they learned about love thy neighbor, during the rest of the week;
3.  Extreme secular proponents that claim Progressive-Naturalism is what life is all about, and that all faiths are "myths."

One must deal with atheists on an individual basis, *as personas,* and start with ideas that we both can agree with first.

Since it rejects or denies the existence of God, atheism is considered a sin against the virtue of religion. This offense can be significantly diminished by virtue of the intentions and the circumstances of the individual. Christians can have more than a little to do with the rise of atheism. To the extent that they are careless about instruction in the faith, or present its teaching falsely, or even fail in their religious, moral, or social personal life. They must be said to *conceal rather than reveal* the true nature of God and of religion.

Practical-Materialism and Atheistic-Humanism, is usually based on ignorance, which might be refuted, granted with some difficulty, by using commonsense (which is not too common today), and reason. The crucial atheistic response is that they reject belief in God because the concept is incoherent or unintelligible. Christians seek to prove the existence of God by His wondrous works in the Universe and Earth, and His Revelations in the Scripture, especially the Gospels of Christ, with arguments that utilize natural reasoning.

## DIALOGUE ON ATHEISM:

In this dialogue, the Atheist's argument is in bold italics:

### *Isn't Christianity about suffering and death?*

Actually, Christianity is really about Life, "The Good News," that Christ came down for our Salvation, to show us the way to Eternal life. Those who preach or over-emphasize suffering, death, hell and damnation, are really deluded. Christ taught forgiveness, mercy and love. Christ spoke more about Hell versus Heaven, because He came to show us mercy, and save us from eternal damnation.

### *If God exists, how can evil and injustice exist?*

The devil (Satan) and humans, by their God-given free will, created evil and injustice, not God. Since "injustice" exists, then "justice" must also exist. We should not expect the Creator to intervene and alter the laws of the universe that He created, to save us from all evil. Nevertheless, God is quite capable of intervening, as in the case of Moses, whenever He chooses to do so.

***Explain the inconsistencies in the four Gospels?*** For example: Matthew 13:55, says that Mary had four other sons. In Mark 6:3, states that Mary had four sons (James, Joseph, Jude, and Simon) and sisters, in addition to Jesus.

The answer is that Joseph was much older than Mary, and Jewish teachings and traditions encouraged many children. Joseph's first wife died, leaving him with his earlier children. Therefore, Jesus had half-brothers and Mary was their stepmother. Anyway, the personal life of Mary and Joseph is not the significant point. Mary was the "pure temple" for the Incarnation of Christ.

Certain perspectives exist between different apostle writings, which should be expected in the reporting of complex events by four different writers, decades earlier. (How many of today's reporters can get yesterday's story precisely right?) Since these variations are included in the Bible, it demonstrates that the -Author didn't revise it, which adds to its creditability. If all the gospels were in perfect agreement about everything, atheists might say it was "fixed." Since fallible men wrote the gospels, no one should accept every word of the Bible, *literally*. A novice needs a guide to help them understand science, business, and a guide is also essential to accurately understanding the Bible.

### *Isn't Evolution and Creationism incompatible?*

Evolution at the micro level is proven science, but evolution between species, has never been proven. Atheists might consider the hierarchies of creation: spirits, humans, animals, plants, micro-organisms and matter. If anything lower is ever to mount to a higher plane, two conditions are required: the higher must come down to the lower; i.e., there must be a descent from above; or, what is lower must surrender its existence to that which is above it. The animal must be subjected to death and fire; the plant must be extracted from its environment. But when these lower things give up their existence, they are taken up into a higher creature; i.e., a thinking, willing, feeling, moving, and loving being; and they become part of a richer existence. They become part of the world of poetry, art, music, science, culture and civilization. Why should this hierarchy stop abruptly with man and woman? Is there not something higher that can come down to man and woman?

Consider the following: Being, Existence and Essence. It is only in the act of thinking about something outside the self, that one knows that one is "a thinking self." Knowledge of things exterior to our self comes first for all humans. The key principle is: existence *precedes* essence. G. K. Chesterton wrote: "Before we know anything about the particular essence of anything, we know there is an 'is.' Before we know self as self, we know that things exist."

Ultimately, wisdom does not come from without; it comes from *within*. Much of what we think we know is not complete knowledge at all. It's about belief or trust in something or someone. One does not seek what one does not feel they can obtain.

Being, reality, thing-ness, unity, identity (as something apart), truth, and goodness are *transcendental*. Each of these transcendental elements are interchangeable, or "being" looked at from various viewpoints. The more unified a thing is, the more intelligible and understandable it is. Truth is the conformity of the mind with reality. Beauty is the goodness of truth. In the end, that ultimate cause of all things, that ultimate intelligence, is the mind of God.

There is a Supreme Being whose essence is beyond the imagination and reasoning of any person in this universe, namely God. (We can only know God indirectly, by His wondrous creations, and by His revelations). Therefore, if man is ever to be elevated into partnership with the Divine, God must come down to man. But there is a significant difference between man going down to lower creation (animals, plants, matter), and God coming to man. These lower things have no personality, no freedom, no liberties, and no rights. Only human persons have "rights." Animals need never consult the plants; plants never consulted the minerals. They confiscate without consultation. But no one can ever lay hold of man without exercising or abusing man's free will. God forces Himself on no one; he breaks down no doors. A condition of man uniting himself with God's nature is that man must "die to himself" as the salt "dies" to its nature, entering into the life of man and woman.

(These hierarchical views were based, in part, on the early teachings of Bishop Fulton J. Sheen).

### *What's the so-called "Design Proof" for God?*

The more widely accepted argument for the existence of God is the "argument from design." If when crossing a field one were to come across an artifact, say a watch (or in today's world, a Personal Computer), one would have to assume that some watch designer (or computer designer) created it. There could be no other explanation for the intricate complex workings of its parts. Analogously, when we look at nature, we see in human beings and animals alike, and indeed in the Universe, a complexity, an amazing order, a pattern, a magnificent design and coordination that can only be explained by assuming they are created by God. Consider the miraculous coordination of the parts of the human body; it can only be adequately explained on the basis that a Supernatural Designer conceived it. Just as a computer and its intelligent software require a designer, so also the intelligently designed human being requires a superior Creator.

If one looks around, they will see that the traditional claim about causality is false. From a tiny seed a huge tree grows. There is no need for proportionality between cause and effect. Moreover, we can only know from observing sequences of events how they arise. It is not the complexity of the watch, and the perfect matching of its parts that leads us to deduce it is an artifact and thus the product of a creator. But, as we have either directly observed or learned from the experience of others, watchmakers make watches; they are artifacts, not part of nature...

In contrast to artifacts, organisms, or seeds are observed to grow in certain determinate, often complex ways without any sign of being designed at all. Going from tadpoles to frogs, or from poppy seeds to poppies are typical examples. We have no reason at all to believe that what we call "nature," is an artifact (that is, intentionally created). Simply having a complex functioning organization is not by itself a sufficient similarity to warrant such an inference. The complex organization of nature, such as the human brain, can be explained in many ways, such as by *Evolution*. Where no explanation exists, at a given time, there is no reason to think a *Naturalistic* explanation will not in time be found. There is no justification for postulating the "supernatural" to explain complex entities or strange events. This implies some "purposeful arrangement of complex parts". See the section on *Intelligent Design* for a more detailed answer to this complex question.

### *Where is the actual evidence that God exists?*

Inductive and deductive reasons for a Supernatural Being include: The existence of the human consciousness; immutable laws of the Universe; and revelations in Scripture. Without belief in God, no sense can be made for: Laws of the Universe and Nature; Existence and Purpose of Life; Human Intelligence and Conscience; Ethics and Morality.

Indeed to explain how there are human beings, with minds, and life itself, one must postulate a Supernatural Creator as a viable option. Consciousness and thinking, and the capacity for Reasoning and Morality, simply could not have emerged as unplanned, unintended by-products of some kind of microevolution.

If God did not exist, what is right and wrong would simply be a matter of individual opinion and whim. Commonsense suggests that Einstein, Edison, Beethoven, Mozart, Michelangelo and Shakespeare could not have evolved from "random accidents" in the universe. Causes must be proportional to their effects.

Ironically, modern cosmology seems to support the Bible chapter on Genesis. For example, Fed Hoyle's "Big Bang" theory, and Hubble's theory that all galaxies are rapidly moving away from each other, and author like George Gamow, among others, happen to result from "Creation-Evolution" (evolution of the universe *after* it was created), an idea that was previously considered contrary to Christian beliefs. Finally, there are 3,200 prophecy verses. Amazingly, *most* of them came true! (See J. Barton Payne's Encyclopedia of Biblical Prophecy Lists).

**What does "God" mean? "I am, who I am," tells Atheists nothing.**

In Judaism, Christianity, and Islam, God is *not* construed as Zeus was in an anthropomorphic sense. Nothing that might count as "God" could possibly be observed, literally encountered, or detected in the universe. God, in such a conception is utterly transcendent to the world. Even when, as Christianity says God is (through Jesus Christ) "Incarnate," He still remains, at one and the same time, "transcendent" (incomparable).

**What does "Transcendent" and "Incarnate" mean?**

God is transcendent (supernatural, incomparable) because He is superior to and above the natural order of everything that we know in His universe. The Creator surpasses the power of all that He created. Christ was Incarnate (took on human form) in order to redeem mankind. To save and teach us, He came down to our inferior human level.

**Atheist Response:**

Christians answer the "intelligibility" problem by saying that the word "God" can only be given sense by the use of descriptions such as "maker of the universe," and "first cause." Anyone, the claim goes, who does not understand such "descriptions" cannot understand the concept of God. But these descriptions are as troublesome as is the term "God" itself, for their key terms are themselves incoherent. We neither know what "eternal," "maker of the universe," or "first cause" refers to, nor in any way understands what they mean. To say they are a "mystery" is just a way of saying you don't understand them?

It is also true that in the case of physics there is no ban on establishing a causal connection between theoretical entities and ordinary everyday things. But no such constant conjunction can be established or coherently asserted between God and the universe, and thus the existence of God is not even indirectly verifiable. There can be no evidential support for God's eternal existence from what we can observe in the world. God's existence, in short, cannot intelligibly be treated as an empirical hypothesis. To say instead that there is an intuitive knowledge of a mysterious ultimate reality—a grasp of the "being" of God—is to make an appeal to something that is not sufficiently clear to be of value. Hypotheses may be formed on a hunch but their truth is not confirmed that way.

### *Christian response:*

If atheists don't know what they are searching for—how will they know when it is found? It is unclear what it would be like to have, or fail to have, evidence for the existence of God. It is not that these God-seekers have to be able to provide the evidence, for if that were so no search would be necessary. But that they must be able at least to conceive what would count as reasonable evidence, so that they would have some idea of what to look for, or some idea of how to proceed in their God-seeking. In any case, *God always seeks them.*

If the stars should suddenly rearrange themselves into a pattern spelling out "God Loves You," this extraordinary occurrence would not give atheists evidence that God exists. They would still be without a clue as to what it would mean to speak of an infinite God, transcendent to the universe. They would be baffled by the occurrence of such an apparently supernatural event in the sky. But since atheists do not understand "infinite God" or "transcendent to the universe" let alone their conjunction, they would not understand what the celestial message meant. Again, we cannot know the essence of God. We know Him by His actions, by His works, and by His revelation.

### *Do Miracles demonstrate God existence? Define Miracles?*

Something that's supernatural. Something that doesn't follow the laws of nature and the universe. Supernatural events cannot be found in natural law. A sample of Gospel miracles includes: Water made into wine at Cana (John 2:1-11); the leper cleansed at Capernaum (Luke 5:12-15); widow's son rose from the dead at Nain (Luke 7:11-17); five thousand fed at Galilee (Mat. 14:15-21); but the only really important, vital miracle is the Resurrection of Christ Jesus.

There are unnatural processes and bizarre laws that we have not yet wholly discovered or fully understand.

Then this discussion is simply an "illusion" and we might as well give up. It's easier to believe in God, than such outlandish phenomena as your *bizarre laws*. It's a question of credibility.

How can one believe Bible stories written from 1,500 BC to 100 AD, by a group of zealots, with a vested interest in promoting their own religion?

The Bible has been the key source of belief for billions of people (about a third of the world today are Christians). Don't dismiss it so recklessly, so thoughtlessly. The Bible is the *only book* that has prophesied 3,200 times, covering hundreds of different events. *All these prophesied events (100%) actually came true!*

### Does God wield evil powers, like wars and despotism?

Again, free will by the acts of the devil and man—not God, produces evil. God often uses the evil acts of others to create good. Many of these evil events caused ordinary people to do extraordinary good acts during wars. People endured hardships and performed heroic acts of love for others. More saints were established in the 20th century than during all prior centuries of history.

### Where is the absolute proof of God?

If God were absolutely provable, beyond all doubt, it would have been settled by now, and *faith would not be necessary*. Scientific reasoning alone cannot provide proof of God, or disprove His existence either. God is not an empirical object. (See *Critique of Pure Reason* and *Critique of Practical Reason and Critique of Judgment* by Immanuel Kant, published 1781-1790).

"If there is no God, everything is permitted," Dostoevsky wrote in *The Brothers Karamazov*. Without God, the weak would fall victim to the strong, moral right or wrong wouldn't exist—and we would experience total chaos. More innocent people died during Atheistic Communism, than all the other wars combined.

***Atheism and Secularism are accepted beliefs of today's society.***
Therefore, they constitute an *implicit* religion; i.e., all who believe that "one should do this, and not do that" represent a system of "religious belief." They also have their particular doctrines that are preached in public discourse in the marketplace. These convictions constitute a particular kind of religion.

***All religions are false, and are clearly based on myths!***
How can one claim that religion is untrue unless they believe themselves to have a superior knowledge? If one asserts that all religions are "untrue," or based on "myths," this is clearly an arrogant claim, which implies that they have "special knowledge," which is superior to all others. The argument fails based on its own irrational logic.

If one claims "there is no way to know the real truth;" that "no one can determine which beliefs are true and which are false," why would one accept the believe of a person who *cannot* determine truth from falsehood? If one starts with faith or trust that God exists, and works backwards, one might find what they are looking for, and most importantly, *find real happiness and joy in the end.*

If one asserts that religious faith must remain private, and never become a matter of secular public policy or discourse, they must define religion. Religion is a set of beliefs that explains:

1. The purpose of life?
2. Why humanity exists?
3. What must one do to have eternal life?

Moreover, Atheism and Secularism represent a kind of "belief," which constitute *an implicit religion*; i.e., "One should do this, and not do that" is a system of beliefs. Atheists also have particular doctrines that are preached in the public marketplace. These convictions collectively constitute a particular kind of religion.

Our most fundamental ideological, philosophical and theological convictions, are based on beliefs that are difficult to justify to those who do not share them. Some past and present ideological convictions include: nationalism, fascism, socialism, communism, atheism, progressive-rationalism, and secularism. It is *impossible* to leave these convictions behind when we attempt to reason together. Proponents of such ideological views do the very thing they forbid others to do—*they cannot leave their sacrosanct beliefs behind.*

How can one claim that no religion is true, unless they believe themselves to have a superior knowledge? If one asserts that all religions are "untrue," or based on "myths," or that they are "relative truths," this is a very arrogant claim which implies that they have a special knowledge which is superior to all others. The argument fails based on its own irrational logic.

If one claims "there is no way to know the real truth;" that "no one can determine which beliefs are true and which are false," why would one accept the believe of such a person who cannot determine truth from falsehood?

Faith and reason are compatible! All science begins with "faith" in an idea, to be proven by experimentation. Theology and Science can never be in conflict. God is the author of all creation and every law that governs it. Science and theology is about discovering God. One may not fully understand and comprehend the purpose of creation, and its laws; nevertheless, if the God is, then His creation and laws cannot be in conflict. If any theory is proven false, then it must be equally false in theology as well, and vice-versa.

Leading Atheists, Anthony Flew has become a Theist. Why did he become a believer after half a century? In the Appendix to his book, *There Is a God*, he wrote: "As I see it, five phenomena are evident in our immediate experience that can only be explained in terms of the existence of God.

- First, the rationality implicit in all our experience of the physical world.
- Second, life, the capacity to act autonomously.

- Third, consciousness, the ability to be aware.
- Fourth, conceptual thought, the power of articulating and understanding meaningful symbols such as are embedded in language.
- Fifth, the human self, the 'center' of consciousness, thought, and action."

## Freedom *from* Religion

It is becoming a familiar refrain: the Freedom from Religion Foundation (FFRF) has utilized its vast amount of time and resources to force a community—in this case, Steubenville, Ohio—to alter its new logo due to the fact that a cross was prominently displayed as a part of it. The horror! Atheists nationwide can rest easy knowing that little old Steubenville is once again open to all citizens, not only the Christian ones.

The FFRF has been on a tear, sanitizing everything they can find of Christian symbols. In the case of Steubenville, the offending cross was attached to Franciscan University's Christ the King Chapel, apparently a Steubenville landmark. It is quite shocking indeed to think that a Christian chapel would have the audacity to display a Christian symbol on its roof. Christ the King was obviously mistaken when they designed their building to reflect their beliefs. Didn't they know that unbelievers would take offense at such a symbol (perhaps Paul was really on to something in 1 Corinthians 1:18)?

The FFRF's ridiculous statement even went so far as to claim: "Steubenville is a theocracy and is a Christian city where non-Christians or nonbelievers are not favored citizens. The city may not depict the university chapel and cross because to do so places the city's imprimatur behind Christianity. The city of Steubenville must not endorse 'faith' and church. While we understand that Franciscan University is part of the City, the City may not depict the University chapel and cross because to do so places the City's imprimatur behind Christianity. This excludes non-Christians and violates the Constitution."

Really? So now that the "city's imprimatur" has been removed from the logo, what do we do about the real cross in the real city? It is still there. If the cross being on the logo is a symbol of solidarity with the church, what message does allowing the actual church to display its cross proudly on its roof send to unsuspecting citizens? If the cross on the logo shows approval, then certainly the wooden cross on the church itself shows it as well. How is removing one and not the other any more honest or less of a "theocracy"? The stupidity is limitless.

Just like the gay agenda setters across the nation, atheist activists interpret everything in light of their (none) beliefs. Most rational people would look at the Steubenville logo, cross and all, and see nothing even remotely close to what the FFRF is claiming. Aside from the fact that the FFRF has no clue what a theocracy really is (hint: think Saudi Arabia, not Steubenville, Ohio), just because they are hyper-offended by any appearance of a cross, does not mean that the rest of Americans are.

In fact, the very name of their foundation is a complete misrepresentation of the First Amendment. You will search in vain to find the phrase "freedom from religion" anywhere in the U.S. Constitution. Forcing the rest of the country to abide by your likes and dislikes is not only the height of arrogance; it has all the hallmarks of being a theocratic behavior. In their efforts to remove any sign of Christianity from American public life, the atheists have become twice the religious dictators they accuse the Christians of being. It should be clear that the FFRF is not actually against religion—they are quite happy to impose their *secular humanism* on the rest of us—they are only against the Christian religion.

## Theological Truths Key Points:

  o The preponderance of evidence shows that faith (trust) is fundamental to all people, not just Christians.
  o Abraham was the first person to have faith and trust in the *one and only God* (the beginning of monotheism).
  o Abraham was the father of Jewish, Christian, and Moslem faiths, which today represents half the world's population.

o   "God reveals Himself to anyone who seeks Him," Blasé Pascal concluded. Pascal found that faith, by definition, is not an intellectual certainty; it is leap into darkness, and that experience brings forth enlightenment.

o   The human person is the only known creature on earth that the Creator has willed for its own sake.

o   The human person *participates* in the light, intelligence, creativity, and power of the Creator's Spirit.

o   God appointed us custodians of earth and our bodies. It is our responsibility to take care of this earth and body.

o   We are temporary residents of this fragile planet. No other creatures have the power to save or destroy our body and the earth except the human species.

o   Charity is the highest form of love. It is unselfish love, which gives of itself without expecting anything in return.

o   Love always implies free will, and with love comes freedom, and with freedom comes responsibility.

o   Only good, not evil should be loved. Love demands indissolubility, fidelity, and faithfulness in definitive mutual giving.

o   God's great mercy and love is [shown] in sending His Only Begotten Son to die on the cross to save all sinners.

o   Jesus Christ said that only two commandments are needed to govern our lives: love of God, and love of neighbor.

# VIII. Ideological Truths

## WESTERN RELATIVISM

Source: Letters between Cardinal Joseph Ratzinger and Marcello Pera, President of the Italian Senate, with special focus on Western Relativism. (Some passages are from George Weigel).

Again, what Drives History? Politics? Economics? Might it be that culture—what men and women honor, cherish, and worship—is the most dynamic element in human affairs, at least over the long haul? Europe is depopulating itself. Generation after generation of below-replacement-level birthrates have created a demographic vacuum… filled by transplanted populations (Moslems, and other cultures) whose presence in Europe is a challenge to Europe's identity, and could become a threat to American and European democracy…. (Democracy requires educated, and well-informed voters). How can we speak of, and defend, "universal human rights" in a cultural climate in which the very idea of "truth" is under sustained assault?

These questions are of urgent importance on both sides of the Atlantic Ocean. The American "culture war" is, in fact an ongoing debate—and continuing political struggle—between those who believe that human beings can, however inadequately, grasp the truth of how we ought to live together, and those for whom any notion of *transcendent truth* involves an unacceptable "imposition" of someone's "values" on someone else.

Excerpts from *Relativism, Christianity, and the West* by Marcello Pera:

Samuel Huntington wrote in *The Clash of Civilizations and the Remaking of the World Order* (*Simon and Schuster*, 1998): "*In the emerging world of ethnic conflict and civilization clash, Western belief in the universality of Western culture suffers from three problems: it is false; it is immoral; and it is dangerous.*"

## Political Correctness:

Political Correctness (P. C.) is the newspeak that the West uses nowadays to imply, allude to, or insinuate rather than to affirm or maintain. ... Everything can be compared and evaluated within the confines of Western culture—be it Coca-Cola with Chianti... Darwinism with Intelligent Design... To me this form of linguistic re-education is unacceptable. I reject it on moral grounds, which are the ultimate reason for refuting an intellectual position. (... We rejected Nazism, Communism, racism, anti-Semitism, and fanaticism... because they offended our consciences, contradicted our deep intuitions about human rights, and violated our fundamental values).

Hypocrisy on the part of people who see no evil and speak no evil to avoid becoming involved; who see no evil and speak no evil to avoid appearing rude; who proclaim half-truths and imply the rest, to avoid assuming responsibility. These are the paralyzing consequences of "political" correctness (as well as intellectual, cultural, and linguistic correctness) that I reject.

In 1992, a French expert on Islam, Olivier Roy, in *The Failure of Political Islam* (Harvard University Press, 1996) wrote that "Political Islam cannot resist the test of power...Islamism has been transformed into a neo-fundamentalism that cares only about re-establishing Islamic law, the *sharia* (law based on the Koran), without inventing new political forms."

To argue that the model of Western democratic institutions and rights is better than the Islamic model does not imply taking any course of action.... According to an old proverb, *it's one thing to say, and another to do.* The dominant culture in the West, however, thinks the opposite, and reveals its prejudices through a major flaw in reasoning. It thinks that "ought" descends from "is." According to this way of thinking, if a person maintains that the West is better than Islam—or, to be more specific, that democracy is better than *theocracy* (government represented by Mullahs), a liberal constitution better than *sharia,* a parliamentary decision better than a *surah* (chapter of the Koran), a civil society better than a *umma* (community of the faithful), a sentence by an independent tribunal better than a *fatwa* (legal opinion or religious decree by an Islamic leader), a citizenship better than *dhimma,* and so forth—then he or she ought to clash with Islam. This is an error of logic that compounds the error of believing that our institutions have no right or basis to be proclaimed as universal (This type of error –the passage from the descriptive to the prescriptive—is made by critiques of Huntington's well-known book, which does not *preach* but rather *predicts* future clashes among civilizations).

For me the opposite holds true. I affirm the principles of tolerance, peaceful coexistence, and respect that are characteristic of the West today. ***However, if someone refuses to reciprocate these principles and declares hostility or a jihad (holy war) against us, I believe that we must acknowledge that this person (group, country) is our adversary. In short I reject the self-censorship of the West. ...that I find unjustified and dangerous.***

Ultimately, not even the most ardent *multicultural relativist* would deny that all human beings, given the choice, prefer to live in conditions of security, respect, health, prosperity, and peace.

Joseph Cardinal Ratzinger wrote that "Relativism ...in certain respects has become the real religion of modern man," and that it "is the most profound difficulty of our day." (*Truth and Tolerance: Christian Belief and World Religions, Ignatius Press,* 2004). Then he raised a series of questions: "The power of Christianity which made it into a world religion (one-third of the world), consisted in its synthesis of reason, faith, and life.... Why is this synthesis no longer convincing today? Why on the contrary, are enlightenment and Christianity regarded today as contradicting each other and even mutually exclusive? What has changed...that it should be so?"

(The foundation of democracy is truth in the value of individuals, dignity, equality, justice, etc.; therefore, if relativism denies these values, it denies the basis for democracy). *... If relativistic-ally speaking, one truth is equivalent to another, what is the purpose of the dialogue?* And if faith contains no truth, how can we be saved? .... In the context of Christian religion, dialogue cannot be an (only) instrument for the discovery of truth, because Revelation plays that role. ...Dialogue is to communicate and foster mutual understanding; and to preach, spread, and advance the message ("Go into the world and preach the Gospel to every creature"). In other words, Christianity is not a process but a *state*, not a becoming but a *being* (Jesus Christ).

## Human Free will:

> *The free will is a good that comes from God, for without it man would be unable to act rightly. Suppose man did not have free will. Under these conditions, he could not act rightly, for the concept of righteous action would have no meaning. To be able to act righteously carries with it inevitably the possibility of acting wrongly.* --St. **Augustine**

**We are all slaves to something!**

### Does Equality Really Exist?

- We are born unequal—physically, mentally economically, and environmentally.

- We don't select parents, tribe, & initial religion.

- Equal Opportunity is good. Equal Outcome is Bad.

- Equality under the law is an "ideal," which society should always endeavor to achieve.

- Thank God we are not all the same; otherwise it would be a very boring world.

> ➢ *Fig 13* Equality*

Those who are opposed to free will, such as Muslims, believe in predestination or determinism. They believe that one has no control over events in life. They would claim that everything has been predetermined. Therefore, no one has a real choice. Yet, without free will (free choice) there can be no morality or system of justice—or true love. If you coerce a person into loving you that is not true love.

> ***Love always implies free will, and with love comes freedom, and with freedom comes personal responsibility.* --Author**

The concept of predestination, assumes that God has predestined everyone and everything. However, if God controls *everything,* then where does evil come from? During the Reformation, Professor Erasmus strongly defended free will, which Martin Luther attacked in his publication *On the Bondage of the Will.* Luther and his followers later moderated their mistaken viewpoint.

In the 21$^{st}$ century, tension between free will and determinism appears in public policy issues, based on modern psychology. They stress that heredity and environment are the primary causes of human behavior, and "evil acts." That kind of belief or modern policy causes people to not take responsibility for their individual acts.

> *In creating beings with free will, Omnipotence from the outset submits to the possibility of defeat (that humans have the power, the ability to ignore and disobey God's commandments). What you call defeat, I call miracle: for to make things which are not itself, and thus to become, in a sense, capable of being resisted by its own handiwork, is the most astonishing and unimaginable of all feats we attribute to the Deity.* **C. S. Lewis**

## World Demographics:

During the first decade of this century, of the 6.9 billion people living on planet earth in 2010, about 57% were Asians; 21% Europeans; 14% from the Americas; and 8% were Africans. About 70% were non-white, and 68% were non-Christian. Jews who only represent about 16 million people worldwide, have a significant voice for such a small minority. Why is that so? Perhaps because they represent the *"root"* of the Christian and Muslim faiths (Abraham), are clearly much better educated, and have lots of political power.

| Rank | Country | Population (thousands 1990 | Population (thousands) 2010 | Growth (%) 1990-2010 |
|---|---|---|---|---|
|  | World | 5,306,425 | 6,895,889 | 30.0% |
| 1 | China | 1,145,195 | 1,341,335 | 17.1% |
| 2 | India | 873,785 | 1,224,614 | 40.2% |
| 3 | United States | 253,339 | 310,384 | 22.5% |
| 4 | Indonesia | 184,346 | 239,871 | 30.1% |
| 5 | Brazil | 149,650 | 194,946 | 30.3% |

| Rank | Country | Population (thousands 1990 | Population (thousands) 2010 | Growth (%) 1990-2010 |
|---|---|---|---|---|
| 6 | Pakistan | 111,845 | 173,593 | 55.2% |
| 7 | Nigeria | 97,552 | 158,423 | 62.4% |
| 8 | Bangladesh | 105,256 | 148,692 | 41.3% |
| 9 | Russia | 148,244 | 142,958 | -3.6% |

***Source: United Nation surveys.***

More Americans call themselves Catholics, by far, than claim allegiance to any other religion. There are about 70 million American Catholics, depending on whether one follows parish reports or official census data. Catholics make up nearly 28 percent of the United States potential voting population, *without* counting a few million Eastern Orthodox Catholics, and about twelve million "undocumented" Mexicans. Protestants of *all* denominations still have at least a two-to-one edge (about 150 million members).

Gallup poll data suggest that Hispanics account for 18% of all *active* Catholics—Hispanic advocates claim numbers that are much higher. The tendency of third-generation Mexican Americans to stop describing themselves as "Hispanic" makes the numbers game murkier. Large numbers of Hispanics, about 20%, have defected to Protestant Evangelical and Pentecostal Churches, which have mounted aggressive recruitment campaigns. Latin America currently represents over *one-third of all* Catholics, worldwide.

The Muslim population is expected to increase by 35% during the next 20 years, from 1.6 billion in 2010, to 2.2 billion by 2030, according to *Pew Research.* If current trends continue, Muslim populations will grow twice as fast as the population of other groups, making up nearly 30% of the world's population by 2050.

The largest populations of Muslims (in millions) are: Indonesia (240m), Pakistan (174m), Bangladesh (149m), Iran, Iraq, Afghanistan, Syria, Malaysia, Palestine, and Saudi Arabia. Millions of Muslims have immigrated to France, England, Belgium, Germany, among other EU countries (9% on average), which will significantly affected economic, social, cultural, religious and government policies.

The process by which Islam grew was nearly the opposite as Christianity had spread. Islam was not (generally) carried to hostile shores by dedicated individuals, such as St. Paul … who made converts by oratory and dedication. Islam went with the armies of the Islamic Empire, so that those who embraced it were joining, not defying the ruling authorities. Islam offered a source of direction and comfort that appealed to ordinary, less educated, and diverse tribes.

## ISLAMIC ROOTS

***Islam is a religion that has some of its roots in the early Bible (OT), and is similarly monotheistic, worshipping the One and Only God, as do Jews and Christians.***

The following are believed to be the *true* about Islam and Christianity. We cannot have any "meaningful dialogue" if one denies these facts. Today one often encounters *extreme* Islamic *and* Christian *fanatics*, who distort the truth of God's message. Individuals also need to have an opportunity to *freely* learn and choose between these different religious doctrines and beliefs.

Do we have the courage to discard earlier claims that can pervert the real truth about theses ideologies? Can we try to make more intelligible this great Islamic *and* Jewish-Christian history, with its message of mercy and love, for 21st century hearers?

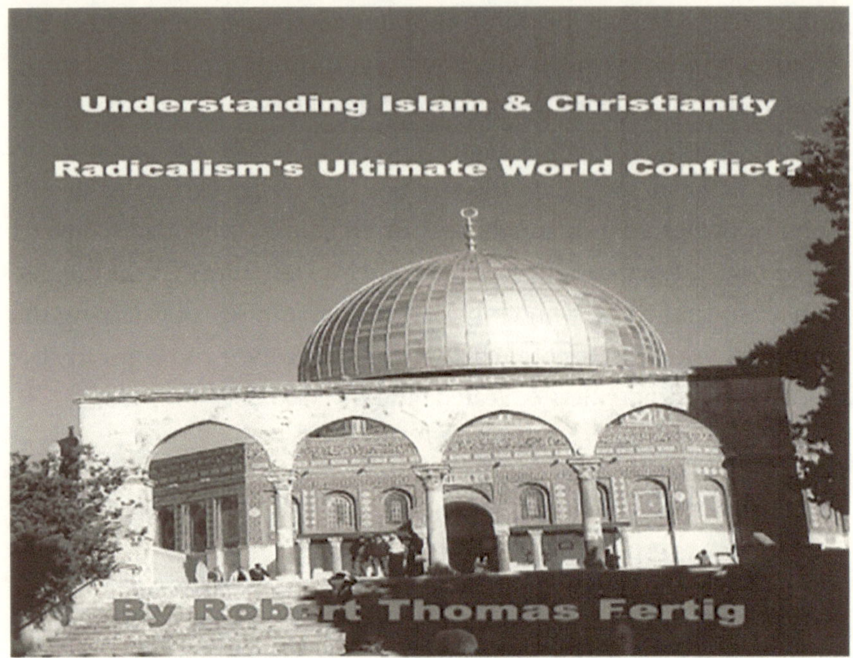


➤ **Fig. Image of the Dome in Israel by the author.**

The Boston bombings, the Fort Hood shootings, events of September 11, and frequent Islamic terrorist activities, are only new to uninformed people, or to those who have a limited sense of history. Our earliest founders in 1805, were familiar with *radical* Islamists. Thomas Jefferson, Ambassador to France, and John Adams, Ambassador to Britain, met in London with Abdurrahman, Tripoli's Ambassador to Britain, in an effort to negotiate a peace treaty. Peace for many Islamist means, *"Surrender to Islam."*

Everlasting peace would cost $160,000 plus the mandatory commission. Moreover, this only applied to Tripoli. Other Muslim nations would also have to be paid. The total amount came to $1.3 million (big money at that time). There was no assurance that the treaties would actually be honored. In vain, Jefferson and Adams tried to argue that America was not at war with Tripoli. In what way did the United States provoked the Muslims? They asked.

Ambassador Abdurrahman explained the finer points of Islamic *jihad* to Jefferson and Adams. In a letter to John Jay, Jefferson wrote, "The Ambassador answered us that it was founded on the Laws of their Prophet, that it was written in their Koran, that all nations who should not have acknowledged their authority were sinners. It was their right and duty to make war upon them, wherever they could be found, and to make slaves of all they could take as prisoners, and that every [Muslim] who should be slain in battle was sure to go to Paradise."

Abdurrahman was paraphrasing the Koran's "rules of engagement" found in the Koran's Surah 47: ***"Whenever you encounter the ones who disbelieve [during wartime], seize them by their necks until once you have subdued them, then tie them up as prisoners, either in order to release them later on, or also to ask for ransom, until war lays down her burdens."***

Unless a nation submits to Islam, that nation is, by definition, at war with Islam. Jihad means, *"to submit."* A non-aggressive nation is still at war with Islam as long as it has not embraced Islam. Islam's goal is to conquer the world, either by the submission of one's will or by the *Sword of Allah.*

When President Jefferson refused to increase the tribute demanded by the Islamists, Tripoli declared war on the United States. A United States navy squadron, under Commander Edward Preble, blockaded Tripoli from 1803 to 1805. After American soldiers from Tripoli, led by the Marines, captured the city of Derma, the Pasha of Tripoli signed a treaty promising to exact no more tribute.

Jefferson, embroiled in a war with Islamic terrorists in his day, wrote, *"Too long, for the honor of nations, have those Barbarians been suffered [permitted] to trample on the sacred faith of treaties, on the rights and laws of human nature!"*

Political and violent Islam goes back to Muhammad, in the seventh century, who massacred the Qurayzah tribe and the Jews of Khybar. In Medina, he started waging war against non-Muslims, and he explained to his followers that they should offer non-Muslims three choices: [1] to convert to Islam; [2] submit as inferiors to Islamic rule, paying the tax and accept the discrimination that Islamic law mandates for non-Muslims in the Islamic state; or [3] die."

## Understanding Islam

In Arabic, Moslem means "submission" to the will of Allah. The five key pillars of Islamic (*hadith*) religious beliefs and obligations are:

1. Admission 'there is no God but One God, and Muhammad was his last Prophet and Messenger.'
2. Daily prayers, five times facing Mecca.
3. Payment of Zakat (alms-tax).
4. Fasting during Ramadan.
5. Pilgrimage to Mecca (if financially and physically possible).

Muhammad preached and promoted the virtues of mercy, justice, integrity, fear of God, and self-restraint to a pagan tribal society. The oral Koran (about 78,000 words in Arabic), with seven Arabic tribal dialects, became their inspiration, their law and guide for their entire society, and centuries later, was strictly followed by most Muslims.

## Koran or Qur'an:

This the Holy Book of Allah's revelation to Muhammad, *allegedly* came from the angel Gabriel, which became the basis for all Muslim doctrine. Within a century of the Prophet's death, Islam (practiced by Muslims), spread throughout the world, from Spain and Morocco, to the Near East, including Central Asia.

Muslim leader Uthman (644-656), the 3rd Caliph, proclaimed the *Book of the Koran* 'official,' about fourteen years after Muhammad died and purportedly went to paradise in 632 AD.

British scholars have suggested that fragments of the world's oldest known Koran, which were discovered [in Aug 2015], *may predate* the accepted founding date of Islam by the Muslim prophet Muhammad. The Times of London reported that radiocarbon dating carried out by experts at the University of Oxford says, the fragments were produced between the years 568 and 645 A.D. Muhammad is generally believed to have lived between 570 A.D. and 632 A.D. The man known to Muslims as The Prophet is thought to have founded Islam sometime after 610 A.D., with the first Muslim community established at Medina, in Saudi Arabia, in 622 A.D.

Keith Small, of Oxford's Bodleian Library, told the **Times**: *"This gives more ground to what have been peripheral views of the Koran's genesis, like that Muhammad and his early followers used a text that was already in existence, and shaped it to fit their own political and theological agenda, rather than Muhammad receiving a revelation from heaven."*

## Simplicity of Islam:

The huge masses of Middle-East people didn't have to do anything to prepare for, or be accepted into the Islamic faith. Islam basically requires one to believe that: "There is no god but God (al-Lah). It has no Catechism, no Baptism, no Bible study (the Koran they believe is the "Word of God," *in Arabic only*), no Apostles Creed, no Sacraments, and (allegedly) no clergy or saints, and no redemption from sins; therefore, no need for salvation.

In *The Crisis of Islam* Bernard Lewis wrote: Islam is not only a matter of faith and practice; it is also [a source of] identity and loyalty—for many an identity and loyalty that transcends all others. In a time of intensifying strains, faltering ideologies, jaded loyalties, crumbling institutions, an ideology expressed in Islamic terms offered several advantages: an emotionally familiar basis of group identity, solidarity, and exclusion; an acceptable basis of legitimacy and authority; an immediate intelligible formulation of principles for both a critique of the present and a program for the future. By means of these, Islam could provide the *most effective symbols* and *slogans* for mobilization, whether for or against a cause, or a political regime.

## Islamic Schisms:

Factional disputes (schisms) eventually developed between the Shiites (representing about 15%, or the minority Muslim sect) primarily in Iran

(Persians), and the Sunni Arabs. Sunni's are the majority, or about 85% of the Muslims, in Saudi Arabia, Egypt, Palestine, Syria, Pakistan, and Indonesia. *There is no unified Islamic nation!* But the faith of the masses survives every coup and dynasty. Unlike the Sunni, Shiites believe that the Imams or Mullahs are the *divinely inspired, infallible spiritual leaders,* such as the late Ayatollah Khomeini of Iran.

In summary, today's 1.6 billion Muslims are diverse in history, ethnic background, language and political experience, as to defy generalization. *Islam (appears to) offer solace in a world of seemingly injustice, continuity in a world of upheaval, brotherhood in a world of strife, and very limited free expression in a world of oppression.* Muslims take up arms against each other (Iraq Sunni vs. Shiite conflicts) at least as often as they take up arms against unbelievers. The vision of a global Islamic community, unified in faith that overrides ethnic, economic, and linguistic differences, is *illusory.* It has been since Uthman (644-656) was 3rd Caliph (he was the leader who proclaimed the *Book of the Koran* 'official,' about fourteen years after Muhammad's death.

## Islamic Beliefs:

Lippman continues: The basic testimony of Islam is called the '*shahada*', the first clause of which states that "*la ilaha illa al-Lah*"—"There is no god but God." In "theory," Islam has no clergy, no saints, no hierarchy, or sacraments. No man stands between the individual and Allah. In practice, they have numerous mullahs, shrines and martyrs. Muhammad (which means "highly praised") was born in 570 AD, in Mecca. He had fourteen wives (some were as young as nine-years), and six children, but only one daughter, Fatima, survived. Not leaving a male heir or designated future leader resulted in many disputes over the future succession to the Prophet, even to this day.

## Origin of the Koran:

No complete texts of the Koran were compiled in Muhammad's lifetime, and he couldn't read or write, so how does one know that his followers accurately quoted the words of the prophet? The Book of the Koran was started by a committee, headed by Zaid ibn Thabit, secretary to Muhammad, under Abu Bakr, the first Caliph, but was not completed until the time of the third Caliph, 'Uthman (644-656), who declared it "official," after burning all other texts.

The work of Zaid and his team remains the only unchallenged version of the Koran, in Arabic, which is considered the *literal* word of God, never to be changed again. However, most of the world's Muslims cannot read Arabic. Therefore, translations into others languages became essential, which could cause some errors to creep into their texts. Even today, major disputes occur over what Muhammad had actually said. Fundamentalism and literalism has crept into the Islam religion (which is perhaps analogous to *some* Bible preaching by irrational Christian fundamentalists).

## ISLAMIC CULTURE:

Lippman wrote: Islam is more than a religion; it's a way of life. Spiritual beliefs and specific rules form equal parts of the Muslim faith, and no distinction exists between doctrine and laws or church and state. At least in theory, Islam is all-encompassing. No thought, act, contract, or relationship is beyond its scope. Christ's injunction to *'Render to Caesar the things that are Caesar's and to God the things that are Gods'* is (totally) alien to Islam. In fact, (it's the) opposite.

**Jihad:** "The Koran and the Prophet taught that Muslims were *required* to fight for the faith and that those who died in its defense were *assured a martyr's reward* in Paradise." Christian martyrs, in contrast, did not generally fight or kill for the faith, except when they were killed for their belief in Jesus Christ, especially during the Roman Empire, and spread of Communism. The (Muslim) concept of jihad, which is customarily but *erroneously* translated as a 'holy war,' inspires collective fear of Islam today. Fundamentalist Muslim leaders contribute to that fear with demagogic talk of jihad in freeing Jerusalem from Israeli occupation.

**Muslim Law (Sharia):** The Prophet said: "The blood of a Muslim may not be spilt other than one of three instances: (1) the married person who commits adultery; (2) a life for a life; and (3) one who forsakes his religion and abandons the community. This law is 'permissive,' *not mandatory* and is generally not used today, except by *fanatical Islamic literalists* that argue that justice demands adherence to acts that applied in the 7th century." Unfortunately, there are many fanatical literalists today in Muslim countries, and these fringe elements have much power. Such acts are not only against Christian principles, they are criminal acts under Western civilized laws.

## MUSLIMS VS CHRISTIANS:

> *Christians must not lose sight of the fact that Muslims, affirm that there is only "One God." In fact, Orthodox Christians in the East, always say in Arabic: In the name of the Father and of the Son and of the Holy Spirit, One God! (Bismilabi wal-ibni war-ruhi-l- quddus, Al-Lah WAHID!).*

Estimates are that about 1% or 3.3 million Muslims live in the United States, and of this total 23% are Arabs. Muslim children, at the age of six, according to Shoebat, *Why I Left Islam*, are taught that *"all Jews are dogs,"* and that Muslims are the current and historical *victims* of the Jews and Americans. It is estimated that over 70% of all Muslims are fundamentalists, again according to Shoebat (other studies suggest that about 20% are *fanatical fundamentalists).*

Muslims don't accept the following important Christian beliefs: the Holy Trinity, the Incarnation of God through Jesus Christ, the Revelation and Redemption, that Jesus Himself is God's Word to humanity. Muslims believe that both the Jews and Christians *perverted* God's Word, in the Torah and the Bible, respectively. They also don't believe in the Original Sin of Adam and Eve, thus they don't see any need for Salvation by Jesus Christ.

The Koran (Qur'an) can be taken to mean that the fate of every individual is sealed from the moment his soul was created: "*Every misfortune that befalls the earth, or your own persons, is ordained before we (Allah) bring it into being* (Sera 57:22)." The important Muslim and Christian differences are explained more specifically as follows:

**Holy Trinity:** How Christians and Muslims conceptualize God is quite different. The emphasis in the Islamic theology of God can be summarized by one word: *tawhid*, which means "absolute unity." Muslims insist that there is no distinction within the Godhead. God is sublimely one. Thus, one of the Islamic quarrels with Christianity has centered on the doctrine of Trinity. Muslims have labeled Christians as "tritheists," guilty of "shirk;" that is, attributing an associate to God. They wrongly think that Christians believe in three gods. This attitude is expressed in the Qur'an: Say not "trinity," for God is One God (4:171). They blaspheme who say: God is one of three in a Trinity, for there is no God except One God (5:76).

Apparently the early Christians, whom Muslims interacted with, misrepresented the *mystery* of the Trinity. Muslims, therefore, came to understand the Christian doctrine of the Trinity in distorted terms. Some Muslims also believed that Christians worship Mary as part of the Trinity. This misunderstanding of the Trinity found expression in the Qur'an itself: And behold, God will say; "O Jesus the Son of Mary, did thou say unto men, "Worship me and my mother as gods in derogation of God?" (5:119).

Interestingly, Muslims honor the Virgin Mary as mother of the "great prophet" Jesus. She is mentioned thirty times in the Koran. In recent times, an apparition of Mary reportedly appeared on the domed roof of a church in Egypt. Many Muslims witnessed this event, and photos were taken to show it happened. Few people realize that Fatimah was also the Moslem name of the only daughter of Muhammad, and his brother-in-law Ali's wife, who is considered by many to be the "Mother of Islam."

In the era of the Qur'an it was assumed by many people that the Trinity was the Father, the Son Jesus, and Jesus' Mother Miriam (Mary).

The Trinity is *incomprehensible* by any human mind. It is presumptuous for anyone to think that they can grasp the mystery of the Godhead! So the fact that the doctrine of the Trinity is not understandable, in terms of reasoning, should not concern anyone, including the Muslims.

The Christian response might be: God has revealed himself to us as Trinity; i.e., Father, the Son and the Holy Spirit. We do not understand this and any explanation that we come up with will be flawed. But since God has revealed Himself as Trinity, we submit to Him as such, even if we do not understand how he can be One God as well as Trinity. The purpose of theology is *not* to bring God down to human reasoning, but to elevate human reason to contemplate the Divine Mystery—revealed mystery in the Gospels—that teaches us that the One God—*incomprehensibly*—exists in three Persons.

One way to enable our Muslim brothers and sisters to understand why God is Trinity is to emphasize Christianity's fundamental teaching, namely that "God is Love." Since love *cannot* be exercised in isolation, God the Father cannot be all-loving *and* alone. *Love is manifested in a relationship*, and for that reason God, who is *perfect love*, exists in a "community within himself," that is, within a community of three persons, among whom their mutual love is so divinely perfect that they, though three, become Perfectly One! This is the fundamental truth underlying the doctrine of the Trinity. One might also argue that humans should never attempt to limit God. If God wills to have a Son, who are we to restrict Omnipotent God?

**Incarnation:** It is from this same viewpoint—that "God is Love" – that we should explain how Jesus is the Son of God. Such a statement is *blasphemous* to Muslims; they believe that God is "far above" having a son. However, since God is all-powerful, one cannot limit Him by saying, *He could not have begotten a Son, or anything else He wills to do.* Christians believe that Jesus, as a testimony to Divine Love, which is so profound (again, beyond human understanding) that God was not content only to bless his creation from outside of it. Thus God became a part of His creation through the Incarnation of His Son, Jesus Christ.

By becoming part of His created order, by taking on a full and complete human nature, God sanctified humanity "from within," as it were.

Both Islam and Christianity agree that God is beyond our comprehension, yet Christians add something different: that God sanctified the world by deigning to become part of it, by loving humans so much that he was willing "to come down from heaven" to become part of His created world. In this bold and wonderful claim, Christianity stands apart from Judaism and Islam, which stresses the total *transcendence* of God, to the point where it is incomprehensible to them that He could become part of His created order.

**Revelation and Redemption:** Christianity believes that God revealed Himself in order to redeem us, to save us—that is, to lead us to the fullness of life, freed from the bonds of sin, both in this world and in the world to come. According to Islam, revelation is *not* for the purpose of redemption, but for the sake of human "guidance"; i.e., God's revelation is meant to provide guidance for living in this world. They also believe in a "master/slave" relationship with God. Christians also believe that God, through His only begotten Son, Jesus Christ, provides us with essential guidance via the Gospels.

In Christianity, one believes (should believe) that the Bible is the Word of God, but one should not believe that God mechanically transmitted it through certain peoples as if they were merely a conduit of some sort. Christians believe that the Holy Bible, written by human beings, was under the divine inspiration of the Holy Spirit. 'Divine Revelation' was thus '*filtered*' through human minds and written in human words, thousands of years ago. That is why Sacred Scripture refers to historical circumstances; it describes not only the divine and mystical revelation of God, but also chronicles His special intervention in history.

**Koran or Qur'an** (Recitation)**:** In Islam, the Qur'an is considered "unmediated" word of God. Islam stresses that in receiving his revelation, since Muhammad was illiterate and couldn't read or write—and hence completely passive—he simply recited what was put into his mouth, without any input or interpretation of his own. The Qur'an is seen as eternally existing in heaven, and simply descended (another name for the Qur'an is 'at-tanzil', that which descended), and was expressed through Muhammad as a passive instrument of revelation.

Since Muhammad was uneducated, admittedly unable to read and write, how can 1.6 billion Muslims know for sure that his words were accurately recorded by many different followers, over many years, and faithfully written as the Koran, fourteen years after his life on earth?

According to linguistic theory, *all communication is mediated*. As soon as a thought is put into words, it is mediated. The very fact that a thought is put into words means that it is 'processed' through the mind. The whole purpose of Revelation is for God, whose thoughts are far above ours, to mediate his communication to us through human language or symbols (art, music, poems, images, and words). God does not think in human terms and language; to say so is to limit His Omniscience, which is far beyond the constraints of any human. Christians should call the Islamic view of "unmediated revelation" into question based on linguistic and theological grounds.

**Eternal Word of God (Qur'an):** It should be understood that Qur'an is much more a 'book-centered' religion than Christianity. It is wrong to assume that what the Qur'an is to the Muslim, as the Gospel is to the Christian. The appropriate analogy is: what the Qur'an is to the Muslim, 'Christ himself' is to the Christian. Christians should not be book-centered; *they should be, Christ-centered!* Muslims say that the Qur'an is the "Eternal Word of God;" but we should not say that the Gospels are the Eternal Word of God. *Only "Jesus Christ" is the Eternal Word!*

Muslims, in affirming the eternity of the Qur'an, face a theological problem that is directly analogous to the one faced by Christians, who affirm that "Christ is the Word, which existed from all eternity." Muslims typically ask: how can Christians say that there is One God, who alone is eternal, and yet claim that Christ existed from all eternity. They accuse us of ascribing an "associate" to God in saying this. But they face the same problem in teaching the eternity of the Qur'an. How can they claim that something besides God—namely the Qur'an—exists from eternity, without also ascribing an associate, an object, rather than a person, to God?

Interestingly, both Christians and Muslims solved these parallel theological dilemmas in virtually the same way: Islam asserts that since the Qur'an is the Word of God, it always coexisted with God—"as part of God," figuratively speaking, since God could never be without his Word. Christians use the same reasoning in defending the doctrine of the Eternity of Christ: as the Word of God, Christ always existed with God the Father. Christ is co-eternal with the Father, since the Father could never exist apart from his Word!

In the Eastern Church, Father Gregory of Nyssa explained this mystery: God eternally spoke his Word (namely, His Son). And when he eternally spoke the Word, there came forth eternally from His mouth the Spirit (namely, the Holy Spirit, "ruh ul-quddus"), by which the Word was spoken. (Breath, after all, is necessary for speech!) *Thus, from all eternity, the Word and the Spirit co-existed with the Father!*

**Word vs. Person:** While both Islam and Christianity affirm that God has spoken and revealed Himself to humankind, there is one *significant difference*: whereas Islam teaches that the Qur'an is God's Word to humanity, Christianity proclaims that Jesus *Himself* is God's Word to humanity. For Islam, God has spoken through a Book. In Christianity, He has spoken through a *Person—Jesus Christ*. In Islam, the written Arabic Book is the marvel; in Christianity, the *Person of Christ* is the marvel! Christians believe that if Almighty God can reveal His will so perfectly in a Book, as Muslims claim, surely He can do so *more perfectly* through Christ. Since He is a personal God, the person, Jesus Christ, is a far better means of revealing Himself than any Book, including the Bible.

**Corruption of Scripture?** This Muslim argument is called the doctrine of 'tahrif'. Articulation of the doctrine of 'tahrif' began with the Qur'an itself. Islam affirmed the veracity of the earlier revelations given to the "People of the Book"; theoretically, they were fully consistent with the Qur'an. Jews and Christians, therefore, were urged to accept the revelation given through Muhammad: O ye People of the Book! Believe in what we have (now) revealed, confirming what was (already) with you. And this is a Book which we have sent down, bringing blessings and confirming (Revelations) which came before it. When Jews and Christians brought arguments against Muhammad and his followers, on the basis of what Scriptures taught, Muslims had to account for the discrepancies. How could the text of the Old and New Testaments contradict that of the Qur'an, if the latter was a confirmation of the former? A number of responses to the problem are found in the *Medinan suras.*

**Perverting God's Word?** The Jews are accused of deliberately perverting the word of God, after having heard and understood it (2:75). Some actually write the Book with their own hands and then say, 'This is from God.'" These transgressors changed the word from that which had been given them." Others corrupt the text by displacing words, changing them from their right places (4:46, 5:14), or by "twisting" their tongues and reading it incorrectly: the charge of concealment (ikhfa') is leveled against the People of the Book. They know the truth as they know their own sons." But some of them conceal it (2:146); they thereby 'swallow fire' and will receive a grievous penalty for their duplicity (2:159; 2:174).

Why do you clothe truth with falsehood," the People of the Book are asked, "and conceal the truth while you have knowledge?" Muhammad is depicted as coming to reveal to them much of what they used to hide in their Book (5:16). Jews are further chided for dismembering the Torah by making it into separate sheets "for show" while concealing its contents (6:91).

Christians, Muslims claim, "forgot a good part of the message that was sent them" (5:15). It was a way of trying to explain the discrepancies between the Qur'an and earlier Scriptures, but it has absolutely no basis in the manuscript tradition. Anyone who has studied the manuscripts of Jewish and Christian Scripture, knows that there is no proof for the corruption posited by the doctrine of 'tahrif'. Actually, the historical evidence substantiates how carefully the texts of the Old and New Testaments were passed down! (In fact, the Qur'an has limited historical manuscript authority).

**Original Sin of Adam and Eve:** Sin and salvation are *central* to Christian theology and spirituality. Christianity teaches that the effects of original sin have corrupted the world and all human beings. In Islam, there is no such a thing as original sin. According to Islamic beliefs, Adam and Eve repented and were forgiven, so their sin had no repercussions for the rest of humanity. The Islamic rejection of original sin is a rejection of 'specific understanding'—a 'narrow' understanding—of original sin. Islam rejects the doctrine of original sin that asserts that all human beings inherited the guilt—the culpability—of the sin of Adam and Eve. This seems unfair to the Muslim: Why should anyone have to accept guilt for someone else's disobedience?

The Calvinists later carried this view of original sin to an *extreme*, saying that the result of Adam's sin is total human depravity; that is, original sin has made human beings *completely incapable of doing anything good, without the assistance of divine grace!* Such a notion is incomprehensible to Muslims! Western Christians need to move beyond the *extremist* Calvinist understanding of original sin, and look toward the Christian East, for what might be a more satisfactory explanation. Eastern Christianity understands original sin in this way: no sin that is committed is without its effect. Every sin that is (was) ever committed—disrupts the entire Cosmos. Your sin has an effect not only on you, but on everyone, throughout the universe (this philosophy is also implicit in many Asian religions).

When the Old Testament claims that "the sin of the father will be visited upon the children," it is not issuing a threat; it is simply describing reality. Is it unrealistic to claim, as Muslims do, that Adam and Eve's sin had NO effect on the world into which all human beings were born? Evil of sin has a "cumulative effect on humanity." It has accumulated throughout history, impacting upon all who are born into the world. What started this off was the sin of Adam and Eve—the first original sin in this process. (Our genes have also micro-evolved from Adam and Eve to ALL humanity).

Eastern Christians say that all who suffer the effects of original sin is not the same as to say that all are "born guilty." Rather, all humans have to deal with the powerful force of evil that has accumulated from the sin of our first parents, until the present day. If one understands original sin in this way, the need for salvation—the ability to break loose from the evil bonds of sin that have grown stronger through the ages—becomes more apparent.

With the effects of evil everywhere around us, all have an undeniable proclivity to sin. Because Islam understandably reacted against their misunderstanding of original sin, it has tended not to be receptive to this more realistic understanding of the pervasive effects of sin on all human beings (except of course, Jesus Christ and His Blessed Mother Mary).

**Salvation:** Islam sees no need for salvation; therefore, they cannot understand how Christ's death and resurrection brings salvation. "Salvation from what?" they ask. Just as it is unthinkable to Muslims that one person should have to shoulder the guilt for another person's sin, it is unthinkable that another person (in this case, Christ) would be able to pay the total penalty for billions of person's sins and their past/present/future evil deeds.

Furthermore, unlike Christianity, Muslims believe that *all prophets are sinless* (this doctrine is known as 'isma'), and it is *blasphemy* to say that Christ died the shameful death of a sinner on the cross. They deny that it was Jesus that was crucified; they claim it was Judas (whom God made to look like Jesus so that he would suffer his rightful penalty for betrayal). By this story, Muslims see themselves as protecting the prophetic integrity of Jesus, since a true prophet, according to Islam, could never suffer the indignity that Jesus accepted. Muslims affirm that Jesus ascended to heaven but strongly deny that he died on the cross.

Because Muslims do not recognize the universal, corruptive power of evil, unleashed as a result of original sin, they see no need for salvation.

Thus they see no need for the saving grace of God (if there is no sin that has a hold on one, they don't need to be saved). According to Islam, one needs to only live a good life, pleasing to God. Submit to God and follow His directives. Religion, to the Muslim, does not mean salvation; it means "following the right path"—which is the *shari'a laws* detailed in Islamic teaching.

**Beliefs vs. Practices:** While Christianity is concerned with "orthodoxy," or "right belief," Islam is a faith concerned *primarily* with "orthopraxy," or "right practice." It is a *religion of laws*, and it sees Christianity's rebuke of the Jewish Laws (as taught by St. Paul in his writings, especially Romans and Galatians) as a serious deficiency in the Christian way of life. This does not mean that Islam is not concerned with right doctrines or that Christianity is not at all concerned with right practices.

However, the difference in emphasis is very important. If one recognizes the pervasive power of sin, salvation is not just an option; *it is a necessity.* Christians lament the fact that a faulty presentation of original sin led early Islam to *"throw out the baby with the bath water,"* with regard to their understanding of sin. By reacting against a wishy-washy understanding of original sin, they have missed what Christians consider to be the *central truth of human existence*: that no matter how hard one tries to conform to "right practices," he or she will fall short of that goal *without God's grace.* We cannot live the kind of life that God wants by our own power.... And that's why salvation was (is) absolutely necessary.

**Religious Community:** What the Church is to the Christians is what the "umma" is to Muslims. Christians and Muslims consider themselves accountable to a community of the faithful. It is not enough to believe in isolation; one must link their lives to brothers and sisters in the faith. There are some noteworthy differences between Christian and Muslims visions of religious community. There is (allegedly) no ordained ministry or "hierarchy" in the Islamic umma (recent Iraqi and Iranian factual events suggest otherwise), and there is much more stress on homogeneity—on a common pattern of life throughout the Islamic world, regulated by the 'sharia', or religious law—than in the Christian church generally.

**Language of the Koran:** Christians try to "incarnate" Christianity as much as possible in local culture. For example, Bible, hymns, and liturgical texts are translated into the local language and modified (somewhat) for the local culture (especially after Vatican II). In contrast, one *must learn Arabic* if one wants to be a "good Muslim." The Qur'an is considered to be "untranslatable"; to the Muslim, the message of the Qur'an is inextricably linked to the original language. One can attempt to render the text of the Qur'an in English, French, etc., but then it is no longer the Qur'an, only an interpretation of it. Arabic is considered a "sacred language"; therefore one can perceive the perfection and inimitability (i'jaz) of the Qur'an, *only in Arabic*.

**Worship Practices:** Muslims and Christians also have different understandings of worship or rituals. It is difficult to talk about "Christian worship" as a single phenomenon because there are many different traditions of worship in Christianity. Different denominations worship in very different ways. In Islam, *all* Muslims worship the same way, throughout the world, with no significant variations, regardless of social and cultural context. When discussing differences between Christian and Muslim worship, one should be aware that Muslims are very attentive not just to the interior aspects of worship, but also to the *external* aspects as well. Muslims have much more in common with Eastern than with Western Christianity, especially Protestantism.

Like Eastern Christians, Muslims use their whole body in prayer. Both religious groups, for instance, make prostrations before God in their worship. This seems strange to many Christians, whose worship consists of sitting (or standing, from time to time) in a comfortable setting on cushioned pews, in air-conditioned churches. What one does with their body in most Western modes of Christian worship seems to be less important. In Islam, the submission of the spirit is symbolized by the submissive gestures of the body, made according to a ritualized pattern. Muslims, therefore, don't understand the overly informal, unregulated worship of the Evangelical Christians.

## DIALOGUE ON ISLAM

The purpose of this dialogue is to show how and where we our Culture is different? Our goal is to encourage Muslims, who live in a *free democratic country*, to try to understand, by means of their *God-given reasoning powers*, what Christinity is really all about. Christians should also appreciate the faith and culture of Islamic people.

Muslim dogma, in alpabetic sequence, is followed by the Christian response (C). The primary sources were: *Inside Islam* by Daniel Ali and Robert Spencer, and *The Holy Koran* translation by S.V. Mir Ahmed Ali:

**Arabic:** Muslims *must* pray in Arabic. However, most don't understand Arabic; they memorize the words of the Koran by rote, and bow towards Mecca. Muslims pledge uncritical allegiance and conformity to all sheikhs.

**C:** Christians pray and worship God in the local language. We believe that God understands *all* languages, even our thoughts before we pray to Him. Christians don't have to bow East or West since God is *everywhere*. We primarily pledge allegiance to the Apostle's Creed.

**Abraham:** Muslims claim that Abraham was the first Muslim and the Father of Islam. The Koran says that at the time of Muhammad, Jews and Christians were in dispute as to which faith Abraham belonged. On the next day, Allah revealed that Abraham (and his children) was a true believer, a Muslim.

**C:** This lacks historical support! The fact is that the Bible clearly indicates that "Abraham was the Father of all three religions," and made his Covenant with God. Abraham, Isaac and Jacob were born many, many centuries before Muhammad was born in AD 610.

**Adam & Eve:** According to the Koran, Adam asks for pardon, and Allah forgives him. That's the end of the matter! Muslims don't believe in Original Sin. According to the Koran, Adam met Moses, who said: "You are the one who made people miserable and turned them out of Paradise." Adam responded to Moses that he was forgiven by Allah.

**C:** If Adam and Eve were pardoned by God, why were they then expelled from the Paradise? That's an illogical *contradiction*! The Bible doesn't support this baseless theory.

**Almoravids:** Morocco Muslims that defeated Alphonso, King of Castile Spain.

C: The Amoravids completely reversed the earlier liberties and toleration of the Jews and Christians, by the Muslim leaders of Spain that existed for nearly 800 years. They created a situation in which they despised Jews and Christians, abhorred all dialogue or debates, treated women as slaves, and established maniacal missionary fanaticism. As a result, these *fanatical* Muslims were ultimately pushed out of Spain by Queen Isabella in 1492. The lesson is that fanaticism ultimately backfires. *Love is far more powerful than hate!*

**Allah (God):** A Master/Slave relationship exists between Allah and all Muslims. The five pillars or practices of the Islamic faith are: Confession of the faith; Prayers five times per day; Fasting during Ramadan; Pilgrimage to Mecca (if possible); and Almsgiving. The six articles of the faith are:

1.  Belief in Allah's unity as One God (no Son);
2.  Belief in Allah's revelations, and that the Jewish and Christian Bibles contain corrupt versions of the original Words of God;
3.  Belief in Allah's 25 prophets (including Jesus Christ), and that Muhammad was the last and final line of all Prophets (claimed to be from Ishmael);

4.  Allah's angel, Gabriel, delivered Allah's revelations written in the Koran, *orally* to Muhammad (who was illiterate);
5.  Belief in fate or destiny, and that everything is controlled by Allah, and humans lack free will;
6.  Belief in Judgment Day, with the *2ⁿᵈ coming of Jesus Christ.*

**C:** Allah to Muslims is a *God of fear*, who is the Master of all, and is not concerned for a personal relationship with His creatures. He is not considered a God of love, as Christians believe.

**Apostasy:** An American Arabic-language textbook teaches: "The unbelievers, idolaters and others like them must be hated and despised ..." Anyone after accepting the Islamic faith, and later expresses unbelief, the penalty is the sentence of death (Surah 16:106).

**C:** Why are Muslims insecure or afraid of people learning about any other religions, especially Christianity? If Islam is the "true faith" they should have no fear of people freely choosing their religion. Where is love, mercy and peace in this faith?

**Bible:** The Koran contains the first five books of Moses in the Bible—Genesis, Exodus, Leviticus, Numbers, and Deuteronomy, plus additional material. Allah is the only speaker (a few exceptions exist). The Koran declares that the Gospel contains "guidance and light ..."

**C:** The Old Testament does not agree with the Koran, so they claim, because it was "corrupted by the Jews." Thus, the Muslim leaders "changed the OT" to fit their Koran, thousands of years later.

**Civil Rights:** The concept of civil rights is a Judeo-Christian concept that's *inadmissible* under Islam law. Testimony of a non-Muslim, the "vilest of creatures" (Surah 98:6), is certainly not valued as highly as a Muslim. A woman's testimony is devalued and inadmissible in some (many) cases.

**C:** These different views on justice and human rights, perhaps explains why some Muslim countries remain significantly underdeveloped. Also, if the required male witnesses cannot be found, a woman's charge of rape becomes an "admission of adultery." In Islamic countries, penalties still include stoning for adultery, amputation for theft, among other draconian methods. Christians in democratic countries, have equal justice under the law.

**Crucified Jesus Christ:** In the Koran, Jesus Christ is defined as a "Prophet," a slave to Allah, but He is later defined as the "Spirit of Allah" (Surah 4:171). The Koran says that Jesus was *not* crucified (Surah 4:157).

**C:** How can God's Spirit be a "slave," or anything other than God Himself?

**Crusades:** The Christians massacred and pillaged thousands of Muslims during the Crusades. Allah caused the Muslims to win this war against unbelievers.

**C:** Muslims conquered Spain in 715, which they held for almost 800 years. In AD 792, the ruler of Muslim Spain, called for a *jihad* into France, which was defeated.

In AD 827, Muslims attacked Sicily and Italy, and in 842 AD France was attacked, causing considerable loss of life and devastation. By 846 AD the Muslim warriors of *jihad* reached Rome, looted Christian churches, terrorized monks, and violated nuns. The facts are that Muslims were bludgeoning Christians and each other, *before* the Crusades stopped them.

Charles Martel (grandfather of Charlemagne) stopped the Muslims at Tours, France in 732 AD; otherwise, Europe might be Muslim today. The Crusades (began in 1095 AD) were mounted over the next two centuries to take back the lands overrun by Muslim invaders, but it didn't fully stem the tide of the Muslim *jihad*. It is true that the Crusades were also brutal. Some immoral Christian leaders murdered and pillaged Jews and Muslims.

Interestingly, the high point of the Muslim expansion was in Vienna, on *September 11th*, 1683. Is the reason for the 9/11 attack on America, where 3,000 innocent lives were lost?

This summary review of factual history, acknowledges that *both* fanatical Muslims, and misguided Christians, have committed brutal acts of violence against innocent people, *in the name of God*!

**Divorce:** *"I divorce you!"* That's all a Muslim man has to say to his wife, three times, if she is not pregnant. She is thereby "officially divorced." If a Muslim couple have children, they live with the father, after the divorce; that is, if he so decides (65:1).

**C:** Christians believe that marriage is a Sacred Blessing between God, man and woman. In contrast, the Muslim wife has great difficulty divorcing her husband, since the testimony of a woman in court does not carry the same weight as that of a Muslim man.

**End Times:** Allah remains unknowable even in Paradise. Humans will never approach, know, or see God.

**C:** Christians believe that *true joy* in heaven is being close to Love itself, which is God. The Islamic vision of Paradise is filled with earthly desires of wine, women, and sex. Such humanistic desires can never be satisfied fully. (All the desires of the flesh on earth, which they declared *forbidden* by Allah, are fulfilled in heaven).

**Evangelization:** Muslims will fight until everyone on earth has converted to Islam. A Christian's life is in danger if they attempt to convert Muslims or preach the Gospel. They are *signing a death sentence* under Islamic law, if they attempt *any* evangelization. Christians are *not* allowed to speak freely about their faith in most Muslim countries. In Saudi Arabia, Christians are not allowed to bring Bibles into the country, or to wear a cross, build churches, or practice the Christian religion in any way while in the country.

**C:** The Koran says Jews and Christians are under Allah's curse, and as a result they have experienced widespread persecution in most Islamic countries. *What are they afraid of?* In contrast, in America and Europe, Muslims are free to practice their faith without fear.

**Fate/Destiny:** In the Koran everyone's destiny or fate is in the hands of Allah: "Say nothing shall ever happen to us except what Allah has ordained for us" (Surah 9:51; 64:11).

**C:** Christians believe that each individual person has *free will* and is responsible for their fate. Muslims don't believe in free will, thus one is effectively not responsible for what happens in their life. Morality cannot exist without free will.

**Fitna:** In AD 909, *Shias* proclaimed a separate government with Sunni Islam, and *ijtikad*, the tradition of independent thought and debate was thereafter forbidden (this is known as *fitna* which is a crime in Islam). Whatever Muslims needed to know was known. Allah's revealed word stands for itself. Muslims must comply-- or else.

C: Christian history, during the Inquisitions, had similar decrees (*"no thinking rules"*), and many heretics were burnt at the stake for daring to question Biblical and Church teachings. It was a sorry time in the Christian past; an overreaction to the Reformation, but it didn't last. Thoughtful leaders of the Church eliminated these diabolical practices, and thereafter encouraged theological debate and toleration of different interpretations of Scripture. Yet, some *extreme* fundamentalist still exist in Christianity.

**God:** Muslims believe that God (Allah) is so far above humanity and His creation, that He can never be known. Muslims will never "see God as He is." He remains radically transcendent, unapproachable, and unknowable. God is *not* Father, or son, but Master, who orders all of His slaves (Muslims) to obey His strict rules.

**C:** In Christianity, God is both transcendent and knowable through His Creation, and especially from His Revelations, through Jesus Christ (His only begotten Son). John 3:2 promises Christians that they will see Him as He is. The Christian God is Merciful and Loving!

**Heaven (Paradise):** Paradise is envisioned as offering physical, sensory, earthly pleasures of wine, women (slaves) and sex, and certainly *not* a "wondrous vision of God."

**C:** Christians believe that the bliss and joy of Heaven is to see and know the magnificent beauty, wonder, and love of God.

**Holy Spirit:** Muhammad received the Koran from the "Spirit" of the angel Gabriel (who was the Spirit of Allah). When Gabriel appeared to Mary and the "Spirit entered in her," as stated in the Koran (66:12): "We breathed in her Our Spirit" (Spirit of Allah).

**C:** Christians and Muslims believe that the Spirit *comes from God*, the Creator of all, when a human is conceived in the womb. Both Christians and Muslims believe that the human soul is *spiritual*, thus it has no parts because it's *not* matter, and cannot be divided because it has nothing *to* divide. Islamic teaching is also that men and women were created from a *single soul*, which seems to contradict logic, or appears to represent a corruption of the Genesis Creation of the Bible, in which the body of Eve is formed from part of Adam's rib (Gen. 2:21-23). *No division of the spirit is ever mentioned in Genesis.*

**Islam:** According to Islamic tradition the prophet Muhammad began receiving revelations (*Wahy*) from Allah, through the Angel Gabriel, in the city of Mecca, in 610. These revelations continued until his death in 632. His followers committed his messages to *memory* and wrote them on whatever was available, which ultimately became the Koran, about 14 years after his death. Muhammad is *not* the founder of Islam, but simply the final prophet.

**C:** How can Muslims really know that Muhammad's followers recorded *exactly* what his revelations were since the prophet couldn't read/write, and these various notes were finalized into a book, called the Koran, fourteen years after Muhammad's death? The historical record is that Muhammad's prophetic mission was acknowledged in its early stages by Waraqa, a priest, a convert from Judaism, who was a Christian heretic. Also, one of Muhammad's teachers *allegedly* was a Persian, Salman Al-Farsi (Surah 39:28).

**Jesus Christ:** The Koran calls Jesus the ***"Spirit of Allah"*** (Surah 4:171), and a messenger of Allah, the ***"Messiah."***

**C:** "Spirit" is the *essence of life* of all living beings! How can God's Spirit be anyone other than God Himself? Therefore, Jesus Christ is "divine," according to this line of reasoning in the Koran. This seems to represent another contradiction within Muslim teaching.

**Jihad:** "Fight in the name of Allah and in the way of Allah. Fight against those who disbelieve in Allah." And Allah's Messenger said, "Know that Paradise is under the shades of swords [jihad in Allah's cause]."

**C:** The "Golden age of Islam" was about the 9th century, when the Caliph (leader) was flexible and reasonable about Jews, Christians and Unbelievers. Jihad is, by definition, a call for violence against *anyone* who does not accept their version of Islam. While Christian inquisitions and missionaries were intolerant toward heretics in past, they ultimately learned that: *love is far more powerful than fear.*

**Judgment Day:** Among the signs of this day, Islamic tradition holds that the greatest of all is the *second coming of Jesus Christ!* It is Christ, not Muhammad, whom Muslims expect to return to earth on the last days *to judge all.* "When Judgment day arrives, Allah will give every Muslim a Jew or Christian to kill, so that the Muslim will not enter into hell fire." (Source: Mishkat Al-Messabih, vol. 2, no. 5552).

**C:** The Second Coming of Jesus Christ *completely contradicts* killing of Jews and Christians! This Islamic idea is bewildering.

**Koran** (Qur'an)**:** Allah is considered the God of Judaism and Christianity in certain Koran texts, yet He is not considered a "Father Image," which is considered blasphemous to Muslims. Still, Muslims vehemently deny that Allah is the God of the Bible. *He is a God to be feared*, who established rules and Allah demands absolute obedience!

**C:** Christians believe in a Merciful and Loving Father *and* Son, One and Only God, which is a great mystery. We believe in a God who cares for all of His creation, especially humanity, is willing to forgive all sinners, and is slow to anger. Forgiveness and mercy are key elements of Christianity. False teachings about God and His nature is the *root cause* of deceptive religious sects and social injustices. The Master/Slave relationship of Allah to humans, can lead to a *legalistic* form of morality. Muslims strive to obey Allah's laws to be saved, out of *fear of God*, and never hope to have a loving relationship with God.

**Love:** Allah's love is only for obedient Muslims. He hates unbelievers, and is transcendent, unapproachable, and unknowable.

**C:** The concept of service to others motivated by divine love, and belief that the Son of God sacrificed Himself for us while we were His enemies (Rom 5:18), is unique to Christianity.

**Martyrdom:** The foremost cleric in Sunni Islam, Sheikh Muhammad Sayyid Tantawi, the Grand Sheikh of Al-Azahar, at the University in Cairo, "emphasized that every martyrdom operation against any Israeli, including children, and women, is legitimate act according to [Islamic] religious law, and an Islamic commandment" (see MEMI Special Dispatch Series No. 363, www.memri.org).

**C:** Christians worship a God of Mercy and Love, not of fear, hatred and terror. The Saudi government will not accept Palestine Muslims as citizens. Yet they finance suicide bombers and award families of martyrs' with money and a trip to Mecca. Christ said: Love your enemies! Forgive all who persecute you in my name. His words from the Cross were: *Father, forgive them for they know what they do.*

**Nullification of Verses (Surah 2:106):** Allah is Divine, and can say and do whatever He likes. If there are contradictions in the Koran, then Muslim theologians determine which parts are *actually* the Word of Allah to be recited and followed, and which verses have been *abrogated* (denied by Allah, at a later date).

The Koran declares that the author of some of these abrogated verses was the Prince of Darkness, Satan. Nevertheless, even on a whim (13:39, 22:52), Allah can change His mind, and say something completely opposite to His earlier word! Allah has revealed that Satan routinely tampers with the messages from the prophets (22:51). Allah later annuls these demonic interpolations. (This is relates to the notorious *Satanic Verses* incident). Islam supports Deuteronomy of the Bible. Deuteronomy 18:22 says that the people should "not to be afraid" of a prophet whose words are proven false.

**C:** How can God's Word be inconsistent? How can "truth itself" be changeable? To assert that God has no need to adhere to the truth is to say that God can be a liar. This is not only gross blasphemy, it *is* impossible! *He is Truth* (John 14:6). If God is *not* immutable and unchangeable, then all that one is taught about faith is open to all kinds of heresies. If the Bible is self-contradictory, no one would believe it! Christians emphasize that an all-knowing, all-powerful God, cannot contradict Himself (Heb. 6:17-18). Since God exists outside of time and space, all reality is present to Him—so God cannot "change His Mind," because change implies limitations of space and time, which are limits that God does not "have."

Nullification is a way for Muslim leaders to change whatever doesn't fit self-contradictory verses in the original Koran, by insisting that Allah doesn't have to be consistent.

The Koran also has some significant historical errors, such as the claim that Alexander the Great was a Muslim in the story of *Zulqarnain* (Surah 18:89-98). But the fact is that Alexander was a *not* a monotheist. Elsewhere, a Samaritan is said to have helped the Israelites to build the Golden Calf (20:19). It is a historical fact that Samaria *did not exist* prior to the existence of Israel (see Ex 32).

Nullification supports *relativism* in society, where traditions, moral values, laws and rules are changeable to whatever fits the current mode of thinking.

**Polygamy:** Muhammad had fourteen wives, including Aisha, a nine-year-old. (See Surah 4:3). A Muslim man today, living in Islamic countries, can have more than one wife (up to four wives).

C: This practice makes it difficult, if not impossible, to eliminate child marriages in the Islamic world today.

**Revelation:** Muhammad was chosen as a Prophet and received his revelations in dreams after long periods of seclusion in the cave of Hira. It is said that the truth came to him orally (he was not able to read or write) from Allah, through the Angel Gabriel (Surah 96:1-5). Afterward his followers committed his messages to *memory* and some wrote them down, and they were collected after his death, about fourteen years later, by the third Caliph, at that time.

C: Humans have very poor memories. In addition, the Caliph burned all notes that seemed to conflict with Muhammad's main message. Finally, since the prophet was illiterate, how could it be verified that Muhammad's followers faithfully wrote whatever he said?

he "Official Koran" was published in 1924. Earlier fragments of the Koran existed in the 8th century. Whereas the Gospel Cannon by Church leaders was certified in the 4th century.

The Gospels are *corroborated* by three of the four books (Synoptic Gospels), and by letters of the Apostle Paul. The Christian faith is *not only* a book, but more importantly, based on the Person, Jesus Christ.

The Bible did *not* make the Church; the Apostles, guided by Jesus Christ and the Holy Spirit, produced the Gospels.

**Satan:** The Koran indicates that Satan routinely tampers with the messages of the prophets (Surah 22:51), and later, Allah annuls these demonic interpolations.

**C:** How can "divinely inspired prophets of God's Word," become corrupted by Satan? In contrast, the words and deeds of Jesus Christ in the Gospel, were prophesied in the Old Testament, up to a thousand years earlier, and did not require any changes!

**Sin:** Muhammad taught that "every human is a sinner by nature, and the best among sinners are those who repent." And, "Indeed man was created impatient" (Surah 70:19). According to Islamic teaching *only* Jesus and Mary were exempt from the touch of Satan at birth; i.e., they were sinless (Surah 3:36). Moreover, even Muhammad was not sinless. In the Koran, judgment proceeds according to the scales. If one's good deeds outweigh his bad deeds, he will enter Paradise; if they do not he will enter Hell (Surah 7:9).

**C:** Christians believe that Salvation is a "gift from God," which is accepted or rejected by us, but *never* earned. If every human being is a sinner by nature, did Allah create Adam's offspring as sinners, or was there a "fall" (of Adam and Eve)? Either Allah did imperfect work in creating human beings, or He produced an indigenous defect in man and woman. Which is it?

Christians believe, as the Bible teaches, that Adam and Eve sinned by their disobedience to God's commandment, by their free will, which has been inherited by all people. God in His great Mercy and Love, however, sent His Only Begotten Son, Jesus Christ to redeem all, *including Muslims.*

**Sunni vs. Shiite Conflicts:** Sunni represents about 85% of all Muslims worldwide. Sunnis follow doctrines and traditions (*Hadith*) from

Muhammad, as *interpreted* by various Muslim scholars. Shiites or Shi'a represent 15%, and are the party of Ali, the husband of Muhammad's daughter Fatima. They have different traditions and practices, such as their belief that *Imams* succeeded Ali, and inherited the "light of Muhammad's prophetic spirit."

**C:** Schisms between these two major Muslim religious groups is not unlike the Christian schisms that developed between the East and West by about 1054, and especially after the Christian Reformation. The point is that Muhammad and the Koran teaches that Muslims may not kill each other; otherwise they will go to Hell. Yet, they continue to slaughter each other, as Christians did in past history. Where is their brotherly love and mercy that God taught them?

**Terrorism:** The Koran says: Muhammad is the Apostle of Allah; those who follow him are merciful to one another, but ruthless to unbelievers" (Surah 829). "Fight against those who believe *not* in Allah …nor acknowledge the religion of truth, from among the "People of the Book" (Jews, Christians and atheists), until they pay the *jizay* [special tax for non-Muslims] with submission, and feel themselves subdued" (Surah 9:29).

**C:** There is no justification in the *Hadith* for the use of lethal force against nonbelievers, and the innocent. In Islam, there is no true peace between the nonbeliever and the devout Muslim. Peace can only exist between those who follow Islam. In fighting the infidels the Koran teaches: … "But those who are slain in the way of Allah, He will never let their deeds be lost. Soon will He guide them and improve their condition, and admit them to the Garden [Paradise] which He has announced for them" (Surah 47:4-6; 3:157).

**Trinity:** Muslims vehemently deny that the Allah of the Koran is the God of the Christian Gospels (although it's the same God as the Jewish Torah). The notion of "Trinity" and "Father" are blasphemous to all

Muslims. Allah is the One and Only "Master" who demands obedience, or else the person ultimately goes to Hell.

**C:** Muslims speak of the "Spirit" of Allah, which Christians consider the "Third Person," the Holy Trinity. The Christian Church says: "The plan of salvation also includes those who acknowledge the Creator, in the first place amongst whom are the Muslims; these *profess* to hold the faith of Abraham, and together with us (Christians) adore the One, Merciful God, *mankind's judge* on the last day." Likewise, many Christians profess to love Christ, but how many really and truly live by His teachings?

**Wahhabism:** Wahhabis of Saudi Arabia represent a significant Sunni subset. Muhammad ibn Abd al-Wahhab (1701-1792) was a reformer, who wanted to rid Islam of everything that developed after the first few centuries. He stressed a "literal" reading of the Koran and Hadith. It is the *most extreme* teachings within the Sunni faith.

C: The only hope for peace between Islamic, Christian and other cultures, is a "Reform Movement" by Saudi leaders. Wahhabism is the KEY problem with Islam today. *They are living in the 7th century!*

**Women:** The Koran teaches male superiority forthrightly: "Women shall, with justice, have rights similar to those exercised against them, although men have a status *above* women" (2:228). Men have authority over women because Allah has made the one *superior* to the other, and men spend their wealth to support them (4:34). Husbands by "divine right" have authority over their wives. Muslim men are entitled to twice the inheritance as women (Surah 4:11).

**C:** All persons are *equal* in America, Europe, and most of the world, and especially in the eyes of God and His Church. Muslim *fanatics* should remember their Koran's warning: *"Allah changes not what is in a people until they change what is in themselves."*

Those who blindly accept *all the teachings* of the Koran and Hadith, literally, are by definition, fanatics! Civilized society no longer follows the outmoded laws of Moses, which were essential to control lawless tribal peoples, before 1400 BC. Islamic Sharia laws are still based on these antiquated laws. Today, such practices are incompatible with the norms of 21$^{st}$ century civilization.

The only solution to this **Cultural Battle** is a "Reform Movement" by Sunni leaders. Wahhabism is the KEY PROBLEM within Islam today.


## IDEOLOGICAL TRUTHS KEY POINTS:

o   Christians, Jews and Moslems should teach the same message of love, compassion, forgiveness, spirituality, and mutual respect.

o   Islam is *incompatible* with Christian Ideology and Theology.

o   Islamic Ideology and Sharia laws are contrary to the American Bill of Rights in the Constitution.

o   Islamic ideology schisms continue to cause millions of deaths between Sunni and Shiites, Jews, Christians, and all "infidels."

o   Most Muslims don't fully understand Christian theology, religious practices, and Western human values.

o   What men and women honor, cherish, and worship—is the most dynamic element in human affairs.

o   Europe is depopulating itself. Generation after generation are below-replacement-level birthrates.

o   Europeans have created a demographic Christian vacuum… filled by transplanted Moslems (among other cultures).

o   This challenge to Europe's identity, could become a threat to European democracy…. (Democracy requires educated, well-informed voters).

o   How can one speak of, and defend, "Universal Human Rights" in a cultural climate in which the very idea of objective "truths" are under sustained assault?

o Moslems believe in the concept of predestination, which concludes that Allah (God) has predestined everyone and everything. Free will doesn't exist!

o In the Middle East there is no sense of distinction between religion and the state. Therefore, what happens in America (the "perception" of immorality), is associated as being part of Christianity by most Muslims.

o The Muslim population is expected to increase by 35% during the next 20 years, from 1.6 billion in 2010, to 2.2 billion by 2030, according to *Pew Research*.

# IX. Spiritual Truths

> *For the Creator, being outside of time [and space],*
> *a flow of events has no meaning. There is no future*
> *in the sense of what will 'eventually' happen. The*
> *future and the past are in the present. An Eternal*
> *Now pervades, like a cloud containing all times, not*
> *in linear progression, but in simultaneity. --Gerald*
> *Schroeder, Science of God.*

The concept of the "Eternal Now" is implied in the explicit name YAHWEH (Ex. 3:14). In Hebrew, the spelling includes the letters of the verb "to be" in its three tenses: I was, I am, I will be. The past, present and future are all contained within the Eternal. (Expressed 6,823 times in the Bible).

Einstein's discovery of the laws of relativity revealed the astonishing fact that dimensions of space, time, and matter are ever changing and always depend upon the way in which they are observed. God is pure spirit, and therefore, outside of time and space.

## SUPERNATURAL BEING:

> *The supernatural nature given to every person at*
> *creation is spirit.*

- **Made in "God's image," means mentally and spiritually. We are *transcendent spiritual* persons.**

- We have a higher purpose and calling by our Creator. How do we discover our calling? Some will discover their purpose in life early, some much later.
- We are constantly in *Pursuit of Wisdom*. Wisdom is defined as Truth, plus Reason, times Experience (W=T+R*E).
- What is this immaterial human spirit or soul? When our body dies, our spirit lives on because it is *immortal*.

For example, people who died *temporarily*, and had Out-of-Body Experience (OBE) told us this when they were revived. Blind people with OBE were able to "see" spiritual beings.

- Some encountered and talked to relatives that were deceased years before this blind person even was born.
- This provides clear "evidence" of the existence of our immortal soul. *That is truly amazing!*
- What do we do with this awareness of our immortal soul? That all thoughts and consciousness continue after death.
- We can train our mind to have "good thoughts" about the *immortals* we deal with in life, and avoid all evil thoughts.
- If we can recognize our own failures *and* goodness, then we might begin to grasp the "goodness within others."

Our mind and spirit are not physical. They are immaterial. They *cannot* be touched or harmed directly. Only negative thoughts and grave sin can harm them. Thus, positive thoughts and virtues can protect them. Soul is the spiritual faculty and principle of all humans, which controls the mind and body. When one speaks of the "heart," they actually mean, *the depth of one's being.* The Conscience is where one decides, for or against goodness or evil. When the immortal soul leaves the mortal body, the body which is physical matter, dies. A person can be essentially brain dead, yet the organs can still function. However, once the soul leaves the body, all human life ends.

> *On a clear calm day, one cannot feel, touch, or see the air, yet we know it's there, and cannot live without it. Light is invisible until it interacts with matter. Then photons of light (particles and waves) cause the atoms of the things they interact with to vibrate and shine, with their particular spectrum of colors. When we dream our eyes are closed, yet we see and hear as clearly as when awake. Our thoughts and prayers are signals, just like the rays of a very faint star that travels millions of light-years to reach us tomorrow. --Author*

## Gospel on Spirits:

The spirit is the seat of supernatural life. Spirit is the vital principle by which the body is animated; namely, the soul. Thus, the body without the spirit is dead (Luke 8:55). After death, the spirit continues to exist" (Heb. 12:23 and 1 Peter 3:19). "Lives of Christians must be spiritual." (Gal. 5:16-18; Rom. 8:9-11).

Ken Wilber writes in *The Marriage of Sense and Soul*: The Spirit knows itself *objectively*, as Nature knows itself *subjectively*. ... The overall sequence of development, from nature to humanity, to [the] divine; from subconscious to self-conscious, to super-conscious; from pre-personal to personal, to transpersonal; from id to ego, to God. Spirit is fully present at each and every stage as the evolutionary process itself. Spirit is the process of its own self-actualization and self-unfolding; its being is its own becoming. ...

For Mind and Nature to be genuinely integrated and unified, a third term is required, above both Nature and Mind and reducible to neither; that term, of course, is Spirit. Only Spirit itself, which is beyond any feelings of Nature, and beyond any thoughts of the Mind, can affect this radical unity.

Spirit alone transcends and includes Mind and Nature. For pre-rational Nature can be seen with the "eye of the flesh," and rational Mind can be seen with the "eye of reason," but trans-rational Spirit can be seen only with the "eye of contemplation," and contemplation is definitely not feelings plus thoughts: it is the absence of both in formless intuition, which, being formless, can easily integrate the forms of Nature and of the Mind, something that either or both together could never do for themselves...

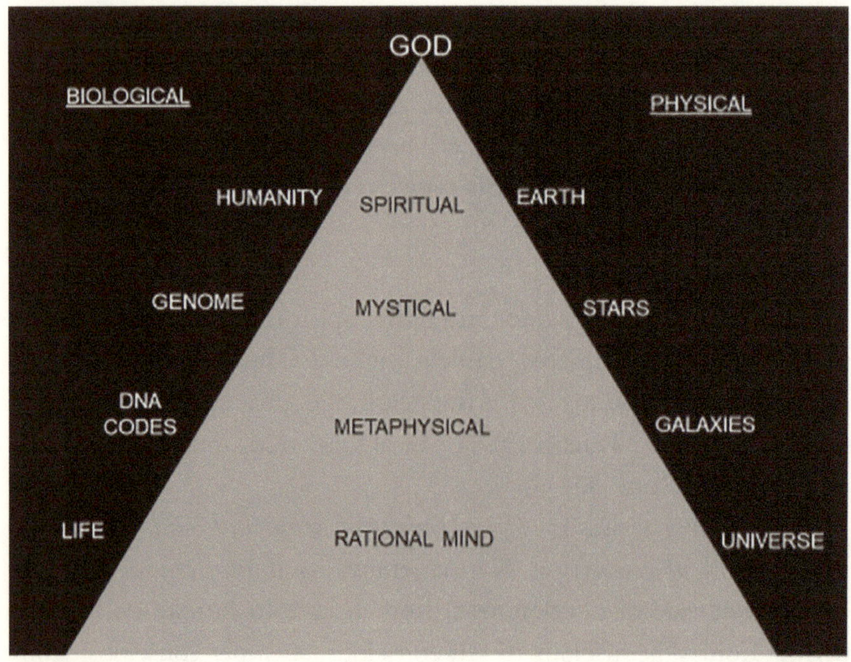


➢ **Fig. 14* Illustration of Dimensions of Creation by the author**

Idealism came very close to integrating the Big Three (I, the WE, and the IT). There was abundant room for arts, morals, and sciences, and they were carefully seen as important and cherished moments in the overall process of Spirit itself. Moreover, the idealist vision was alive to the currents of development ... Idealism integrated Spirit and Evolution as perhaps the only convincing way, namely, by recognizing that evolution is simply Spirit-in-action ... This lustrous vision saw the entire universe—from physical matter, to biological organisms, to societies, cultures, minds, and souls—as the radian unfolding of a luminous Spirit, bright and brilliant in its way, never- ending in its liberating grace, as illustrated above by the author.

As Hegel put it, "Everything that from eternity has happened in the heaven and earth, the life of God and all the deeds of time simply are the struggles for the Spirit to know itself, to find itself, be for itself, and finally unite itself to itself; it is alienated and divided, but only so as to be able thus to find itself and return to itself. ... "

## CONSCIENCE:

*He always listens to his conscience—that inner voice that warns him when somebody's watching.* **--Anon**

Conscience or Awareness is the interior quintessentially human voice that speaks to us of goodness and duty. It's the voice we must obey if we are to keep our integrity. It counsels doing good, while avoiding evil, and serves as a referee to rule on what is questionable. What is more, conscience *requires action*, not just conviction. It demands that we live according to the *truth* as we know it. ... Now, if the world were perfect, everyone would agree on what the truth is and all our consciences would be pulling in the same direction. In the flawed and imperfect world that *really* exists, this is not the case.

### Pluralism:

Source: *"The Right to be Wrong,"* by Kevin Seamus Hasson

Pluralism results more or less inevitably from these three factors about conscience: It's not infallible but it is in charge—and it demands action, not just belief. [It is] an interior voice that is often right, sometimes wrong, but always authoritative [and] will predictably lead different people to embrace the different religious convictions they believe to be true, and to live accordingly.

America began with religious beliefs and traditions about God, and the convictions of former European Christians, primarily Puritan Protestants. Later Catholics became the single largest Christian group (about 28% of the population today), and Jews, Moslems, Mormons, and many other religious minority sects have been accepted in society. It is neither good nor bad in itself. It can't be outlawed and needn't be glorified. *It simply is!* The question *is not* how to maximize diversity, or how to minimize it. The question is how to live authentically in the midst of it, while allowing others to do the same.

Certain factors in American culture, especially the Puritan tradition of self-sufficiency and Thoreau's ideas of Civil Disobedience, have led to our understanding of conscience only as individual and personal choice, as in a decision or judgment about right or wrong.

Conflicts between the individual conscience and groups or government authority have been part of our history: Dr. Martin Luther King defying discriminatory laws in the name of conscience. Young men protesting the Vietnam War as: "conscientious objectors." Soldiers who refuse to carry out orders, which they consider immoral or unjust. Couples practicing contraception with the words, "We've got to follow our conscience."

## True Conscience:

According to Bishop Fulton J. Sheen "[In] *Christian Theology*, a true conscience is not of our making; otherwise we could induce it always to testify in our defense. Conscience cannot come to us from the rulings of society; otherwise it would never reprove us when society approves us, nor console us when society condemns.

A sound conscience stands firm, no matter whether we dislike its findings, and no matter whether those around us are opposed to them or not. (This presumes that basic faith beliefs, moral conduct, and traditions are taught in the home by parents and schools, which is not generally the case today).

The very existence of conscience implies that there is outside us a Divine Lawmaker, Who legislates—a Divine Executive, Who witnesses our correspondence with the law—and a Divine Judge, Who passes sentences. At all times, we feel that there is confronting us an unseen witness in whose inner praise we rejoice, in whose inner reproof we blush with shame; and this witness is God.

The very word conscience means knowing with—knowing with whom, but God? For conscience is the impact of Divine Truth and Goodness on our inner self."

## Grammar of Assent:

John Henry Newman (1801-1890) was one of the greatest champions of the human conscience, with his *Grammar of Assent*, published in 1870. He viewed conscience in two ways—as an Inner Light and as Personal Choice. In religious matters, Newman fully realized that the mind desires certitude (self-evident, utmost conviction), "a consciousness of being right." Certitude can be established from self-evident information, but the problem is how the mind passes from a conditional inference to certitude.

In actuality, all sciences make use of our senses in the collection of data. We must trust our senses and logic to get to final conclusions. Our senses themselves can and must, in the end, be the instruments through which one finds out about the limitations of their senses. The truth is that refined science can (does) utilize what the senses give to increase our understanding, but it is the senses that provide that essential information in the first place.

However, we can come to false conclusions from our limited senses, as in a closed moving train with the window covered, wherein we believe we are motionless. Most of us lack senses to "see" the spiritual nature of humans, yet we "sense" that we and they are spiritual beings. How? Because they (we) act spiritually.

> ***Just as a candle cannot burn without fire, men cannot live without a spiritual life.*** **Buddha**

## Newman's Conscience:

Source: James Murray Elwood on: *John H Newman*

Newman's contribution to religious thought was significant. He said, the mind, in accepting generalizations of science and the great outlines of history, is guided by probabilities founded on certainties, so the mind is also a guided in religious affairs by a method described as *"cumulating probabilities."* They are independent of each other, arising out of the nature and circumstances of the particular case which is under review; probabilities too fine to avail separately, too subtle and circuitous to be convertible into syllogisms, too numerous and various for such conversion, even were they convertible.

The ability of the mind to discover certitude in a mass of converging probabilities is termed by Newman *"the illative sense."* The human mind judging and correlating, or analyzing and synthesizing principles, doctrines, facts, testimonies, memories, experiences, and proceeding to "an accumulation of probabilities … and from probabilities we may construct legitimate proof, sufficient for certitude. …"

However brilliant Newman's defense of human freedom is it should be noted that he did *not* view conscience only as personal choice. Newman's understanding of *"the light within"* is far richer and much more profound than the way it has been interpreted by "civil libertarians."

The role of conscience is to offer us an interior light by which we would not only become more and more sensitive to the presence of God within our hearts, but would be led to a more intimate union with him. Conscience also helps us sort out right and wrong and assert ourselves against injustice. *Act upon your light, though in the midst of difficulties, and you will be carried on, you do not know how far.*

Abraham obeyed the call and journeyed, not knowing whither he went. So if we follow the voice of God, we shall be brought on step by step into a New World, of which before we had no idea. This is His gracious way with us: He gives, not all at once, but by measure and season, wisely.

Newman was very concerned that conscience be understood as the *"voice of God."* It was not only that obedience to His "kindly light" had led him to take the momentous steps in his own life (conversion from the Anglican Church to Catholicism) –despite the loss of university position, great loss of public reputation and loss of the affection of his family and friends. But he knew that obedience to conscience, as the voice of God, would lead to obedience to the Gospel as the Word of

God. For fidelity to a personal request is far more demanding than loyalty to abstract ethical principles.

Sensitivity to God's presence can reorient the direction of a person's whole life and have enormous consequences in his or her quest for happiness. Many saints have experienced this special spiritual influence that caused them to perform incredible acts of charity. Is this "inner voice" a reality or only a Victorian cleric's way of describing what modern psychology now calls "guilt feelings?" Newman was well aware of psychological states such as neurotic guilt and free-floating anxiety (which he called "fidgets"), but he saw our overwhelming awareness, commanding insights and sudden prompting in terms of their ultimate origin; they were, in Callista's beautiful phrase, but *"the echo of a person speaking to me."*

These feelings have their source in an inescapable "Someone": Inanimate things cannot stir our affections; these are correlative with persons. If, as is the case, we feel responsibility, are ashamed, are frightened at transgressing the voice of conscience, this implies that there is One to whom we are responsible, before Whom we are ashamed, Whose claims on us we fear . . ..

"These feelings in us are such as require for their exciting cause an intelligent being: we are not affectionate toward a stone, nor do we feel shame before a horse or a dog; we have not remorse or compunction on breaking mere human law; yet, so it is, conscience excites all these painful emotions, confusion, foreboding, self-condemnation and on the other hand it sheds upon us a deep peace, as sense of security, a resignation, and a hope, which there is no earthly object to elicit."

## Human Ego

*If true freedom is to be found within ourselves, the ego must yield itself to the birth of our true personality.* **--Bishop Fulton J. Sheen, Ph.D. in his book: "Lift up Your Heart."**

The story of Dr. Jekyll and Mr. Hyde is the story of every man born of woman, for their lives within each one of us two selves—the ego and the 'I.' The ego is what we think we are—the self. The ego is the spoiled child in us—selfish, petulant, clamorous, and spoiled—the creation of our mistakes in living.

The 'I' is our personality made in the image and likeness of God! The lives of the two selves cannot be lived simultaneously. If we attempt to do so, we suffer remorse, anxiety, and inner dissatisfaction. Key points of Bishop Sheen's thoughts on when the Ego dominates:

We blame little faults on others, and excuse great offenses in ourselves;
We wrong others, and deny that there is any guilt;
We hate others, and call it "zeal";
We flatter others because of what they can do for us, and call it "love";
We lie to them, and call it "tact";
We selfishly push others aside, and call it "getting our just rights";
We judge others, and say that we are "facing the facts";
We pile up more wealth than is necessary in life, and call it "security"
This becomes a major obstacle to the acceptance of faith in God. Students are told by parents and teachers and become convinced that this is the "thing" that is most important *"if you want to get ahead you must do this."* The masses of the world have made this their "god." They spend their very life and waking moments to achieve this. They know not poverty of the "3rd World" and could care less).
We resent the wealth of others, and call ourselves "defenders of the downtrodden";
We deny inviolable principles of law, and call ourselves "liberal";
We want so much to be loved, that we forget to love;
We possess money, and think that therefore we have worth;
We judge our virtues by the vices from which we abstain;
We refuse to make up our minds, and boast that we are broadminded; and
They develop a vicarious interest in solving problems, which do not concern them, as a substitute for tackling their own problem of selfishness.

These are some of the temptations to which we are all prone when we allow the ego in us to become supreme. In talking about other people we often ask: "*Why doesn't he recognize his own faults?*" The reason is that "he" has never practiced self-introspection; his ego has obscured his "I"; his egotism has drowned out his personality. Constantly busied with appearances and with their own surface emotions, such people become incapable of love in the true sense of the word; they love the experience of love, but they do not love any person, because they are hardly persons themselves. Frightened to look inside themselves, they abhor silence and quiet; for only the peaceful soul can live with themselves.

The ego asks: Why should anyone tell me what is right or wrong? How do I know there is God? The little infractions of youth become the grave rebellions of maturity. For what crime is long inexcusable if one makes his own conscience the standard? If each man is to be his own judge, who will be condemned? If the ego's "right" is identified with cupidity, then what injustice will it not espouse?

The Dalai Lama adds: If the "self" had intrinsic identity, it would be possible to speak in terms of self-interest in isolation from that of others. But because this is not so, because self and others can only be understood in terms of relationship, we see that self-interest and others' interest are closely interrelated. Indeed, within this picture of dependently originated reality, we see that there is no self-interest completely unrelated to others' interest. Due to the fundamental interconnectedness which lies at the heart of reality, your interest is also my interest. From this, it becomes clear that 'my' interest and 'your' interest are intimately connected. In a deep sense, they converge.

## Passions & Emotions:

Feelings are good, since they are a gift from the Creator. Yet, excessive emotional passion can be treacherous, and precarious, if that's all we live for. They force us back into our selves—our egos—*what I want is what I feel, is what I need.*

Feelings can trap us within ourselves. A more mature man and woman, or married couple, must go beyond this initial stage—that's when they begin to know true love for each other. That's how it is with God—you grow and reach that higher stage in your relationship with Him, a much deeper love, real joy, such as experienced by saints, like St. Catherine of Siena, St. Teresa of Avila, St. Teresa of France, and especially, St. Francis of Assisi.

## Evil & Suffering:

> ***Evil as disordered love, disordered will; it is a wrong relationship, and nonconformity between our will and God's will. --St. Augustine***

Evil is *not* a being, or substance, or "thing." All of creation is good, *ontologically*. Things are not evil, within themselves. One must distinguish between the natural forces of nature, and human moral evil. Moral evil is caused by the human heart, the will, and our free choice, the *intention* of the mind and soul. One must also separate the evil acts towards someone, from evil done to us by others.

> ***We have met the enemy—and he is us. --Walt Kelly***

The Greek term for evil: *kakia* means "what is bad," what one desires to avoid, such as sickness, misfortune, suffering, fear, grief, terror, and confusion. The Christian meaning does not include physical or emotional misfortune, but rather moral evil, which comes from the human heart (see *Morality and Conscience*). "What shall we do?" *There are moral absolutes*, which are founded on reality that can be understood, providing real knowledge on how humans should behave. Good is related to order and final causality. Every agent acts toward an end. Humans are rational, material and spiritual agents.

One does that which is evil or good with every deliberate human choice and act (or inaction). One also develops habits that cause them to *automatically* do what is good or evil. Evil is often done under the auspices and attraction to what we "think" is good.

If one kills innocent people for a "good cause," as some "brain-washed" terrorists do, in the name of Allah. The person(s) committing the act may or may not be guilty, depending on the *specifics of their mental state*: did they know right from wrong? Did they know that the deed was evil? Nevertheless, the act itself remains evil. Reason determines what is good and evil. The *normal* human mind makes moral judgments, called conscience, which means 'with knowledge' (*con scientia*). In a court of law, mentally sick villains cannot be judged guilty, if they didn't know right from wrong.

## Group Evil:

M. Scott Peck, M.D., an expert of the human psyche, writes in *People of The Lie,* (Touchstone) about cases of really evil people, and group evil, that he encountered in his practice, which psychiatrists and psychologists are unwilling to acknowledge as "evil." People have been "possessed" before, during and after the time of Christ. Dr. Peck witnessed Exorcisms and concludes that only through the intercession of many prayers and *real love* by priests and family for the victim, can they drive out such evil spirits, and it is essentially only through the saving grace, mercy and love of Jesus Christ.

The only reasonable solution to the wave of school, church, and airport mass killings is: "profiling." *It works in Israel!* Everyone has a cellphone, which should be used to report suspicious persons, *confidentially.* Unfortunately, trained guards, *with guns*, must also be in every large school and college, with metal detectors installed at all entries to schools. Databases containing incidents of anti-social behavior must be established, and authorities *must take action* on all validated activities. Mental health needs to be much better addressed in America, and violent movies must be controlled by authorities.

> ***Individual civil rights are meaningless when you're dead!*** *–***Author**

## Bad Things Happen to Good People:

Just as there are natural laws of nature (physical and biological), there are moral laws, as well. Many good and innocent people have experienced physical or biological tragedies (sickness, cancer, terrorism), and great wars and suffering. One might also ask: why are millions in Africa, Asia and Central America are born into a life of poverty, and hopelessness? One answer: it's a test to see if those who are better situated will feed the hungry, care for the sick, and cloth the naked?

Nevertheless, it is said that the humble and poor get to heaven easier than most of the proud and wealthy. Christ said (Luke 6:20*): "Blessed are you who are poor, for yours is the kingdom of God. ..."* God gives each of us a cross to carry of different weight. Our goal is to carry it, with the grace of God to help us. (For the impact of sin and evil in our lives, see also 1 Cor. 10:13).

Extreme Nationalism, at beginning of the 20th century, produced extreme evil forces that were planted at the end of World War I. The British, French, and American victors demanded *extreme* penalties, which unjustly caused suffering for the collective German people. Thus the past evil of World War I, produced even greater future evil, such as Nazism during WW II, and Communism during the long Cold War. It's like a cancerous organism that spreads unceasingly. Other examples of evil and suffering included: the Irish famine, Stalin's Great Purge, Mao's Red Brigade, and the Jewish Holocaust, where millions of Jews *and non-Jews* died.

Many Jews had a clear choice when Hitler was becoming the new dictator: they could stay or leave Germany with their families. Some prudently left, but many stayed. The reasons for not avoiding this "Gathering Storm" of obvious evil forces varied: some thought this would soon pass; others didn't want to leave their positions of power, businesses and wealth behind; and others were passive, in the face of such pending great evil.

Thomas Aquinas said of suffering, as Aristotle had said of shame, "that it was a thing not good in itself, but a thing which might have certain goodness in particular circumstances. If evil is present, its pain [can be] recognition of the evil being a kind of knowledge, and that is relatively good. The alternative is that the person should be ignorant of the evil or ignorant that evil is contrary to its nature 'either of which,' says the philosopher 'is manifestly bad.'"

"Suffering reminds us of what all others endure, it serves as a powerful injunction to practice compassion and refrain from causing others pain. …, though potentially a source of anger and despair, it has an equal potential to be a source of spiritual growth (depending on our interpretation and response)," writes the Dalai Lama.

> *The true lesson is this: just as the sins of the guilty harm the innocent, the sufferings of the innocent can redeem the guilty. The key to this powerful problem is not to be found in our words, but from His dying words from the cross: "Father, forgive them for they know not what they do."*

Rabbi Harold Kushner wrote a bestseller book in 1983, *When Bad Things Happen to Good People* (Avon Publishing. 1983). Kushner's tone is humble, compassionate, and he is obviously a man of significant biblical scholarship. When Kushner's son Aaron was three, he and his wife learned that he had a rare disease known as *Perihelia* (rapid aging). They both suffered greatly while watching their son slowly waste away, until he died at the young age of fourteen. The book is a masterpiece, in terms of its feelings about the human dilemma, which grew out of this very personal tragic experience.

Nevertheless, the main thesis of this excellent work by Rabbi Kushner, in this author's view, *is erroneous*: "Since good people suffer unfairly, God must lack either goodness or power," Kushner believed. He concludes that: God is good, but abandons belief in His infinite power. He writes his book *"for all those people whose love for God and devotion to Him led them to blame themselves for the suffering and are persuaded that they deserved it."*

Rabbi Kushner perhaps didn't fully consider that the reasons people suffer is because, while most children are born healthy and physical normal, not all do. Nature has its own level or kind of random-like freedom. Moreover, moral evil is done to us by others (See Mt 25:41, 46 and Luke 3:16-17).

Adam and Eve upset the balance of the universe with their disobedience. Satan (in essence) argued that since God cast him out of heaven for his sin of disobedience, how can humans who were also disobedient be reconciled? Thus, God sent His only begotten son, Jesus Christ into the world, to suffer and die, in order to justify *all* repentant sinners. *Universal justice was then re-established!*

Suffering and death are great trials, and also a prodigious challenge for family members and friends to see how well they respond to their neighbor's suffering. Do they pass this test?

> **The Human package: Great grief always comes with the greatest love! The supreme example is Jesus Christ on the Cross.** Author

Our trials on earth are only a preview of what's in store—a small sample of the enormous joy and suffering to come. Job in the Old Testament deals with this profound human theme: Why do people suffer, if God is in control? That problem has exercised the best minds of every society, from the beginning of civilization.

The answer: God will not interfere with *free will*, our ability to act as we choose—for good or evil. Nonetheless, He is certainly not helpless and is decisive when it suits His divine plan, as when He heard the pleas of the Hebrews in Egypt, and sent Moses to free them. However, He does *not* allow unrestrained evil to exist.

By tasting a bit of hell (and sample of paradise) in this life, we are driven to ponder what we may face in the next. In this way our current trials may be "acts of mercy." For some, they may represent God's way of placing obstacles in our otherwise headlong rush to hell. For others it may motivate them to finally make peace with their Creator, before it's too late.

> ***Human souls are the battlefield on which spiritual battles are fought, on a daily basis. Without God's saving grace, we are lost.***

A moment is that split second between past and future. Everything that we do and say, feel and experience will soon pass. One cannot freeze that special moment. *It's transitory!* We cannot hold onto it, no matter how precious it may be. Yet, each moment of every day of our short lives has eternal consequences. The stakes are enormous. Like Pascal's wager, *winners take all; and losers sacrifice everything.*

Every individual has his or her own particular cross to carry in life. Only through true faith and prayer, can one uphold their cross. We cannot save ourselves or anyone else by our acts alone. We are dependent on the grace of God. We must cooperate with this grace, by trusting His mercy and love, and then accept the challenge.

> ***When one is close to God, the beauty, the love, the wonder of His presence is so phenomenal, that nothing else really matters—including great pain and the many problems of life.* ---Author**

## Anthropos Morphism:

> ***Greek expression: Man giving human form to God's words or acts; fallible man attributing to God what He never commanded.***

You don't tell a story or report events, such as the Bible, like one would deliver a loaf of bread. When one writes, delivers or sends information there are different mental processes involved between the writer or sender, and reader or receiver:

1. Apoplectics: Intended purpose of the sender and results.
2. Pragmatics: Expected action and the implemented action.
3. Semantics: Ideas of the sender and understood meaning.
4. Syntax: Language employed, understood and its context.
5. Translation: Errors that alter true meaning of the story.

Since God Almighty is merciful, loving and absolutely good, **He is incapable of evil**. Accordingly, this author has serious questions about *some* Bible Old Testament claims: In 1 Samuel 15, 16, and 19, the prophet asserts: This is what the Lord Almighty says: *"I will punish the Amalekites for what they did to Israel… now go (King Saul) and attack the Amalekites and totally destroy everything that belongs to them. Do not spare them: put to death men, women, children and infants."*

Saul didn't fully follow this *supposedly* God-given order by Samuel. He didn't kill everyone and gave some of the booty to his commanders. According to Samuel: *"Now the Spirit of the Lord had departed from (King) Saul, and an evil spirit from the Lord tormented him."*

In this story, not only did God *allegedly* send Saul an "evil spirit," He also caused the king of Israel to not have free choice, the ability to choose between good and evil. This clearly doesn't fit with a merciful and loving God. Moreover, *Saul cannot be considered guilty if he lacked free will.* These contradictions suggest misrepresentations of what God really commanded. How is this possible? Because these writers were not superhuman; they were not dictation machines, thus errors creeped into the text.

Moreover, these ancient authors wrote during an era when culture, language, and the symbols used to express meaning, were very different from our 21ˢᵗ century. Haven't many of us experienced difficulty communicating what we really mean today, even when the dialogue is between people of the same culture and language?

Those who preach that one must accept *every word* of the Bible, as the "exact words of God," are doing a disservice to the very people they are trying to win over to Christianity. Faith built on a foundation of sand will be shaky at best, imprudent at worst. We must be able to see the forest from the trees, to be able to understand the meaning of the message from the particular details of stories. This is a *literalist* version of Christianity that equates God's love with Biblical Genocide, cannot be defended historically or in today's world.

## Temptation:

> *Temptation can strengthen us, with the grace of God, to help us overcome it. Without temptation, we would never be tested.*

Free will makes little sense without temptation; the making of our choice(s) between that which is good versus that which is less good, or evil. After all, Satan even tempted Christ in the desert. Without the knowledge that Revelation gives of God, we cannot recognize grave sin clearly. One usually explains it as merely a development flaw, a psychological weakness, a mistake, or the consequence of an "inadequate social environment."

> *Sin is an abuse of the freedom, which God gives to all persons, so that they are capable of loving Him, and loving one another.*

Temptation can strengthen us morally, or corrupt us. The Hebrew word *Satan* means: to be hostile toward, to attack, to act as an adversary. Temptation first appears in the *Book of Job*. It is easier for anyone to avoid sin if they live a good, healthy, happy life, and are infrequently exposed to the temptations of the evil. Whereas a person who is constantly bombarded by temptation (e.g., drugs, sexual), is bound to give in to sin. Nevertheless, through sincere and constant prayer, the special grace of God is provided, even a person living in a cesspool of sin, can rise above it, for the glory of God.

A perfect case is that of the earlier sinful life of St. Augustine. His mother, St. Monica prayed for the conversion of her son for nineteen years. Her prayers were finally answered: He soon became one of the greatest saints and doctors of theology in all Christianity.

There are many physical disasters in nature—droughts, floods, earthquakes, fire, epidemics, and the like. In some Eastern Religions, this is "evil" which is attributed to Karma (force generated by a person's actions held in Hinduism and Buddhism to perpetuate transmigration and in its ethical consequences to determine the nature of the person's next existence).

Cause and effect from individuals, groups, and national thoughts, words, and deeds spring from ignorance. Is this what caused World Wars? Evil thoughts and deeds by people, with free choice, that allowed themselves to be seduced by evil leaders (Hitler, Stalin, Mao)? Most Germans thought Hitler was "The Savior," who rescued his people from the great injustices following World War I.

**State of Journeying:**

**The way of the world is to praise dead saints and persecute living ones. --Nathaniel Howe**

The Creator willed to create a world *"in a state of journeying"* toward its ultimate perfection. The process of becoming involves the existence of the more perfect alongside the less perfect; the constructive and destructive forces of nature. With moral good there exists also moral evil, as long as creation has not reached perfection. Angels and men, as intelligent and free spirits have to journey toward their ultimate destinies by their free choice, preferential love. They can therefore go astray. Thus, moral evil entered the world. God in no way, directly or indirectly, is the cause of moral evil. He *permits* evil because He respects the freedom of His creatures, and knows how to derive great good from everything.

## Virtues & Vices:

*Men imagine that they communicate their virtue or vice only by overt actions, and do not see that virtue and vice emit a breath every moment. --R. W. Emerson*

Virtue is an activity of the soul in obedience to good reasoning. The hindering factors of virtue are ignorance, lack of self-control, insufficient training, lack of good intentions, and weak will. Virtue is a routine, a determined disposition to do what is good. It causes a person not only to perform good acts, but also to give the "best of themselves," each and every time.

The virtuous person tends towards the good with all their mental and spiritual powers. He or she pursues what is good and chooses it with concrete actions, according to reason. The hindering factors of good virtues are ignorance, lack of self-control and training. It's *essential* however to have early training in good virtuous habits.

There are three classes of virtues: moral, intellectual, and theological. Moral virtues are acquired by human effort.

There are four "cardinal" moral virtues: prudence, justice, fortitude, and temperance. They are called cardinal because all other virtues may be classified under these four major virtues: Prudence disposes the practical reason to discern, in every circumstance, true good and to choose the right means to achieve it. Justice consists in the firm and constant will to give God and neighbor their due. Fortitude ensures firmness in difficulties and constancy in pursuit of the good. Temperance moderates the attraction of pleasures of the senses and provides balance in the use of created goods.

Moral virtues grow through education, deliberate acts, and perseverance in struggles. Divine grace of God purifies and elevates them. Intellectual virtues are: stable dispositions of the intellect and the will, which govern our acts, order our passions, and guide our conduct in accordance with reason and faith.

The three theological virtues are: faith, hope, and charity (Rom. 5:1-8). They dispose Christians to live in a relationship with the Holy Trinity, and have God for their origin, motive, and object.

The nine "fruits of the Holy Spirit" are: love, gladness, peace, long-suffering, kindness, goodness, fidelity, mildness, and continence or self-restraint (Gal. 5:22-23). The seven gifts of the Holy Spirit are: wisdom, understanding, counsel, fortitude, knowledge, piety, and fear of the Lord.

Virtues may be natural, i.e., acquired by good habits that are increased by naturally doing good acts, or supernatural. God infuses supernatural virtues into the soul, so that one may perform supernatural acts, as many great saints have done in the past.

## Extremism:

> ***What is dangerous about extremists is not that they are extreme, but that they are intolerant. The evil is not what they say about their cause, but what they say (and do) about their opponents. --Robert F. Kennedy***

Feelings or passions are emotions or movements of our sensitive appetites that inclines us to act or not to act in regard to something felt or imagined to be good or evil. Passions are natural components of the human psyche; they provide the essential connection between the life of the senses and the mind. Passions are evil, if that which is loved is evil, and good, if that which is loved is good.

The following thoughts are from The Dalai Lama: ... Restraining our response to negative thoughts and emotions is not a matter of just suppressing them: insight into their destructive nature is crucial. Merely being told that envy, a very powerful and destructive emotion, is bad, cannot provide a strong defense against it. If we order our lives externally but ignore the inner dimension, inevitably we will find that doubt, anxiety, and other afflictions develop, and happiness eludes us.

> ***Thousands of candles can be lighted from a single candle, and the life of the candle will not be shortened. Happiness never decreases by being shared.* Buddha**

We can conceive the nature of mind in terms of water in a lake. When the water is stirred up by a storm, the mud from the lake's bottom clouds it, making it appear opaque. When the storm passes, the mud settles and the water (mind) is left clear once again.

... Unlike physical discipline, true inner—or spiritual—discipline cannot be achieved by force, but only through voluntary and deliberate effort. The undisciplined mind is like an elephant. If left to blunder around out of control, it will wreak havoc. But the harm and suffering we encounter as a result of failing to restrain the negative impulses of mind, far exceed the damage of a rampaging elephant can cause.

...The undisciplined mind—that is, the mind under the influence of anger, hatred, greed, pride, selfishness, and so on—is the source of all our troubles. ... Afflictive emotions destroy one of our most precious qualities, namely, our capacity for discriminative awareness. Robbed of what enables us to judge between right and wrong, to evaluate what is likely to be of lasting benefit and what is merely temporary benefit to self and others, and to unable to discern the likely outcome of our actions, we are no better off than animals.

Afflictive emotions deceive us. They seem to offer satisfaction but they do not provide it. ... This energy is essentially blind. Decisions taken under its influence are often a source of regret. When we become angry, we stop being compassionate, loving, generous, forgiving, tolerant, and patient altogether. We thus deprive ourselves of the very things that happiness consists of. If we are burned by fire, there is no sense being angry with fire, it is the nature of fire to burn. In fact, for every negative state, we find that we can identify one which opposes it (positive state). For example, humility opposes pride; contentment opposes greed; and perseverance opposes indolence. Inner peace, which is the principal characteristic of happiness, and anger, *cannot* coexist without undermining one another. Indeed, negative thoughts and emotions undermine the very causes of peace and happiness.

**Peace comes from within. Do not seek it without.**
**Buddha**

Negative emotions are the source of unethical behavior. Each act affects not only people closest to us but also colleagues, friends, community, and, ultimately the world. Our every act has a universal dimension.

> **Are desires and emotions separate or merely modes of
> the same type of behavior? One point is very certain,
> both are distinguished from the mental logistic faculty,
> the sole expression of form, and are wholly subject to its
> decisions. How? By the power of ideas, hardened into
> reasoned judgments. --Author**

## EXPERIENCE & KNOWLEDGE:

> **Experience is the worst teacher; it gives the test before
> the lesson. --Vernon Law**

Knowledge is based on one's correct application of reason and experience. Certain knowledge, not probable knowledge, is beyond reasonable doubt. It's unity of the knower and the thing known. Different levels of knowledge start from experience (or an information base of past experiences), and builds conclusions (or chains of conclusions), used to build, derive, and establish some final level of conclusion.

Intellect is what is essential (in different degrees) compared to phantasms (images) of the object or thing under consideration. Passive intellect forms a conscious idea about the thing, subject, or object. Intellect is not material. Matter or objects of being are specific. Ideas within our intellect are general and immaterial.

In the early Christian Church, outside of Israel, most of the faithful were recruited from uneducated pagans. Over 90% of all people in the Roman Empire were pagans, including laborers, and 75% were slaves, the common people, and many were outcasts. When it is seen how our Lord chose the commonest men for His apostles and world evangelism, it is apparent that there are other factors at work besides the intellect.

It does not take knowledge to save a soul; it takes trust and love of God, and love of neighbor. "My brethren, if one of you strays from the truth, and a man succeeds in bringing him back, let him be sure of this: to bring back erring feet into the right path means saving a soul from death, means throwing a veil over a multitude of sins." (James 5:20).

True lovers of God and wisdom are never content with what their eyes can see, but are ever searching with reasoning for the invisible, pure and immutable essence of things. They distinguish the idea from the objects that participate in the idea. Our conceptual knowledge does not reveal all the particular determinations of an idea.

> *Man is the mineral that blooms, the plant that feels, the animal that speaks. Intelligence makes man spokesman of the universe. He carries the whole universe back again to its Creator God, by his intelligence. No reason can be established, without another reason. Truth is eternal though its verbal expression (is) localized in time and space. --R. W. Emerson*

Intelligence is generally necessary to produce a work of art, music, painting, poetry, etc., and for its appreciation. Yet some art forms can provide a "spiritual" experience that transcends the purely rational, scientific and objective truth capabilities of human beings.

Knowledge, in and of its self, is neither good nor evil. *How we apply that knowledge is the key point!* The more we know, the greater are the risks and rewards, and the greater is our responsibility towards human nature and our global environment. Human knowledge cannot be denied, since it is God-given. The more we understand the forces of the universe, the more we should appreciate the beauty, wonder, and glory of the Creator.

## Sciences ("ITs"):

> *Science seeks to understand the objective facts about the universe; religion provides the purpose, the meaning. Science is concerned with measurable, deducible facts. The object of religion is that knowledge and study that concerns the Creator. ---Author*

Whether one plots the progress of science and technology beginning 10,000, 1,000 years ago or 100 years ago, the result is much the same. There was an enormous span of time unmarked by any conspicuous activity, until about 10,000-6,000 BC. There were important changes, such as horticulture, but no measurable departure from what went before. Then, about 4000 BC, sometime after Abraham, there was a distinct increase in technological innovation (agrarian societies). At about 2,100 years ago, during the time of Christ, the rate of change quickened. Taking always the whole globe as a unit—for local areas have retreated as well as advanced, the rate of pace continued to increase rapidly, to well beyond the Industrial Revolution. Adapting to change, not to stability, is the normal aspect of human progress.

## Civilization ("WE"):

> ***Civilization is human culture and society characterized by significant size and complexity and by widespread influence, often associated with developments as writing, the arts and sciences, and establishment of cities.***

The term "civilization" may also be applied to a specific culture or society that has attained this status. Thus, one may speak of "American civilization" or "Western culture." As a culture, civilization is a way of life, our values, a more or less coherent body of convention, or view of the nature of things, that characterizes a particular community. As a society, it is a group of people who live in social communion with each another. However, the boundaries of the society and the culture do not always coincide. This question of boundaries gives rise to some of the principal problems examined by students of civilization.

The above definition of civilization as a special type of culture or society must be distinguished from other related meanings that have been attached to the word. In the 18th century, "civilization" came to be used to describe a *rational and enlightened* way of life as contrasted with the neglected ways of life of the feudal period. The word "civilization" was sometimes used as a synonym for "culture." Some writers have restricted the term to the rational and technical outlook of a culture, which they contrast with such aspects as morals and the arts that are ends in themselves, and are not usually judged on rational grounds.

The generally accepted criteria of civilization, which is found in ancient civilizations of both the Old and the New World are:

1.   Large compact settlements;
2.   Differentiated people;
3.   Taxes for those who govern;
4.   Public buildings;
5.   Ruling class exempt from manual work;
6.   Writing; and some forms of science;
7.   Foreign trade; and
8.   Specialized craftsmen and the arts;

This view sees civilization in terms of technological achievement, complexity and the magnitude of political and social life.

Of all civilizations, that which we call "Western" is merely the upstart or prodigy. During most of history, Europe was isolated, peripheral, and culturally dependent on the Mediterranean. Its people were primitive tribesmen long after other civilizations (e.g., Chinese, Egyptian, and Maya) had come to full development as a civilization. Only during the Middle-Ages did Europe become comparable.

During the last three centuries European civilization carried out radical expansion, and revolutionary transformation of the world. In about the last 150 years, nearly all areas of the world, civilized or primitive, confronted the creative vitality of the West, and the impact of its values, ideas, religion, political power, military superiority, and Western technology. The world is rapidly evolving into fewer interdependent regions, characterized by a "worldview," or universal way of life that tends to dilute what was previously local and traditional. A few ancient civilizations, and the newer widespread modernity, have so far coexisted.

## Science & Faith:

> ***Science must be at the service of the human person, of
> his/her inalienable rights, for his/her true and integral
> good, in conformity with the plan and the will of God.
> It is an illusion to claim moral neutrality in scientific
> research and its applications.***

The Creator gave humans the authority, knowledge, and stewardship over all that He created. The purpose of the scientific-technological phase of evolution was to give humanity the capacity to transcend the early creature-human condition. The "new" earth can be a more natural, more cooperative, in which the works of humanity and nature are lovingly tended, preserved, enhanced, and consciously evolving as a steady-state balanced environment.

> ***The shores of truth are girt by a wide and stormy
> ocean; the natural home of illusion... We always find
> the thing obscure which we wish to prove, and that
> clear which we use for proof."***—**R. W. Emerson**

In *The Marriage of Sense and Soul*, Ken Wilber wrote: Truth, in the sense of *objective* truth, is described in 'IT' language. This is the domain of objective realities, realities that can be seen in an empirical and mono-logical fashion, from atoms to brains, from cells to ecosystems, from rocks to solar systems, all of which are described in 'IT' (scientific) language.

Thus, when we say that Modernity differentiated the spheres of individual and art, morals, and science, this also means that modernity differentiated the realms of I (individual morality and beauty), WE (collective morality), and IT (objective truths).

Because modernity differentiated the WE and the IT, political or religious tyranny (of the WE) could no longer determine what was objectively true. This differentiation of the WE and IT led directly to the rise of the Empirical Sciences, including ecological sciences, systems theory, and quantum-relativistic physics (see *Equations that Changed the World*). Pre-modern societies produced [fewer] of these empirical sciences, in part because they lacked this differentiation.

Because modernity differentiated I and the WE, the collective WE could no longer dominate [the] individual I. That is, each individual I (person) had rights that could not be violated by the state, by churches, or the community in general. This differentiation of I and WE contributed directly to the rise of liberal democracies, where each I was extended the political rights of Equality and Justice.

## SPIRITUAL TRUTH KEY POINTS:

o   Conscience is the interior quintessentially human voice that speaks to us of goodness and duty. It's the voice we must obey if we are to keep our integrity. It counsels doing good, while avoiding evil, and serves as a referee to rule on what is questionable.

o   The ego is what we think we are—the self. The 'I' is our personality made in the image and likeness of God! The lives of the two selves cannot be lived simultaneously.

o   The supernatural nature given to every person at creation is spirit or soul. All spirits are not necessarily good. Spirits can become sons or daughters of God, or of the devil.

o   The mind and spirit are not physical. *They are immaterial.* They cannot be touched or harmed directly.

o   Only negative thoughts, emotions and sin can harm them. Thus, only positive thoughts, emotions and virtue can protect them.

o   Soul is the spiritual faculty and principle of all humans which controls the mind and body.

o   Evil is *not* a being, or substance, or a "thing."

o   All of creation by God is good, *ontologically.*

o   Moral evil is caused by the human heart and will, our free choice, the *intention* of the mind and soul.

o   God Almighty is absolutely *incapable* of evil.

o   Virtue is an activity of the soul in obedience to good reasoning.

o   The hindering factors of virtue are ignorance, lack of self-control, insufficient training, lack of good intentions, and weak will.

o   Knowledge is based on one's correct application of reason and experience.

o   Certain knowledge is something beyond reasonable doubt. It's unity of the knower and the thing known.

o   Civilization is human culture or society characterized by significant size and complexity and by widespread influence, often associated with writing, the arts, and sciences, and the establishment of cities.

o   Science is a significant expression of man's dominion over creation. Science must be at the service of the human person. It is an illusion to claim moral neutrality in scientific research and its applications.

# X. Cultural Challenges & Solutions

*A climate of opinion, like a physical climate, is so pervasive a thing, that those who live within it and know no other take it for granted.* --Ralph W. Emerson

What kind of culture have we created lately? Is it a culture of compassion, love and life? Is it a culture of greed, violence and death? We remember the great evil of Nazism and Communism of the 20th century. We will encounter similar challenges in the 21st century. Why is this so? Because of the lack of empathy and contentment—which sows seeds of envy and aggressive competitiveness, which in turn, produces a society lacking in compassion for others. Advanced technology *multiplies* the effects of such evil, and ultimately produces home-grown terrorism.

*Freedom without purpose, without individual responsibility, and without spirituality, produces fundamental discontent. Clearly, that's exactly what we have today— deep-rooted discontent.*--Author

Many earlier Empires rose and declined in the history of humanity. Most declined from lack of moral leadership and *corruption from within*. America is experiencing a lack of morals, which has to be taught in the home, and the absence of ethics by government public officials, as well as business leaders. In today's society, bribes and "golden parachutes" seem to be the order of the day. Scandals run rampant and dishonesty seems to be accepted as the "new normal" way of doing business.

Such behavior has its *roots* in the lack of teaching children morality, the absence of good role models by parents, especially in early childhood years. We know this to be true, because my editor and spouse, Miriam, experienced lack of ethics by our youth, during her 40-years of teaching, at all levels, both private and public schools—*and it's getting much worse!*

Society has rejected Nazism, Fascism, Communism, Racism, and Terrorism… because they offend our conscience, contradict our human rights, and violate America's fundamental values. Unless this current trend is stopped, *and reversed*, we will face, in the next decades, and even greater moral decay in Western and American cultures.

## CHRISTIAN CHALLENGES:

We will continue to experience the following challenges:

- Disintegration of the basic family unit.
- Weakening of elementary moral values.
- Inadequate religious education.
- Progressive-Liberalism, and Atheism.
- Profusion of Occults' such as Scientology.
- Illicit Substance and Opioid epidemics.
- Sexual permissiveness, and lack of responsibility.
- Abortion-on-demand and Euthanasia.
- Materialism and absence of compassion for others.

Our youth are ill-prepared for the next onslaught of evil forces because of the inadequacy of public education systems, and insufficient Christian teaching, in particular. Where will children learn about morality, if not in their home? Who will be their future role models? What will inspire them? Whom will they emulate as adults? What is the role of Christianity?

## THE AWAKENING

The Coronavirus-19 Pandemic awakens us to our mortality, and the realization of our temporary existence on planet earth.

**Recent Pandemics**

## Examples of Plagues & Pandemics

**1. CORONAVIRUS PANDEMIC (2019-2021)**

Death Toll: 1-2 million. Cause: Corona-19 Virus

**2. HIV/AIDS PANDEMIC (2005-2012)**

Death Toll: 36 million. Cause: HIV/AIDS

**3. FLU PANDEMIC (1968)**

Death Toll: 1 million. Cause: Influenza

**4. ASIAN FLU (1956-1958)**

Death Toll: 2 million. Cause: Influenza

**5. FLU PANDEMIC (1918)**

Death Toll: 20-50 million. Cause: Influenza

**6. BLACK DEATH (1346-1353)**

Death Toll: 100 - 200 million. Cause: Bubonic Plague

➢ **Fig 15* Past Pandemics ***

During the *great pandemic in Rome in 590 AD*. Pope Gregory the Great, pleaded with God, and led a spiritual procession, with an image of the Blessed Mother of Christ, around the streets of Rome.

As they approached Hadrian's Tomb, Pope Gregory saw a vision of Michael the Archangel atop the tomb overlooking the city, sheathing his sword, a sign that the procession is pleasing to God. *That plaque ended immediately!*

## Bishops Key Role is to Save Souls

- The Church has *never* closed its doors to Christians who need access to the Sacraments in its 2,000-year history—until 2020

- Even during world wars, epidemics & pandemics, priests and bishops have served the people's needs.

- Saint Pope John Paul II, when he was a priest, held secret masses, during the Nazi and Communist era.

> ➢ **Fig 16 Bishops key role***

- If we awaken to this truth, we might realize that there is a more important meaning to life than mere existence, procreation, accumulation of wealth, status and power.
- We might recognize that we are *transcendent spiritual beings* with human bodies and remarkable "eternal souls."
- By *allowing* a "evil virus" to spread in the world, the Lord places an obstacle in our persistent path to damnation.
- The *positive* aspect of this pandemic is that God loves His creation that is good, especially humanity, and wants to save those who are otherwise heading towards the abyss.
- He turns Chinese Communist Evil Lies and Pandemic into a powerful message, while also respecting our free will to choose which path to take on our journey in our life.

This pandemic, in many respects, is worse than a "hot war," because it spreads silently and swiftly worldwide, killing hundreds-of-thousands of the good and bad, rich and poor, weak and strong, and the powerful, without any warning.

### *Those who demand "Equality;" this is the "Great Equalizer!"*

People are restricted, without families and loved ones. They must now think about their priorities in this life:

- What is it all about?
- Why did I waste so much time?
- How will my family survive this disaster?
- What does the future hold for me, and for humanity?

Many will turn to the Lord, and pray more passionately for forgiveness and salvation. Some will curse, become resentful, and fall away from their churches and temples. Millenniums will *suddenly* have to grow-up and somehow, reluctantly perhaps, become much more responsible.

The root cause of this Cultural Crisis is "lack of contentment"—which is greed—that then sows the seeds of envy and competitiveness, which then leads to a society of materialism, and lack of compassion for others.

While there are (unfortunately) dissimilarities between many Christian churches, as explored in my chapters on Spiritual, Moral, and Theological Truths, *all* accept the Apostles Creed. While one can and should openly debate important issues of faith, we all agree that there is a close and inescapable connection between *Wisdom and Goodness*. Right and wrong are no secret to anyone—until they begin to deny that evil exists. All of our ideas about human virtues: kindness, compassion, tolerance, charity, and the dignity of human beings—regardless of religion, gender, race, and status— originated in Holy Scripture. Is it not crucial that these virtues be prominently emphasized in the future?

Psychologist Martin Seligman, in *Learned Optimism* (Knopf), suggests that the loss of religious belief in the 1960s (during the drop-out, love-in, drug culture) was partly responsible for the dark mood and [some] national disasters—from race riots, to the immoral Vietnam War, to national disillusionment—of that era. We know, or should know, that grave sin breeds misery; and faith and hope breeds' optimism. In times of crisis and war, people need God. In times of plenty they forget Him, and worship "things." Of course *fanaticism* and false religious beliefs are pathological, and have caused considerable evil in the world. Christianity was supreme during times of great adversity, such as world wars, and rarely at its best during times of prosperity. *There are no atheists in foxholes!*

## Islamic Challenges:

The seeds of radical Islamic terrorism are *principally* due to Cultural and Ideological (Worldviews). It is conflicting values between Eastern and Western society. If our *fundamental* beliefs, human values and laws are incompatible, how can we possibly have meaningful agreements? Should we continue to compromise Western values for the sake of peace?

Islam needs to experience *"Reformation."* Fanatical Muslims are still living in the 7th century. "Wahhabism" supported by Saudi money, and taught in Madrassas schools, continues to "brainwash" young children with absurd ideas and laws that have not been changed in 1,500 years. These *uncivilized* beliefs and laws include: slaughtering Jews and unbelievers; cutting off limbs of anyone who steals; stoning adulterers (mostly women); honor killings of those who refuse to obey their parent's will; killing Muslims (Sunni vs. Shia) that are not "orthodox," including those who dare to question the Koran and Mohammed's teachings.

Some Christian leaders continue to preach: *we must live peacefully together.* Are they living in another world? We must wake-up to the reality of terrorism, and counter such evil ideological forces *firmly*, by use of political, and when necessary, military power. A peaceful solution can only be found by directly countering false, evil ideology, and by meaningfully changing Islamic laws, and teaching Muslim children about love. *Hate is never an invitation to dialogue.*

Islamic poor nations, which lack everything, including the essentials to live, especially education, naturally envy Western societies that appear to have everything, and seem to dominate the world. Nevertheless, we can never trust or make agreements with "Evil Dictators." These endless evil forces have *not* gone away, yet the power to do enormous harm has *multiplied* during the new millennium due to technology. (After all, we almost didn't make it in the last century, if one considers all the bloody hot and cold wars and the Cuban nuclear missile crisis, in 1962).

In summary, the evil forces of this world have much greater power, both in terms of Weapons of Mass Destruction (WMD), and control of world opinion, than has ever existed before in history. The ability to kill by chemical, germ, and nuclear weapons has increased orders-of-magnitude. Current "hotspots" include not only Afghanistan, Iran, Pakistan, Iraqi, and Syria, but also North Korea, China, and Russia. The ability to manipulate less educated masses, through global networks and the Social Media is also greater than ever before.

> **We must learn to live together as brothers or perish together as fools. Martin Luther King, Jr.**

## Environmental Challenges:

Similarly perilous are the environmental challenges that will become severe in this century. China, with its nearly 1.5 billion people, is burning sulfur coal at an alarming rate (Coal supplies 73% of China's energy according to *Time)*. China will represents over 20% of the world's population in a few decades. What will be the environmental effect, as they become the world's No.1 dirty coal and oil users, tripling their fossil fuel consumption? In addition, underdeveloped countries are burning wood, which increases deforestation, exacerbating air pollution. This global effect, when it actually happens, will result in massive regional destruction and enormous migrations of people, thereby unsettling other regions.

On the other hand, a major global freeze (mini-Ice Age) might occur, caused by uncontrollable natural forces, such as a slight alteration of the tilt of earth's axis, decreasing the sun's heat, or more likely, caused by huge volcano eruptions that block-out the sun (e.g., recently in Iceland), resulting in a greater impact on earth and all humanity. We must face this objective truth: *we cannot control our global environment!* Should we spend trillions-of-dollars in an attempt to alter the earth's temperature by one or two degrees? What if we spent these enormous sums to educate and feed poorer nations? Which is the more compassionate and realistic solution?

## Mass Media Mania:

Meaning is context dependent. Language creates and distorts, discloses and hides, enables and inhibits, oppresses and enriches. Everything that one sees and feels with their five senses and scientific instruments (that enhance our limited senses), is a product of mind and spirit. Perceptions are actually conceptions, mental thoughts are not merely empirical truths. We create visions of our empirical world, and if those images match our conception of that world, we *think* we have found real truth.

Whom do you really trust and believe for news about your world? Conflicting news services attack each other, and too often give us *distorted* views about the real world. How many educated listeners can determine the truth? Many of these reporters purport to be "the authority" on what the news really means to less educated audiences. Some "manufacture" fake news stories. Of course, sensational news is what sells in our materialistic society. *Positive news does not sell!* This is a psychological fact. *It is the "nature of the beast!"* How can we change "Mass Media Mania?" Only by the public *demanding* much higher standards of excellence.

## Symbols & Images:

> **"We are what we think. All that we are arises with our thoughts. With our thoughts, we make the world."-- Buddha**

Most of the great works of art and architecture was originally created by ancient Chinese, Greek and Roman cultures. The Christian Church was one of the first patrons of our recent culture: the arts, music, architecture, and sciences, which became the foundation for further great works of art and sciences. Most readers may not realize that monks, during the middle-ages, were the first to establish industries (olive oil, wine and bread), and they also invented capitalism (exchange of goods and service for money).

There are many symbols used in the secular world to represent things, objects and important ideas for teaching, for business, for entertainment. Symbols are in many ways part of that which it symbolizes, and calls up feelings associated with it; e.g., the Cross of a Christian Church; the Star of David in Synagogues; the Crescent on top of a Mosque. Symbols are a kind of entryway into the Culture of Society—the essential chain of associations that are endless.

## Society Challenges:

In the past, families and small ethnic communities were closer knit together to insure their survival, and if they took into account their neighbor's welfare, so much the better. Such is no longer the case. *We are now a global society!* The "population meltdown" in Western Society, due to government supported birth control, abortion, aging populations, euthanasia, and the filling of this "demographic gap" by many Islamic immigrates, which is now nearly 10% of the European Union population, has and will continue to impact Western values, culture, and politics. (Paradoxically, Europe leaders pushed out the Muslims during the 15th century, and now they are coming through the front door, in the 21st century). This economic and *cultural upheaval* is producing more unemployment, and greater crime among minority groups, and further eroding Christian values. Unlike most immigrants, *Muslims, will not assimilate!* And, they certainly will not accept any Western views about fundamental human rights!

## Immigration Challenges:

In the United States the challenge is dealing with about twelve million *undocumented* Hispanic immigrants, many of which are Mexicans, and those from South and Central America. More than 18% of the total *legal population* are Hispanics (defined as those who speak Spanish).

That's fifty million people who can and should vote, and this number is increasing *very rapidly*. Hispanic communities are family oriented, conservative, and certainly very serious Christians. It is estimated that 70% of all 3rd generation young Hispanics speak English. Why is this so? Because *Hispanics want to assimilate!*

Governments exist *fundamentally* to provide security and protection for its citizens, among other requirements, such as healthcare and education. How can government agencies be responsible for basic needs of its citizens, especially considering the war on terrorism, drug trafficking, and future pandemics, while achieving these essential objectives, *humanly?*

First, we must identify who's who? Any illegal persons, should be given about one year's time (a grace period) to register and receive a tamperproof ID card. Government can encourage them to register by promising to allow all who do not have a criminal record to stay and work for perhaps five-to-ten years. During that time, they will be entitled to basic education and health care services, and must file to obtain citizenship.

Second, government enforces this new policy by severely fining any company that hires the undocumented, without this special ID card, for every abuse of the law. In addition, those without IDs will not be entitled to jobs, education and health services (except in emergencies).

Third, those that get the new ID's must learn English, pay taxes, and must not be involved in any criminal activities. Education and health services will be paid by the states, *subsidized* by the federal agencies responsible for oversight and enforcement.

Fourth, those who refuse to register and/or have criminal (felon) records, or those that are not loyal to America, are expelled *permanently*. If the *illegal* persons cannot find work, and have no access to basic services, they will obviously migrate back to the original country.

Fifth, concurrent with this new policy, our government must build an *electronic fence* (which is far more effective than a physical wall) across the border, with advanced technology that can detect all breaches, with sufficient guards to protect and enforce our borders.

The facts are that the aging American population will *unquestionably require* much younger, educated workers from other countries. Otherwise the American economic system will collapse. Furthermore, social security and other "entitlements" will become bankrupt, without millions of younger Hispanic and other skilled workers. (We should remember that Hispanics actually arrived in America 500 years before the Pilgrims).

## Technological Challenges:

The seductive and corrupting influence of the mass media, especially television and social media has had a profound impact on young adults. While many TV programs are both educational and entertaining, too many provide a daily diet of *extreme violence and sex*, which will have a serious influence on the emotional and psychological health of our youth. "TV kids" have (will) become addicts, who grow up to become emotional delinquents (some adults also fall into this category).

Over 70% of all TV programming is highly violent and sexual, a five-fold increase in about twenty years. Our youth are wasting away, watching programs that can pollute *any* impressionable young mind. This is most alarming at best! Also, conservative Muslims families who see this trash, believe that Western society is "obviously corrupt"; that's one major reason why they avoid assimilating into American and European cultures.

While we are properly concerned about "environmental pollution," why do we allow "audio and video pollution" to invade our homes? The major web distributors (Facebook, Netflix, and Amazon) *claim* that they have little control over this significant source of this trash. *That's really fallacious!* Nevertheless, the only *practical solution* is for parents to accept their responsibility for the mental health and moral wellbeing of their children, by exercising control over this trash—and, *just turn it off!*

Complete "freedom" and "equal rights" is irrational without responsibility. Rights are not a given! Rights have to be earned by our youth by demonstrating that they are trustworthy and responsible. The key point is *not* censoring artistic creation, but rather controlling what our children watch, until they have developed mentally and emotionally.

## Neo-Darwinism Challenges

Source: Jonathan Wells, Ph.D. Abstract from this recent work follows:

Harvard evolutionary biologist Stephen Jay Gould wrote in 1977: *"Biology took away our status as paragons created in the image of God."* Darwinism teaches that we are accidental byproducts of purposeless natural processes, that had no need for God, and this anti-religious dogma enjoys a taxpayer-funded monopoly in America's public schools and universities. Teachers who dare to question it openly, have in many cases lost their jobs.

*Wake up America!* The issue here is not "Micro-Evolution" – a broad term that means very small changes within existing species (which no one doubts). The issue is "Macro-Evolution," or Darwinism – which claims that *all* living things are descended from a common ancestor, modified by natural selection, acting on random genetic mutations.

The truth is Macro-Darwinism is *not* a scientific theory, but a materialistic *myth*, masquerading as science. It is first and foremost a weapon against all religions. This is becoming increasingly obvious to the American people, who are not the ignorant religious dogmatists that Darwinists make them out to be. Darwinists insult the intelligence of taxpayers, and at the same time depend on their taxes for support. This is an inherently unstable situation, and cannot last.

## Cultural Challenges:

"Culture Battles" focused primarily on past and present Scientific, Societal, Philosophical, Spiritual, and Ideological truths. We also addressed future challenges facing Western and Eastern Cultures and Ideologies. This author and thinker would like to leave readers with a summary of my recommendations: At the beginning of the 21st century, a "revolution" is dawning that is upsetting earlier progressive-liberal controversies, in at least five important areas: (1) Cosmology, (2) Biology, and (3) Psychology, (4) The Constitution, and (5) Education.

**Cosmology:** The "Big Bang" theory (defined in the chapter on **Scientific Truths**), suggests that the universe began nearly 14 billion years ago, as an enormous explosion, and has been expanding ever since. This theory first coined by Fred Hoyle, and the "Anthropic Principle," described by Carter, has completely overturned former false theories about a static, random universe. One has to conclude that there is intelligence that designed the universe expressly for all life, not unlike what Genesis first proclaimed. Thus, one must ask: *If there is an intelligent design, who is the designer?*

**Biology:** Stephen Jay Gould, Harvard Paleontologist (see the **Being & Life** chapter), overturned Darwinian fundamentalists' belief which previously insisted that mechanisms of "natural selection" hold the *entire keys to evolution*. Expert biologists now believe that the manner in which organisms evolve is determined more by internal *and* external signals (intelligence within DNA), and by intelligent adaptation to signals from the outside environment. Order is *not* simply created by random trials and adaptation; it comes from somewhere else. The fossil record does *not* show gradual, steady change over time—but rather, *sharp jolts of change*. Natural selection is not the "silver bullet" biologists once thought it was. The evidence also indicates that Intelligent Design *and* Darwin's Micro-evolution are compatible. Once again, if intelligent design exists in the DNA for all of nature, *there must be an intelligent designer!*

**Psychology:** Herbert Benson, in his publication *Timeless Healing*, exposed Freud's views of religion as "entirely fallacious." In *The Future of Illusion*, Sigmund Freud, perhaps the most extreme Atheist of the 20th century, concluded that faith is a form of mental disorder, a "universal obsession neurosis," rooted in "infantile narcissistic" patterns of thought.

"No nation outside of Germany and Austria was more hospitable to psychoanalysis than America," notes Mark Edmondson in *"The*

*Death of Freud.*" Freud understood that we would embrace his theories. *"We are bringing them the plague,"* he reportedly told colleagues when disembarking in New York, *"And they don't even know it."*

Freud predicted to his circle of followers that presumably strait-laced Americans would never embrace his ideas *"once they discover the sexual core of our psychological theories."* But of course, in America, sex sells; indeed, it is probably one of the biggest reasons that Freud's theories gained such currency. As so much else, he was wrong about that, too. (Source: *One Hundred Years of Freud in America, Wall Street Journal,* August 7, 2009).

Ironically, recent scientific research has shown that, far from being a neurosis, religious belief is one of the "most consistent correlates of overall mental health and happiness." Study after study show a powerful relationship between religious belief and practice, and healthy behaviors in such vital areas as:

- Reducing suicide rates (Kubler-Ross, *On Children and Death,* Collier);
- Lowering drug abuse (Melvin Morse, *Closer to the Light,* Ivy Books);
- Declines in divorce rates (Fenwick, *The Truth in the Light,* Berkley);
- Curtailing depression ((Melvin Morse, *Closer to the Light,* Ivy Books).

This writer certainly does *not* propose eliminating psychotherapeutic treatment, especially where other therapies have failed. However, much of the empirical data runs contrary to the earlier consensus of the profession. For example, David B. Larson, former National Institutes of Health psychiatrist, writes in *"Have Faith: Religion Can Heal Mental Ill's,"* (Insight on the News, Mar. 6, 1995): If a new health treatment were discovered that helped to reduce the rate of teenage suicide, prevent drug and alcohol abuse, improve treatment for depression, reduce recovery time from surgery, lower divorce rates and enhance a sense of well-being, one would think that every physician in the world would be scrambling to try it. Yet, critics denounced this treatment as harmful, despite research findings that showed it to be effective more than 80% of the time.

Which would you believe—the assertions of critics based on opinions, or results of the clinical trials based on solid statistical data and research? The "health treatment" Larson is talking about is *Christian faith*.

**The Constitution Solution:** Many of today's political leaders would *not* have signed the Declaration of Independence, because it contains words they can't accept today, such as: "Creator," "Truth," and "Equality." Recent changes in the Supreme Court Judges have shifted it back from its Progressive-Secular orientation. Hopefully this will alter some earlier *irrational* rulings on individual rights, especially abortion-on-demand, gay marriages, sex transformation, burning of the American Flag, prohibiting Christmas and Jewish symbols in the marketplace, and the "right" to allow terminally ill patients to have a so-called: "happy death." As these laws are changed, this country may once again become: *"One Nation under God."*

## Educational Challenges:

> *If you think education is expensive, try ignorance.*
> **Derek Bok**

The American public education system clearly needs a major overhaul. *It will never happen unless it is forced to change.* Everyone seems to cry for "free choice," or "woman's choice," and "sexual orientation choice." Why not "school choice"? Democracy cannot function *without* an educated and well informed society. (That's also a true for numerous Middle-East nations). Democracy depends on an educated population.

Our Universities have become a solid bastion for extremely liberal viewpoints, as demonstrated by two articles in a recent issue of the scholarly journal *Current Reviews*. One article presents a *survey of academic social scientists*, which we will not review here, because it's NOT just about Republican versus Democrats; it's about *attitudes*. A second article studied voter registration of California college professors and found that the ratio of registered Democrats to Republicans is 5 to 1, with sociology departments with a ratio of 44 Democrats to 1 Republican, but economics departments employ 2.8 Democrats for each member of the GOP.

While liberal professors often think that they are "open-minded," Daniel B. Klein of George Mason University, believes that they often think that "we're smarter" than those outside of academia, *which gives them a right to "discriminate against people who get it wrong."* In their ["group-think"] many social scientists marginalize heterodox thinkers, Saunders suggests. As a result many conservative professors [are] afraid to share their points of view, which may cause colleagues to turn on them. (Source: This edited summary is based on *St. Petersburg Times*, Aug. 5, 2006 column, titled: *Academia's Stultifying Swamps* by Debra J. Saunders).

## Thinking for Yourself:

A recent survey claims that there are twelve times more Democratic than Republican professors in our colleges and universities. While such a high ratio is debatable, one cannot ignore the fact that our education system is primarily progressive. Some would claim, *extremely left leaning.* How will this imbalance affect America's future society?

Why do students attend any university? We believe it's to develop their reasoning abilities, to exercise free will, to use their intelligence, and to discover what the universe is all about. Basically, it's to understand and appreciate their world and the universe. That requires them to be exposed to *multiple* ideas, from different sources. If they are "brainwashed" by professors, it becomes much more difficult for them to develop a balanced, and more rational worldview.

> ***Change the university system—and you change the world!***

The American public education system has to have serious competition from the private sector, before it will change, says editor, Miriam Fertig, who retired after 40 plus years as a devoted educator. *"We need to reward good teachers and rid the system of apathetic, biased teachers,"* she says. Active parental participation is also most important; they must be represented on all school boards. We must measure and reward "excellence," wherever it is found. After all, if a business enterprise couldn't measure its own performance, reward good results, and correct poor results, its stockholders would fire management, and/or it would quickly go out of business. Taxpayers are the stockholders of all education enterprises, and they must demand no less from its institutional managers.

## A Self-Model Solution:

All behavior of humans in Western society (particularly in American society) is based on, and motivated by, the approval and perception of others; that is, *"What will the Jones' think?"* This is "fear" based on what "others" think and approve—including society in general, disregarding what one may actually "think," "desire" or "feel." Many individuals fall into this trap created by society and culture that condones or accepts this role, *without question.* These persons ransom their own identity and individuality to the whims of others. They sacrifice their "self-concept" in return for approval of others. One might ask: Where are the mavericks, the risk takers, and the futuristic innovative "thinkers and doers?" Where are the "wild ducks," that refuse to fly in formation? Where will our future leaders come from? Not surely from passive, submissive persons, who are the sacrificial lambs, who so willingly submit to others. These persons actually turn over the reins of control to others, the reins of their very lives. They are at the mercy of those who are willing to lead and exploit them for their own selfish purposes. *It's manipulation on a grand scale!*

One should set one's own major goals in life to achieve happiness. *"Be true to yourself!"* Therein is the key solution to self-fulfillment and happiness. *Anything overriding this goal dooms one to a life of unhappiness!* As one is born with free will, who is it that has "freedom of choice?"

why would anyone so willingly give up this precious God-given right by surrendering to the pressures of any group in our society? The Constitution guarantees this most valued right. Astonishingly few exercise, value or assert this right! Are we becoming "a nation of sheep?" Consider nations in history (USSR, North Korea, China, Iran, and Cuba) that gave up this most cherished right. Where are they today? Will one continue to follow the "whims of society" and turn over their destiny to the "Jones'?"

## Truth Speaks to Power:

*Times have changed. Journalism has become like a "work of fiction." One can actually report the "real truth" better with a novel.--Author*

In order for truth to speak to those with political or business power, one must agree on "what is truly truth?" That's what this book is all about; getting students and young adults to acknowledge that truth actually exists in the sciences, biology, and most importantly, in the spiritual sphere.

One must acknowledge that "subjective truths" also exist in the arts, music, ethics, secular laws, and most importantly, in love.

Truth Shall Prevail!

The Ultimate Truth is simply, "Love." Jesus Christ comes down to be crucified. He takes on the lowly form of a poor human creature, to save *all* from eternal death, and this becomes the model, the guide of what love is. "*We love because He first loved us,*" wrote St. John.

## Why Are We Here?

*You are here for a brief instant (30,000 days, on average), considering the timelessness and vastness of cosmological time. Why do we exist at all in this tiny flickering moment, in the theoretical 14 billion-year*

**history of the universe? We're a mere blip on this enormous time horizon.--Author**

The ideas presented in this book points to the fact that the universe and humanity were *intentionally created* by an infinitely superior, intelligent, merciful, and loving Creator, who gave us free will to evolve—physically, mentally and spiritually towards perfection. The evidence shows that "Intelligent Design" exists at *all* levels, from bacteria to plants, to all creatures, including humans, and the entire universe.

In *Generic Entropy Mystery of the Genome*, by Dr. J. C. Sanford *confirms* that there is a gradual decline in all living things. That human beings that built Stone hedge, the Pyramids, the Aztecs, and the Incas, had an advanced intelligent civilization behind them. Yet they experience both good and evil forces, which eventually ended their civilizations.

## What's Our Purpose?

Your purpose is not wealth! Your purpose is not power! Your purpose is not pleasure! Your real purpose is to discover the Creator, from His Word, from His Works (universe, nature, humanity), and to glorify Him to all people. We are "Agents" of His mercy and love. As Isaiah 49:6 declared: *"You are to be my salvation to the ends of the earth, a light to the nations."*

## Where are We Going?

We have all experienced a taste of heaven and hell on earth. Heaven is a *spiritual state of being* where one can finally know and love the Creator, in His Beatific Wonder, Goodness and Magnificent Glory.

## How will We Get There?

We all have *freedom* to choose. We have the amazing human power to accept, or reject the Creator's plan for us, and follow the "Good News," with His merciful and loving guidance. What are you waiting for? Have you not experienced many stern warnings: two World Wars; the Korean, Vietnam, Afghanistan and Iraqi Wars; seventy years of "Cold War"; and now domestic Terrorism, Tsunamis, and Epidemics? No one is going to tap you on the shoulder, and say, "you have a few days to get your act together!" ***It will come suddenly, without warning!***

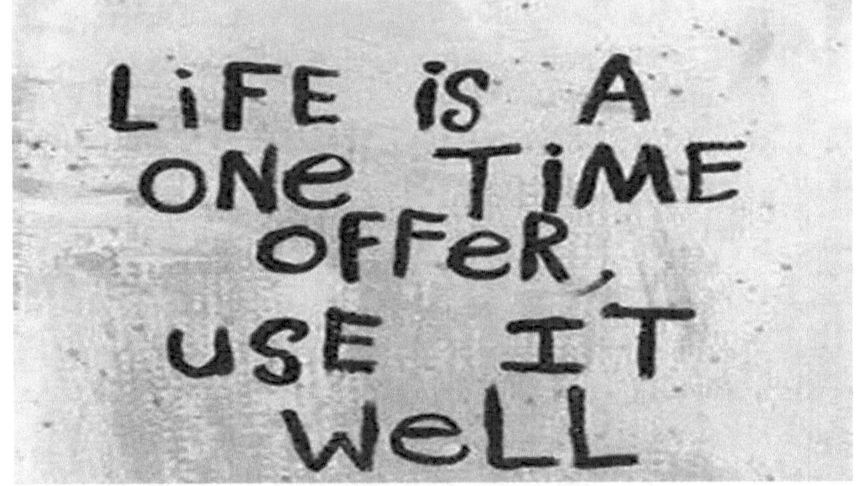



**To Be Continued …..**

# Appendix

**Ex-Nuncio Accuses Pope of Failing to Act on McCarrick's Abuse**

Testimony of His Excellency Carlo Maria Viganò, Titular Archbishop of Ulpiana, Apostolic Nuncio by Edward Pentin

In an extraordinary 11-page written testament, a former apostolic nuncio to the United States has accused several senior prelates of complicity in covering up Archbishop Theodore McCarrick's allegations of sexual abuse, and has claimed that Pope Francis knew about sanctions imposed on then-Cardinal McCarrick by Pope Benedict XVI but chose to repeal them.

Archbishop Carlo Maria Viganò, 77, who served as apostolic nuncio in Washington D.C. from 2011 to 2016, said that in the late 2000s, Benedict had "imposed on Cardinal McCarrick sanctions similar to those now imposed on him by Pope Francis" and that Viganò personally told Pope Francis about those sanctions in 2013.

Archbishop Viganò said in his written statement, simultaneously released to the Register and other media, (see full text below) that Pope Francis "continued to cover" for McCarrick and not only did he "not take into account the sanctions that Pope Benedict had imposed on him" but also made McCarrick "his trusted counselor." Viganò said that the former archbishop of Washington advised the Pope to appoint a number of bishops in the United States, including Cardinals Blase Cupich of Chicago and Joseph Tobin of Newark.

Archbishop Viganò, who said his "conscience dictates" that the truth be known as "the corruption has reached the very top of the Church's hierarchy," ended his testimony by calling on Pope Francis and all of those implicated in the cover up of Archbishop McCarrick's abuse to resign.

On June 20, Vatican Secretary of State, Cardinal Pietro Parolin, on the order of Pope Francis, prohibited former Cardinal McCarrick from public ministry after an investigation by the New York archdiocese found an accusation of sexual abuse of a minor was "credible and substantiated." That same day, the public learned that the Archdiocese of Newark and the Diocese of Metuchen in New Jersey had received three accusations of sexual misconduct involving adults against McCarrick. Since then media reports have written of victims of the abuse, spanning decades, include a teenage boy, three young priests or seminarians, and a man now in his 60s who alleges McCarrick abused him from the age of 11. The Pope later accepted McCarrick's resignation from the College of Cardinals.

But Viganò wrote that Benedict much earlier had imposed sanctions on McCarrick "similar" to those handed down by Cardinal Parolin. "The cardinal was to leave the seminary where he was living," Viganò said, "he was also forbidden to celebrate [Mass] in public, to participate in public meetings, to give lectures, to travel, with the obligation of dedicating himself to a life of prayer and penance." Viganò did not document the exact date but recollected the sanction to have been applied as far back 2009 or 2010.

Benedict's measures came years after Archbishop Viganò's predecessors at the nunciature — Archbishops Gabriel Montalvo and Pietro Sambi — had "immediately" informed the Holy See as soon as they had learned of Archbishop McCarrick's "gravely immoral behavior with seminarians and priests," the retired Italian Vatican diplomat wrote.

He said Archbishop Montalvo first alerted the Vatican in 2000, requesting that Dominican Father Boniface Ramsey write to Rome confirming the allegations. In 2006, Archbishop Viganò said that, as delegate for pontifical representations in the Secretariat of State, he personally wrote a memo to his superior, then Archbishop (later Cardinal) Leonardo Sandri, proposing an "exemplary measure" be taken against McCarrick that could have a "medicinal function" to prevent future abuses and alleviate a "very serious scandal for the faithful."

He drew on an indictment memorandum, communicated by Archbishop Sambi to Cardinal Tarcisio Bertone, then Secretary of State, in which an abusive priest had made claims against McCarrick of "such gravity and vileness" including "depraved acts" and "sacrilegious celebration of the Eucharist."

According to Viganò, his memo was ignored and no action was taken until the late 2000s — a delay which Archbishop Viganò claims is owed to complicity of John Paul II's and Benedict XVI's respective Secretaries of State, Cardinals Angelo Sodano and Tarcisio Bertone.

In 2008, Archbishop Viganò claims he wrote a second memo, this time to Cardinal Sandri's successor as sostituto at the Secretariat of State, then Archbishop (later Cardinal) Fernando Filoni. He included a summary of research carried out by Richard Sipe, a psychotherapist and specialist in clerical sexual abuse, which Sipe had sent Benedict in the form of a statement. Viganò said he ended the memo by "repeating to my superiors that I thought it was necessary to intervene as soon as possible by removing the cardinal's hat from Cardinal McCarrick."

Again, according the Viganò, his request fell on deaf ears and he writes he was "greatly dismayed" that both memos were ignored until Sipe's "courageous and meritorious" statement had "the desired result."

"Benedict did what he had to do," Archbishop Viganò told the Register Aug. 25, "but his collaborators — the Secretary of State and all the others — didn't enforce it as they should have done, which led to the delay."

"What is certain," Viganò writes in his testimony, "is that Pope Benedict imposed the above canonical sanctions on McCarrick and that they were communicated to him by the Apostolic Nuncio to the United States, Pietro Sambi."

The Register has independently confirmed that the allegations against McCarrick were certainly known to Benedict, and the Pope Emeritus remembers instructing Cardinal Bertone to impose measures but cannot recall their exact nature.

In 2011, on arrival in Washington D.C., Archbishop Viganò said he personally repeated the sanction to McCarrick. "The cardinal, muttering in a barely comprehensible way, admitted that he had perhaps made the mistake of sleeping in the same bed with some seminarians at his beach house, but he said this as if it had no importance," Viganò recalled in his testimony.

In his written statement, Viganò then outlined his understanding of how, despite the allegations against him, McCarrick came to be appointed Archbishop of Washington D.C. in 2000 and how his misdeeds were covered up. His statement implicates Cardinals Angelo Sodano, Tarcisio Bertone and Pietro Parolin and he insists various other cardinals and bishops were well aware, including Cardinal Donald Wuerl, McCarrick's successor as archbishop of Washington D.C.

"I myself brought up the subject with Cardinal Wuerl on several occasions, and I certainly didn't need to go into detail because it was immediately clear to me that he was fully aware of it," he wrote.

Ed McFadden, a spokesman for the Archdiocese of Washington, told CNA that Wuerl categorically denies having been informed that McCarrick's ministry had been restricted by the Vatican.

The second half of Viganò's testimony primarily deals with what Pope Francis knew about McCarrick, and how he acted.

He recalled meeting Cardinal McCarrick in June 2013 at the Pope's Domus Sanctae Marthae residence, during which McCarrick told him "in a tone somewhere between ambiguous and triumphant: 'The Pope received me yesterday; tomorrow I am going to China'" — the implication being that Francis had lifted the travel ban placed on him by Benedict. (Further evidence of this can be seen in this interview McCarrick gave the National Catholic Reporter in 2014.)

At a private meeting a few days later, Archbishop Viganò said the Pope asked him "'What is Cardinal McCarrick like?'" to which the archbishop replied: "He corrupted generations of seminarians and priests and Pope Benedict ordered him to withdraw to a life of prayer and penance." The former nuncio said he believes the Pope's purpose in asking him was to "find out if I was an ally of McCarrick or not."

He said it was "clear" that "from the time of Pope Francis's election, McCarrick, now free from all constraints, had felt free to travel continuously, to give lectures and interviews."

Moreover, he added, McCarrick had "become the *kingmaker* for appointments in the Curia and the United States, and the most listened to advisor in the Vatican for relations with the Obama administration."

Viganò claimed that the appointments of Cardinal Cupich to Chicago and Cardinal Joseph Tobin to Newark "were orchestrated by McCarrick," among others. He said neither of the names was presented by the nunciature, whose job is traditionally to present a list of names, or *terna*, to the Congregation for Bishops. He also added that Bishop Robert McElroy's appointment to San Diego was orchestrated "from above" rather than through the nuncio.

The retired Italian diplomat also echoed the Register's reports about Cardinal Rodriguez Maradíaga and his record of cover-up in Honduras, saying the Pope "defends his man" to the "bitter end," despite the allegations against him. The same applies to McCarrick, wrote Viganò.

"He [Pope Francis] knew from at least June 23, 2013 that McCarrick was a serial predator," Archbishop Viganò stated, but although "he knew that he was a corrupt man, he covered for him to the bitter end."

"It was only when he was forced by the report of the abuse of a minor, again on the basis of media attention, that he took action [regarding McCarrick] to save his image in the media," wrote Viganò.

The former U.S. nuncio wrote that Pope Francis "is abdicating the mandate which Christ gave to Peter to confirm the brethren," and urged him to "acknowledge his mistakes" and, to "set a good example to cardinals and bishops who covered up McCarrick's abuses and resign along with all of them."

In comments to the media Aug. 25, Viganò said his main motivation for writing his testimony now was to "stop the suffering of the victims, to prevent new victims and to protect the Church: only the truth can make her free."

He also said he wanted to "discharge my conscience in front of God of my responsibilities as bishop for the universal Church," adding that he is an "old man" who wanted to present himself to God "with a clean conscience."

"The people of God have the right to know the full truth also regarding their shepherds," he said. "They have the right to be guided by good shepherds. In order to be able to trust them and love them, they have to know them openly, in transparency and truth, as they really are. A priest should always be a light on a candle, everywhere and for all."

After requests from EWTN News for comment, the Vatican press office has declined to give immediate response to Viganò's letter.

**Lepanto Institute's Report**

On June 23, the CCHD-funded People Organized for Westside Renewal (POWER) demanded the defunding of the Los Angeles Police Department, which led to a reduction of $150 million from department funds. The first weekend in July brought a 100% increase in shootings and homicides in Los Angeles.

In Chicago, the CCHD-funded Southside Together Organized for Power (STOP), which marched to chants of "F**k-12" against the police, and Organizing Neighborhoods for Equality Northside both called for the defunding of the Chicago PD and advocated for Black Lives Matter. The 4th of July weekend in Chicago left the city with 87 people being shot and 17 killed, including 7-year-old Natalia Wallace.

"The USCCB fell all over itself in its rush to denounce racism and police brutality over the death of George Floyd, but were silent regarding the murder of a 7-year-old girl by organizations they fund is nothing short of disgusting!" said Hichborn. "We warned a month ago that CCHD-funded groups were engaging in revolutionary and violent activity that would lead to bloodshed, and now here we are."

**On June 6, the Lepanto Institute published a report** on eight CCHD-funded organizations engaged in revolutionary anti-police behavior. One CCHD-funded organization participated in a march with chants of "Death to the racist pigs."

"What the CCHD is funding is nothing short of Marxist Revolution, and it knows it!" said Hichborn. "There is no plausible deniability here and there is no excuse that can possibly be made for Catholic funding to be going to organizations engaged in the behavior we just profiled."

The Lepanto Institute's latest report can be read here: https://www.lepantoin.org/violence-erupts-as-more-catholic-funded-groups-call-for-defunding-of-police/

Author Marcantonio: "The Dictator Pope: The Inside Story of the Francis Papacy." Infiltration by Dr. Taylor R. Marshall.

Pope Paul VI's appointments to the American Episcopate accentuated the [Catholic] problem. The United States hierarchy was transformed by the nominations made by the Nuncio Archbishop Jadot (1973–1980), who appointed 103 bishops and promoted fifteen archbishops. Example, Archbishop Hunthausen of Seattle, whose management later provoked Vatican intervention, and above all Archbishop Weakland of Milwaukee, who resigned after he paid $450,000 from diocesan funds to a male lover, threatening him with a lawsuit.

Cardinal Carlo Maria Martini, for most of his years of under John Paul II and Benedict XVI, is the leading figure of the Church's *liberal faction*. A reading of Martini's interviews and writings gives a hint as to Bergoglio's enthusiasm for his "declared mentor"; many of the cardinal's favorite terms and phrases reappear in Pope Francis own writing and off-the-cuff speeches.

Most Catholics have forgotten the Ten Commandments. Catholic leadership seems to ignore #1 Idols in Churches, and #3 Excusing Sunday Mass and #6 Excusing Adultery. This commandment includes *fornication*, which is sex between unmarried people, homosexual acts, same-sex marriage, and allowing Holy Communion for divorcees.

# Historical Dates

**Dates:**

**BCE**

5000 Egyptian (pre-dynastic) communities

3000 Hieroglyphic Writing

2500 Abraham Father of Jews/Christians/Moslems

1700 Hebrews enslavement in Egypt, caused by famine

1200 Moses rescues Hebrews from Egypt, Ten Commandments

1200 Iron Age in Europe and Trojan War

1100 Israel established by Jews in Palestine

1000 King David, 2$^{nd}$ Jewish King; succeeded by King Solomon

900 Assyrians in control of Judea

750 Rome established by Romulus & Remus

586 Temple in Jerusalem destroyed

540 Persian Empire conquers Babylonia, Palestine, Egypt

510 Roman Republic founded

399 Socrates convicted of corrupting the youth of Athens

387 Plato establishes Academy in Athens

335 Aristotle establishes Academy in Athens

334 Alexander the Great controls Near-East

200 Dead Sea Scrolls first produced

150 Rome expands after the Third Punic War

49 Civil War in Rome (46-49 AD)

46 Julian calendar established (365 days per year)

44 Julius Caesar assassinated

37 Herod King is leader of Judea

27 Octavian becomes Roman Emperor Augustus
5-4 Jesus Christ is born

## CE/AD
30 Jesus Christ is Crucified & the Resurrection
70 Romans suppress 1st Jewish Revolt
115 Roman Empire reaches its peak of power
133 Romans suppress 2nd Jewish Revolt
161 Devastating Plague in Rome
175 Marcus Aurelius writes *Meditations*
192 Civil War in Rome
250 Christians further persecuted by Roman Empire
312 Constantine becomes Roman emperor
330 Christianity becomes Religion of Roman Empire
378 Visigoths invade Europe
375 Roman Empire divided into East & West
420 St. Jerome produces first Latin Bible (Vulgate)
455 Vandals sack City of Rome
478 End of the Western Roman Empire
529 Benedictine Order founded
632 Muhammad and Islam beginning
635 Islamic Koran partly completed
711 Arabs expand power throughout North Africa
800 Charlemagne expands Frankish control to Germany, Italy, Spain
800 Holy Roman Empire established in Europe
1020 Italian City-States established
1054 Schism divides Roman and Eastern (Greek) Churches
1097 First Crusade defeats Turks and Muslims
1209 St. Francis of Assisi found the Order of Friars
1215 Magna Carta in England produces "Due Process" of Laws
1229 Sixth Crusade recaptures Jerusalem
1237 Mongols raid Europe
1252 Catholic Inquisitions begins
1295 First Parliament in England

1337 Hundred Years War (until about 1453)

1341 Renaissance begins in Italy

1347 Black Death (bubonic plague kills 25-30% of Europe)

1450 Gutenberg invents printing press (1ˢᵗ Bible printed in 1455)

1492 Columbus reaches the Americas

1517 Reformation by Luther and Calvin (1536)

1529 King Henry VIII severs ties with Church of Rome

1545 Council of Trent Reforms Catholicism

1588 Spanish Armada defeated by England

1611 King James English Bible published

1620 Mayflower Compact in Mass.

1679 Enlightenment Age (1588-1778)

# Bibliography

This book's is based on the works of over seventy-five authors, and would not have been possible without their contribution.

## Selected Reference Sources by Topic:

Micro-Evolution: The *Origin of Species* by Charles Darwin is a classical work that has affected Christians and non-Christians alike for nearly 150 years, and cannot be ignored by any serious writer about biology, philosophy and Christianity.

Intelligent Design (I.D): *Politically Incorrect Guide to Darwinism and Intelligent Design,* and *Icons of Evolution* by Jonathan Wells, Ph.D., Senior Fellow at Discovery Institute. Also, *Darwin Strikes* back by Professor Thomas E. Woodward, Ph.D.

Biology and I.D.: *Darwin's Black Box,* and *Edge of Evolution* by Michael Behe, Ph.D., Professor at Lehigh University. We also quoted Stephen C. Meyer's paper on I.D.

Cosmos: *The Privileged Planet* by Guillermo Gonzalez, Ph.D. Assistant Research Professor at Iowa State University, and Jay W. Richards, Ph.D., Senior Fellow of the Discovery Institute in Seattle.

Epigenetic: *The Biology of Belief* by Bruce Lipton, Ph.D. covers new research on cell functions and the missing link between life, the environment and consciousness.

Physics: Paul Davis is a theoretical physicist. He was recipient of the 1995 Templeton Prize for the *Philosophical Meaning of Science.* His outstanding work is *God & the New Physics.*

Poet/Essayist: Ralph Waldo Emerson was a philosopher, essayist, poet, and minister, who challenged conventional thinking, emphasized human intuition as the way to perceive reality, and believed that nature is *one* of the Revelations of the Spirit of God.

Human Suffering: Rabbi Harold Kushner wrote about this key issue. Our dialogue on Suffering and Evil motivated an earlier Jewish reader to recommend his books: *Who Needs God*, and *When Bad Things Happen to Good People*.

Human Conscience: John Henry Newman is a great thinker and leader of his time. We found his ideas on the *Conscience*, that "inner-light," intriguing.

Fundamentalism: *The Battle for God* by Karen Armstrong; and *Rescuing the Bible from Fundamentalism* by Bishop Spong. While we *disagree* with their liberal viewpoints, some of their candid thoughts are nevertheless brilliant.

Theology: The *Summa Theologiae*, by St. Thomas Aquinas (1225-1274). This masterpiece represents one of the major theological foundations of Christianity. St. Augustine (354-430). Also, *The Basic Writings of St. Augustine* (by Whitney J. Oates) contains a wealth of beautiful theological thoughts from this ancient (yet still current) saint.

Jesus Christ: We depended mostly on the NIV version of the Bible. Also, *the Hidden Jesus: A New Life* by Donald Spoto, Ph.D. in Theology from Fordham University.

Spirituality: *The Marriage of the Sense and Soul* by Ken Wilber. Ken's ideas about the "I" (Individual and Beauty), the "We" (Collective Morality), and the "It" (Objective Truths) was of particular interest to us in integrating these forces.

Ethics: *Ethics for the New Millennium* by the Dalai Lama emphasized that: "ultimately the whole purpose of religion is to facilitate love and compassion."

Gospels: The best synthesis and analysis of the Gospels was: *An Introduction to the New Testament* by Raymond E. Brown.

Islam: *Understanding Islam*, we depended on the leading expert, Thomas W. Lippman, for this important subject.

Christian Principles: *Joyful Christian* and *Mere Christianity* by C. S. Lewis. Who can say it better than he? Lewis was an atheist who later converted to Christianity.

Philosophy: *Science Before Science—A Guide to Thinking* in the 21st Century by Anthony Rizzi, is the link between science and our deepest questions, and helped us to more fully appreciate the fundamental foundation for *all* the sciences, which is philosophy.

History of Christianity: Multiple viewpoints are provided on the Bible and History of Christianity from: J. P. Meier, *A Marginal Jew*; and *The Victory of Reason* by Rodney Stark.

Western Relativism: *"Without Roots"* is based on an exchange of letters between Joseph Ratzinger (Pope Benedict XVI) and Marcello Pera, President of the Italian Senate. We think their view are extremely interesting.

Worldviews: *Universe Next Door* by James W. Sire contributed to our better understanding of different Worldviews; that is, Ideologies, Philosophies, and Religions that evolved over many, many centuries.

Science: *The Science of God* (1997) by Gerald L. Schroeder Ph.D. from MIT. His distinguished work on the convergence of scientific and biblical wisdom was discovered weeks before our first manuscript was published. We came to some of the same conclusions.

## Readers may find books by searching using author's name.

Alan Guttmacher Institute Abortion Surveys & Statistics,

Aquinas, Thomas Summa Theologiae, 13th Century

Aristotle Metaphysics

Armstrong, Karen, the Battle for God; the History of God, Random House

Aurelius, Marcus Meditations Publisher unknown, 1950

Barzun, Jacques From Dawn to Decadence, Harper Collins, 2000

Behe, Michael Darwin's Black Box; Edge of Evolution

Blum, Harold the God of Exodus

Brown Dan, the Da Vinci Code, Random House

Brown, Raymond E. An Introduction to the New Testament, Doubleday, 1997

Buckley, Michael J. A the Origins of Modern Atheism Yale Univ. Press,

Cahill, Thomas the Gift of the Jews, Doubleday, 1998

Carter, Brandon Anthropic Principle

Chaves, Mark Statistics on Church Attendance Notre Dame

Collier's Encyclopedia Collier Newfield, Inc., 1997/98

Darwin, Charles Origin of Species Reeves, Arcade Publishing, 1996

Darwin, Charles the Decent of Man

Davis, Paul God & The new Physics Simon & Schuster, 1983

Dalai Lama, Ethics for the New Millennium

Dembski, William A. the Design Revolution, IVP Books

Edwards, Paul the Encyclopedia of Philosophy Macmillan & Free Press, 1967

Emerson, Ralph Waldo Essay's Various publishers

Freud, Sigmund Interpretation of Dreams

Gonzalez & Richards, the Privileged Planet

Green, Michael Evangelism in the Early Church Eerdmans, 1970

Guillen, Michael Five Equations that Changed the World

Hansson, Kevin Seamus, The Right to be Wrong

Hewitt, Hugh Searching for God in America

Hume, David The Natural History of Religion Oxford Univ. Press, 1976

King James Version The Complete Bible Compton New Media, 1995

Kung, Hans Does God Exist? Crossroad Publishing, 1991

Kurshner, Rabbi Harold, When Bad Things Happen to Good People

Lapati, Americo J. H. Newman Twayne Publishers, 1972

Lewis, C. S. Mere Christianity; Joyful Christian; the Four Loves, Macmillan, 1960

Lipton, Bruce Mind over Genes; Biology of Belief

Lombard, Peter, Books of Sentences (Theology)

M. Scott, Dr. People of the Lie Simon & Schuster, 1989 Hart

Madalyn Murry, All About Atheists, American Atheist Press, 1988

Martin, Micheal, Atheism: A Philosophical Justification, Temple Univ. Press,

Mayr, Ernst What Evolution Is

McLaughlin, Robert A. Separation of Church & State

Meyer, Stephen the Origin of Biological Information & the Higher Taxonomic

Michael H. Persons in History Citadel Press, 1987

Morris, Charles R. American Catholic Random House, 1997

Meier, J. P. A Marginal Jew, Doubleday, 1991

Morris, Thomas V. God and the Philosophers University Press, 1994

Newman, John Henry The Gamma of Assent

Palau, Luis God Is Relevant Doubleday, 1997

Pascal, Blaise Pascal's Pensees Peck

Paul VI, Pope Humanae Vitae (Of Human Life) Vatican

Peck, M. Scott, M.D. People of the Lie, Touchstone

Penrose, Roger, Big Bang, Oxford Press

Pius XII, Pope Humani Generis Vatican

Plato's Republic, various -Author

Polkinghorne, John Gifford Lectures

Ratzinger, Joseph (Pope Benedict XVI), Without Roots, Basic Books, 2006

Ratzinger, Joseph Cardinal, Catechism of the Catholic Church Liguori Publications, 1994

Ratzinger, Joseph Cardinal, Christianity and the Crisis of Cultures, Ignatius

Rizzi, Anthony, Science before Science

Robert N. Statement on Euthanasia Nat. Conf. of Catholic Bishops

Ross, Hugh The Creator and the Cosmos NavPress, 1993

Sartre, Jean-Paul The Psychology of Imagination 1966

Schaff, Philip History of the Christian Church

Schroeder, Gerald L. The Science of God, Broadway Books

Schwartz, Hans The Search for God Augsburg, 1975

Shanks, Hershel, The Meaning & Mystery of the Dead Sea Scrolls, Doubleday

Sheen, Fulton J. Life Is Worth Living McGraw-Hill, 1955

Sheen, Fulton J. Lift Up Your heart McGraw-Hill, 1955

Stein, Gordon An Anthology of Atheism & Rationalism, Prometheus, 1980

Stark, Rodney, the Rise of Christianity, Princeton Univ. Press

Stark, Rodney the Victory of Reason, Random House

Spoto, Donald, The Hidden Jesus

Spong, Bishop, Rescuing the Bible from Fundamentalism

White, David Manning The Search for God Macmillan, 1983

Walter M. Abbot The Documents of Vatican II Guild, 1996

Weigel, George, The Cube and the Cathedral

Wells, Jonathan Icons of Evolution; Darwin and Intelligent Design

Wells, Jonathan the Politically Incorrect Guide to Darwin and Intelligent Design

Whitney J. Oates, Basic Writings of Saint Augustine, Random House,

Wilber, Ken, Marriage of the Sense and the Soul.

# About the Author

**Robert Thomas Fertig** is a veteran of the USAF. At the Columbia University Graduate Physics Lab, he was responsible for setting up science experiments for graduate students. At General Electric, he taught computer programming, nationally. At Sperry Univac, Mr. Fertig was a Competitive Analyst and authored monthly marketing newsletters. He later became Vice President of Advanced Computer Techniques Corporation in NYC, where he research and wrote technology reports forecasting trends. He established Enterprise Information Systems, Inc., the IT Consulting Firm, in Greenwich, CT.

Mr. Fertig is the author or co-author of a dozen books, such as Pursuit of Wisdom, Guardianship Realities, Middle East Quicksand, Consequences, Beauty and Wonder of Transcendent Truths, Culture Battles, Miraculous, Software Revolution, and Best Interests of the Children. He was a five-year volunteer with Guardian ad Litem, and also a five-year Eldercare Guardian, in Florida. Robert and Miriam Fertig have been married nearly 60-years, and have three children.